FEMINIST INTERPRETATIONS OF THEODOR ADORNO

RE-READING THE CANON

NANCY TUANA, GENERAL EDITOR
This series consists of edited collections of essays, some original and some previously published, offering feminist re-interpretations of the writings of major figures in the Western philosophical tradition. Devoted to the work of a single philosopher, each volume contains essays covering the full range of the philosopher's thought and representing the diversity of approaches now being used by feminist critics.

FEMINIST INTERPRETATIONS OF THEODOR ADORNO

EDITED BY RENÉE HEBERLE

THE PENNSYLVANIA STATE UNIVERSITY PRESS
UNIVERSITY PARK, PENNSYLVANIA

Chapters 3 and 4 were originally published in the journal *New German Critique*.
"Adorno's Siren Song" by Rebecca Comay appeared in *New German Critique* 81 (2000):
21–48. "A Feminine Dialectic of Enlightenment? Adorno and Horkheimer Revisited" by
Andrew Hewitt appeared in *New German Critique* 56 (1992): 143–70. Reprinted with
permission.

Library of Congress Cataloging-in-Publication Data

Feminist interpretations of Theodor Adorno / edited by Renée Heberle.
    p.   cm.—(Re-reading the canon)
Includes bibliographical references (p.   ) and index.
ISBN 0-271-02879-3 (cloth : alk. paper)
ISBN 0-271-02880-7 (pbk. : alk. paper)
1. Adorno, Theodor W., 1903–1969.
2. Feminist theory.
I. Heberle, Renée, 1962– .
II. Series.

B3199.A34F46   2006
193—dc22
2006001243

Contents

Preface

Nancy Tuana

Take into your hands any history of philosophy text. You will find compiled therein the "classics" of modern philosophy. Since these texts are often designed for use in undergraduate classes, the editor is likely to offer an introduction in which the reader is informed that these selections represent the perennial questions of philosophy. The student is to assume that she or he is about to explore the timeless wisdom of the greatest minds of Western philosophy. No one calls attention to the fact that the philosophers are all men.

Although women are omitted from the canons of philosophy, these texts inscribe the nature of woman. Sometimes the philosopher speaks directly about woman, delineating her proper role, her abilities and in-abilities, her desires. Other times the message is indirect—a passing remark hinting at women's emotionality, irrationality, unreliability.

This process of definition occurs in far more subtle ways when the central concepts of philosophy—reason and justice, those characteristics that are taken to define us as human—are associated with traits histori-cally identified with masculinity. If the "man" of reason must learn to control or overcome traits identified as feminine—the body, the emo-tions, the passions—then the realm of rationality will be one reserved primarily for men,[1] with grudging entrance to those few women who are capable of transcending their femininity.

Feminist philosophers have begun to look critically at the canonized texts of philosophy and have concluded that the discourses of philosophy are not gender-neutral. Philosophical narratives do not offer a universal perspective, but rather privilege some experiences and beliefs over others. These experiences and beliefs permeate all philosophical theories whether they be aesthetic or epistemological, moral or metaphysical. Yet this fact has often been neglected by those studying the traditions of philosophy. Given the history of canon formation in Western philosophy, the perspective most likely to be privileged is that of upper-class white males. Thus, to be fully aware of the impact of gender biases, it is imperative that we re-read the canon with attention to the ways in which philosophers' assumptions concerning gender are embedded within their theories.

This new series, *Re-Reading the Canon*, is designed to foster this process of reevaluation. Each volume will offer feminist analyses of the theories of a selected philosopher. Since feminist philosophy is not monolithic in method or content, the essays are also selected to illustrate the variety of perspectives within feminist criticism and highlight some of the controversies within feminist scholarship.

In this series, feminist lenses will be focused on the canonical texts of Western philosophy, both those authors who have been part of the traditional canon, and those philosophers whose writings have more recently gained attention within the philosophical community. A glance at the list of volumes in the series will reveal an immediate gender bias of the canon: Arendt, Aristotle, Beauvoir, Derrida, Descartes, Foucault, Hegel, Hume, Kant, Locke, Marx, Mill, Nietzsche, Plato, Rousseau, Wittgenstein, Wollstonecraft. There are all too few women included, and those few who do appear have been added only recently. In creating this series, it is not my intention to rectify the current canon of philosophical thought. What is and is not included within the canon during a particular historical period is a result of many factors. Although no canonization of texts will include all philosophers, no canonization of texts that excludes all but a few women can offer an accurate representation of the history of the discipline, as women have been philosophers since the ancient period.[2]

I share with many feminist philosophers and other philosophers writing from the margins of philosophy the concern that the current canonization of philosophy be transformed. Although I do not accept the position that the current canon has been formed exclusively by power relations, I do believe that this canon represents only a selective history of the tradition. I share the view of Michael Bérubé that "canons are at once the location, the index, and the record of the struggle for cultural representation; like any other hegemonic formation, they must be con-tinually reproduced anew and are continually contested."[3]

The process of canon transformation will require the recovery of "lost" texts and a careful examination of the reasons such voices have been silenced. Along with the process of uncovering women's philosophical history, we must also begin to analyze the impact of gender ideologies upon the process of canonization. This process of recovery and examina-tion must occur in conjunction with careful attention to the concept of a canon of authorized texts. Are we to dispense with the notion of a tradition of excellence embodied in a canon of authorized texts? Or, rather than abandon the whole idea of a canon, do we instead encourage a reconstruction of a canon of those texts that inform a common culture?

This series is designed to contribute to this process of canon transfor-mation by offering a re-reading of the current philosophical canon. Such a re-reading shifts our attention to the ways in which woman and the role of the feminine are constructed within the texts of philosophy. A question we must keep in front of us during this process of re-reading is whether a philosopher's socially inherited prejudices concerning woman's nature and role are independent of her or his larger philosophical frame-work. In asking this question attention must be paid to the ways in which the definitions of central philosophical concepts implicitly include or exclude gendered traits.

This type of reading strategy is not limited to the canon, but can be applied to all texts. It is my desire that this series reveal the importance of this type of critical reading. Paying attention to the workings of gender within the texts of philosophy will make visible the complexities of the inscription of gender ideologies.

Notes

1. More properly, it is a realm reserved for a group of privileged males, since the texts also inscribe race and class biases that thereby omit certain males from participation.

2. Mary Ellen Waithe's multivolume series, *A History of Women Philosophers* (Boston: M. Nijoff, 1987), attests to this presence of women.

3. Michael Bérubé, *Marginal Forces/Cultural Centers: Tolson, Pynchon, and the Politics of the Canon* (Ithaca, N.Y.: Cornell University Press, 1992), 4–5.

Acknowledgments

This volume would not have come to completion had it not been for the support and interest of a number of people. William D. Rose and Hannah Heberle-Rose top the list of those who make my life of work and family possible and sane. Several essays were presented at the 2003 Western Political Science Association meeting, where Judith Grant took on the task of discussant, encouraging the forward movement of the project. Patricia Jagentowicz Mills introduced me to the work of Theodor Adorno in graduate school. Ann Ferguson encouraged my ongoing interest in the value of his work for feminist purposes. I had the opportunity to present my work on Adorno at the University of Canterbury in Christchurch, New Zealand, in the spring of 2005. I thank Victoria Grace and the Sociology/Anthropology Department for that opportunity. Mary Franks gave some valuable help in a tight spot with some of the work. All the contributors have been a pleasure to work with. Thanks to the Department of Political Science at the University of Toledo for their support. Many thanks go to the editors working on this series, to Nancy Tuana and Sanford Thatcher, and to the anonymous reviewers at Penn State Press for their supportive responses to this work.

1

Introduction: Feminism and Negative Dialectics

Renée Heberle

The contributors to this volume look at issues in feminism using insights from Theodor Adorno and reread Adorno using insights from feminism. While Adorno had many thoughts about women, about modern feminism, and about sexuality, he offered little in the way of sustained argument about them. Nonetheless, given the questions feminism raises and the questions raised about feminism, there are good reasons to "go back to Adorno."[1] In this introduction I will elaborate on some of these reasons. I cannot possibly do justice to the scope and complexity of Adorno's thinking here, nor do I wish to attempt an introductory explanation of his ideas to the reader.[2] The contributors do the work necessary to move the reader into the arguments. However, I do hope to highlight some of his most compelling insights and ideas about the task of philosophy, to show some affinities between Adorno and feminist concerns, and thus entice the reader into an engagement with the chapters that follow.

Feminism is critically reflexive about its status as a protest against conditions that make it possible; that is, it is simultaneously diagnostic and symptomatic. It is a field of inquiry that grows in intensity and effectiveness precisely through its disagreements and resistance to closure. Critically examining the troubled and troubling status of "woman" is among the many projects of feminism and contributes to its vitality as a field of inquiry and politics. And the contingent status of "women" drives the restless, conflictual quality of feminism in theory and in practice. In patriarchy, women are conceptually interchangeable. Concretely, they are not. Conceptually, *woman* refers to an object of inquiry. Concretely, that object comes diffusely apart as critical attention is paid to the terms of its existence and its particularity. Much of Adorno's thinking predicts some of these basic conundrums of feminist theorizing.

Adorno was born to a Catholic mother and a Jewish father in Frankfurt, Germany, in 1903. He was raised an only child of privilege in a solidly middle-class milieu. His mother was a professional singer, and his aunt, who helped raise him, was a pianist. It is commonly remarked upon that he was raised by women in an extremely protected environment and that this may have something to do with his sensitivity toward the suffering of women as participants in bourgeois society as well as with his seeming nostalgia for the nineteenth-century ideal of the family as a space of nurturance for the autonomous bourgeois individual. There is little else in the way of biographical information that would tell us in any direct fashion how we as feminists might approach Adorno's work. His Jewishness plays a profound part in his thinking, for it created the historical circumstances that forced him into exile. It was his experience of exile that inspired some of his famously melancholy works. Rebecca Comay, in Chapter 3, reflects on how the interpretation of the *Odyssey* in the *Dialectic of Enlightenment* stands in for Adorno's own exile and relationship to the feminine. Adorno spent his later life in Germany as a well-established figure in academia. In Chapter 6, Lisa Yun Lee takes as her point of departure an intensely personal experience that has traditionally been interpreted as indicating Adorno's aversion/distance from the body, particularly the feminine body. Lee shows this interpretation to be wrong, pointing out that Adorno's work is deeply informed by concern with the body and with somatic suffering and that the body figures deeply in his philosophical work. Apart from these biographical references, it is Adorno's work in itself with which authors in this volume engage, bringing it to feminism and bringing feminism to it.

While it is clear that Adorno concurs with many feminist sensibilities about Western philosophy and Enlightenment thinking, our goal here is not simply to judge whether his thinking is good for women, as if each were a predetermined object, with one waiting to be applied to the other. Rather, authors in this volume rethink his work in light of historically specific challenges faced by feminism and in light of diverse understandings of our present condition. Adorno himself would protest the "application" of his work—as if we were testing it for feminist purposes. He was famously opposed to instrumentalizing thought. Further, litmus tests of the intent of thinkers regarding the lives of women or analyses of gender relations typically obscure more than they reveal about the possibilities for thinking about women and gender relations offered by Western philosophy. Following the pattern established in other volumes in this series, each contributor rereads Adorno against the grain of his or her own thinking. Adorno's work may have unintended (by him) consequences for feminism that can only be discerned through open-ended and experimental approaches to his work, which is open and experimental in its own right. The chapters that follow are written in this spirit.

Adorno was criticized, indeed sometimes vilified, for his apparent inattention to the accessibility of his work. However, for him, "[d]irect communication to everyone is not a criterion of truth. We must resist the all but universal compulsion to confuse the communication of knowledge with knowledge itself, and to rate it higher, if possible—whereas at present each communicative step is falsifying truth and selling it out. Meanwhile, whatever has to do with language suffers of this paradoxicality."[3] These kinds of questions continue to alternately plague and inspire feminists. Judith Butler was recently criticized specifically for using difficult language; the value of her ideas was dismissed as the question of whether her work was or should be accessible to a general readership became the issue. Critics of her work often suggest that it is not feminist of her to use complex language to express ideas.[4] Adorno would have scorned this rhetorical dismissal of critique that demands serious and prolonged attention from the reader. The difficulty of his form and style of writing was inherent in what he regarded as the task of critique: to express the complexity of what only seems simple to the common sense prevalent in the historical moment, to render the familiar strange, and to open pathways to alternative thinking and practice.

For Adorno, critical theory is not about finding final answers or revealing truth. It is about articulating the irreconcilable quality of the movement of thought and experience in history. In *Negative Dialectics*, he says, "Unlike science, philosophy knows no fixed sequence of question and answer. Its question must be shaped by its experience, so as to catch up with the experience. Its answers are not given, not made, not generated; they are the recoil of the unfolded, transparent question."[5] Feminism's questions have been shaped by experience. This is a legacy of the insight that "the personal is the political" in its nonproscriptive, most political (as in opening up new spaces for public contestation) sense. Learning how to ask questions about that which is most taken for granted in everyday life is a crucial concern for feminists.

Adorno was committed to the project of philosophy as interpretation. Further, he considered form to be as important as content to the meaning of any written text. This, he argued, philosophy has in common with art, though the two remain significantly different enterprises. Unlike art, philosophy is about truth, but it does not work with or tell the truth. It is about a truth that challenges history, not one that will presently or ultimately merge with it. Truths, for Adorno, as for Hegel, unfold from within history itself. Thus Adorno is committed to a philosophy that engages in immanent critique, which Susan Buck-Morss explains as "argumentation from within, on the basis of philosophy's own inherent, historically developed logic, in order to break out of bourgeois idealism and into revolutionary materialism."[6] However, Adorno departs from Hegel (and Marx) in suggesting that there is no potential reconciliation of subject and object, of self and other, of concept and object. In his materialism the dialectic remains negative. Adorno rejects the notion that any concept is adequate to its object or that the nature of the object could ever determine the truth of the concept. The excessive quality of thought and the instability of the object conditions philosophical inquiry. Thus he supported speculative thinking against positivism, empiricism, and what he called the dogmatics of ontology.[7]

Walter Benjamin was arguably the contemporary by whom Adorno was most influenced.[8] Departing from orthodox Marxism, yet indebted to its insights, both men engaged in a kind of materialism that took the moments of reality as riddles to be solved rather than as given facts to be identified. History does live in the object but is neither determined by nor determines its nature. The following quotation best sums up Adorno's understanding:

> The central difference [between science and philosophy] lies far more in that the separate sciences accept their findings, at least their final and deepest findings, as indestructible and static, whereas philosophy perceives the first findings which it lights upon as a sign that needs unriddling. Plainly put: the idea of science (*Wissenschaft*) is research; that of philosophy is interpretation. In this remains the great, perhaps the everlasting paradox: philosophy persistently and with the claim of truth, must proceed interpretively without ever possessing a sure key to interpretation; nothing more is given to it than fleeting, disappearing traces within the riddle figures of that which exists and their astonishing entwinings.[9]

In common with that of feminists, Adorno's philosophy challenges the dualisms that structure Western thinking. He did not suppose he would reconcile through theory the contradictory forces of nature and history, culture and social structure, or desire and Reason. Rather, he considered the work of deconstructing these dualisms to be ongoing. They would not be thought away in their immediacy, but worked against each other to show their untruth as independent things-in-themselves. Susan Buck-Morss shows how the use of antithetical concepts provided Adorno with a method, of sorts, of critical cognition. "That which appeared as rational order in bourgeois society was shown by Adorno to be irrational chaos; but where reality was posited as anarchic and irrational, Adorno exposed the class order which lay beneath this appearance. . . . Where nature confronted men as a mythic power, Adorno called for the control of that nature by reason; but where rational control of nature took the form of domination, Adorno exposed such instrumental reason as a new mythology."[10] This is echoed in feminism. Where some feminists have shown the historicity of presumably natural qualities of sexed existence, others have shown the irrational, mythic, naturalizing force of historically constituted notions of masculinity and femininity.

Further, Adorno tells us, "The task of philosophy is not to search for concealed and manifest intentions of reality, but to interpret unintentional reality, in that, by the power of constructing figures, or images (*Bilder*), out of the isolated elements of reality it negates (*aufhebt*) questions, the exact articulation of which is the task of science, a task to which philosophy always remains bound, because its power of illumination is not able to catch fire otherwise than on these solid questions." This is the materialism Adorno advocates. "Interpretation of the unintentional through a juxtaposition of the analytically isolated elements and illumination of the real by the power of such interpretation is the program of every authentically materialist knowledge."[11] From Walter Benjamin, Adorno borrowed the term *constellation* to describe what they were doing in interpreting "reality." Constellational thinking rejects identity thinking and challenges dualistic presuppositions. It is thus significant for feminist purposes.

As it is for feminists, concrete, lived experience is fundamental to Adorno's work, but not because it tells the truth about oppressive social conditions. For Adorno, access to authentic experience withered with the possibilities of an authentically individualist social order in late capitalism. He considered the popular responses of his time to this decay to be dogmatic; whether they were existentialist (Heidegger, Sartre) or Marxist (Brecht, Benjamin) in orientation, he argued that these approaches obscured the tragic dimensions of lived *dialectical* tensions between the extremes of mythology and Enlightenment rationalism and between nonhuman nature and inhumane history.

Adorno's major philosophical work, *Negative Dialectics* (1966), elaborates his theory of the nonidentical, which speaks to feminist concerns about essentialism and identity politics (see particularly Gillian Howie's contribution to this volume, Chapter 15). Feminism is concerned with the difference that is "woman" and the differences that constitute the category of "women." Essentialism became a problem rather than a solution to the question of unity among women as black feminism and feminists of color told white feminists not only that having gender identity in common is partial in its constitutive power, but also that unconditionally identifying women as such obscures as much as it illuminates about the quality and experience of oppression in general. Further, and in part as a response to these criticisms, as some feminists adopted poststructuralist and deconstructionist approaches to interpreting gendered experience, pursuits of origins and causal explanations for oppression were brought into question. Thus feminist theorizing has become increasingly attuned to its contingent, conditional status as a field of inquiry. This is an attunement that should lead not to pessimism or paralysis, but rather to heightened sensitivity of the transformative possibilities offered by not taking anything for granted about one's object of inquiry. Adorno's insistence on the primacy of the object encourages this nonidentitarian approach to knowledge.

Adorno's claim about nonidentity is, at base, fairly straightforward. It is that the object does not go into its concept without remainder and that the space between indicates simultaneously the failure and the hope of Enlightenment thinking.

Contrary to widely held belief, Adorno was not anti-Enlightenment.[12] He self-consciously used reason to critique the categorical Reason of traditional philosophy. As noted above, his constellatory thought insists on the primacy and many-sidedness of the object. For Adorno, rationality should not be subject centered, partly because we cannot know ourselves completely and therefore will always be obscuring, perhaps irrevocably, parts of the self that are "objectively" conditioned by historical circumstance. He says of constellations:

> The history locked in the object can only be delivered by a knowledge mindful of the historic positional value of the object in its relation to other objects—by the actualization and concentration of something which is already known and is transformed by that knowledge. Cognition of the object in its constellation is cognition of the process stored in the object. As a constellation, theoretical thought circles the concept it would like to unseal, hoping that it may fly open like the lock of a well-guarded safe-deposit box: in response, not to a single key or a single number, but to a combination of numbers.[13]

Constellations suggest a move away from what have been some defining terms of feminist method: determinist thinking wherein we can know in advance the source of woman's suffering; social constructionism, which is more historical, but still drops subjectivity from the equation; or essentialism, which will find the truth of "woman" within the subject. My own contribution (Chapter 10) offers insight into how "experience," a concept crucial to feminist theorizing and one that is often subjected to the forms of thinking just described, might be understood through constellational interpretations. I proffer an alternative to thinking about experience as either an authoritative source of truth or as a construction we can only understand through the conditions of its emergence and articulation, but not as an object in itself.

Adorno writes, "The truth of music is inextricably bound to its tran-
siency." This claim can be applied to his thinking about the truth of the
self and experience. The truth is not in them, but is in their historical
movement, not only in forward motion, but in lateral motion as well.
Feminism approaches this understanding in many of its modes of theorizing. It can pick up some cues from Adorno in order to take another look
at some basic conundrums of feminist work, theoretical and political.

Adorno and Praxis

Adorno died in 1969 at the age of sixty-six. His untimely death came at
the height of the new leftist and student movements, and coincided with
the burgeoning women's movement, in Western industrialized countries.
His life and work had been profoundly marked by the rise and subsequent
violent demise of the Fascist state in Germany and by his own experience
of forced exile to England and the United States just before the war. He
became a significant, even leading, figure in radical intellectual circles
in Germany upon his return to that country in 1949. The *Dialectic of
Enlightenment*, written with Max Horkheimer, served to focus students'
attention on their felt alienation from bourgeois consumer society. It is a
founding text of the Institute for Sociological Research, popularly known
as the Frankfurt School. It departs from orthodoxies about the necessity
of the domination of nature and the inevitability of progress that were
found in orthodox Marxist critiques of capitalist administrative society.

However, Adorno's critique of progress; his skepticism toward all forms
of positive theory; and the profound aura of melancholy, even pessimism,
that emanated from his work ultimately made him an unlikely figure to
inspire those who came to assert the need for a programmatic critique
that would guide radical social action. Adorno did actively avoid association with collective politics and action. But his reasons for doing so deserve our attention. In all his writings he addressed questions about the
relationship between thinking and political commitment, between art
and political commitment, and the place of critique in contemporary
mass society. These questions are addressed by other thinkers, but typically as an afterthought or as an otherwise minor consideration. For
Adorno the relationship between theory and practice is a critical point
in the constellation of concrete concerns that drove his life and work.[14]

In spite of this wealth of material, critical theorists, including feminists, in the United States have, since the early 1970s, been slow to pick up on Adorno's work. Herbert Marcuse and, after him, Jürgen Habermas have remained the most visible representatives of the critical tradition spawned by scholars associated with the Institute for Sociological Research. Marcuse's optimistic use of Freud and Marx to resolve modern forms of alienation from self and other and Habermas's faith in the potential for transparency in rational forms of communication have been important references for contemporary feminist theorizing of conditions of gendered and sexual freedom. However, interest in Adorno, always at a steady but rather low ebb among critical thinkers, has reemerged as the debates about modern and postmodern theorizing have become somewhat threadbare.[15] I would argue that Adorno's nuanced theorizing about the constitutive quality of the object; his consequent insistence on the complexly mediated quality of intersubjective relationships; and crucially, his thinking about suffering and memory may help contemporary critical thinking point beyond itself.

The Contributions

We open the volume with an interview with Drucilla Cornell. Cornell is probably best known for her theorization of the imaginary domain as a site of individuation and freedom. The interview with Cornell reveals the ways in which Adorno continues to influence her thinking about legal, cultural, and feminist matters.

The interview shows how she weaves the idea of negative dialectics into her feminist theorizing about ideality as a space of struggle. She discusses the re-presentation of the feminine in the feminist pornography of Ona Zee, showing how Zee demonstrates the concrete materiality of women's bodies, which always already negates the male fantasy of women as always absolutely knowable as an object. After several minutes of what appears to be a "normal" porn scene, Zee stops the sex acts to show what women who are menstruating must do in order to continue to work on porn sets during their period. This highlights the negativity of women's bodies against which the male fantasy must always work to sustain a phallocentric ideal of the feminine. For Cornell this is the negative dialectic in action.

Cornell's conceptualization of the imaginary domain as a never fully constituted space that should be protected by law provides a corrective to the liberal notion of a self that is always already there to be protected. Following the insights of critical theory that it is not only that our preferences as preconstituted subjects are shaped by the culture industry but also that our subjectivity itself is "pounded into a being who has lost the ability to distance ourselves from the bombardment of images that promotes the endless push to consume more and different products," Cornell recognizes the difficulty of conceptualizing such a space. Her theory of the imaginary domain does rely on the liberal idea of individuality as critical to freedom, but it is indebted to dialectical theory in that for Cornell, individuation is a process that moves within and against the limits of the individual's own horizons, which are in turn continually shaping and shaped by her relations with others. The interview shows how a critical reading of Adorno can inform contemporary feminist theory and activism and challenge our thinking about the relationship between theory and activism.

Apart from an excellent collection of essays on feminist sociocultural theory titled *Adorno, Culture, and Feminism* (2001), edited by Maggie O'Neill, there has been little feminist attention to Adorno's work. In this volume we include only two previously published works, those by Rebecca Comay (2000) and Andrew Hewitt (1992). Comay, in Chapter 3, rereads the *Dialectic of Enlightenment* as representative, even symptomatic, of Adorno's own troubled exile. The vulnerabilities of the bourgeois patriarch are critically elaborated in the excursus on Odysseus, and the melancholy hope for something different is lodged in complex ways in the various deployments of woman as allegory for the seductions of modernity. In Chapter 4, Hewitt allows us to see how the *Dialectic of Enlightenment*, in spite of its own critique of instrumental thinking, instrumentalizes the "feminine" as a cipher for the deindividuating effects of modernity.

Comay draws out the ways in which Adorno's personal experiences haunt the *Dialectic of Enlightenment*. Adorno's volume of aphorisms, *Minima Moralia* (1947), written shortly after the *Dialectic*, is purposively personal, even intimate, in tone and content. Eva Geulen, in Chapter 5, looks at this most intimate of Adorno's works to show the place of love and desire in Adorno's thinking generally. Love as that which can be most consuming and most particular in human experience has been the subject of much philosophical concern. Geulen argues that "none of

Adorno's theorems—neither those pertaining to art and aesthetic experience or to history and social relations, nor those addressing problems of literary or musical expression—can be sustained at all if their roots in erotic desire are severed." She shows how Adorno finds his way through and around the traps of existentialist proclamations of authenticity in love as a model for relations between the individual and the social. His references to erotic experience, to the transitory selflessness experienced in the moment of love, tell us about his thinking about mimesis in all its complex guises.

While Adorno's most intimate of reflections include some of his most stereotypical references to women, Geulen describes how he turns the "truths" of those references against themselves to illuminate the contradictions inherent in the lived condition of "being woman." Such readings as Geulen's draw out of a frustrating lack of closure, which causes some readers of Adorno to dismiss him as hopelessly obscure and self-contradictory, the very insight into human experience we may need to continue to hope for something different in damaged conditions.

We go back to *Minima Moralia* in Chapter 6, as Lisa Yun Lee explores Adorno's thinking about an object associated with intimacy and central to feminist critique. Similar to Geulen's critical recovery of the importance of the erotic to Adorno's work, Lee's thesis identifies the centrality of the body, in its most visceral corporeality, in his writings. She uses the (in)famous scene of Adorno's humiliation in the seminar room when, frustrated by his inattention to activism and collective organizing, students planned a protest. Radical students became "disenchanted" with his apparent scorn for direct action and street politics. In 1969 female students embarrassed Adorno during a lecture by rushing to the podium in a planned moment and baring their breasts while caressing him and throwing rose petals over his body. The protest was inspired by contemporary radical thinking about sexuality and corporeality and was intended to highlight the assumed disjuncture between Adorno's work and political praxis. Lee takes as a point of departure the interesting fact that female bodies were deployed as substitutes for the praxis the students were "reminding" Adorno about. As in the case of his thinking about "love," what the students were missing, according to Lee, is that the body is written in all over Adorno's work; his attention to sentient suffering and his critique of the occlusion of the body from philosophical concern is addressed in several of the chapters that follow. Adorno does not offer any systematic comment on the body in *Minima Moralia*. This is in keeping with his commitment to the Nietzschean form of aphorism that reflects his more general commitment to the practice of philosophy as an unriddling of the object. It is only through teasing out the combined and incomplete insights offered that one might put together, as does Lee, an argument about Adorno's thinking on the body.

Ultimately she shows that his concern with the body is related to his concern with the subordinate forms of manual labor and with praxis. He does not reclaim the body in any direct fashion, as he is aware that simply reversing the mind/body dualism might as readily lead to Fascism as to freedom. Thus attention to the body is best given through immanent critique that exposes its naturalized status and illuminates its position of negativity. The body is philosophy's negative as in its suffering it signifies philosophy's failures. Adorno does not try to fill in its absence from Western philosophy but uses the absence of the body as such. Through metaphor and language that evokes visceral bodily experience, Adorno reminds us, sometimes jarringly, of our embodied condition and the dialectical relation between mind and body. It is in his critique of the modern insistence on the mind/body dualism, of the division of mental and manual labor, and of traditional ideas about subject-object relation that one finds the concern for and about the body in Adorno's work. Lee shows how these dualisms are related to one another in a complicated fashion, the first nested within the second, which reflects the more general epistemological status of subject-object relations in traditional philosophy.

With Bruce Martin's contribution (Chapter 7), we move from the critical recovery of terms relevant to feminism in Adorno's work to an exploration of how Adorno contributes to thinking about ongoing ecological crises and coming catastrophes. Martin explores the multifaceted philosophical life of mimesis. Moving from aesthetic to ecological and scientific deployments of mimesis, he elaborates the distinct possibilities rendered when we acknowledge the mimetic quality of identity, when we acknowledge that we engage in a necessary process of projection in and through others as we engage in becoming selves. This projection, the movement of subjectivity through others, whether those others be of human, of natural, or of aesthetic type, can have repressive/regressive or emancipatory effects. Martin shows how Adorno's work can inform a radical feminist ecological project that avoids identitarian effects, the collapsing of subject and object (human and nature) into a totalitarian state of reconciliation. Adorno values mimesis for its partiality, as an inconclusive means to the end of recognition of the nonidentity of self and other.

Sora Han's contribution (Chapter 8) is, again, a critical retrieval of sorts. She is retrieving the concept of *intersectionality*, first introduced by Kimberlé Crenshaw in 1991, from an untimely dismissal by critical race theorists. Han suggests that the criticisms of and efforts to move past intersectionality miss an opportunity to realize its potential as a term of critique necessary to any progressive move against forms of simultaneously racial and gendered violence. She argues that coalitional efforts against increasing levels of violence against women and the egregiously disproportionate rates of incarceration of men of color need intersectionality as a critical concept. However, it is not, in Han's reading, a static social positioning or an alternative identitarian category of being. It is, instead akin to an aesthetic sensibility. Han uses Adorno's aesthetic theory, specifically references to his appreciation of aesthetic appearances that capture the apparitional quality of the subject as under the spell of the social, while nonetheless providing the subject (who sees or reads or hears the art object) with a corporeal experience of the "shudder" that momentarily, at least, breaks the spell. On Han's reading, intersectionality is not merely a more complicated version of identity politics or an assertion of a space from which truth might be told. Rather, it invokes that which is not intelligible yet must be attended to if politics, in this case, an antiviolence politics, is to move forward.

Mary Anne Franks turns to Adorno's assessment of the culture industry's effects on mass consciousness to think about pornography and sexual violence. Franks is not interested in arguing a causal relationship here. She is more concerned with how pornography creates the conditions in which sexual violence can thrive, in spite of the moral indignation and horror that is expressed at its occurrence.

Adorno and Horkheimer critique the culture industry for its anesthetic effects on consciousness. They compare it to anesthesia in medicine, which does not remove the pain itself, but only the memory of it. Patients' bodies thus experience the pain, but they know nothing consciously of the pain afterward. Adorno's suspicion of the pleasure aroused by the culture industry is not that cultural commodities allow us to escape an untenable reality. Like the surgery patient, we are not escaping a painful "reality"; instead, we are experiencing pleasure that comes with the freedom from having to think about, and thereby potentially resist, the untenable conditions of the world. This is the anesthetic effect Franks

claims pornography imposes. It anesthetizes consumers to their own suffering and to that of others, not by removing the suffering but by negating
active remembrance of it.

Franks does more than argue that the 12-billion-dollar pornography
industry desensitizes us to the suffering other. She uses the liberal arguments about the difference between looking and doing and consent and
coercion against themselves. She shows that in viewing pornography the
consumer has no way of discerning the difference between a consensual
act and an act of rape. It could always be either, and, indeed, if "fake
rape" is as "erotic" as "real rape," then the issue of consent means little in
our ethics about sexuality. The pornographic anesthetizes our sensibilities
about sexual violence by blurring, even eradicating, the boundaries between consensual and coercive sex. We may have a visceral response to
hearing about sexual slavery and violence, but an active memory is effectively wiped out by pornography.

One of Adorno's basic concerns was with ethical self-other relations.
Traditional philosophy sustains the subject as primary and the object as
the subordinate, as that which is to be known, mastered, and altered
according to the subjective will. Adorno's negative dialectic challenges
the primacy of the subject, viewing the object as the constituent of the
subject. In my own chapter (Chapter 10), I work through this approach
to the knowledge of and representation of objective experience. My concern is with the representation of suffering in an integrative world that
erases difference in the interest of managing knowledge and furthering
exchange relations. Women's suffering has a particularly difficult time
becoming intelligible in its own right, given the weight of stereotypical
forms of femininity, each of which can explain or make sense of woman's
suffering in noncritical ways. I argue that feminists must take note of
Adorno's negative dialectics and rather than mourn the impossibility of
representing reality as it really is, make critical use of the distance between material experience and experience as represented in the public
world. Knowing that representations of even the most visceral suffering
will be performative may help ward off despair when the world does not
respond to the "reality" of suffering. There will always be distance between an experience and the representation of that experience. This
makes room for telling stories that do not "fit" with stereotypical notions
of femininity and masculinity, for a telling of experience that remains
aware of how that telling will travel and, as object, will in turn become

constitutive of subjective possibilities. It may help create a more strategic sense of what we are doing as we represent suffering to the world.

Paul Apostolidis is also concerned with ethical self-other relations. In Chapter 11, he takes Adorno's ideas into a space through which Adorno himself would have been unlikely to travel, into a meeting between migrant-labor organizers, workers, and community members in a small town in eastern Washington State. Apostolidis reads the form and content of the meeting using categories he takes from Iris Young's *Inclusion and Democracy* (2000): greeting, rhetoric, and narrative. Pushing Young's thinking beyond where she goes in her book, Apostolidis advocates the integration of these forms of self-other interactions into the space of public deliberation. In the tradition of feminism and critical theory, Apostolidis regards rational argument and instrumental reason as Western, masculinist forms of address that inherently exclude or marginalize forms of address deployed by historically marginalized persons. Whether marginalized groups are such because they use such forms of address or use such forms of address because they are marginalized is not the question. Rather, the issue is how to bring them into the conversation in such a way that self-other relations are rendered more receptive and less instrumental. Apostolidis is concerned with re-forming democratic interactions according to principles that may not be specifically feminist, but that certainly reflect and inform feminist activism. The gender politics of the meeting is made clear in his discussion, interwoven with a discussion of the ethical challenges involved in organizing and engaging in the event.

Apostolidis suggests that Young does not take far enough her own insight into the critical potential of the forms of address she theorizes; she leaves them as a kind of preliminary to the "real" doings of deliberative democratic debate. Apostolidis is concerned, as I am, with how progressive persons can live with negative dialectics, even act it out, in a world wherein conditions of social inequality will inhibit, or even render more damaging than helpful, the most well intentioned gestures of solidarity. In the meeting he describes, relatively privileged students and community members come to listen to the experiences of workers in local meat-packing plants and the organizing strategies of union leadership. Apostolidis weaves greeting, rhetoric, and narrative into his discussion of the meeting, showing how deployment of these forms of address can counter the instrumental reason of which the relations of privilege present in the room are an effect. He suggests that the reception by listeners

can move well beyond that of sympathy to the plight of others to a mutually constitutive interactive relationship. Adorno was attuned to the politics of suffering, but also to Nietzsche's various admonitions about
ressentiment: the will to power of the weak that drives the impulse to
hold the strong to account while obscuring the attachment of the weak
to their status as victims. Apostolidis takes these dynamics into account
in rendering an interpretation of the meeting that subverts these relations and creates a different model for unity among differences.

The three chapters that follow Apostolidis's take up Adorno's aesthetic theory. Adorno is well known for his advocacy of aesthetic autonomy against those who would instrumentalize art toward political ends.
Against Bertolt Brecht and Walter Benjamin, Adorno held that it is in
the very uselessness of art that its potential for critique lies. Contemporary feminists, by contrast, have held that feminist art must be committed
art. They have argued that the disembodied and abstract formalism of
modern art reflects masculinist values, marginalizing and objectifying the
embodied and always particular feminine. Art must deliberately engage
with and challenge masculinist values in the name of transforming gender roles. Feminist art must be committed to a social agenda. In Chapter
12, Lambert Zuidervaart takes up this debate, ultimately claiming that it
is not helpful to argue for or against aesthetic autonomy on its own terms;
it is to the historical conditions and relations of production that Zuidervaart would also look as we think through the critical potential of art.

Zuidervaart does lean toward aesthetic autonomy as the critical gesture, but wishes to broaden its meaning. He turns to Adorno's theory for
insight into how feminist art might hold to its legitimate criticisms of
the masculinism inherent in most versions of aesthetic autonomy while
avoiding absorption and integration into the status quo that Adorno
pointed to as the necessary failure of committed art. Zuidervaart outlines
how Adorno works through a theory of autonomous art that lives up to
Kant's purposiveness without purpose yet issues its own form of critique.
This critique lives in the dialectical relation between form and substance
in the artwork itself and in its relative autonomy from the very capitalist
forms that make its existence possible. Zuidervaart argues that Adorno's
sense of aesthetic autonomy is limited, because Adorno only addresses
the relationship between art and the state or between art and monopoly
capitalism as the measure of its social autonomy. Adorno misses the importance of civil society, of voluntarist productions of art and cultural
practices. For Zuidervaart, the critical move is to avoid colonization by

corporate and governmental influence and control. He sees potential in nonprofit, cooperative, or communal forms of production of art that would, at least in part, sustain its critique as a potent force and help it resist integration into the culture industry.

Thus, Zuidervaart advocates expanding Adorno's notion of aesthetic autonomy to include consideration of the practices involved in creating and experiencing art. It makes a difference, then, whether, to view art, one goes to the Museum of Modern Art in Manhattan or to the East Side docks. The entire aesthetic experience, from production to engagement with the work of art, would become part of the critical aesthetic experience.

Zuidervaart offers a version of aesthetic autonomy that takes into account more than the internal autonomy advocated by Adorno. He argues that we should consider a whole range of factors in considering aesthetic value, including its communicability and sociability, which Kant considers a part of aesthetic judgment. It would look at alternative spaces in civil society and alternative economies that produce works of art. Importantly, Zuidervaart regards aesthetic autonomy not as something to be for or against in the abstract, but as an aspiration to be struggled for and assessed in historical context.

Jennifer Eagan, in Chapter 13, also looks at the culture industry, exploring the potential for a critique of suffering in art. Eagan seeks to draw connections between Adorno's theory of suffering and his understanding of culture. Feminists strive to think and speak beyond the constraints that they themselves have so effectively exposed and struggled with. Eagan uses Judith Butler's work as an exemplar of the contemporary feminist critique of gender as an instantiation of suffering. Eagan then looks to Adorno's aesthetics for insight into how that suffering might be represented without reiterating the terms of the status quo.

Eagan locates suffering at the intersection of the body and the social-linguistic order that inscribes meaning onto the experience of that body. It is neither pure feeling (pure pain) nor reducible to discursive representation, but is constituted dialectically as an effect of that relation. Eagan uses concrete examples of how AIDS and breast cancer are captured in discursive spaces, showing that those who suffer are never expressing the "truth" of their suffering in an unmediated fashion. Rather, their mediations make possible the intelligibility of their experience to the world, rendering the reality of it far beyond any terms to which the subject can fully consent. Suffering changes the lens through which we view the world and the world shapes possibilities for representing suffering.

Neither Butler nor Adorno offer straightforward means by which to escape the status quo. The value of their work lies primarily in the recognition of the complex relation between any cultural gesture and the reality of suffering. Eagan looks to Adorno's immanent critique of culture and Butler's theory of nonfixed performative identities for an approach to thinking through the conundrums of representing the lived experience of suffering.

Mary Caputi, in Chapter 14, accepts Adorno's challenge with respect to the internal autonomy of the work of art. She takes up the early performance art of Cindy Sherman, seeing it as exemplary of art that, in form and content, implodes the common sense of gender. Sherman's art works as immanent critique, unhampered by the guilt of complicity with the culture industry. Sherman self-consciously deploys as her venue art's entanglement with the status quo. Rather than resigning herself to a necessary entanglement, Sherman exposes that entanglement with each aesthetic gesture of her performance art. Caputi offers an appreciation of what she calls Sherman's "staid rebellion," one wherein Sherman offers no apologies for complicity as she insistently demonstrates, rather than expressing or explaining, the indeterminacy of gender. Sherman only gestures toward the possibility of something different from that which we think we know so well. Art here acts as a double agent. It works within the stereotypes of femininity to expose the instability of femininity as a category of being. Caputi notes that Sherman moves in and out of the stereotypical guises of femininity with ease, showing their very indeterminacy through that movement. She uses her body and costume and form to perform femininity as a recognizably contingent subject. "Art does not come to know reality by depicting it photographically or 'perspectivally' but by expressing, through its autonomous constitution, what is concealed by the empirical form reality takes."[16]

Our volume ends with a chapter about identity and difference in third-wave feminist thought. *Third-wave thought* is loosely understood here to refer to feminists who are critical of the essentialist tendencies of feminism in the 1970s and 1980s. We might generally include in this category feminists of color and those who turn to postmodern theory for insight as to identity and difference. Gillian Howie, in Chapter 13, shows how Adorno's form of materialism allows us to see that there is simultaneously truth and untruth in our identifications. Howie explains some distinctions between identification as a benign cognitive exercise and that which is complicit with social relations of domination. She suggests that there are concrete, though historically contingent, truths about the nature of group identity, but that the thought of identity should always be suspected of obscuring social interests.

Feminists struggle with the normative values implicit in any gesture toward identification. Howie suggests a way in which to identify exploitative interests that are served in grouping women together and that should not be reiterated in progressive movements. Her careful delineation of the relationship between identity, cognition, and injustice lays some groundwork for asserting or forming groups in a way that challenges rather than affirms or mirrors the status quo.

An Inconclusive Conclusion

As a philosopher Adorno had immense integrity. He stands as a thinker who sustained an absolute commitment to the life of the critical mind, one that works toward the cause of an enlightenment that can bring real freedom. His context is not ours. However, he predicts and speaks directly to many questions that go to the heart of contemporary feminist theory, including questions about interpretation, the relation between theory and practice, representation, identity, and historical memory. The chapters that follow keep the faith with Adorno's attunement to historicity and offer some insight into how we might continue to think about those questions through the prism of his thought.

Notes

1. Robert Hullot-Kentor, "Back to Adorno," *Telos* 81 (1989): 5.
2. For a fine introduction to Adorno's thinking and some biographical information, see Martin Jay, *Adorno* (Cambridge, Mass.: Harvard University Press, 1984).
3. Theodor Adorno, *Negative Dialectics* (New York: Continuum, 1987), 41.
4. For an attack on Butler's work that includes the claim that her writing is obscure, see Martha Nussbaum, "Professor of Parody," New Republic Online, 2 February 1999.
5. Adorno, *Negative Dialectics*, 63.
6. Susan Buck-Morss, *The Origin of Negative Dialectics: Theodor Adorno, Walter Benjamin, and the Frankfurt Institute* (New York: Free Press, 1977), 66.

7. See Theodor Adorno, *The Positivist Dispute in German Sociology* (London: Heineman Press, 1976) and *Jargon of Authenticity* (Evanston: Northwestern University Press, 1973).

8. For an excellent review of the influence Benjamin had on Adorno's thinking and development of the theory of negative dialectics, see Buck-Morss, *Origin of Negative Dialectics*.

9. Theodor Adorno, "The Actuality of Philosophy," in *The Adorno Reader*, ed. Brian O'Connor (London: Blackwell, 2000), 32.

10. Buck-Morss, *Origin of Negative Dialectics*, 58.

11. Adorno, "Actuality," 32.

12. Jürgen Habermas, *The Philosophical Discourses of Modernity*, trans. Frederick Lawrence (Cambridge, Mass.: MIT Press, 1987).

13. Adorno, *Negative Dialectics*, 163.

14. While Adorno was certainly not an activist figure, it is broadly inaccurate to say that he was uninterested in communicating with the public at large. In the introduction to a recently published collection of his essays, Henry Pickford points out that Adorno participated consistently in radio discussions of contemporary issues in Germany from 1950 until 1969. When appropriate he worked conscientiously to make his language accessible to a nonspecialized audience of listeners, even having the sound technicians tell him in their own words what they thought he said in order to measure the comprehension of his ideas and refine his expression. To briefly speculate, this may be the result of a difference he understood between listening to complex ideas and reading them with the time to struggle with complexity. He was intensely involved in educational reforms in Germany in the postwar era. In short, there are many aspects of Adorno as a public intellectual that have yet to be explored.

15. For recent readers, edited collections, and single-author works on Adorno, see the Selected Bibliography in the present volume.

16. Theodor Adorno, *Notes to Literature*, vol. 1 (New York: Columbia University Press, 1991), 227.

2
An Interview with Drucilla Cornell

Questions by Renée Heberle

RH: Your intellectual trajectory has moved across dialectical and psycho-analytic theory into, more recently, thinking defined in relation to arguments associated with neo-Kantian liberalism. How would you describe the influences from your lived experience as a feminist activist and intellectual that inspired this trajectory?

Drucilla would like to thank Claudia Leeb for her input on Adorno's view on such diverse issues as Adorno's notion of iterability, the culture industry, politically committed art, and homosexuality. Each of these issues is addressed throughout the interview.

DC: My intellectual history has always been through German idealism, particularly the writings of Kant and Hegel. So there is a sense in which I have always been concerned with what remains true about German idealism, first, against certain versions of materialism and Marxism and, later, against certain versions of deconstruction and what has been called postmodernism more generally. But my activism has also brought to the fore the importance of ideals in day-to-day struggles. Through the struggle for freedom, we continuously redefine the meaning of freedom, both for ourselves and, often, for larger political agendas, such as, for example, socialism. As I have written earlier, even the struggle to be "in union" and to act in solidarity implies an idealized definition of acting together. An obvious example of these famous "in union" struggles is a scab who breaks rank during a strike.

When I became an academic, there was great skepticism about ideals, particularly as they normalized the parameters of the political and thus set limits on politics itself. Ethical limits on the political were at the forefront of my writing from its earliest stages, including in my first essay, "Should a Marxist Believe in Rights?" a question that I answered in the affirmative. Undoubtedly it was a certain version of Marxism's rejection of ideals, specifically as this was manifested in the Marxist-Leninist groups I was in, that not only led me to see their importance to people in political struggles, but also compelled me to understand them both as aesthetic and ethical reminders of what we were fighting for and not merely against. I am aware that Adorno himself would worry that I am authorizing here a certain "jargon of authenticity." But what I am arguing is that we are inescapably caught up in idealizations of ourselves, including ourselves in struggles. And that all these idealizations are not equal simply because they can be understood as idealizations or as attempts to appeal to an authentic self. What I am suggesting instead is the example of the scale. Its solidarity does indeed risk exclusion if it is based on an ethical ideal, and yet at the same time we need to risk solidarity through ideals as a way in which to pull ourselves together in order to struggle for a better world. There are dangerous aspects in that struggle, but the dangers and the awareness of them does not release us from our *responsibility*; a word that Adorno seems to replace with *consciousness*. My point was that we must risk those dangers precisely because of the power of ideals. Gramsci famously writes that the struggle around ideals is crucial to any class struggle, as this struggle takes place within an ideological battlefield, one that can be as important as any actual political or military confrontation. Thinkers like Laclau and Mouffe understand the big signifiers of freedom and equality to be ultimately empty except as they mark the struggle for hegemony itself. My addition has been to argue that there is a sense in which ideals are never able to be known simply through their demarcation as signs of an ideological battlefield, but that precisely because we are interpellated by the ideals that we defend—we are as much defined by their definitions as their definitions are defined by us. Therefore, they never actually come to us as empty, but are always already filled in as we struggle over competing ethical and moral justifications for the direction of those ideals. For us as participants in politics, justifications for ideals always turn us back to the spectrum of definitions and representations of the ideals themselves.

I've suggested that the big ideals such as freedom be thought of as aesthetic ideas in Kant's sense; ideas that can figure but not entirely conceptualize the meaning of what is to be signified by the ideal. For example, John Rawls's veil of ignorance, which attempts to figure the free moral subject, the noumenal self, as imagined behind the veil of ignorance, exemplifies this attempt to configure what cannot be conceptualized—the noumenal self. I am not here defending Rawls's own hypothetical experiment in the imagination; I am defending the idea that, whatever one thinks of Rawls's actual deployment of an aesthetic idea, there is such a place for ideals in political philosophy, and also that they are vital in any attempt to advocate a position within a given political movement—advocate not in the legal sense, but in the sense of defending, for example, the ideal of perpetual peace, as against the United States' continuation of its infinite "war on terror."

At the end of his life, Adorno explicitly addressed the question of whether or not he was resigned in the face of the thoroughgoing colonization of the culture industry by capital. He argued that as long as there are people who are thinking, and insisting on the slowed-down pace of thinking that goes entirely against the grain of the endless turnover of trend after trend in the culture industry, that there are people who are not resigned. I agree with him here that thinking itself is a disruptive activity, as an activity that runs against the temporality of the culture industry. Yet I also believe that at times, we have no choice but to be activists and, in the course of struggle, defend ideals and different representations of ideals as crucial to the struggle itself. The broad-based coalition we built named United for Peace and Justice—and not United for Hegemonic Victory—in some sense says it all. Of course in the end, we are fighting for a hegemonic victory against the reigning administration of the United States. But my point is that we can only engage in that struggle on an ideological battlefield that implicates us all in the struggle for or against ideals. And as political actors we are not simply manipulators of political ideals.

RH: Adorno is most often understood as being radically pessimistic with respect to the potential for resistance and certainly with respect to social transformation. The administered society allows for no "peeping out," as he says in *Negative Dialectics*. In a recent essay that draws on Adorno's reading of Kant, you defended the importance of ideality against the notion that ideals are empty of content, emergent from a struggle for hegemony ultimately driven by power and violence. How would you describe the defense of ideality that you find in Adorno? What is the significance for feminism?

DC: Actually, Adorno and I part ways in my defense of ideality. Adorno became very suspicious of the possibility of immanent critique's relying on the great ideals of the bourgeois Western revolutions, because those ideals had been so captured by the culture industry that they had been drained of anything like a critical edge. Remember, for example, that the war in Iraq was ultimately called Operation Iraqi Freedom. So in the end, our disagreement over ideality takes us back to the first question, where I write that there is much greater space for representational politics in the two senses in which I define it there: in actual struggles (for example, for porn workers to represent themselves in a union [see below]) and in finding new ways to represent both our relationships with one another and the ideals through which we imagine them. After all, most of Candida Royale's films are about the ideal of love. It is not just that I think there is space for peeping out of the administered society. It is that, in our resistance to it, we are also reshaping the very apparatus of administration. Just to make clear what I'm trying to say: remember that Ona Zee [see below], in her sex education films, by bringing the administrative apparatus of the pornography industry into view, actually frees herself from her reduction to an administered object and opens our eyes to what that apparatus is in the first place. I refuse all forms of what I see as a form of historical reductionism, where an ideal can be completely reduced in meaning to the determination imposed upon it by its historical locale. For me, ideals actually matter, as they give form not only to our politics, but to who we imagine ourselves to be. The ideal of freedom was and continues to be clearly manipulated in the Iraq war, but this manipulation shows the power of the ideal over people's imaginations. In order for the war to be "sold" to the public, it had to be sold through the ideal of freedom. Ideals, in other words, can be manipulated in part because they continue to mean something to people, both in the sense that they actually have significance, where people have understandings of them, and in the sense that they have significance to people who believe in them as part of their both personal and national identity as citizens of the United States. The struggle over ideals and the meaning of ideals can become important if you take Adorno at his word that cynicism is the ideology of advanced capitalism. Cynicism in the sense that all ideals are simply manipulations, then, can dangerously play into what Adorno himself saw as the profound ideological danger of a neoliberalism that assumes that all idealists are in the end nothing but self-interested utility maximizers dressing up their self-interest so as to sell their product.

RH: The texture of the relationship between law and the possibilities of individuality is different from that between the culture industry and individuality. The dynamics of the former are ultimately coercive, for example, while the dynamics of the latter are persuasive. Is the protection of the imaginary domain from and through the law significant in the context of the culture industry? If so, how?

DC: The ideal of the imaginary domain as both a moral and a legal right is justified in the name of protecting the space for individuation, which assumes the vulnerability of individuality that Adorno consistently returns us to. For Adorno there is a profound sense in which the culture industry results in something close to the liquidation of individuality. In a sense, it does so by taking away the very space I'm seeking to protect in the imaginary domain. As we are consumed by the products that we are supposedly simply consuming, we lose any identity other than that of the consumer. But this importantly is a consumer who is unaware that what is operating here is not choice but rather a produced set of images that have taken over our ability to distance ourselves from the aspirations to live up to some ideal as advertised on television. Almost every magazine targeted at women bombards us with new remedies for weight loss, new tonics and toners to reverse the aging process, and so forth, all so that we may perhaps acquire a purportedly sexual body for men. We are offered thousands of kinds of hair dye, of course premised on the assumption that no one wants to go gray. Adorno forces us to questions whether those who dye their hair really chose to do so, or on the other hand whether we have been eaten up by the distorted desire to maintain the youthful image necessary for, as we so often read, dating after fifty. Adorno goes beyond the critique that our preferences are shaped, to make the much stronger point that it is we who are pounded into a being and as a result have lost the ability to distance ourselves from the bombardment of images that promotes the endless push to consume more and different products.

Note that in the examples I have just given, I have mainly been writing about women. It could be interpreted that I think that it is women who are more easily consumed by the culture industry. Adorno often insinuates that women seemingly are more easily manipulated than men. For example, he talks about how women are enticed to get suntans. "In the sun-tan, which can be quite fetching," Adorno muses, "the fetish character of the commodity lays claim to actual people; they themselves become fetishes. The idea that a girl is more erotically attractive because of her brown skin is probably only another rationalization. The sun-tan is an end in itself, of more importance than the boy-friend it was perhaps supposed to entice."[1] Adorno frequently refers to women being much more vulnerable to their own fetishization than men. It is clear in such statements that he considers women to be prey to the masquerade that is femininity and therefore easily seduced by the culture industry, leading him to use women as examples of the beings who have had their individuality completely eclipsed. This unconscious sexism, however, is not necessary for his argument. But at the same time, it shows that Adorno tends to associate, on a very deep level, individuality and masculinity. It is not merely a coincidence that almost all his metaphors for the effective undermining of individuality are related to feminization, rendering us unable to stand up in any meaningful way to assert ourselves as our own persons.

Adorno reflects unconscious assumptions about the antagonism between feminine sexual difference and personhood. The imaginary domain has as its political justification the need to protect as a matter of right the very spaces in which we are able to imagine ourselves beyond this unconscious antagonism between women and personhood. Part of its work, if you will, as an ideal is to elaborate that this connection between woman and personhood must be given space even as it is recognized psychoanalytically as a struggle that can only be carried out over a lifetime. I am arguing that legal rights can play an important role in protecting the moral space needed by us to reimagine our personhood, and ourselves as sexuate beings who can be persons. Certainly law is a coercive system by definition, and I take seriously all the critiques of a feminism that turns itself over to a state protection to answer feminist aspirations to liberation and freedom. Law itself has only too clearly become a part of the culture industry, as we have seen in the spectacles of legal trials—who can forget the O. J. Simpson "affair." Of course in the O. J. Simpson trial fantasies about race and particularly sex between a black man and a white woman is part of the "attraction." That black women function as the unimaginable shows the effectiveness of the culture industry in producing a thoroughly racialized view of women and sexuality. I strongly defended the reasonableness of those women jurors and tried to bring attention to the one book about the trial that did not become a best seller.[2] Adorno can certainly help us understand whose book becomes a best seller and why law can indeed function as an important weapon against the production of legal trials as a TV attraction. But on the other hand, a right such as the imaginary domain, and this is of course following a Hegelian insight, actually constitutes the conditions and possibilities of the person rather than simply recognizing it, as if it were a pregiven attribute or aspect of every individual. In this way, you might say that the constitution of personhood is itself left open to more possibilities if the imaginary domain is protected, than if it is not.

RH: Does Adorno's thinking about the culture industry ring true for you, or is your reading, for example, of the culture and business of pornography and its role/effect/purpose quite different from what he might say?

DC: What rings true for me in Adorno's analysis is that the notion of the artist as a critic of the homogenization imposed by advanced capitalism has now been replaced by the managed artist. The managed artist, in all too many circumstances, has no say in either what she produces as her art, or how she herself is to be produced as the thing that has to match the expectations that the culture industry promotes as both the subject and object of its purpose—profit and consumption. Culture becomes one industry like any other under capitalism, driven solely by profit. The culture industry, then, is only able to produce commodities, whether in the form of art objects of culture, or in the form of the produced stars who are controlled by the very objects they put into circulation—their art. The managed rock star is a classic example of what Adorno is speaking about. All aspects of her life are managed and controlled, including often the voice, and the music itself, for the production of an image that sells along with its product. It is a commonplace joke that Brittany Spears cannot sing, but Adorno's point is that the management of the production of Brittany Spears is not only the production of a certain kind of female sexuality, particularly teenage female sexuality, but also of a thoroughgoing and tamed heterosexual message in the form of her songs. She in a sense portrays managed femininity, and her lack of a voice becomes a metaphor for the way all of us are silenced by an industry that seeks to promote a thoroughgoing commodification of what used to be associated with creativity and the imagination. Adorno does not speak to the specific production of a tamed feminine sexuality, but certainly the projection of an artist consumed by her own produced image is thoroughly Adornian.

It would seem that the mass production of pornographic videos would certainly fit into Adorno's searing critique of the culture industry, since pornography has been a big business in the United States. I say "has been" because the pornography industry itself, if one means by the industry the production of pornographic videos, has been negatively affected by the pervasiveness of Internet pornography. Internet pornography might well be for Adorno the absolute epitome of how advanced capitalism completely inverts the meaning of human contact; sex, which at least traditionally was thought of as contact, is now carried out through the very lack of touching. As such, the alienated, frightened individuals, who Adorno sees as the victims of advanced capitalism, have now reached the pinnacle of their degradation. In the place of dreams and fantasies, we have the safety of a form of sex that demands nothing of us in the way of imagination. As I answer this question, I've already been invited to enlarge the penis I do not have, and to tune into Internet images of two teenagers having sex. I chose to keep answering the question. And this may be why I still agree with Adorno, that as long as we keep on thinking, we are not completely resigned to our alienated condition.

What Adorno seems to understand as pornography, though, is neither the Internet nor the video industry, but rather pornographic books. Indeed when he speaks of examining the possibility of negative effects of pornography on young people in "Sexual Taboos and Justice Today," he writes that the experiment would take the form of having two groups, only one of which reads pornographic books.[3] Adorno defends pornography, understood as books, as giving pleasure to adults, and its regulation as an interference with personal freedom. But the billion-dollar industry of video production with its endless display of stereotypical heterosexual scenes of male violence actually comes quite close to one of the most damaging effects Adorno associates with television—the reduction of human activity to deadly repetition. Feminist critics of the pornography industry have argued that the stereotypical and deadly repetitive scenes of heterosexuality displayed in pornography announce the death of sexual passion, but also that the women in porno films are depicted as both desirable and despicable. Or perhaps more accurately, desirable because they are despised.

In one very literal sense a porn worker is a prostitute because she has actual sex in exchange for money. For Adorno, prostitutes are both tolerated and hated because they represent the false pleasure of bought sex and legal persecution of prostitution will always be ineffective because the false pleasure it represents is the only kind of pleasure left open in a world where sexuality is simply one commodity among others. This ambivalence toward prostitutes, which Adorno attributes to the lingering sexual taboos in Germany, is now taken on the screen in the stereotypical scenes of the porn film and thus turned into the material of the pornographic film itself. The violence enacted on women is crucial to the presentation of women and women's bodies as desirable, precisely because they are the space for violation.

I have argued, following insights of Jacques Lacan, that the dismembered feminine body often displayed in pornographic films is a safe object that saves men from having to come to terms with their fear of the maternal body. The maternal body can only be remembered as always already in pieces, so that the horrifying figure of the phallic mother cannot rise against the man and suck away his individuality. For someone like Catherine MacKinnon, this is not merely the representation of violence against women; it is violence against women. According to MacKinnon, no woman who was her own person could consent to her reduction to what she aptly refers to as the "fuckee." Interestingly enough, MacKinnon's analysis of pornography shares many insights of Adorno's analysis of the culture industry. For MacKinnon, pornography actually produces the final word on who and how we can be, as women, particularly in matters of heterosexual love. Thus for her, this commodification of women as violent objects is the truth of women. Here she echoes Adorno's insight that we no longer create culture, but are produced as its objects. Pornography, like the culture industry, creates a deadly circle in which what is produced for consumption actually consumes those for whom the objects are produced.

But I disagree with Adorno, and MacKinnon, when I defend the possibility for something like a re-representation of the scene of pornography. Although Adorno provides deep insight into understanding the loss of the space and creativity of imagination in culture, his argument, for me, is ultimately too encompassing. For Adorno, we have, in the deepest and most profound sense, been consumed by the culture we once might have been thought to create. Thus, there is very little space left for the productive imagination to grapple with the constraints on the representational field that is pushed on us as all we can see, believe, or dream. To be fair to Adorno, the necessity for repetition, even as managed performance, leaves something like the freedom of what Jacques Derrida would call iterability; in any repetition there can always be difference. Still, through Adorno we cannot defend, as I have, the possibility of the re-representation of the scene of pornography. I understand this possibility in two senses: first, in terms of a re-presentation of sex and gender that challenges prevailing stereotypes of femininity and, second, as representation in terms of the unionization of its workers. There lies the possibility of a new representational space, and indeed a new representational politics, that shifts the meaning of the scene itself.

In the 1990s, Ona Zee sought to organize women and men porn workers into a union. She had great success with her efforts, notwithstanding the ultimate collapse of her union because of a lack of any meaningful political or legal support. Using techniques she explicitly associated with Brecht, Ona Zee not only tried to show that porn workers were workers who indeed could be in the subject position, but also sought to break up the stereotypical, repetitive scenes of traditional pornography. In *Sex Academy*, Ona Zee steps in and out of her role in the film, showing how women porn workers manage to keep working throughout the month. The first ten minutes of *Sex Academy* would have you believe it to be a traditional porn film; Ona Zee after all is having sex with a much younger man. But then she breaks from the sex act to tell you that she has her period, proceeding to show in graphic detail what a woman has to wear in order to keep working during her period. The period becomes the material that a traditional pornography movie cannot represent. Ona Zee uses that material itself to remind us that these are real women with real bodies and that this is indeed difficult labor. She concludes by calling for double time for women who are working during their period, making her argument rather forcefully by demonstrating just how arduous sex is then, in order to appear on film.

In her films Ona Zee, who by the way is the Meryl Streep of the porn industry, not only directly uses alienation effects to show how the films are produced. She also tries to help people develop ways of engaging their own sexuality so as to free them from the constraints of the stereotypical scene of pornography—which she does in part by refusing to have plastic surgery and hide her age. Her film *Learning the Ropes*, a six-hour sex education film, is about sadomasochistic sex for poor, working-class people. In the film, Ona Zee, with her husband, aspires to actually free people to be able to explore their sexuality by removing some of the taboos against playing, and for her it should always be playing, with desires for domination and submission. As *Learning the Ropes* teaches us, we should never actually use ropes in sadomasochistic sex because ropes can in fact hurt people. Ona Zee instead uses flexible elastic bands that can be adjusted to the size of the person and that can actually be used for other purposes than sadomasochistic sex, such as hanging up pots and pans for flexible kitchen organization. She indeed inserts breaks into the film to show how one can use these bands for household purposes. But her hope is that these videos actually open the space for forbidden fantasies and free up desires from the deadly repetition she associates with some of the more boring pornography films. Her representational politics then implies both a representation of workers and an opening up of new spaces for the representation of sexuality. Other "femme" pornographers—for example, Candida Royale—have sought to do the same. As I argue in *The Imaginary Domain* (1995), these pornographers seek to rework some aspects of a feminine imaginary, which allows for a reimagining of a feminine body, a body that is able to represent its own pleasure as a whole woman rather than as the feared and despised sex, which is only a hole. The ideal of the imaginary domain, as a moral and psychic space, is one that we need to keep open to rework even the repressed materials of the imaginary; it is one that requires us to promote and support both forms of these representational politics in the pornography industry.

Adorno would be unlikely to think of the possibility of such representational politics as feasible. Indeed, he would perhaps have even condemned it as dangerously implying that we can work the culture industry almost as much as it can work us. More strongly put, Adorno would have been highly critical of Ona Zee's politically committed films. Think, for example, of Adorno's engagement with Brecht. For Adorno, plays such as *Mother Courage* can only demand, rather than compel, a change of attitude. This demand not only can remain unheard, but worship puts the politically committed artist in the position of the supply cart, that is, the one who is asking on her knees. Such a demand and such a position is hardly the one that Adorno associates with great works of art, which refuse an accommodation to the culture industry. Ona Zee is explicitly following Brecht in her alienation procedures but she is also doing it with a state of political purpose in mind. Thus, Adorno's critique of Brecht could clearly apply to Ona Zee's porn films. He also most likely would have been skeptical of the very idea of the porn worker as a subject, let alone as a subject of her own sexuality, although in *Minima Moralia* he writes eloquently about how women's bodies are circulated in a representational field so as to give men, because they can control them, the illusion of control and empowerment. An ideal like the imaginary domain ultimately turns on a faith in the reproductive and productive imagination that goes beyond what Adorno indicates as possible under the conditions of the culture industry. For Adorno, the deformation of the imagination is a key effect of the culture industry; then, the danger of articulating an ideal such as the imaginary domain can seem to go against the profound necessity of remaining true to a relentless critique of how the imagination has been deformed.

Although I accept aspects of his critique, I further argue that it is not only in iterability that we can find freedom. The imagination itself, particularly what I have called the feminine imaginary, can never be completely encompassed by the culture industry because of the paradox that feminine sexuality itself represents. That paradox is that the feminine sex in pornography is always depicted as simply there for her manipulation by others and yet the materiality of our bodies is for us always different from that fantasy. Remember Ona Zee's graphic demonstration of how a woman has to work the material of her period in order to stay at work in a porn movie. The porn industry sought to repress Ona Zee's films because it was not pornography, but gynecology, sick, unclear, or unsexy; but it is the paradox that the material of our sex is never reducible to anyone's fantasies of what it is because it is there for us as something we live with even if as we join with Ona Zee in demanding ever greater spaces for "it"—representation. When represented as managed, feminine sexuality is already being represented through the fantasy of a controlled woman, one who is absolutely knowable as object. The two forms of representational politics that I describe in the porn industry explicitly stage the inadequacy of the dismembered woman's body to the woman herself in different ways. By so doing, they challenge the idea that the imagination can ever be completely caught up by the culture industry. In this way, feminist pornography becomes an interesting example of a cultural product working through the conditions of its own production, so as to show what cannot be imagined within the constraints imposed upon the industry. That very demonstration indicates an imagination that goes beyond those constraints. In the end, it is the phantasmic dimension of sex and of feminine sexual difference that prevents it from ever being effectively turned once and for all into a tool for the culture industry.

RH: Though I do not find him ever finally defining its terms, but rather discursively developing the reader's notion of it through the style and content of his prose, Adorno does rely on some notion of a societal un/subconscious to articulate some of the contradictions and aporias of late-modern experience, particularly with reference to sexuality and sexual taboos. What might feminists do with this aspect of his work? Is it superceded by the sophistication of feminist appropriations of Freudian and Lacanian theory? Or do you find anything in it that is particularly helpful for feminist theory and politics?

DC: Adorno offers us an interesting analysis of the continuing use and manipulation of sexual taboos in modern society—a society in which more and more of those taboos seem to have been lifted. We have much we can still learn from Adorno about how sexual taboos are used and how they continue to operate in such a society. However, the problem with Adorno is that for him there is some sense to the taboo against homosexuality. For him, homosexuality is not a mature form of sexuality, but is one that leads to dangerously extreme sexual fantasies, fantasies that some psychoanalytic schools might base on an overidentification with and incomplete separation from the mother. For Adorno the lingering sexual taboos in Germany predispose especially homosexuals to totalitarianism because they are eaten up by sexual fantasies they aim to get rid of by projecting them onto out-groups. To be fair to Adorno, he, at least in one article, argues that homosexuality should not be legally repressed, because that only further blocks the "homosexual" from having any possibility of achieving something like maturity. It will always only be "something like" maturity, because a "homosexual" by definition, for Adorno, has not achieved mature sexuality. But interestingly enough, this overidentification with the mother has positive consequences for Adorno; so many gay men are "smart," he notes. We should note that Adorno does not speak of lesbians. They are simply erased in his discussion of homosexuality. You might say that for Adorno, the taboo on lesbianism runs so deep that he himself could not allow it to come into his view. It is as if the lesbian, as the subject of her own sexuality, could not even be imagined by Adorno, which of course paradoxically shows us the importance of his understanding of sexual taboos; they block the range of the imagination. In this way I would claim Adorno an ally of the imaginary domain.

RH: The politics of representation with respect to suffering, most particularly sexual suffering, has been the subject of recent debates in feminist theory and politics. Wendy Brown's articulation of the issue uses Nietzsche's theory of ressentiment to develop a critique of what she sees as a dangerous strain of moralistic reaction defining the terms on which feminists think they should engage politically. The Holocaust constitutes a defining event/moment for Adorno's thinking. Thus suffering and its remembrance are central to his sense of how we might live ethically in the post-Holocaust world. Can you share your thoughts about the representation of and the place of the suffering subject in politics?

DC: I opened my first essay on Adorno, in *Philosophy of the Limit*, with the epigraph "The need to let suffering speak is the condition of all truth." As I wrote there, we need to put Adorno's engagement with Schopenhauer's ethics of pity within the materialism or indeed the centralism of Adorno's philosophy of redemption. Adorno's dialectic of natural history reminds us that neither history nor nature can be turned into a first principle. To quote Adorno, "If the question of the relation of nature and history is to be seriously posed, then it only offers a solution, if it is possible to comprehend historic being in its most extreme historical determinacy, where it is most historical, as natural being, or if it were possible to comprehend nature as historical being where it seems to rest most deeply in itself as nature."[4] Suffering in Adorno is not merely recognized as historical or natural necessity; rather, suffering, from the standpoint of the particular who endures it, is senseless. The only answer adequate to the suffering physical is the end to suffering, not a new version of the meaning of what has been undergone. In this sense, Adorno is rebelling against Hegel's attempt to give a philosophical meaning to the suffering of actual human beings in history. The last thing Adorno seeks to do is to reconcile human beings with their suffering by making it "make sense." This is what Adorno thought of as the antispiritual side of spirit, the promise of happiness that the desiring individual has been denied. Adorno's materialism as deployed in his nonidentity thinking carries within it a profound refusal of the continual denial of happiness that is demanded. In Adorno's words: "The telos of such an organization of society would be to negate the physical suffering of even the least of its members, and they negate the internal unreflexive forms of that suffering."[5] The dialectic of natural history for Adorno not only serves to expose the hardening of social formations into a "second nature"; the dialectic also potentially returns us to what has been forgotten within ourselves—our own physicality and vulnerability. The reminder that we too are the suffering physical is simultaneously expressed in both a destructive moment and a contrary moment that promises hope. The feeling of vulnerability can push us further to the identity logical thinking that seeks to control the other by appropriating it to an idea or conceptual schema adequate to its full description. By *identity logical thinking*, Adorno means the attempt to conflate subject and object through the attempt to conceptualize their identity. Adorno's main target here is Hegel, whose philosophy of reconciliation attempted to come full circle and reconcile the dichotomies that seem inevitable in modernity. Adorno was rebelling against Hegel's specific conceptualization of reconciliation as a particular kind of naturalized history in which who and what humanity is and has undergone is ultimately given meaning through its incorporation into a totality famously known as *Geist*. Adorno does not entirely reject reconciliation, but rewrites it by trying to keep the rift between the physical and the meaning that has been given in Hegel's second nature so that that physical and the suffering with it is not encircled in an immanence that defends itself paradoxically against the promise of happiness. But the contrary moment in the reminder of the suffering physical is that the vulnerability points beyond the very conceptual schemes that seek to give meaning to the unhappiness. For Adorno, to remember ourselves as the suffering physical is to hold on to the physical moment within ourselves, and with it the goal of our longing—sensual ease. Put somewhat differently, for Adorno the suffering physical demands its own redemption in a reconciled world, a world in which sensual ease is not blocked by the striving to control a world of both nature and culture so as to avoid confronting its own vulnerability. To consciously understand oneself as a "natural" suffering being is to retrieve a kind of innocence. To deny a physicality is to deny a kind of suffering. The materialist in Adorno honors the pledge to otherness by its adherence to suffering. His reading of Hegel's historical idealism leaves out its relentless attempt to capture historical truth as the ultimate meaning of humanity. As Adorno writes, he seeks to "read transcendence longingly rather than strike it out." The longing of the suffering physical is to be protected as a sign of what might be, of what I call Adorno's utopia of sensual ease. Suffering, then, speaks against meaning, but Adorno means this in a very specific sense. As he writes, "What would happiness be that was not measured by the immeasurable grief at what is."[6] This "grief" is not meant to hold on to any meaning that registers as a form of address or appeal that seeks to preserve the wounded attachment through an underlying asserted identity of the attachment and the suffering. In some sense, the opposite is the case. We need to break out of the ways that we have both defined and given meaning to the suffering and, at the same time, deny the full weight and brutality that bears down on all of us that would seek a world in which we didn't take enormous deprivation as the condition of humanity. Compassion for Adorno is not rooted in, for example, Schopenhauer's wisdom of disillusionment, but in the recognition of the shared human plight that comes from the subject's shared reflection of her "natural side." The mindfulness of nature, our grasp of our existence as the suffering physical, allows us to be soft. We find truth in tenderness for the subject's reflection on his or her own otherness.

RH: Feminists have struggled with how certain articulations of what the world is like for women constrain and circumscribe involvement and or possibilities of feminist politics. For example, Catharine MacKinnon's articulation of the present condition of woman as "the walking embodiment of male desire" seems to leave no space for differences to matter among women as they engage in politics. Could you reflect on the relationship, as you see it through your reading of Adorno and Kant, between how we understand and describe what the world is like for women and the political struggles of feminists?

DC: Adorno's relentless critique of historicist and reductionist thinking as a form of identity logic could not be more relevant here. MacKinnon is ultimately a positivist in exactly the sense that Adorno spent a lifetime demonstrating as itself a form of a hierarchical, patriarchal way of comprehending reality. For Adorno, instrumental reason fails at the very moment it asserts itself as having fully grasped the world it encounters. What one runs up against is exactly the concept as other to what it seeks to understand. Adorno is following Kant in a very specific sense here. When human beings conceptualize their world, they are caught in a regress that ultimately leads them to an intuition of space and time upon which all concepts are ultimately based. In other words, we never get to simple reality in Kant; reality is only graspable through a complex set of deductions that in the end take us back to an acknowledgment of the finitude of reason—finitude understood as Kant's recognition that reason itself is always limited by the transcendental imagination that makes it possible.

Thus, Adorno's nonidentity logical thinking proceeds from two seemingly opposite points of departure. First, from the quasi-Kantian recognition that we never simply think beyond our concepts and therefore our concepts themselves are always limited by what is other to them, the transcendental imagination. Second, it proceeds from the otherness that itself reminds us that what is natural or physical, the otherness we confront, is never just a concept. In one of my earlier essays on Adorno and feminism, an essay I wrote with my colleague and former student Adam Thurschwell, we argued that Adorno actually broke up the attempt to reduce woman to a paradoxically unknowable position, as, for example, Jacques Lacan does. Famously, Lacan argued that women are beyond the symbolic order because they are the embodiment, in fantasy at least, of what is the lingering remnant of a presymbolized subject. We argued that Adorno potentially shows us that the concept of gender can never be adequate to its masculine subject or its feminine object and that this "inadequacy" can alternatively never be captured within the repostulation of the feminine within sexual difference, as it is itself the mark of this inadequacy.

Now MacKinnon has to assume a one-way relationality between the masculine and the feminine, so that the masculine is in no way contaminated in its assertion of supremacy by the very otherness it seeks to suppress. Adorno shows us that this contamination is always an excess beyond the confines of a categorically gendered subject. The I of the feminine subject may cling to the subversive power of the negative that disrupts the categorical definition of feminine sexual difference, and yet at the same time does not position woman as the Negative as Lacan does.

Both Lacan and MacKinnon at the end define woman as the one with nothing to say. She is only there for man as the boundary and the limit to confirm his identity. Reified gender differentiation, then, must assert itself against Adorno's relentless attempt to show that any claims to the positive truth about who we are as men and women ultimately falls prey to the identitarian logic that unravels at the moment that it asserts itself against that which it seeks to and yet ultimately cannot control.

RH: In *Minima Moralia* and elsewhere, Adorno expresses concern for the role of the intellectual. Feminists have struggled with tensions between what we might loosely call academic or scholarly feminism and activist or street feminism. Would you please reflect on how you view this relationship and how Adorno's insights contribute to your thinking?

DC: At the end of his life, Adorno defended the idea that there is a utopian impulse in thinking itself and, at times, pseudoactivity, including activism, can actually operate against that utopian impulse. I want to quote Adorno on this point, because it is important for feminism's relationship between theory and practice: "[T]he uncompromisingly critical thinker, who neither superscribes his conscience nor permits himself to be terrorized into action, is in truth the one who does not give up. Furthermore, thinking is not the spiritual reproduction of that which exists. As long as thinking is not interrupted, it has a firm grasp upon possibility. Its insatiable quality, the resistance against petty satiety, rejects the foolish wisdom of resignation. The Utopian impulse of thinking is all the stronger, the less it objectifies itself as Utopia—a further form of regression—whereby it sabotages its own realization. Open thinking points beyond itself. For its part, such thinking takes a position as a figuration of praxis which is more closely related to a praxis truly involved in change than in a position of mere obedience for the sake of praxis."[7]

Here Adorno reminds us of the central lesson of *Negative Dialectics*. We need to step back and allow for a slowed-down pace of thinking in order to estrange our world and see what is all too familiar as *unheimlich* in order to keep in touch with what is speeded up by the culture industry. I deeply agree with Adorno on the relationship between thought and critical distance, and this means that within feminism we should never demand that all thinking have an immediate practical application. I have been at many conferences in which the tension between those committed to "theory" and those committed to "practice" reached such a point of heat and dispute and regrettable name-calling that a debate over what was really at stake was impossible. Let me be clear: I do think that there is an important place for theory that is practical and that takes up the position of advocacy—I have for example, defended the imaginary domain as both a legal and moral right. But I am also arguing that not all philosophy or thinking need, even in trying times like our own, find only one validation for itself, that is, that it advocates a specific program of reform. But what I would like to further suggest here is that what has torn apart so many feminist conferences has to do with an elitism that is inseparable from the way in which class plays out in the university itself. Many universities in the United States have up to one-half of their teaching staff in the position of adjunct faculty—adjuncts who work long hours, keep up with unbelievably demanding teaching schedules and receive little pay and no benefits. Perhaps one of the demands that has grown out of the union movement of adjuncts and graduate students is that they be given the time and money to think. But this would mean that the right to think and the kind of support that thinking demands, from financial assistance to light teaching loads, be much more equally distributed in the university than it is now.

If we were to recast the debate within the academy between theory and practice as being about a struggle against elitism and class hierarchies within the university then we would get to what is truly at stake in so much of the debate between so-called feminist theorists and feminist activists, since those who are labeled the "theorists," are often associated with fancy positions at fancy universities, while those who are the "activists" are either implicitly or explicitly questioning feminist identifications with elite positions at elite universities. In the end, of course, there is no simple reality in which theorists have the fancy position and the activists do not. Is there place in the world for both? Of course. Do many of us try to be both? Of course. I have been an activist all my life and in recent years formed an organization called "Take Back the Future" to struggle against the politics, or lack thereof, that have stemmed from the infinite "war on terror." I think there are times in which we are called on to take our place in the streets and that we cannot be somehow excused from that responsibility. When the country in which we live engages in an illegitimate war, we have to either accept that responsibility or turn from it, but we cannot at the end escape from it altogether. In other words, sometimes we have no choice but to put down our books and risk getting our hands dirty in the deepest sense with activist politics. But in the end the temptation to fit in and indeed be patted on the head for appearing smart to those in power is harder to resist than many of us had thought. Perhaps we can end with an important reminder of Adorno, which causes us to reflect on our position as professionals in the academy: "The depart-mentalization of mind is a means of abolishing mind where it is not exercised ex officio, under contract. It performs this task ex officio, under contract. It performs this task all the more reliably since anyone who repudiates the division of labour—if only by taking pleasure in his work—makes himself vulnerable by its standards in ways inseparable from elements of his superiority. Thus, in order ensured: some have to play the game because they cannot otherwise live, and those who could live otherwise are kept out, because they do not want to play the game."[8]

Notes

1. Theodor Adorno, "Free Time," in *Critical Models: Interventions and Catchwords*, trans. Henry Pickford (New York: Columbia University Press, 1990), 170.

2. Toni Morrison and Claudia Brodsky Lacour, eds., *Birth of a Nation'hood: Gaze, Script, and Spectacle in the O. J. Simpson Case* (New York: Pantheon, 1997).

3. Theodor Adorno, "Sexual Taboos and Justice Today," in *Critical Models: Interventions and Catchwords*, trans. Henry Pickford (New York: Columbia University Press, 1990).

4. Cited in Drucilla Cornell, *The Philosophy of the Limit* (New York: Routledge, 1993), 26.

5. Cornell, *Philosophy of the Limit*, 26.

6. Cornell, *Philosophy of the Limit*, 17.

7. Theodor Adorno, "Resignation," reprinted in *Critical Models: Interventions and Catchwords*, trans. Henry Pickford (New York: Columbia University Press, 1990).

8. Theodor Adorno, *Minima Moralia: Reflections from a Damaged Life*, trans. E. F. N. Jephcott (London: Verso, 1985), 21.

3

Adorno's Siren Song

Rebecca Comay

Excursus on an Excursus

In a lengthy "excursus" or appendix to the first chapter of the *Dialectic of Enlightenment*—a detour in a book which constitutes itself essentially as an extended patchwork of such appendages—Adorno reads Homer's *Odyssey* as an allegory of the dialectic of enlightenment. Odysseus himself would be the quintessential figure of *homo oeconomicus*, his voyage an extended business trip, his passions the usual affairs men fall into when they have a devoted wife at home. So domesticated is Odysseus's wanderlust, so conventional his calculations, that Adorno indeed reads the ancient epic as a modern novel, the bourgeois genre par excellence.[1]

In his reading of the Sirens episode Adorno reckons sharply just what the costs of Odysseus's enlightenment might be. If reason can only assert itself as the domination of an alien nature, this is in turn inseparable from a self-domination which becomes self-mutilation at its extreme. Reason becomes unreason when pushed to its conclusion: the attempt to free oneself from external bondage to the Other unleashes an endless ritual of sado-masochistic bondage games in which the subject has himself tied up tight. In the face of the Sirens' singing—a voice of nature, a voice of pleasure, a voice of the past, and, yes, a voice of women—both the danger and the solution would be extreme. The Sirens are not the first or last women to try to seduce Odysseus. Calypso, Circe, even Nausicaa, in her own fashion, represent the "other woman" in all the essential ways. But if Odysseus could afford to succumb, provisionally, to the druglike charms of the other temptresses, this time he has to keep a grip. Always one to cut his losses, he wants to have it both ways: famously, he plugs up his sailors' ears so they can row on undistracted while he has himself tied to the mast so as to listen in solitary safety. By Adorno's reading, such a strategy would institutionalize the upright posture as the posture of domination. Expressed in the physical distance between Odysseus above (inert but "sensitive") and the sailors below (deaf but active) is the founding opposition between intellectual and manual labor on which class society as such depends. The sailors with their plugged up ears are like the factory workers of the modern age: busy hands, strong arms, senses dulled by the brutalizing boredom of wage labor. Odysseus strapped to the mast in solitary delectation would be the bourgeois as modern concertgoer, taking cautious pleasure in "art" as an idle luxury to be enjoyed at safe remove.

Setting aside the question of just what it means for Adorno to be reading the Odyssey as an allegory—suspending, that is (though this is perhaps the ultimate question) the precise relationship between "philosophy" and "literature"—I'd like to consider what might have gone unread here. Let me propose that what is foreclosed in this reading may determine. Adorno's thinking at crucial junctures. What if the Odyssey chapter, far from being an episode contained within the larger economy of the work, in fact resurfaces just where it seems most safely set aside? If the "appendage" or "excursus" in fact absorbs the book? If Adorno is inscribed within the Odyssey rather than the other way around? If what is presented as a provisional excursus or diversion—an excursion with a fixed return—ends up being a sea voyage without an end in sight? If Adorno's own Odyssey remains unfinished? And if, then, the Sirens' song still haunts?

If I speak of "Adorno" here, I'm using the name partly as a metonymy (for the overly cumbersome "Adorno-and-Horkheimer" pair); partly because there is reason to think that the Odysseus excursus is in fact largely Adorno's own work;[2] but mostly because the repercussions of this reading are perhaps most visible in the discussion of the "culture industry" (music, technological reproduction, propaganda) which bears the unmistakeable stamp of Adorno. But as we'll see, Horkheimer's writings on the family are not irrelevant to this discussion.

Antinomies of the Upright Posture

This cowardly and tranquil pleasure, this moderate pleasure, appropriate to a Greek of the period of decadence who never deserved to be the hero of the *Iliad*; this happy and confident cowardice, rooted in a privilege which set him apart from the common condition . . .

—Blanchot

What Adorno and Horkheimer leave understated is just how precarious Odysseus's prophylactic remedy ultimately is. But perhaps they underestimate the Sirens' real temptation. It was not simply the lure of "nature" which seduced Odysseus. And thus it was not just domination-over-nature-in-general which had to be reasserted. Nor was it just the temptation of a primordial past running counter to the work of civilization, with its major discontents and its minor triumphs. Perhaps that domination took a more specific form. And perhaps the real temptation remained unthinkable.

It was not simply the erotic promise which was so alluring. And it was not just that peculiar blend of sex and knowledge which was for Odysseus, as for so many others, irresistible. Nor was it simply sexual difference which represented the greatest danger. Perhaps even more dangerous for Odysseus than sexual difference was the possibility that this very difference might be subverted. Such a possibility would undermine the standard organization of such difference—opening the play of sexuality beyond the oppositional economy governing the conceptual space of work and power, to the point that "difference" itself might come to receive the name "indifference." And by this I don't mean neutrality.

What the Sirens threatened, perhaps above all, was the sexual identity of those who listened. Not that their own identity was all that secure.[3] If their song was sweet and sensuous—"female," according to the terms of Homer's day (and ours)—what proved most irresistible to Odysseus was in fact the ("male") promise of a knowledge so absolute it would rupture the bonds of finite subjectivity by assuming the impossible standpoint of the whole.

The promise of history is at stake here—history in its totality, as totality, in total recollection. The Sirens claim to "know all the pain the Greeks and Trojans once endured on the spreading plain of Troy." To know, in fact, "all that comes to pass on the generous earth."[4] In offering Odysseus to sing "his" song—to let him hear the whole epic story of his heroic exploits[5]—they had effectively offered him the total perspective on life which is, strictly speaking, only possible post-mortem.[6] How could Odysseus, living, hear his own song? If all autobiography is, at its limits, allothanatography (to hear your own true story—the whole story—you must be someone other than yourself and you must be dead),[7] the Sirens' promise would threaten to disturb the very economy of life and death on which the very order of narrative depends.[8] For the living Odysseus to hear of his own heroic *kleos* would be to transgress the very logic of self-consciousness. It would have been an invitation to his own funeral. A hypertrophic memory—Odysseus's anticipation of his own posthumous reputation—would be indistinguishable from the lethal oblivion which would make a living death of every present.[9]

The "honeysweet fruit" (*meliedea karpon*) of the lotus-flowers (9.94) had made the men forget the voyage home. Circe's beautiful song (10.221) and honeyed wine (10.234) made them forgetful of their fatherland. Calypso with her beguiling voice (1.56) voice and nectar (5.93) had promised immortality, but at the cost of fame. The Sirens' "honeyed voices" (*meligerun op'*) (12.187),[10] in contrast, promise a kind of memory, but at the cost of life. Such fame—premature, private, fame which therefore contradicts itself as fame—would swallow up its listener, leaving only shriveled skins and bone-heaps, the anonymity of the unmourned dead. By hearing his own fame, Odysseus would, in fact, negate it.[11] If desire feeds on the narcissistic will-to-knowledge, the honeymoon would soon be over. Memory would become forgetfulness. Culture—song—would relapse into "nature." Levi-Strauss reminds us that honey (an uncooked but processed food, "natural culture" at its most alluring) is structurally ambivalent from the start.[12] If honey is a traditional funerary offering to the dead (24.68, cf. *Iliad* 23.170)—a standard ingredient, too, of Greek embalming—in this case its "cultural" attributes would result in the excessive naturalness of an unmarked death: the corpse would be left to rot unremembered in the open air. The evidence of the rotting corpses (*andrôn puthomenôn*) (12.46) lying strewn on the Sirens' flowery meadow— Vernant reminds us that "meadow" (*leimôn*) in Greek signifies also the female genitals[13]—would be a warning to those who would ask too many questions (*puthomenôn*).[14] Those who would hear an omniscient Pytho (*Puthô*) in the Sirens' meadow would find, ultimately, just the snake in the grass which is the temptation of forbidden knowledge. Between Calypso's (5.72) and the Sirens' flowery meadow, between this blissful ignorance and that rapturous knowing, the distance would seem, then, to be quite slight. The woman who would sing back to Odysseus his heroic glory and the woman whose charm would make him forget all about it (thereby rendering him, in turn, forgotten) would equally subvert the narrative order of time and history, replacing epic remembrance with the premature recall which has oblivion as its end.

But if the Sirens promise omniscience—a "masculinity" so total it would end up paradoxically reducing its bearer to a heap of bones—their appeal is sexually ambiguous in other ways as well. What would it mean to seduce through song? Was the threat of the song not precisely that it assailed the passerby through the ear, reducing his body to an open orifice, impregnated by whatever calls? In letting that viscous sweetness penetrate would not the man become, in effect, a woman?[15] Understandably, Odysseus's only counter-spell to the Sirens' magic involves an emphatic reassertion of the phallic position. If the ear is in fact the essential organ of equilibrium and the erect posture, its labyrinthine confusion would render precarious the sense of balance and the upright gait. Hence the seasickness which accompanies every disturbance of the inner ear.

But what would be the force of Odysseus's strategy? Would it not reinstate the very ambiguity it was to cure? In filling his men's ears with wax, preempting the Sirens' aural rape by pressing the "honeysweet" (*meliedea keron*) (12.48) substance into their open orifices, he simultaneously both denies and confirms their sexual confusion. Not to mention his own. For in closing up those gaping holes he must first enter them, must therefore acknowledge what he would most deny, becoming, therefore, at once both female seductress to the sailor men and male rapist to the sailor women. Odysseus himself—who, moreover, is able to spellbind (*thelgein*) any audience with his own singing eloquence (e.g., 11.333, 17.514ff.),[16] who has administered "honeysweet wine" (*meliedea oinon*) (9.208) and "honeyed words" (*epessi meilichioisi*) (9.363) to the Cyclops prior to mutilating him, and who has similarly soothed his own men with words of honey softness (*meilichiois epeessi*) (10.173, 10.547)—this honeyed, honeying Odysseus becomes at once both seductive Siren and supreme victim of the Sirens' power.

What does it mean for Odysseus to reassert his phallic position by having himself tied to the mast with cords? Odysseus—who was taught all about knots from the sorceress Circe (8.447)—is no neophyte in bondage games. Earlier, to get the besotted sailors away from the honey-sweet fruit of the lotus-flowers, he had dragged them back weeping to the boat and tied them, horizontal, beneath the rowing benches (9.99f.).[17] Now, above board and securely vertical, he insists that the plugged-up men tie him hard. "Until it hurts" (*en desmô argaleô*) he says, a rather touching detail in no way necessary to the strategy and in any case not part of Circe's original instructions. But what is this body pinned immobile against the mast, arms and legs helpless, torso reduced to a giant ear, like a sail growing swollen with the Sirens' swell,[18] like the "inverse cripple" of which Nietzsche writes:

> An ear! An ear as big as a man! I looked still more closely—and indeed, underneath the ear something was moving, something pitifully small and wretched and slender. And, no doubt of it, the tremendous ear was attached to a small, thin stalk—but this stalk was a human being! If one used a magnifying glass one could even recognize a tiny envious face; also, that a bloated little soul was dangling from the stalk. The people, however, told me that this great ear was not only a human being, but a great one, a genius. But I never believed the people when they spoke of great men; and I maintained my belief that it was an inverse cripple who had too little of everything and too much of one thing.[19]

Odysseus, all ears for the Sirens' song, stiff with the erection that masks a deeper fearfulness, Odysseus would be just this cripple.[20] Ptolemy Chennus, a satirist from the second century C.E., suggests that Odysseus's nickname "Outis" ("nobody") indeed comes from the fact that he had big "ears" (*ôta*).[21] With ears like this does it matter what there is to hear? Kafka wonders whether the Sirens were not, indeed, quite silent; whether it was not Odysseus who seduced himself with his own drive to mastery;

whether it was not indeed the cure itself which was in the end the real disease. Who could withstand the vertical exaltation (*Überhebung*) induced by the experience of the upright stance? "Against the feeling of having triumphed over them by one's own strength, and the subsequent exaltation [*Überhebung*] that bears down on everything before it, no earthly powers could have remained intact [*widerstehen*]."[22] And what would be the effect of such a binding? What if the binding which was homeopathically to counter the enchanting song—for in Greek, as in other languages, "binding" and "spellbinding" share a common semantic thread[23]—was only to redouble its constricting power? If the Sirens themselves were stringing Odysseus along with promises as binding as they were untethered? According to at least one etymology, the word "Siren" relates to *seira*, the word for "cord" or "line" or "bandage": the enchanters would be, then, the enchainers.[24] Suggesting, finally, that the binding power is from the outset split and doubled. A double bind.

Adorno's Sirens

I have experience, and I am not joking when I say that it is a seasickness on dry land.

—Franz Kafka

Adorno of course had his own Sirens to contend with. By the 1930s the autonomous bourgeois subject had been, as he saw it, liquidated beyond repair, having succumbed to the faascinations of the culture industry, to the hypnotic spell of a power which no longer needs to mask itself as such. Such a submission would have already disrupted the possibility of every *nostos*, shortcircuiting every scene of recognition, preempting all return. If Odysseus is the figure of eventual return-to-self and homecoming, the modern exile is unable to find his way back home.

Odysseus was a scarred man, but the scar would have found its uses. Odysseus's scar had been the very locus of self-identity. Fully healed, full of memory of childhood, of family, and of tender convalescence, the scar also marked the place where immediate recognition (by the servant woman Euryclea) could first take place. It was a scar born in privilege, signifying the security of lordly pedigree, giving back to "Nobody" (*outis*) his proper name. If the scar recalls the "pain" or "trouble" which is *odussamenos Odusseos*'s paternal destiny (19.407–9), its sutured smoothness would be a sign that all that pain had been put to work. Pain (in Hegelian fashion) is neutralized in the labor of the Concept; the event of recognition coincides precisely with the restoration of the *etymon* or proper name.

Recall the famous scene. Odysseus has arrived home in Ithaca, disguised as a beggar, stripped of heroic appearances, divested of his name. Nobody recognizes him except for his dog—who promptly drops dead (17.326)—and particularly not Penelope. His wife is kind to the old beggar anyway, and puts him up for the night, telling Eurycleia the nurse (Odysseus's own servant since infancy) to wash the stranger's feet. As Odysseus gets undressed, Eurycleia catches sight of a scar on his thigh (the hero's identifying mark) at which point there is a long camera freeze. Just at the point where the nurse is about to exclaim aloud in recognition, Homer indulges in a lengthy flashback, recounts how as a young man Odysseus had been gored by a wild bore while hunting at his grandfather's country estate, how well he was taken care of by his relatives, how many gifts he received, and so on. There is a second flashback contained within the flashback: the mention of the grandfather reminds Homer of how Odysseus was named at birth: his name means "troublemaker" or "troubled" (*odussamenos*, middle voice) (19.407). When Homer is through with these details, everything snaps back into position, the nurse utters her long deferred exclamation, and the recognition scene is consummated. In a sense the interruption, together with its narrative overcoming, functions structurally as a microcosm or synecdoche of the *Odyssey* as a whole.

The description of the scar in Book 19 would be the digression to end all digression: a little circle inscribed within the larger circle which is the hero's wandering journey home. Auerback points out that the syntactical digression introduced by the scar's description—the steeplechase of reminiscence unleased by Odysseus's unveiling of his leg, conjuring up name, ancestry, patrimony, property—in no way threatens the coheren narrative of the recognition scene. The relaxed economy of the epic present, he says, can tolerate such a digression without a strain.[25] Particularly, perhaps, when it is the patriarchal details of Odysseus's birthright which are being interpolated into the text, and particularly when it is a servant woman who is waiting in the wings.

Odysseus's scar thus is, and signifies nothing other than, the very image of the home. By contrast, the modern wound—unending, unhealing—would have made impossible any such enonomy of return. Adorno knew such exile. In America, he wrote: "every intellectual in emigration is, without exception, mutilated."[26] He went on to speak of this wound as the universal diaspora which marks modernity as such. Heine lived his exile as a wound. That wound, says Adorno, has become our own. "Now that the destiny which Heine sensed has been fulfilled literally . . . the homelessness has also become everyone's homelessness; all human beings have been as badly injured in their being and in the language as Heine the outcast was."[27]

The threat of shipwreck has become a universal fact. Once more it is a question of distraction and dispersal. Once more a question of a premature and hence preemptive pleasure. Once more it is a question of an impossible relationship to death. Once more it is a question of seduction through the ear. The propriety of the phallic subject is once more threatened by an emasculating voice which penetrates everywhere because it is located nowhere in space and time.

Who are the modern Sirens? If music's very essence is to be the "surviving message of despair from the shipwrecked,"[28] it is the sign of the times that it falls on deaf ears. Or rather: it is a degenerate form of music which would have already infantilized its listeners, reducing the alert, autonomous subject to the spellbound consumer, identifying with what he hears, acquiescent to whatever calls. "Vulgarization and enchantment, hostile sisters, dwell together"[29] in the reified productions of mass music.

Benjamin suggests that by Kafka's day, the Sirens have fallen silent because music as such—the last "token of hope"—has been permanently gagged.[30] This will not prevent them, perversely, from exerting a certain hypnotic spell. In "Josephine the Singer" (Kafka's final testament, written on his deathbed while his own voice, was, under the impact of tubercular laryngitis, disappearing[31]) the mass mouse audience fails to appreciate the pathetic squeaking which nonetheless, they insist, "enchants" them.[32] Having missed out on proper childhood, these rodent exiles—"nearly always on the run"—are at once too "childish" and "too old for music," and hardly notice when the enchanting Josephine, on strike for better working conditions, stops singing.[33]

Music for Adorno epitomizes the degradation of modern culture. As the "most immediate expression of instinct,"[34] it both carries the greatest emancipatory potential and would be therefore the most vulnerable to distortion. As the least obviously representational of all the art forms (a "non-mimetic mimesis") music would seem to have the supreme advantage in fulfilling art's utopian mandate which is the expression of the inexpressible. But in its privilege lies its weakness. Its very autonomy from signification, its "monadic" tendency to introversion, would entail a certain blindness to material origins which is the mark of every fetish. Insofar as music has to be performed in order to be realized, thus harbouring within itself its own congealed self-imitation or self-interpretation,[36] its production and its reproduction would be in logical symbiosis from the outset. It is in this sense half phantasmagorized from the start. It anticipates its own alienation in its inner form. It would thus seem to submit most readily to the commodifying force of capital, easily alienated from its own performance, easily cut off from its own source. Under the impact of sound recording, says Adorno, reproduction overwhelms production and thus the self-alienation of music becomes complete. Its components become interchangeable, abstract entities, like standardized parts on an assembly line,[36] like the commodities they have indeed become. Identifying with this process of abstraction, its listeners become the undifferentiated consumers whose life, says Adorno, has become a film. Processed music becomes the conformist, repetitive spell which turns its listeners into the retarded, children who keep on asking for the same old dish.[37] "Es ist babyfood."[38]

Because of the listener's hallucinatory identification with the apparatus, it becomes unclear who is consuming whom. If the audience has been reduced to pure orifice—a "great formless mouth with shining teeth in a voracious smile"[39]—it is just as true, for Adorno, that it is swallowed by the junk it swallows. No less than the child devours the babyfood, mass culture (like Charybdis) devours him. "Being consumed, swallowed up, is indeed just what I understand as 'participation' [Mitmachen] which is so totally characteristic for the new psychological type."[40] It is equally unclear who is hearing whom. Delusional projection on the part of the listener strips him of the inner "voice of conscience" which provides the very possibility of self-reflection. Lacking inner speech he now hears voices from the outside.[41] The "alien" product, "cut off from the masses by a dense screen, . . . seeks to speak for the silent." Lacking both voice and ear of his own, the modern listener finds the sirens providing an instant self-interpretation, predisgesting what they offer, constituting their own audience before the fact. "The composition hears for the listener."[42]

If "human dignity"—for Adorno as for Bloch—consists of the "right to walk,"[43] the culture industry would have crippled the orthopaedia of the upright posture. Reification produces the "stiffness" or "rigidity"[44] which signify the compensatory erections of Medusa's victims. Like Odysseus stiff against the mast, writhing in an ecstasy born of deepest deprivation, the spellbound listeners' hard and jerky movements betray the impotence which is their fate. Adorno comments, somewhat tartly, that people no longer know how to dance. "As if to confirm the superficiality and treachery of every form of ecstasy, the feet are unable to fulfill what the ear pretends."[45] Jazz listeners are the castrati who experience their own mutilation as an aesthetic pleasure. The "whimpering" vibrato[46] or "eunuchlike sound"[47] of the jazz singer croons the comforts of impotence—stepping out only so as to step back in line—expressing only the "premature and incomplete or orgasm"[48] which keeps on cheating you of the real thing.

Circe's magic had turned men into snuffling pigs (10.239). Civilization's defense, Freud insisted, was to institutionalize the upright posture in its repression of the sense of smell.[49] But if the advertising industry would guarantee *homo erectus* his hard-won dignity in the form of "shining white teeth and freedom from body odor,"[50] Adorno reminds us that such vertical appearances can be deceptive. Beneath the surface of the upright subject would be the distorted creatures of Kafka's imaginary— mice, moles, dogs, hunchbacks—until we come, finally, to Gregor Samsa, traveling salesman turned insect, crawling in grotesque rapture towards his sister's violin.[51] Adorno's modern Circe has transformed men into "savages" and in turn into insects.[52] In a sadomasochistic parody of sexual ecstasy (or, remarks Adorno, like the hideous convulsions of a wounded animal) the "jitterbugs"—in Adono's unusually vivid description— "whirl about in fascination."[53] The siren-bonds are tight. The jitterbugs only "entangle" themselves all the more tightly in the next of reification the more frantically they try to break away.[54]

According to a familiar Platonic formula, and with perhaps a similar gender subtext, the uncontrolled reproducibility of the artwork expresses itself as an infinietely regressive mimetic flux. A genealogical catastrophe would hve disordered the very process of reproduction. Copy and original become indistinguish, the voice becomes a simulacrum of itself, the original no longer holds. After the "birth of film out of the spirit of music,"[55] life itself becomes just like the movies. The "performance sounds like its own phonograph recording,"[56] the voice becoming like an imitation of itself,[57] the "hit song" becoming an advertisement for itself, sending out its own title as the only content it would announce. "Today every giant close-up of a star has become an advertisement for her name, every hit-song a plug [*zum Plug*] for its tune."[58] "Only the copy" appears.[59] Utopia becomes "merely a gilded background projected behind reality"[60]—i.e., for those like Plato's prisoners, or perhaps for those in Calypso's cave.

In Home, there was already a fine line between the song "itself" and its own announcement or replication. Odysseus's Sirens, promising to sing of "everything," sing of nothing other than the fact that they are to sing: a song about itself, says Todorov, a song about all song.[61] A song, says Blanchot, directed towards a singing which is always "still to come."[62]

> . . . they burst into their high, thrilling song:
> 'Come closer, famous Odysseus—Achaea's pride and glory—
> moor your ship on our coast so you can hear our song!
> Never has any sailor passed our shores in his black craft
> until he has heard the honeyed voices pouring from our lips.'
>
> (12.183–88)

What would the difference between the promising song and the song which is promised? Promising is of course the paradigm instance of the performative utterance of which the "saying" and the "doing," the announcement and the act, are indistinguishable. In Homer, the Siren's promise sounds as sweet as the honeyed voice it promises: certainly its allure is as lethal. The culture industry, by Adorno's account, would have transformed such a radical performativity into the teasing specularity of sheer performance. Radio assumes the phatic/phallic function of noise for the sake of noise, penetrating all orifices, invading all space. "The gigantic fact that speech penetrates everywhere replaces its content."[63] Sound becomes the echo advertising nothing but its own publicity: "Advertising becomes art and nothing else, just as Goebbels—with foresight—combines them: *l'art pour l'art*, advertising for its own sake, a pure representation of social power."[64] In an infinitely circular deferral, the ad promises the product, which in turn "incessantly reduces to a mere promise the enjoyment which it promises as a commodity."[65] The spectacles of Hollywood reduce the consumer to Tantalus,[66] tantalized with a fore-pleasure so numbing it would preempt the greater urge to happiness. By stimulating a desire which it thereby frustrates (pornography in its essence), the culture industry makes the promise the very articulation of which would be its own denial. Art's *promesse de bonheur* ("once the definition of art"[67]) would have been eliminated. The "medicinal bath" of "fun" (*das Fun*)[68] scrubs away the last utopian traces of happiness. The menu replaces the meal:

> The culture industry perpetually cheats its consumers of what it perpetually promises. The promissory note which . . . it draws on pleasure is endlessly prolonged; the promise, which is actually all the spectacle consists of, is illusory: maliciously, all it signifies is that the real point will never be reached, that the diner must be satisfied with reading the menu.[69]

In the totalitarian state, the promise preempts its own fulfilment: every promise becomes a threat, every invitation a call to panic. Sound becomes, indeed, a screeching siren, blocking hearing, blocking thought. The new sirens are described as follows:

> The radio becomes the universal mouthpiece of the Führer; his voice rises from street loud-speakers to resemble the howling of sirens announcing panic—from which modern propaganda can hardly be distinguished anyway. The National Socialists knew that the wireless gave shape to their cause just as the printing press did to the Reformation.[70]

Reproductive Aberrations

It is perhaps unnecessary to emphasize that there is a certain gender subtext underlying Adorno's denunciations. According to a familiar Platonic logic, an uncontrolled mimetic series would be indistinguishable from the wanton propagation which makes potential bastards of every offspring. Even Telemachus is not so sure who his father is (1.216). Reproductive confusion at the aesthetic level suggests as always the fragility of the sexual contract. If the unproductive foreplay of the culture industry yields only the simulacral pleasures of false adversiting, its demonic self-replication would both soften the virile "firmness" of every subject and corrupt the legitimacy of every birth.

> The decomposition of the subject is consummated in his self-abandonment to an everchanging sameness. This drains all

firmness [*Feste*] from characters. What Baudelaire commanded through the power of images, comes unbid to will-less fascination. Faithlessness and lack of identity, pathic responsiveness to situations, are induced by the stimulus of newness, which already, as a mere stimulus, no longer stimulates. Perhaps mankind's renunciation of the wish for children is declared here, because it is open to everyone to prophesy the worst: the new is the secret figure of all those unborn. Malthus is one of the forefathers of the nineteenth century, and Baudelaire had reason to extol infertile beauty. Mankind, despairing of its reproduction, unconsciously projects its wish for survival onto the chimera of the thing never known, but this is equivalent to death.[71]

But the generational disturbance goes in both directions. If children have become the death wish of a fatherless society which has replaced authentic propagation with sterile propaganda, Adorno suggests that the genealogical relationship to the past is distorted along parallel lines. A "disturbed relationship" to the ancestors.[72] A mourning gone astray.

Memory itself is at issue. In its complicity with mass culture, Wagner's music has the mnemotechnic versatility that writing once did for Plato—music "designed to be remembered, intended for the foregetful."[73] Berlioz's *idée fixe* puts the listener "under the spell of an opium dream."[74] The detached or morcellized musical "theme" impresses itself indelibly in our memory, thereby confirming our general amnesia, making us memorize what we cannot remember, idiotically inscribing what cannot be learned.[75] It is death itself, of course, which goes most unremembered. If mourning itself is, as Adorno says, the very "wound of civilization"[76]—a pure purposeless activity which challenges the functional efficiency of every order—it would be naturally the first thing in an exchange society to undergo liquidation. That which is not put to rest by proper mourning, says Freud, will always keep coming back to haunt us. And this is just what happens, adds Adorno, in the recycled tunes of the music industry.

The atomized, spatialized time of serial music expresses just the rage against the past—Nietzsche's "revenge" against the "it was"—which is the mark of inauthentic memory. (Nietzsche's vengeful listener danced, if not the jitterbug, the whirling "tarantella.")[77] Regressed listeners "kill time because there is nothing else on which to vent one's aggression."[78] In their frantic need to be "*Uptodatesein*," they ridicule that with which only yesterday they were most infatuated, hating the old and out-of-date as if to avenge the fact that their own ecstasy has been, to begin with, fake.[79] In a note "On the Theory of Ghosts," Adorno relates the modern atomization of time to a radical failure of mourning. The hatred of the past is itself the inability to give proper burial. Immigrants wipe away all traces of their past life. Out-of-print books get set aside. The unburied bones on the Sirens' beach become, for Adorno, the ornaments of the crematorium. The modern funeral with its beautified Corpse" and take-home bottled ashes suits the "hardened" survivor mentality of the guilty[80]—a reification of life which has continued even unto death, a cheating of the dead, a "homecoming without a home."[81]

But let us not ignore the gender assumptions determining this whole discussion. According to Freud, some sort of misfired mourning leads directly to the phantasmagorias of "mass psychology."[82] What would proper mourning be? Oedipal autonomy—and Freud recognized no other kind—required the son's internalization of the father's prohibition: the acquisition of a super-ego would be the only proper monument to the dead. "Mass" psychology has no such memory. Lacking a proper father to bury, the sons project an archaic father imago before whom they fuse prostrate in helpless identification. The "leader" would be the simulacral supplement for the missing father, who can be neither mourned nor, therefore, overthrown. The group's ties would remain all pre-Oedipal:[83] the incorporation of the mother's body rather than the introjection of the father's law. The prohibition on enjoying the mother's body has not been registered or internalized: the father's "No" remains unheard. From ear to mouth, from father to mother, from Oedipal to pre-Oedipal: on this triply regressive axis—body, gender, stage—mass psychology's perversions would seem to turn.

According to Adorno's almost verbatim transcription of the Freudian group psychology, the decline of the Oedipal family leads directly to the aberrant mourning patters of mass culture.[84] If freedom presupposes the internalization of a prior authority, the adult capacity for resistance requires precisely that there be strong fathers to overcome. Jessica Benjamin has outlined the issue well.[85] By Adorno's and Horkheimer's gloomy reckoning, the decline of entrepreneurial capitalism would have dislodged the patriarchal order, turning the self-reliant businessman into the scrambling employee, replacing the authority of the father with the power of administration, replacing the self-legislating son with the compliant child who does whatever he is told. Replaced as well would be the traditional "warm and loving mother" whose very exclusion from the world of work and power had meant (imagined Horkheimer) a certain utopian transcendence of the principle of exchange.[86] The "professional mother" ("Mom"[87]) turns affection into "hygiene."[88] Woman "bustles about after cultural goals like a social hyena."[89] And so on. (I parody, but only slightly—since I'm actually quoting—both the rhetoric and the substance of Adorno's and Horkheimer's argument.)

Monopoly capital has dispensed, says Adorno, with the need for superegos. Governance no longer requires the internalization of social norms. The family is no longer necessary or sufficient to provide a buffer for and from the demands of civilization. The administration now works directly on its subjects, rendering the detour through (self-) repression superfluous and obsolete. With the erosion of the bourgeois family goes the last vestige of guilty inwardness—but at the same time, notes Adorno somewhat sadly, the final possibility of revolt:

> When the big industrial interests incessantly undermine the economic basis for moral decision by eliminating the independent economic subject, partly by taking over the self-employed entrepreneur and partly by transforming the workers into the objects of a trade union, the capacity for reflection must also atrophy. . . . There is no longer an internal, instinctual or motivational conflict to be adjudicated, by which the tribunal of conscience is formed. Instead of the internalization of the social command which not only made it more binding and at the same time more open, but also emancipated it from society and even turned it against the latter, there is an immediate and direct identification with stereotyped value scales.[90]

Although Adorno is not exactly nostalgic for the patriarchal bourgeois family—I must stress this lack of nostalgia and note that on this score he differs markedly from Horkheimer[91]—he notes sharply that its demise would mean just the eclipse of the last opportunity for independent thought. "With the family there passes away, while the system lasts, not only the most effective agency of the bourgeoisie, but also the resistance which, though repressing the individual, also strengthened, perhaps even produced him. The end of the family paralyses the forces of opposition.[92]

In the absence of effective paternal prohibition we find an endless melancholic consumption substituting for the authentic work of mourning. In fascism, identification reverts to the pre-Oedipal, narcissistic cannibalism which subverts the (male) achievement of normal growth. In his essay on fascist propaganda, Adorno suggests that the relative absence of paternal authority in the present creates the projective phantasm of the "leader image." Instead of internalizaing a real authority, the orphaned masses simply absorb what they themselves put out: they embellish their own psychic overflow and go on to devour their own creation as an external thing. Like positivists, they "discover" what they have in fact "made"—and proceed to eat it.[93]

Where legitimate authority has withdrawn—Adorno suggests thereby that it once existed—an amorphous (almost Foucauldian) "power" steps in to fill the vacuum left by the unmourned dead. But because the leader himself is only deputizing for the powerless individuals who have, in fact, invented him, the leader is just an actor, playing the role of "leader" to an enchanted public who cannot tell the real thing from the fake. "They look like hairdressers, provincial actors, and hack journalists," writes Adorno.[94] The phantasmagoria of fascist demagogy are the final dissimulations of a banished mimetic impulse, an "organized imitation of magic practices," a "mimesis of mimesis."[95] "Group psychology" is jut this fiction.[96]

And what better figure for such a fiction than the figure of "the feminine"? Lacking a proper father whose authority they might internalize, the masses become, in the end, a woman. "Just as women adore the unmoved paranoiac, so the nation genuflects before fascism."[97] Or again: "Now emotion is reserved to power conscious of itself as power. Man surrenders to man, cold, bleak and unyielding, as woman did before him. Man turns into a woman gazing up at her master. . . . The seeds of homosexuality are sown."[98] And thus we find Adorno, finally, chiming in with the nineteenth-century male imaginary—mass culture as woman—the fantasy of a lethal lassitude or an oceanic engulfment, the fantasy of a watery grave. Andreas Huyssen has outlined the issue well.[99] From Nietzsche's polemic against Wagner's hypnotic effeminacies through Le Bon's description of the sphinxlike crowd to Eliot's depiction of the lure of mass society as a return to an encompassing womb, little is left to the imagination. Early Weimar film theory, too, was quick to pronounce on the dangers to hygiene posed by the "dark hole" (Kracauer[100]) of the movie theater: the stuffy air, the risk of disease, the blurring of class and gender divisions, the risk of sexual contact itself.[101] If Adorno does not exactly reproduce these fearful fantasies, he doesn't exactly dispel them either. Leaving us to wonder, finally, where this modern Odysseus has a leg to stand.

Penelope

When Ulysses and Penelope are in bed and telling their stories to one another, Penelope tells hers first. I believe a male writer would have made Ulysses's story come first and Penelope's second.
—Samuel Butler

Or is there another sexual economy at play? I haven't mentioned Penelope—few do. Even in antiquity she was considered too boringly good to be mythologized. What was there to say? She was faithful, she wove, Odysseus came home. Later tradition turned her into a slut. By the Hellenistic period the fantasies were going full steam.[102] Apollodorus speaks of her promiscuity, sleeping with the suitors, being sent away in disgrace upon Odysseus's return.[103] As Hyginus tells it, she ends up marrying Telegonus—Odysseus's illegitimate son by Circe, who appears one day in Ithaca to murder his father—and bearing Italus, after whom Italy was named.[104] (Telemachus meanwhile is said to go on to marry stepmother Circe, fathering Latinus in the process, but that is another story.)[105] By the Renaissance, Penelope's web had become the very image of feminine prevarication, a sign of promiscuity and diversion, a spider's web, a trap.[106]

But even in the *Odyssey* her identity was less secure than one tends to think. Agamemnon backhandedly compares her to a Clytemnestra (11.433f., 24.200f.). Athena insinuates that she's just hunting for another man (15.20–23). Telemachus doesn't trust her to protect the family property in his absence (15.88–91). He complains bitterly that to the eager suitors she won't say yes or no (1.249f., cf. 16.730). Penelope herself professes to understand Helen's adultery as, after all, a normal "error" (23.209–30). She dreams with pleasure about her collection of pet geese (19.537).[107] The men she feeds among the pigs become just like the pig-victims of Circe's magic.[108] Odysseus, who rarely sees fit to mention her on his travels, treats her with jealous suspicion on his return. His homecoming takes place while he's wrapped in a slumber so "sweet" (*hedistos*) it's compared to death (13.79–81). If homecoming is said to be "honeysweet" (as Teiresias puts it[109]), its allure would be perilously close to the distracting exile it was to end.

Certainly the suitors see her as another Siren. Penelope too knows

ЁЁЁ

how to "enchant" (*thelgein*) men's hearts with "words of honey" (*meilichiosis epeessi*) (18.283): she too knows how to "fan" and "inflame" their passion (18.160f.) until their "knees slacken" and "hearts dissolve" of her web routine (2.89). Her prevarication is itself the ultimate promise that so defers itself that it unravels its own point. The weaving proves not only to be deceptive but to be quite fatal. The slaughtered suitors are described as fish caught in a net (23.384f.).

In 1897, Samuel Butler reads the *Odyssey* and concludes that a woman must have written it. The telltale signs are numerous: the obsession with womanly matters; the trivial housewifely details; the various inconsistencies and bad logic;[110] and finally the whitewashing of Penelope's name. The "authoress" of the *Odyssey*" has no feel, he complains, for what it's really like to be a man in love. It would have been easy enough for Penelope to get rid of the suitors if she had really wanted. "All she had to do was to bolt the door."[111] After all, she must have been a good forty, "and not getting any younger," Butler adds. "Did she every try snubbing?" he asks.

> . . . and then there was boring did she ever try that? Did she ever read them any of her grandfather's letters? Did she sing them her own songs, or play them music of her own composition? I have always found these courses successful when I wanted to get rid of people. . . . Did she ask [them] to sit to her for her web—give them a good stiff pose, make them stick to it, and talk to them all the time? Did she find errands for them to run, and then scold them, and say she did not want them? Or make them do commissions for her and forget to pay them, or keep on sending them back to the shop to change things. . . . In a word, did she do a single one of the thousand things so astute a matron would have been at no loss to hit upon if she had been in earnest about not wanting to be courted? With one touch of common sense the whole fabric crumbles into dust.[112]

But was not Penelope's weaving quite essential? Did it not represent a desire so vertiginous that it could not come to term? Penelope's "seductiveness" is in fact inseparable from her weeping. For like her weaving, Penelope's grief cannot end. When the bard Phemius charms the entire company with his singing (1.337–44), Penelope is the only one to resist his siren spell. Her "unforgettable sorrow" (*penthos alaston*) (1.342) (in her words) won't accept the drug of musical comfort; it is a sorrow which is "unforgettable" simply because it cannot come to term. Not knowing whether Odysseus is dead or alive—not knowing, therefore, the full measure of her loss—she can neither mourn nor abstain from mourning. In this tension between mourning and desire, Penelope's own double bind now comes to light.

Neither mourning nor not-mourning, she does not in fact recognize her returning husband. Unlike the dog, the nurse, the son, the swineherd, and the father, this wife demands an infinity of proofs. Unseduced even when Odysseus appears in dazzling, greased-up splendor—the very charm that worked well enough on Nausicaa (6.230–35)—Penelope remains stony and inert. If Penelope's faithfulness is said to be the very condition of Odysseus's heroic reputation (24.192–202), if h is glory requires that his wife wait patiently at home, it is ironic that Penelope herself won't participate in the general recognition she renders possible.[113] Her reticence is at once both the condition and the limit of his heroic *kleos*: she withdraws from the intersubjective arena she opens up. Her son reproaches her for her hardheartedness (23.97–103). Her nurse reproaches her for being "untrusting" (23.72). The word in Greek is *apistos*: it means in fact both untrusting and untrustworthy. But could a wife in such a circumstance ever be fully *pistos*? To trust and to be trusted would seem here to be at odds. (In Homer, typically, it's only male companions like Patroclus and Achilles who get the familiar epithet of *pistos*.) Were Penelope to allow herself to be seduced too quickly by Odysseus, her trust would betray her real untrustworthiness. To trust and to be trusted are, for this woman, quite irreconcilable. The double bind of being Odysseus's wife.

Perhaps, at moments, Adorno himself had glimpses of this Penelope. In the *Aesthetic Theory*, he writes of the endless longing which feeds off an infinite loss. No comfort could assuage this. The stubbornness of its attachment introduces within mourning a desire which refuses the consolation of every partial nourishment and thus stakes a claim on a happiness outstripping every fact. In its tenacity would be its urgency, in its patience its greatest zeal. In *Prisms*, Adorno writes: "Like knowledge, art cannot wait, but as soon as it succumbs to impatience it is doomed."[114] Such burning patience feeds on a grief which knows neither healing nor recompense. This grief would be, like Penelope's, quite "unforgettable"— endless precisely where it is most uncertain what exactly has been lost.

In *Minima Moralia*, Adorno writes that for "the one who no longer has a homeland," writing itself becomes the only place to live.[115] Such a place would be the non-place of a permanent wandering, an odyssey without a final end. But here Odysseus would have become none other than Penelope. His intransigence would have become just her expectancy: a kind of "seasickness," as Kafka remarked, which now is felt everywhere on dry land. The bonds would loosen just where they would seem to be the tightest. In such a loosening, the text as such is formed.

"Properly written texts," writes Adorno, "are like spiders' webs: tight, concentric, transparent, well-spun and firm."[116] In the *Aesthetic Theory*, he writes of the special "cunning" of the artwork. It unravels its own will to mastery and incorporates its own failure to totalize as an esssential moment of its truth. The paradigm of this cunning is none other than Penelope.

> The unity of logos, because it mutilates, is enmeshed in the nexus of its own guilt. Homer's tale of Penelope, who in the evening unraveled what she had accomplished during the day, is a self-unconscious allegory of art: What cunning Penelope inflicts on her artifacts, she actually inflicts on herself. Ever since Homer's verses this episode is not the addition or rudiment for which it is easily taken, but a constitutive category of art. Through this story, art takes into itself the impossibility of the identity of the one and the many as an element of its unity. Artworks, no less than reason, have their cunning.[117]

In *Fear and Trembling*, Kierkegaard writes of the "infinite resignation" which sacrifices without hope of restitution. Such renunciation is not (yet) compromised by the consolations of religion, with its comforting hope of recompense. It thus installs a mourning which is not yet that of the knight of faith, whose leap—and this is of course precisely what Adorno was to find most irritating about him[118]—involved the absurd conviction that he would somehow get his own back. "Infinite resignation" would have no such knightly confidence. Its melancholy would exceed the economy of every homecoming; in its rigorous hopelessness would lie its only strength. Kierkegaard writes:

> Infinite resignation is that shirt we read about in the old fable. The thread is spun under tears, the cloth bleached with tears, the shirt sewn with tears; but then too it is a better protection than

iron and steel . . . The secret in life is that everyone must sew it
for himself, and the astonishing thing is that a man can sew it
fully as well as a woman.[119]

Notes

1. Theodor Adorno and Max Horkheimer, *Dialektik der Aufklärung, Gesammelte Schriften* vol.
3 (Frankfurt: Suhrkamp, 1981), 64 ("Abenteuerroman"), 80 ("Robinsonade"). Hereafter cited as
GS. In English as *Dialectic of Enlightenment,* trans. John Cumming (New York: Continuum, 1969),
46, 61. Hereafter cited as *DE.* Throughout this chapter I will be citing the standard English translations of Adorno with some modifications as indicated.

2. Although Robert Hullot-Kentor argues that Horkheimer's influence is evident in this chapter as elsewhere in the *Dialectic of Enlightenment.* See Robert Hullot-Kentor, "Back to Adorno," *Telos*
81 (1989): 5–29.

3. Early Greek representations of the Sirens show them as sexually ambiguous, frequently
bearded figures. See John Pollard, *Seers, Shrines, and Sirens: The Greek Religious Revolution in the Sixth
Century* (London: Allen and Unwin, 1963), 140.

4. Homer, *Odyssey, Homeri Opera,* ed. David B. Munro and Thomas W. Allen (London:
Oxford University Press, 1917); in English, trans. Robert Fagles (New York and London: Penguin,
1996), Book 12, lines 205–7. All references will henceforth be given in the text by book and line
numbers only (Greek edition).

5. On the connection between the Sirens and the Iliadic Muses, see Pietro Pucci's remarkable
rhetorical analysis in "The Song of the Sirens," *Arethusa* 12 (1979): 121–31.

6. Cf. Jean-Pierre Vernant, "Feminine Aspects of Death in Ancient Greece," *Diacritics* 16
(1986): 54–64.

7. Cf. Philippe Lacoue-Labarthe, "L'Écho du sujet," *Le sujet de la philosophie: Typographies I*
(Paris: Aubier: Flammarion, 1979) 217–303. It is striking that at the court of the Phaeacians, Odysseus speaks of his own heroic glory (*kleos*) in the first person ("I am Odysseus, son of Laertes, known
to the world for every kind of craft—my fame has reached the skies" [9.19f]). Charles Segal remarks
that it is unusual in Greek to speak of "my *kleos*" (*kleos* or fame normally enunciated only in the third
person—not for a speaker to advertise about himself—and typically only after the hero's death). See
"*Kleos* and its Ironies in the *Odyssey*," in Harold Bloom, ed., *Homer's The Odyssey* (New York:
Chelsea House, 1988), 128f. The trip to Hades in Book 11 (prior in the order of experience, posterior
in the order of telling) has already given Odysseus a premature taste of death, a death before death,
rendering him, as Circe aptly remarks, twice mortal (*disthanees*): "doomed to die twice over—others
just die once" (12.22). And indeed, in response to Alcinous, Odysseus announces his tale, the story
of his own *kleos*, as a mourning performance, a narrative grief which redoubles the grief which his
life as such has, according to him, become. "But now you're set on probing the bitter pains I've
borne, / so I'm to weep and grieve, it seems, still more. / Well then, what shall I go through first, /
what shall I save for last?" (9.12ff.). The very compulsion to narrate would seem to transgress the
bounds of what "I" can say of myself, thus making the act of speech not only an act of mourning for
the lost object but, indeed, a form of self-mourning, an impossible mourning for the lost subject.

8. Cf. Odysseus's urge to impart sequential order to his narrative of grief, a grief which in its
excessiveness threatens precisely to explode such sequence, or render it arbitrary: "Well, then, what
shall I go through first, / what shall I save for last? / What pains—the gods have given me my share. /
Now let me start by telling you my name . . ." (9.15–17).

9. On the mythological connection between the Sirens and the underworld, and the possibility that the Sirens themselves were seen at some point as mediating between the living and the dead (early Greek paintings represent the Sirens as birds, thus corresponding, perhaps, to the Egyptian *ba* or soul-bird), see Georg Weicker, *Die Seelenvogel in der alten Literatur und Kunst* (Leipzig: Teubner, 1902), and K. Buschor, *Die Musen des Jenseits* (Munich: Bruckmann, 1944). See also the critical discussion by Karoly Marot, *Die Anfänge der griechischen Literatur* (Budapest: Ungarische Akademie der Wissenschaften, 1960), 106–87. For a good survey of the issue, see Siegfried de Rachewiltz, *De Sirenibus: An Inquiry into Sirens from Homer to Shakespeare* (New York: Garland, 1987), 254–75, as well as Gerald Gresseth, "The Homeric Sirens," *Transactions and Proceedings of the American Philological Association* 101 (1970). It is worth recalling here that in the allegory of the afterlife in the last book of the *Republic*, Plato has the soul encounter the Sirens (eight of them, almost Muselike) presiding over the spindle of Necessity, singing the music of the spheres (616b–617d).

10. According to at least one etymology, the word for Siren is related to the word *seirén*—' 'inherited from some Mediterranean language"—signifying a mantic bee. See Gabriel Germain, "The Sirens and the Temptation of Knowledge," in George Steiner and Robert Fagles, eds., *Homer: A Collection of Critical Essays* (Englewood Cliffs: Prentice-Hall, 1962) 96. The association is particularly interesting insofar as the industrious bee was typically valorized in Greece as the very image of feminine virtue. See for example the Homeric hymn to Hermes and Laurence Kahn's superb essay, *Hermès passé ou les ambiguités de la communication* (Paris: Maspéro, 1978).

11. Pietro Pucci points out that the Sirens, despite the proximity of their attributes and diction to the (Iliadic) Muses, do not actually speak of *kleos* by name. See "The Song of the Sirens," 130n9. Charles Segal makes the parallel point that, like Hesiod's Muses, the Sirens speak not of memory but of a kind of immediate "knowing" (*idmen . . . idmen*, 12.205–7); see "Kleos and its Ironies in the *Odyssey*," 145.

12. Claude Lévi-Strauss, *From Honey to Ashes*, trans. John and Doreen Weight (New York: Harper and Row, 1973). On the semantic field of "honey" in early Greek literature, see Pietro Pucci, *Hesiod and the Language of Poetry* (Baltimore: Johns Hopkins University Press, 1977). See also Jan Hendrik Waszink, *Biene und Honig als Symbol des Dichter und der Dichtung in der griechische Literatur* (Opladen: Westdeutscher, 1974) and Kahn, *Hermès*.

13. Jean-Pierre Vernant, "Feminine Figures of Death in Greece."

14. Emily Vermeule (*Aspects of Death in Early Greek Art and Poetry* [Berkeley and Los Angeles: University of California Press, 1979], 203) relates the *andrôn puthomenôn* of 12.46 to the pun on the rotting Python at Delphi.

15. We know that Odysseus (who "does not resemble an athlete" [8.164] and whose "legs have lost their condition" [8.233]) is rather prone to cry at music. Upon hearing Demodocus's epic chant at the court of Alcinous, he was reduced to tears (8.86–93), compared, indeed, to a widow weeping over the body of her dead husband (8.521–29). At 10.410ff. Odysseus's men cluster around him as calves around a cow. On the question of "role reversal" in general in the *Odyssey*, see Helene P. Foley, " 'Reverse Similes' and Sex Roles in the *Odyssey*," in John Peradotto and J. P. Sullivan, eds., *Women in the Ancient World* (Albany: SUNY Press, 1984), 59–78.

16. Odysseus is also compared to a bard at 11.368 and, indirectly, at 21.406–11. It is worth noting that in late antiquity Orpheus sometimes stands in for Odysseus in the Sirens episode. Apollonius of Rhodes has Orpheus outwit the Sirens by playing their own game—literally outsinging them with his lyre. See *Argonautica* IV.891–92, trans. R. C. Seaton (Cambridge, Mass.: Harvard University Press, 1912).

17. The escape from Polyphemus's cave similarly involved tying the surviving sailors (horizontally) onto the back of the Cyclops's male sheep (9.429f.), Odysseus himself having mutilated the Cyclops with a (vertical) beam the size of a "mast" (9.322). Later, back home in Ithaca, in a kind of parodistic redoubling of the Sirens episode, and in terms which semantically link the Sirens with the prophylactic remedy against them, Odysseus will have the treacherous cowherd Melanthios tied up with a "braided rope" (*seirén plektén*) and hoisted up a "high column" (22.175f.).

18. On some of the psychoanalytic resonances of wind fertilization, see Ernest Jones, "The Madonna's Conception Through the Ear," *Essays in Applied Psychoanalysis*, vol. 2 (New York: International University Press, 1964).

19. Friedrich Nietzsche, "On Redemption," *Thus Spoke Zarathustra*, *The Portable Nietzsche*, trans. Walter Kaufmann (New York: Viking, 1968), 250.

20. Cf. Sigmund Freud, "Medusa's Head," *Standard Edition of the Complete Works of Sigmund Freud* 18, trans. and ed. James Strachey (London: Hogarth, 1974), 273.

21. Or, even more suggestively, in Homeric Greek dialect, *ouata*. See John Winkler's essay, "Penelope's Cunning and Homer's," in *The Constraints of Desire: The Anthropology of Sex and Gender in Ancient Greece* (New York: Routledge, 1990), 129–67, here 144.

22. Kafka, "The Silence of the Sirens," *Parables and Paradoxes*, bilingual edition, ed. Nahum Glatzer (New York: Schocken, 1961), 88f.

23. See Pedro Laín Entralgo, *The Therapy of the Word in Classical Antiquity* (New Haven: Yale University Press, 1970), 21. Entralgo points out that when Odysseus's hunting companions "bind up" (*dêsan*) his wound and staunch the bleeding by means of a "charm" (*epaoidê*) (19.457) the medical and magical aspects of the cure are inseparable and indeed indistinguishable. Cf. *Eumemides* 331–33 on the song of the Furies, "binding brain and blighting blood in its stringless melody."

24. See August Friedrich von Pauly, *Real-Encyclopädie der classischen Altertumswissenschaft*, Neue Bearbeitung begonnen von Georg Wissowa (Stuttgart: J. B. Metzlersche Verlagsbuchhandlung, 1927), Zweite Reihe, Bd. 3.A.1, cols. 289f. Other etymologies of *seirené* include *surizo* ("hiss," "pipe,") *seirios* ("scorching,") and the Semitic *sir* ("song"). See on this last point Gerald Gresseth, "The Homeric Sirens," 204 n.

25. Eric Auerbach, *Mimesis: The Representation of Reality in Western Literature* (Garden City, N.Y.: Doubleday, 1957).

26. Adorno, *Minima Moralia: Reflexionem aus dem beschädigten Leben*, *Gesammelte Schriften* 4 (Frankfurt: Suhrkamp, 1974); in English, trans. E. F. N. Jephcott, *Minima Moralia: Reflections from Damaged Life* (London: NLB, 1974), §22. (Hereafter cited as MM.)

27. Adorno, "Die Wunde Heine," *Noten zur Literatur*, *Gesammelte Schriften* 2 (Frankfurt: Suhrkamp, 1974), 100; in English, "Heine the Wound," *Notes to Literature*, trans. Shierry Weber Nicholsen, 85.

28. Adorno, *Philosophy of Modern Music*, trans. Anne Mitchell and Wesley Blomster (New York: Continuum, 1985), 133. I cannot resist citing the rather free translation. The original is more sober. "Sie ist die wahre Flaschenpost." *Philosophie der neuen Musik*, GS 12:126. (Hereafter cited as PMM.)

29. Adorno, "Über den Fetischcharakter in der Musik und die Regression des Hörens," GS, 14:28; in English, "On the Fetish-Character in Music and the Regression of Hearing," in Andrew Arato and Eike Gebhardt, eds., *The Essential Frankfurt School Reader* (New York: Urizen, 1978), 281. (Hereafter cited as F.) (Translation modified.)

30. Walter Benjamin, "Franz Kafka," *Gesammelte Schriften* 2.2 (Frankfurt: Suhrkamp, 1977), 416; in English, trans. Harry Zohn, *Illuminations* (New York: Schocken, 1969), 118.

31. Ernst Pawel, *The Nightmare of Reason: A Life of Franz Kafka* (New York: Vintage, 1984), 443.

32. Franz Kafka, "Josephine the Singer, or the Mouse Folk," *The Complete Stories* (New York: Schocken, 1971), 362.

33. "Josephine the Singer," 364, 369. See Laurence Rickels's suggestive essay, "MUSICPHANTOMS: 'Uncanned' Conceptions of Music from Josephine the Singer to Mickey Mouse," *Sub-stance* 58 (1989): 3–24.

34. GS, 14:14; F, 270.

35. Adorno, *Ästhetische Theorie*, GS 7:190f.; in English, trans. Robert Hullot-Kentor, *Aesthetic Theory* (Minneapolis: University of Minnesota Press, 1997), 125f. (Hereafter cited as AT.)

36. Adorno (with the assistance of George Simpson), "On Popular Music," *Studies in Philosophy and Social Science* 9 (1941): 19.

37. GS, 14:39; F, 290.

38. GS, 3:305 (supplement not included in English edition of *DE*).

39. GS, 14:35; F, 287.

40. "Notizen zur neuen Anthropologie," quoted in Susan Buck-Morss, *The Origin of Negative Dialectics* (New York: Free Press, 1977), 189.

41. GS, 3:214; *DE*, 189.

42. "On Popular Music," 25.

43. GS, 4:182; MM, §102.

44. "Alle Phänomene starren . . ." See "Kulturkritik und Gesellschaft," *Prismen*, GS 10:29; in English, trans. Samuel and Shierry Weber, "Cultural Criticism and Society," *Prisms* (Cambridge, Mass.: MIT, 1982), 34.

45. GS, 14:42; F, 292.

46. Adorno, "Über Jazz," GS, 17:99; trans. Jamie Owen Daniel, "On Jazz," *Discourse* 12 (1989–90): 67. (Hereafter cited as *J*.)

47. "Zeitlose Mode—Zum Jazz," GS 10:133; in English, "Perennial Fashion—Jazz," *Prisms*, 129.

48. GS, 17:98; *J*, 66.

49. Freud, *Civilization and Its Discontents*, *Complete Works*, 2:99–100n1. Adorno picks up this scent at GS, 3:209, 266; *DE*, 184, 233, and refers it specifically to the Circe episode at GS, 3:90; *DE*, 71.

50. GS, 3:191; *DE*, 167.

51. Kafka, "The Metamorphosis," *The Complete Stories*, 130f. For Adorno's response to the theme of animality in Kafka, see "Notes on Kafka," GS, 10:254–87; in English, *Prisms*, 245–71.

52. To twist the matter even further: recall that the Sirens themselves were, at least in one tradition, related to insects (cf.n. 10 above). In the *Phaedrus*, Socrates, trying to speak against the background noise of the cicadas, warns Phaedrus of the narcoleptic temptation of their buzzing drone, which he refers to, indeed, as a "bewitching Siren song" (259a). The cicadas themselves are said by Socrates to descend from men who became so drunk with pleasure from the music of the Muses that they forgot to eat or drink and "died without noticing it" (259c). By such an allegory the "Sirens" would be, then, both the perpetrators and the first victims of musical seduction. See, for some interesting remarks on the *Phaedrus* myth, J. Ferrari, *Listening to the Cicadas* (Cambridge: Cambridge University Press, 1987).

53. GS, 14:42; F 292. Adorno also refers to the "jitterbugs" in "Jazz—a Perennial Fashion," GS, 10:132; *Prisms*, 128.

54. GS, 14:41; F, 292.

55. Adorno, *Versuch über Wagner*, GS, 13:102; in English, trans. Rodney Livingstone, *In Search of Wagner* (London: NLB 1981), 107. (Hereafter cited as *W*.)

56. GS, 14:31; F, 284.

57. GS, 14:23; F, 277.

58. GS, 3:187; *DE*, 163 (translation modified).

59. GS, 3:165; *DE*, 143.

60. GS, 3:166; *DE*, 143 (translation altered).

61. Tzvetan Todorov, *Poetics of Prose* (Ithaca: Cornell University Press, 1977), 56.

62. Maurice Blanchot, "The Song of the Sirens," *The Gaze of Orpheus*, trans. Lydia Davis (Barrytown, N.Y.: Station Hill, 1981), 105.

63. GS, 3:183; *DE*, 159.

64. GS, 3:186; *DE*, 163.

65. GS, 3:185; *DE*, 162 (translation modified).

66. Cf. GS, 3:162; *DE*, 140.

67. GS, 14:19; F, 274. Cf. GS, 7:26; AT, 12.

68. GS, 3:162; DE, 140.

69. GS, 3:161; DE, 139 (translation modified).

70. GS, 3:159; DE, 159.

71. GS, 14:270; MM, §150 (translation modified).

72. GS, 3:243; DE, 215.

73. GS, 13:29; W, 31.

74. GS, 13:29; W, 31.

75. GS, 14:27; F, 281.

76. GS, 3:244; DE, 216.

77. See Nietzsche, Thus Spoke Zarathustra, "The Tarantulas."

78. GS, 14:44; F, 294.

79. GS, 14:45; F, 295.

80. GS, 3:244; DE, 216.

81. GS, 13:139; W, 149.

82. See Freud, "Group Psychology and the Analysis of the Ego," SE, 18:67–144.

83. Cf. Janine Chasseguet-Smirgel, Sexuality and Mind: The Role of the Mother and Father in the Psyche (New York: New York University Press, 1986), 81–91.

84. See, in particular, "Freudian Theory and the Pattern of Fascist Propaganda," GS, 8:408–33; The Essential Frankfurt School Reader.

85. Jessica Benjamin, "The End of Internalization: Adorno's Social Psychology," Telos 32 (1977): 42–64; "Authority and the Family Revisited: or, A World Without Fathers?" New German Critique 13 (1978): 35–57. See also Klaus Theweleit, Männerphantasien, 2 vols. (Frankfurt: Roter Stern, 1977–78). Also, Patricia Jagentowicz Mills, Woman, Nature, and Psyche (New Haven: Yale University Press, 1987), 93–116.

86. Horkheimer, "Authority and the Family," trans. Matthew O'Connell, Critical Theory (New York: Seabury, 1972), 114; "Authoritarianism and the Family," in Ruth Nanda Anshen, ed., The Family: Its Function and Destiny (New York, Harper, 1959), 390.

87. Cf. Philip Wylie, Generation of Vipers (New York: Rinehart, 1942).

88. Horkheimer, "Authoritarianism and the Family," 389.

89. GS, 3:288; DE, 250.

90. GS, 3:224; DE, 198 (translation modified).

91. This lack of nostalgia becomes particularly clear in Adorno's sharp critique of Huxley in "Aldous Huxley and Utopia," 10:97–122; Prisms, 97–117.

92. GS, 4:23; MM, §2.

93. GS, 8:417–19.

94. GS, 3:270; DE, 236.

95. GS, 3:209; DE, 185.

96. GS, 8:432–33.

97. GS, 3:216; DE, 191.

98. GS, 3:290; DE, 252.

99. Andreas Huyssen, "Mass Culture as Woman," in Tania Modleski, ed., Studies in Entertainment: Critical Approaches to Mass Culture (Bloomington: Indiana University Press, 1986).

100. Kracauer, "Langeweile," Das Ornament der Masse: Essays (Frankfurt: Suhrkamp, 1977), 322. For an examination of some of the gender assumptions determining Kracauer's film theory, see Sabine Hake, "Girls and Crisis—the Other Side of Diversion," New German Critique 40 (1987): 147–64.

101. This has become a central theme in feminist film criticism focusing on the Weimar period. See, in addition to Sabine Hake (cited above), Heidi Schlüpmann, "Kinosucht," frauen und film 33 (October 1982): 45–52; Miriam Hansen, "Early Silent Cinema: Whose Public Sphere?" New Ger-

man *Critique* 29 (1983): 147–84; and Patrice Petro, *Joyless Streets: Women and Melodramatic Representation in Weimar Germany* (Princeton: Princeton University Press, 1989).

102. For a survey of the classical literature, see Pauly and Wissowa, *Real-Encyclopädie der classischen Altertumswissenschaft*, Erste Reihe, Bd 19.1, cols. 479–82.

103. *Epitome* VII:36–38, in *The Library of Apollodorus*, trans. James Frazer (London: Heinemann, 1921). Apollodorus presents two alternative scenarios. In the first instance, Penelope is seduced by Antinous, is sent away by Odysseus to her father Icarius, and proceeds to get pregnant with Pan by Hermes. (On Penelope as the mother of Pan, see also Cicero, *De Natura Deorum* III.xxii.56, trans. H. Rackham [London: William Heinemann, 1933]). In the other instance, Penelope is seduced by Amphinomos and is killed in punishment by her returning husband.

104. Hyginus, *Fabulae* CXXXVII, ed. H. I. Rose (Lugduni Batavorum: A. W. Sythhoff, 1963).

105. Hyginus, *Fabulae* CXXVII.

106. Cf. Patricia Parker, *Literary Fat Ladies: Rhetoric, Gender, Property* (New York: Methuen, 1987), 26.

107. For a psychoanalytic reading, see Georges Devereux, "Le caractère de Pénélope," *Femme et mythe* (Paris: Flammarion, 1982), 259–70.

108. To tighten the identification still further, Calypso and Circe, conversely, are outfitted with looms (5.62 and 10.222), the latter of which is associated with the suspicion of a trap or snare (*dolos*) (10.232, 10.258)—the same cunning attributed later to Penelope's weaving (19.137)—and, throughout, of course, to Odysseus himself. See John Winkler, "Penelope's Cunning" and Marcel Détienne and Jean-Pierre Vernant, *Cunning Intelligence in Greek Culture and Society* (Sussex: Harvester Press, 1978).

109. 11.100. Cf. Odysseus's own invocation of home sweet home at 9.34.

110. "I do not say that this is feminine, but I can find nothing like it in the *Iliad*." Samuel Butler, *The Authoress of the Odyssey* (London: a. c. Fifield, 1897), 151.

111. Butler, 126.

112. Butler, 130.

113. On Penelope's non-recognition, see Sheila Murnaghan, "Penelope's *Agnoia*: Knowledge, Power, and Gender in the *Odyssey*," *Helios* 13 (1986): 103–15.

114. Adorno, "Arnold Schönberg 1874–1951," *GS*, 10:171; *Prisms*, 165.

115. *GS*, 14:96; *MM*, §51.

116. *GS*, 4:95; *MM*, §51.

117. *GS*, 7:278; *AT*, 186f.

118. Adorno, *Kierkegaard: Konstruktion des Ästhetischen, GS*, 2; in English, trans. Robert Hullot-Kentor, *Kierkegaard: Construction of the Aesthetic* (Minneapolis: University of Minnesota Press, 1989).

119. Kierkegaard, *Philosophical Fragments*, trans. Howard Hong and Edna Hong (Princeton: Princeton University Press, 1985), 56.

4

A Feminine Dialectic of Enlightenment?

Horkheimer and Adorno Revisited

Andrew Hewitt

One of the reasons for the continued influence exercised by Horkheimer and Adorno's *Dialectic of Enlightenment*[1]—a work which could scarcely be more clearly marked by the historical context of its creation—upon current theoretical debates in the realms of politics, aesthetics, and sociology, is the paradigm shift it marks in the analysis of power. Wedged between the dual threats of American consumerism on the one hand and Nazism on the other, *Dialectic of Enlightenment* effects a move away from the analysis of domination as an essentially binary structure and toward the examination of power as a complex system of mediation. Stated plainly: it is no longer a question, in this work, of analyzing the subject's domination of its object, but rather of exploring that discursive system of power in which effects of domination—oriented around notions of Subject and Object—are possible, and, indeed, inevitable. Both Subject and Object, dominator and dominated, function as bearers of a power which neither actually possesses. To this extent, *Dialectic of Enlightenment* offers a rigorous historical recontextualization of the master-slave dialectic, pushing the Hegelian model to that extreme point where the very category of enslavement crumbles beneath the coercive weight of universal consent. Motivated by an attempt to understand the emergence of fascism as a popular movement, Horkheimer and Adorno aim to understand why it is that both participants in the complex of domination should connive at the system which in turn dominates them. That the dominator—who, for all that he is dominated by a broader system of power, does not cease to dominate—should trade off his own subordination to a network of power in order to maintain his own direct privilege is, perhaps, all too understandable. The question, then, would be directed toward the dominated—what stake do *they* have in this continued subordination?

This shift in analysis is dictated not by methodological imperatives, but rather by the twin historical phenomena of Nazism and mass consumerism. Horkheimer and Adorno do not offer an epistemology of the subject, and of the historical implementation of that subject—à la Foucault—but rather they insist upon a historical mutation in the structure of subjectivity, a mutation brought about by capitalism as the rationalized instantiation of Enlightenment thought. At the same time, however, the somewhat vague historical contours of the very term "enlightenment"—as it is used in this work, to cover an historical period stretching back as far as the Greeks—threatens to cloud the historical and political clarity of the analysis. As an analysis of fascism, meanwhile, *Dialectic of Enlightenment* can be read alongside other early attempts to understand the movement as something more than a massive confidence trick played upon an unsuspecting democracy.[2]

If, however, we present the ideological structure of fascism as such that the dominated—by means of an escalation of domination, a superimposition of hierarchy upon hierarchy—can always point to a situation in which they, in turn, held power over a group even lower down the ladder (even if that power is but power over external nature, or over an unruly internal nature), then we will have missed the specificity of Horkheimer and Adorno's analysis of the etiology of power. While it may be possible—if not necessarily correct—to analyze fascism in terms of a pure domination, in which the experience of being dominated is always effaced by one's own domination of others, such a presentation fails to examine the pathology of domination itself. The logic and desirability of power (as domination) is thereby assumed. It is precisely this assumption that Horkheimer and Adorno seek to address.

Thus, though *Dialectic of Enlightenment*—complete with its theses on anti-Semitism—clearly responds to the historical phenomenon of fascism, the specificity of its analysis of power is more directly attributable to the exile experience in America. If, on the one hand, fascism could no longer be accounted for as an aberration or a swindle, the same was true for capitalism. Moreover, the specific organization of capitalism served to radicalize the critique of the complicity of the dominated. For consumer capitalism—in its purest form—would consist precisely in the refusal to subordinate fundamental categories of economic exploitation to compensatory political and ideological structures of domination. The religion of the market-place would, classically, reject the false gods of "ideology" so central to fascism. Thus, for Horkheimer and Adorno the specific form of swindle central to capitalism—the swindle of the exploitation of labor—could no longer be analyzed within an agonistics of domination, but had to be explained within a language game of consent. In the America of the New Deal—that is to say, in the period of capitalism's potential resurgence as a welfare state—power could no longer be thought purely in terms of the economic. Exploitation, as the economic modality of repression and domination, needed to be rethought.

In a sense, of course, power is always already the field of possibility of domination, its philosophical metadiscourse. At the same time, domination is always the syntagmatic instantiation of power—even when it is no longer experienced as such. It goes without saying that *Dialectic of Enlightenment* cannot be read from a poststructuralist perspective as a model or precursor of theories of totalitarianism. Clearly this text does not analyze totalitarianism as a blanket term covering both fascism and communism: the key analytical observations arise from the insights afforded by the comparison of *capitalism* and fascism. While this observation is in itself banal, it nevertheless obliges us to delineate more clearly just how power—as "totality"—operates in this work. What Horkheimer and Adorno are analyzing is political power not as a given, but as a specific manipulation of the more fundamental power of representation.

Power—as a collusive system of domination—is taken as a system of *representation* in *Dialectic of Enlightenment*: "Just as the capacity of representation [*Vertretbarkeit*] is the measure of domination [*Herrschaft*], and domination is the most powerful thing that can be representated in most performances, so the capacity of representation is the vehicle of progress and regression at one and the same time" (34–35). Domination would, it seems, be the monopolization of the means of representation (as exchange)—and power the impossibility of such a monopoly. What makes possible the movement from a dyadic model of domination to a complex and mediated analysis of power-systems is the domination—or, perhaps, mediation—of domination itself by representation. In other words, while we might wish to read Horkheimer and Adorno's analysis in the tradition of the master-slave dialectic, the analysis is, in fact, a response to a specific, historical reconfiguration of domination as power. Power is domination by representation—it is the system in which even the putative origin of domination must itself be constituted representationally.

The analysis of representational power in *Dialectic of Enlightenment* cannot, however, be reduced to the level of an analysis of ideology; this work is *not* primarily an analysis of hegemonic strategies. Indeed, the absence of a cohesive theory of hegemony in the work might be seen as the source of its pessimism. Within power, it can no longer be a question—at least at the level of individual intentionality—of the struggle *for* power, since individuation itself is a process which can only occur *within* rather than *against* power: "the individual—the self—is man no longer credited with the magical power of representation [*Stellvertretung*]" (51).

One does not possess power—one is possessed *by* it; one does not, as an individual, possess the power to represent—one is represented. This does not necessarily mean that the analysis of power negates the concept of domination—only that power has become the condition of consciousness and has therefore rendered inaccessible the *experience* of domination. It is this loss of experience that Horkheimer and Adorno seek to repair. If the loss of experience (of domination) cannot be made good, perhaps it can itself be experienced: such would seem to be the subterranean hope of the *Dialectic of Enlightenment*.

There are moments when it seems that some restoration of experience, some escape from the totality of power, might be possible; and yet such a restoration necessarily risks a return to the direct experience of domination. Politically, at least, such a return seems to be a dead-end. What is notable, however, is that where such possibilities are articulated in terms of a potential agency, it is in and around figures of women—or, perhaps, a fantasm of the feminine—that they are collected. In fact, the very rethinking of power as representation is inextricable from the thematization of woman in the *Dialectic of Enlightenment*. For the representation of woman is not simply one representation among many—it occupies a pivotal role in the work and binds together the various strands of a critique oriented now toward philosophy, now toward science, now toward art, now toward politics.

Above all, Horkheimer and Adorno are aware of the exclusion of women as a condition of possibility of the philosophical discourse within and against which they work. They comment explicitly on the issue of philosophy's phallocentrism in passages such as the following:

> By virtue of the claim to universal validity, the philosophic concepts with which Plato and Aristotle represented the world, elevated the conditions they were used to substantiate to the level of true reality. These concepts originated, as Vico puts it, in the marketplace of Athens; they reflected with equal clarity the laws of physics, the equality of full citizens and the inferiority of women, children and slaves. (22)

It is not enough, however, simply to problematize this exclusion, for power is about *inclusion*. It is necessary to ask how are women included—or rather, how are they constituted within an all-inclusive discourse. This seems to be the key issue which confronts any attempt at a feminist reading of *Dialectic of Enlightenment*, yet I would suggest that women are included in this work—somewhat paradoxically—precisely *by* their exclusion. Women are instrumentalized as the representatives of the possibility of exclusion understood as an *escape* from the all-inclusive system of power. In other words, the initial—and damning—exclusion of women from the philosophical project is reworked as a potential exemption from the totality both of power as ontologized domination and of reason as a system of closure.

To work within the tenuous utopian margins of the feminine in the *Dialectic of Enlightenment* is necessarily to embroil oneself in a series of performative contradictions. On the one hand, historical necessity demands that one work within an analysis of power, and yet to work on such an analysis is necessarily to work within a masculine discourse. Of course, this is a classic dilemma of feminist theory, and one which Horkheimer and Adorno's analysis dramatizes in its attempt to instrumentalize woman as a way of escaping the closure of traditional philosophical logic. That such an attempt entails a number of contradictions is clear even at the level of *Dialectic of Enlightenment*'s own operation as a linguistic performance. For example, Horkheimer and Adorno problematize man's discursive domination of woman in the following terms:

> Man as ruler denies woman the honor of individualization. Socially, the individual is an example of the species, a representative [*Vertreterin*] of her sex; and therefore male logic sees her wholly as standing for nature, as the substrate of never-ending subsumption notionally, and of never-ending subjection in reality. Woman as an alleged natural being is a product of history which denaturizes her. (111)

While more recent feminist analyses of the identification of woman and nature may have rendered it difficult for us to appreciate the originality of Horkheimer and Adorno's presentation of feminine nature as a historical construct, their formulation nevertheless retains an exemplary clarity in its very ambiguity. For it is important to mark the unavoidable performative contradiction that the assertion involves, a contradiction already operative in the simple statement that "Man as ruler denies woman the honor of individualization." To which "woman" does man deny this honor? Clearly, it is to no woman *in particular*, but rather to woman in general that the interdiction extends. But this is precisely the problem: woman is always "in general"—by virtue of that very interdiction. In other words, Horkheimer and Adorno are obliged to repeat the generalizing gesture they condemn. How can it be asserted that "woman" is denied the honor of individualization without once again denying her the honor of individualization, by forcing her into the singular yet generic category of "woman"?

This is not a "mistake" on Horkheimer and Adorno's part, a "slip" which I—another male critic—need simply point out. One must be careful not to suggest that Horkheimer and Adorno somehow "got it wrong" about women. What must be questioned is the possibility of ever "getting it right."[3] While one might wish neither to examine a putative primary object and its subsequent representation, nor to ontologize the impossibility of representation as a characteristic of that object, in reality—and in language—it is virtually impossible not to do one or the other. How is it possible—simply at the level of semantics—to critique Horkheimer and Adorno for once again denaturizing "woman," without partaking in the same violent abstraction? How, in other words, can women be thought and represented at all? Yet how, once again, can theory resist thinking precisely as that which cannot be thought or represented?

The problem extends from the dilemma as to whether to use singular or plural nouns—whether to "rectify" or accept as unavoidable the generic effacement of women/woman—to the problematic notion of any notion of the "feminine" itself. When I use "the feminine"—or any such term—am I referring to a construct whose ideology Horkheimer and Adorno already critique? Or perhaps to an alternative model which they propose in their more "utopian" moments? Or perhaps I am operating with some unspoken notion of my own? The question is strictly undecidable. The critic's most earnest disavowel of any desire to reimpose a notion of "the feminine" is itself profoundly paradoxical. Such a move would involve arrogating to oneself the power to deny that one has the power to impose such a notion; the power of intentionality is invoked in order to be denied. An analysis of the rhetoric of *Dialectic of Enlightenment* is not, then, simply a way of obscuring Horkheimer and Adorno's "intention." For what is at stake—both in my critique and in theirs—is the possibility of isolating any such intention once the philosophical discourse in question has been accepted as a framework for analysis.

If the problem is exacerbated for the male reader, the nature of the philosophical rhetoric is such that the same question remains for a woman reader also. There is something in the rhetoric of reading which tends to masculinize in order to elicit an "adequate" response. This, perhaps, is the inescapable element of totalitarian logic which informs the critique of rational totalization worked out in *Dialectic of Enlightenment*. What response, for example, would be adequate to the assertion that "Man as a ruler denies woman the honor of individualization"? One might answer: "Yes, and there you go again. In isolating 'woman' as something which is always collectivized, you once again collectivize her." A second response would be: "Yes, such is the discursive violence practiced by a masculine discourse, and something must be done about it." And a third reply might go as follows: "Yes, but let us look at the possibilities this cooptive inclusion opens up for women in the interstices of the philosophical system." But these are only the answers possible in the affirmative. What would be the implications of *disagreement?*

To disagree with the statement would open even more possibilities and double binds, which illustrate the complicity of Horkheimer and Adorno in a certain coercive rhetoric of assent. On what authority might one disagree? Primarily, it could be argued, as a woman. But in claiming the authority of woman, one claims the authority of the very nonindividualized generality one seeks to deny. This is more than just a play with words; the impossibility of negation dramatizes the difficulties of simply exempting oneself from the philosophical discourse. The problem is as follows: if woman *is* denied the "honor of individualization," if she *is* held to be "an example of the species," how is she to be theorized *except* in terms of that same male logic? In other words, if even to speak of "woman" is to speak in terms of a male logic, around what sort of categories could a "feminist philosophy" or a "feminist politics" orient itself? If the politics consists in a rejection of subjugation to the species, does that politics also entail both a negation of the conceptuality of philosophy and the disqualification of any feminine collective? To question the necessity of so precipitous a retreat from whole realms of discursive practice is to raise the possibility that the assertion—by the male theoriests, Horkheimer and Adorno—that man "denies woman the honor of individualization" itself serves as a further strategy of exclusion. By instrumenting a set of performative double-binds the text attempts to foreclose the possibility of a feminist philosophy. In other words, the masculine self-indictment of philosophy serves in fact—and despite itself—as a rear-guard action of precisely that phallocentric tradition which is supposedly under attack.

This, then, is the double-bind of Horkheimer and Adorno's analysis of the place of woman within a masculine discourse of rationality—the impossibility of either agreeing or disagreeing with their assertions. The critic is obliged to read woman not as the possibility of a real opening up of the boundaries of the work, but as a figure whose utopian possibilities are entirely bound to the presuppositions of the discourse in question. It is by virtue of the "honors" denied her that woman acquires a liberational potency. Thus, for example, man's denial of the honor of individualization to woman becomes potentially positive when read within the context of that more general alienation which is the book's theme. Recalling the earlier observation that "the individual—the self—is man no longer credited with the magical power of representation" (51), one can question whether the so-called "honor of individualization" does anything more than rob us of power—the power of representation. Furthermore, if woman escapes this paradoxical self-constitution and self-negation of individualization, might she then be supposed to *retain* "the magical power of representation," whose loss Horkheimer and Adorno otherwise deplore? But to valorize woman in this way again involves a performative contradiction. It can be asserted that woman is exempted from the masculine philosophical and representational dilemma only if we replay that gesture of denial which man practices upon woman. We can exempt her only by including her, by accepting the definition offered by the philosophical system from which she is to be excluded.

Beyond the difficulties involved in responding to *Dialectic of Enlightenment*—beyond the problem of speaking of "woman" at all in terms which are not always already compromised—there is the more fundamental question of the instrumentalization of woman within the discourse of the male Frankfurt School theorists. The question of women's liberation is always subordinated to that of a more general human (that is, male) liberation at the same time as the inapplicability of such a model to women is taken as the cornerstone of that rather tenuous process of liberation. Let us reconstruct the general model of alienation. The movement from domination to power which I have isolated as a fundamental critical observation in *Dialectic of Enlightenment* can be traced through thee basic stages of alienation. First, in their alienation from Nature: "Men pay for the increase of their power [*Macht*] with alienation from that over which they exercise their power. Enlightenment behaves toward things as a dictator toward men. He knows them only in so far as he can manipulate them" (9).

Instrumentalization and reification are the first stages of the process, then: the subject-object relation is established with regard to external nature. This structure is replicated at a second stage which involves man's alienation from other men, and radically internalized in a final stage that consists of man's alienation from himself: "It is not merely that domination [*Herrschaft*] is paid for by the alienation of men from the objects dominated: with the objectification of spirit, the very relations of men— even those of the individual to himself—were bewitched" (28). Man's self-alienation marks the closure of the system, the escalation of domination into seamless power. It marks the domination of the dominator by the very system which ensures his domination over others. Domination becomes total—becomes power—through alienation.

This alienation, however, cannot be thought simply as the alienation of an originally unified subject from him—or (still, at this stage of the argument) herself—for it is only through this process of alienation that any such subject comes into existence. Horkheimer and Adorno argue that:

> Man's domination over himself, which grounds his selfhood, is almost always the destruction of the subject in whose service it is undertaken; for the substance which is dominated, suppressed, and dissolved by virtue of self-preservation is none other than that very life as functions of which the achievements of self-pres-ervation find their sole definition and determination. (54–55)

Subject-oriented discourse is grounded upon the death of the subject it creates. The individual emerges only within a system of representation which he cannot control. This dialectic of subjectification—the need to subjugate the self in order to become a subject—takes places both at the level of psyche and at the level of the individual's relationship to the power of representation.

This is why the analysis of representation—and a critique of significa-tion—are so central to the pathology of power. Power is not simply repre-sented—power *is* domination *as* representation. But where do women feature in all of this? If, for example—as Horkheimer and Adorno have already insisted—the identification of woman and nature is a grounding commonplace in Western literary and philosophical discourse, then is the first stage of alienation—man's domination of nature—synonymous with man's domination of woman? The problem with any such assertion, of course, would be that the domination of woman takes place *by means of* her identification with nature. To assert that the domination of woman is the domination of nature is to accept—at some level—the very process of identification (of woman and nature) which serves to dominate. In other words, man does not simultaneously dominate nature and dominate woman and subsequently conflate the two in some form of metonymy of domination: to argue thus would be to underplay the role of representa-tion in the genesis of power. Man does not dominate woman *and* identify her with nature—he dominates *by* identifying her with nature. In this repressive identification, of course, will be bound up the utopian instru-mentalization of woman as the means of a (copulative) reconciliation with nature.[4]

Horkheimer and Adorno do not shy away from the fact that the identi-fication of woman and nature serves to subjugate woman at the first stage of alienation. But does this mean that woman (at least as an ideological construct) never passes through the second and third stages of alienation which effect the shift from domination to power? This would mean, on the one hand, that the subject-object split central to alienation would not be a feminine experience and, on the other, that women's oppression would still need to be thought within the model of domination operative at the first stage of alienation rather than within the subsequent model of power.[5]

The problem with both these assumptions is that they accept, in the name of woman, the ideological constructs of the philosophical tradition. Consequently, to accept the extrapolation—from the alienation model—that the subject-object split is itself alien to feminine experience and then to orient a politics of feminism around this assertion would be both to accept—at another level—the identification of woman and nature and to hypostatize a condition of ontologized feminine nondifferentiation as a political telos. The second conclusion—namely, that women's oppression would need to be thought in terms of domination rather than power—poses, above all else, questions of tactics. How, given the general en-trenchment of a collusive system of power, is it still possible to articulate a model of domination without seeming hopelessly inadequate theoreti-cally? Moreover, doesn't theory find itself at odds hwere with the empiri-cal movement of political outcome from the shift from a politics of domination to a politics of power, it has been the movement beyond the economic category of exploitation as the sole locus of political action. Whereas the politics of feminism, of homosexual liberation, and of racial equality both empowers and is empowered by the move *beyond* a purely economically-oriented model of domination, here we seem to be arguing that this analysis of power is actually alien to woman's experience of domination. The question which poses itself is: whether "woman's expe-rience" retains any substantive value for Horkheimer and Adorno—as something specific—or whether it is not lost under the fetishization of experience itself (as a dwindling category)—whether it is not subsumed under that *category* of the specific which supposedly resists totalization, but which does so only within a totalized model.

On the positive side, however, the persistence of a notion of domina-tion does help to differentiate *within* the model of power. As the most casual critic of the power model might observe: it is all very well to talk of totalized power-structures, when nothing is being done about specific, local domination. Power does not effact domination; it simply ontologizes or abstracts it. However, in focusing upon the category of (masculine) self-domination, Horkheimer and Adorno ignore the persistence of outer-directed domination—man's domination of woman, for example. The central role played by the category of alienation (which I use here to characterize the completed third stage of the process) allows them to focus, among other things, upon: "male domination, which—as a permanent deprivation of instinct—is nevertheless a symbolic self-mutilation on the part of the man" (72).

That male-domination involves a certain self-immolation on the part of the male may well be true—very probably, it is—but the thrust of the argument here is to bypass man's domination of woman in the rush to get at the crux of the issue, the "real" heart of the matter: man's alienated domination of himself.

Clearly, there can be no systematic way out of the totality of system. Rather than expanding upon the figure of woman as a way out of the text, it ssems necessary, instead, to read one's way further into it, to analyze some of the paradoxes which seem to have been embodied in the figure of woman. For the reading I offer here, what this involves is a closer engagement with the text *as* text, rather than an evaluation of the text as a programmatic political statement; in other words, a reading of this text as a performance which is itself caught in the very psychosocial structures it takes as its object.

Within *Dialectic of Enlightenment* there seem to be two basic strategies for dealing with woman—models within which woman is presented less as the subject of experience than as a figure *for* experience itself, as a phenomenon threathened by the totalizing systems of power. In the first instance, woman is forcibly included in the general model. Men's domination of women is viewed from the perspective of feminine self-alienation. Thus:

> Prostitute and wife are the complements of female self-alienation in the patriarchal world: the wife denotes pleasure in the fixed order of life and property, whereas the prostitute takes what the wife's right of possession leaves free, and—as the wife's secret collaborator—subjects it again to the order of possession: she sells pleasure. (73–74)

Woman's labor as wife or whore is assimilated to the model of self-alienation implicit in all labor. Moreover, the wife and the whore seem to be engaged in some kind of plot against the male—a plot to rob him of pleasure. They are themselves, in fact, collaborators in a patriarchy of which *men* seem to be the primary victims. This tactic for the inclusion of women in the general schema is based entirely upon the perspective of male pleasure and deleterious effect of women upon it.

The second attempt to account for the experience of women within the power model consists in tendentially excluding them from it. Women—in accordance with their subjugation at the first stage of alienation—experience domination, not power. Thus, for example, the woman's experience of power is mediated even in advanced industrial societies by the family, in which authority is asserted as straightforward domination. In this case, woman's experience of domination within the patriarchal family actually serves a quasi-utopian function for Horkheimer and Adorno. It is an experience supposedly closed to men, for whom power has always already displaced domination. Since the experience of domination is crucial to break through the totalized non-experience of power, domination serves almost as a mark of privilege for the dominated. It is not difficult to see what Horkheimer and Adorno are trying to articulate here—the opening and subsequent closure of pockets of resistance constituted by the anachronistic persistence of domination within the apparently seamless fabric of power. But this often leads to such potentially conservative social positions as the observation that: "Before, thralldom in her father's house would awaken an emotion in a girl which seemed to point to freedom, even though it was actually realized either in marriage or somewhere else outside. But now that a girl has the prospect of a job before her, that of love is obstructed" (107).[6] At the very least—we are given to understand—"thralldom in her father's house," precisely because it was experienced *as* thralldom, maintained in the young girl a notion of liberation, an experience which capitalism closes off. Patriarchy, it seems, is an imperfect model of social organization precisely because it leaves such "gaps." As a social structure, however, patriarchy is retained within capitalism, which only gradually displaces it, as it becomes aware of the incommensurability of patriarchal domination with the seamless power of capital. What is often seen as a nostalgia for patriarchy in Horkheimer and Adorno, is—in a sense—nostalgia for a system of domination in which injustice can be experienced—and resisted—as such. It is the category of experience itself which is to be retained in and through "the feminine": and experience means pain.

At the same time as woman figures experience, however, marriage as a process of socialization might be taken as an allegory of sorts—an allegory, that is, of the passage of dominion into power. In escaping from the home of her father into her own home as wife and mother, the girl merely rejects direct domination by her father and "chooses" domination by the husband. As an alternative to this second-order patriarchy the "prospect of a job" offers only direct socialization, the (non)experience of power, and the closing of the possibility of ever conceptualizing oppression. At first sight, then, the political potential of woman in *Dialectic of Enlightenment* seems to reside in the very category of "experience" itself. Since, as we have seen, power and alienation result from certain dialectical tensions already inherent in the model of domination and since—within the non-contemporaneous social organization of capitalism—women are still in a position to experience domination, they are, presumably, in a position to short-circuit the escalation of domination into power. The problem, it would seem, is that in liberating themselves from domination, women merely liberate themselves into a more complex system of power.

Politically, the project which seems to emerge from this analysis is woefully inadequate: Horkheimer and Adorno are not attempting to re-politicize *Kinder, Kirche, Küche* as a blueprint for political liberation. The aporias of their analysis only persist, however, so long as the figure of woman is accepted *within* a certain system of representation. The "way out"—which is really a "way in," a way into the very heart of representation—that Horkheimer and Adorno offer consists in articulating in and through the figure of woman a critique not only of the social relationships made possible within a certain system of representation but a critique of the representational system itself. It is primarily in and through the reading of myth that this critique is implied. In so far as *Dialectic of Enlightenment* does attempt to offer some kind of feminist counternarrative, it does so not *within* any given system of representation, but rather as the narrative of a mythical *succession* of systems of representation. To reach this level of the text it is necessary to reconstruct an ethnology of sorts from within the analysis of the *Odyssey*.

There is something paradoxical—or just plain complicitous—in offering a narrative of the emergence of narrative as the discursive form whereby patriarchy (and, in Horkheimer and Adorno's presentation, scientific discourse as its epitome) establishes dominance. Again, it is a paradox—a complicity—neither Horkheimer and Adorno nor I can avoid. However, *Dialectic of Enlightenment* does assess the stakes of persisting with narrative and even flirts with the possibility of a "relapse" out of structured narrative. The nondifferentiation of woman—that so-called "natural" state which in fact denaturizes her—is more than just a position assigned to women *within* a masculine logic. It is also the state into which that logic fears it might slip: "The dread of losing the self and of abrogating altogether with the self the barrier between oneself and other life, the fear of death and destruction, is intimately associated [*verschwistert*] with a promise of happiness which threatened civilization in every moment" (33). Women are both that which threatens philosophy *and* philosophy's "*promesse de bonheur*." This threat is transformed into knowledge's fear of a collapse back into "prehistoric myth, from whose womb it tore itself" (32), a fear of "mythic prehistory." It is a "healthy" and necessary fear of resubsumption in the mother.

What Horkheimer and Adorno must attempt to problematize is that initial identification of woman with the nondifferentiation of nature, which presents any falling away from dominant narrative structures as a fall into nature, a fall into the feminine. Complicating the simple opposition of nature and culture as a way of carving up narrative, Horkheimer and Adorno analyze instead a process of representational escalation: "One after the other, mimetic, mythic, and metaphysical modes of behavior were taken as superseded eras, any reversion to which was to be feared as implying a reversion of the self to that mere state of nature from which it had estranged itself with so huge an effort, and which therefore struck terror into the self" (31). The fear of nondifferentiation, philosophy's fear of "becoming-woman" is the same fear which drives us from one system of representation to another, from mimesis to metaphysics. It is in this context that the *Odyssey* is read as an ethnology—as a history of social development and systems of representation, and it is possible to extrapolate the makings of a feminist critique of representation by interweaving this narrative with the analytic project of the first chapter. This critique will—for Horkheimer and Adorno—take on the characteristics of "magic."

The analysis of the *Odyssey* begins by grounding the ethnological reading philologically:

> If we follow Kirchoff in his assumption that Odysseus' visit to the Underworld belongs to the most ancient level of the epic—that of saga—it is this oldest layer, too, that most decisively features (for example in the tradition of the visits of Heracles and Orpheus to the Underworld) something extending beyond myth: indeed, the theme of the forcing of the gates of hell, the annulment

of death constitutes the very core of all antimythological thinking. (76)

The most ancient level of the epic is the visit to the underworld. And, as
Horkheimer and Adorno also point out, the "souls which the adventurer
sees on his first visit to the realm of the dead are primarily the matriarchal
images banished by the religion of light" (75). In other words, the earliest
stage is prenarrative, antimythological and matriarchal. The images encountered in Hades, however, are "impotent, blind and dumb." That
which myth cannot accommodate it presents as silence and death. So
long as it is thought within myth, the feminine must remain dumb.

In opposition to the patriarchal myth, Horkheimer and Adorno propose not matriarchy—an alternative mythology, and thus no alternative
at all—but magic. But what is magic? *Dialectic of Enlightenment* offers the
following description: "On the magical plane, dream and image were not
mere signs for the thing in question, but were bound up with it by similarity of names. The relation is not one of intention but of relatedness. Like
science, magic pursues aims, but seeks to achieve them by mimesis, not
by progressively distancing itself from the object" (11). Magic, it would
seem, is the name of a certain form of representation. Consequently,
if patriarchy goes hand in hand with disenchantment, then this must
simultaneously entail a disempowering of the feminine. Instrumental cognition of the world involves a distantiation and objectification, whereas
"the world of magic retained distinctions whose traces have disappeared
even in linguistic form" (10).

The characterization of magic is highly complex, it would seem. On
the one hand, there is an insistence upon distinction—the individualization, perhaps, which men deny women. It is important to note—and this
has been often overlooked by an overemphasis upon instrumental reason
as the key to the critique of *Dialectic of Enlightenment*—that magic is
differentiated from science *not* by virtue of its opposition to purposive
rationality. Magic too "pursues aims." Moreover, it is not enough to say
that magic pursues its aims in a fundamentally different—"mimetic"—
way. Even Bacon implicitly invokes mimesis when observing that: "now
we govern nature in opinions, but we are thrall unto her in necessity: but
if we would be led by her in invention, we should command her by action" (4). Furthermore, it will subsequently be quite specifically the mimetic "concordance between the mind of man and the nature of things"
which will be criticized as "patriarchal" (4). Mimesis will even prove

itself to be the principle of the very rationality which supposedly displaces it, for: "the *ratio* which supplants mimesis is not simply its counterpart, it is itself mimesis: mimesis unto death" (57).[7]

The question remains, therefore: what is specific about magic? One can only answer by an apparent tautology—what is specific about magic is its specificity! The specificity, that is, of its mode of representation: "In magic there is specific representation [*Vertrebarkeit*]. What happens to the enemy's spear, hair or name, also happens to the individual; the sacrificial animal is massacred instead of the god" (10). First and foremost, then, it is the fracturing of the conventional relationship of signifier and signified which constitutes magic—a so-called "relation of relatedness," a metonymic motivation of the sign. If there is no ground here for a specifically feminist or "feminine" politics, there may be grounds, at least, for an aesthetic, or a rethinking of representation. Put differently, perhaps the aesthetic might *provide* the grounds for a feminist politics. After all, the privileging of the aesthetic throughout *Dialectic of Enlightenment* is likewise legitimated by the assertion made in the first chapter that the "work of art still has something in common with enchantment" (19).

Once again, however, it is important to exercise a little caution and to question what is involved in this specific form of representation. As a model of representation, the "relation of relatedness" seems merely to hypostatize that image of woman as nondifferentiation which the Enlightenment itself perpetrates. Is magic simply being offered as a model of insignificance, that is, as a model of nondifferentiation within the sign itself, as the elision of signifier into signified? And if this is the case, are Horkheimer and Adorno not guilty of a regression—albeit on a more sophisticated level—to that practice of domination which figures woman as nondifferentiation? In the very midst of specificity—the specificity, that is, of magical representation—the nondifferentiated reasserts itself as the conflation of signifier and signified.

The text's subsequent mutation of magic into a somewhat vaguely developed notion of "the symbolic" seems to bear out these fears. There is, on first hearing, something scandalous about the symbolic—it is the voice of the muted feminine: "The representations [*Darstellungen*] of creation in which the world comes forth from the primal mother, the cow, or the egg, are symbolic—unlike the Jewish genesis" (17). Matriarchal myths of creation are symbolic—and the symbolic is the medium of magic. But how does it function? First of all, it should be noted that the symbolic can be articulated at all only once it has been manipulated by mythic religion. Thus: "The doctrine of the priests was symbolic in the sense that in it sign and image were one" (17). Here we clearly hear echoes of that magical relation of relatedness:

> Just as hieroglyphs bear witness [bezeugen], so the word too origi-
> nally had a pictorial function, which was transferred to myths.
> Like magical rites, myths signify self-repetitive nature, which is
> the core of the symbolic: a state of being or a process that is
> presented as eternal, because it incessantly becomes actual once
> more by being realized in symbolic form. Inexhaustibility, unend-
> ing renewal and the permanence of the signified are not mere
> attributes of all symbols, but their essential content. (17)

The symbolic would seem to be a form of representation which "bears witness"—it is pictorial and is likened to the hieroglyph. In it, "sign and image were one"—that is, undifferentiated. What is being stressed in the symbolic is the nondifferentiation of reality and representation, though not in the sense of a manipulative Baconian "concordance" of mind and matter, nor within an idealizing tradition which would hypostatize the reality of the concept.

So, this is *how* the symbolic represents, but *what* does it represent? "Like magical rites," Horkheimer and Adorno have observed, "myths sig-nify self-repetitive nature, which is the core of the symbolic." The sym-bolic seems to function as the catalyst for the taking up of magic into myth, as an historical transition crucial to the emergence of the domi-nant patriarchal discourse. The core of the symbolic is self-repetitive nature. But there is something about myth—and, remember, the matriar-chal is figured as *anti*mythological, a part of the ancient *nostos*—which usurps the symbolic. Mythic mimesis is the repetition of self-repeating nature. That is to say, it becomes through mimesis nature itself—nature in its self-repetition. Myth is not simply the signification of an autono-mously self-repetitive nature—it *is* the repetition of nature in mimetic, narrative form. What is supposedly "the core of the symbolic"—repetition—signifies within the mythic the possibility of mere tautology. That is to say, the symbolic—offered as a short-circuiting of significa-tion—finally serves to *ground* that form of self-identity which is at the heart of *logos*. Rather than opposing myth, the symbolic seems to reach through it toward the systematicity of administered truth. Once a place is assigned to the symbolic—and the feminine—*within* myth, woman no longer threatens anything more than an impossible self-fulfillment of the signifying system, a moment of completion and perfect mimesis in which the signifier-signified difference is elided, a moment in which representation becomes repetition. This is the sense in which mimesis feeds into rationality—the mimetic repetition functions as the supplement to self-repeating nature.

It is this instrumentalization of the category of the symbolic which Horkheimer and Adorno are at pains to resist by insisting upon the specificity of signification in magic. "Magic," we are told, "is utterly untrue, yet in it domination is not yet negated by transforming itself into the pure truth and acting as the very ground of the world that has become subject to it" (9). This invocation of magic as an experience of domination which does not seek to legitimate domination as truth is obviously reminiscent of the status accorded women throughout *Dialectic of Enlightenment*. The experience of domination, however, is no guarantee of truth, and magic instituted within a systematic discursive context is magic no longer. If, on the one hand, self-repetitive nature gives rise to a logocentric model of tautologous truth, the insistence upon the specificity of the magical also feeds into a similar form of self-sublation.

Magic as a specific instance of specific representation becomes what Horkheimer and Adorno call "sacrifice": "Substitution [*Substitution*] in the course of sacrifice marks a step toward discursive logic. Even though the hind offered up for the daughter, and the lamb for the first-born, stil had to have specific qualities, they already represented the species. They already exhibited the non-specificity [*Beliebigkeit*] of the example" (10). The entire feminine problematic of the relationship of the specific to the general, the individual to the species, is raised in sacrifice. The specificity of the sacrificial object—that which makes it "unfit for exchange"—is always already the specificity *of* exchange, the specificity of that which has replaced (as sacrificial signifier) the signified which is to be spared (the hind for the daughter, and so forth). The same gesture which establishes discursive logic—namely the ability to displace in its entirety one thing by another, or a thing by a word—sets a paradigm for the subjugation of women under the rule of the general. It is not, perhaps, a coincidence that the first example of sacrifice is the offering of the hind for the daughter—for what is sacrificed in sacrifice is the specificity of a feminized magical representation. A woman can no longer even *be* sacrificed—what *is* sacrificed is her specificity. In sparing the woman and sacrificing the hind, we sacrifice women to the realm of discursivity and to nonspecificity.

Ritual is still, however, a threshold experience. It is not yet fully rationalized, for: "the holiness of the *hic et nunc*, the uniqueness of the chosen one into which the representative enters, radically marks it off, and makes it unfit for exchange" (10). The specificity operative within the system of magical signification—that is, as a semiotic—has been displaced onto the context. This notion of the *hic et nunc* grounds the specificity of the magical and of the aesthetic also, but can do so only within the institutionalized limits of a structured public sphere. What Horkheimer and Adorno finally reach is a double bind in respect of philosophy's ability—or inability—to think "the feminine." The specificity of the feminine seems to be conserved, on the one hand, in the *hic et nunc* of experience—but in the discursive marking of the here and now, there is an inevitable shift into the register of "then and there," that is, into the discourse of the "other." There is no speaking of the "here and now"—outside of the here and now itself—except as "there and then." The specificity of context is necessarily de-differentiated within the philosophical text. On the other hand, to insist upon the specificity of the representation of self-repetitive nature serves only to ground—as the virtual goal of logocentric discourse—the rhetorical formula of truth as tautology: philosophy as the self-repetition of nature. In a sense, then, the feminine has become *not* that which is excluded from masculine philosophical discourse, but rather that which grounds it—either as its other or as its essence.

That Horkheimer and Adorno should refer to the sacrificial object as "unfit for exchange" serves as some indication of the direction in which they wish to develop this analysis of forms of representation. Sacrifice stands as a link between an analysis of models of representation and a critique of the relations of exchange intrinsic to capitalism. It is clear that for Horkheimer and Adorno, the notion of ritual sacrifice is the key to understanding not only the establishing of a certain philosophical tradition, but also of specific social and economic relations. Thus, they will subsequently argue in their reading of the *Odyssey* that: "If barter [*Tausch*] is the secular form of sacrifice, the latter already appears as the magical pattern of rational exchange, a device of men by which the gods may be mastered: the gods are overthrown by the very system by which they are honored" (49). If ritual sacrifice is the sacrifice of woman—as specificity—then it is a sacrifice made at the twin altars of capitalism and philosophy.

That such a reading of sacrifice can be pursued directly into a critique of social and economic relations under capitalism is indicated by subsequent invocations of the *hic et nunc* of sacrifice within *Dialectic of Enlightenment*. Thus, for example, in Horkheimer and Adorno's reading of the *Odyssey*, it is specifically the role of the wife which is linked to the nodal moment of sacrifice. When Penelope suggests that marriage—as a promise of permanence—brings down the wrath of the gods, it is observed that: "Even if the contract between the partners only calls down that age-old enmity, nevertheless, peacefully growing old together, they can vanish at the same moment like Philemon and Baucis: just as the smoke of the sacrificial altar turns into the wholesome smoke of the fireside" (75). We have returned, perhaps, to the rebellious daughter who chooses married servitude over paternal domination. Capitalism, logocentrism, patriarchal marriage—all seem the outcome of ritual sacrifice, a sacrifice in which the specific woman is spared: spared as woman, sacrificed as specificity, sacrificed to categoriality. The specificity of a woman would be possible only in her death, it would seem, in her sacrifice—or in her silencing—hence the mythicized silence of the dead matriarchs of Hades.

Having isolated the moment of sacrifice as a turning point in the philosophical representation and social encoding of woman, it is not really necessary to trace here in detail Horkheimer and Adorno's ethnological reading of the *Odyssey*. It is a reading which establishes a continuum from premythic matriarchy, through the savagery of the lotus-eaters—who represent the nostalgia for "a stage more ancient than agriculture, cattle-rearing, and even hunting, older, in fact, than all production" (63). From here develops the barbarism of the cyclops—"defined as the absence of any systematic agriculture, and the lack of any systematic organization of labor" (64)—and, finally, "the civilized marriage with Penelope," which "while older in literary terms, represents a later stage of the objectivity of the patriarchal order" (72). Women only seem to figure either—as in the case of Penelope—as the guardians of a patriarchal order vacated by the patriarch, or—as in the case of Circe—as figures of historical regression and oblivion. Wife and whore are more than just valorizations of woman *within* the patriarchal narrative—they are fundamental to its very discursive organization.

If the notion of a premythic, prepatriarchal order is raised—through the feminine figures of Hades, for example—it is clear that a critique of patriarchal mythic structures cannot be articulated as a return to an ear-lier stage. The easy incorporation of Penelope ("older in literary terms") into the fabric of the myth indicates the way in which any such return might be preempted. Woman as historical regression is already located outside of the process of rationalization being described in this text. Con-sequently we must refrain from locating woman at any stage of the con-tinuum—within a matriarchy, for example. To return to the passage quoted earlier: "One after the other, mimetic, mythic, and metaphysical modes of behavior were taken as superseded eras, any reversion to which was to be feared as implying a reversion of the self to that mere state of nature from which it had estranged itself with so huge effort, and which therefore struck terror into the self" (31). Woman as regression becomes a structural—or, perhaps, a deconstructive—principle, which consis-tently thwarts or threatens linear progress. To think woman as a *stage* of a process is problematic because it is precisely this form of thinking which leads us to give content to a purely formal fear of regression and to iden-tify woman with that to which we might regress—that is, to the nondif-ferentiated. The threat of nondifferentiation posed by Circe "constitutes the nature of promiscuity" (69), we are told. Nondifferentiation and sex-ual indifference are conflated. The principle of nondifferentiation as-signed to woman within masculine discourse—the nondifferentiation, that is, which designates her, nondifferentially, *as* woman—makes of Circe a prostitute.

In fundamentally opposing ways, the two female figures central to Hor-kheimer and Adorno's reading of the "civilized" discourse of the *Odys-sey*—the wife and the whore, Penelope and Circe—both threaten the temporality of narrative. The one (Circe) represents the threat of histori-cal "failure," of regression, while the other (Penelope) is the threat of fulfillment—an end of history in the sense of history's self-fulfillment— history's return home. Again, the threat posed by these two figures to the hegemony of male pleasure is one in which "the wife denotes pleasure in the fixed order of life and property, whereas the prostitute takes what the wife's right of possession leaves free, and—as the wife's secret collabora-tor—subjects it again to the order of possession" (74). Woman is danger-ous both to progress and narrative, and to masculine pleasure. Women seem to challenge a specifically masculine "pleasure of the text."

The joint analyses of marriage as a development of the sacrificial mode of representation and of masculine discourse as an effacement of woman and of specificity meet in Horkheimer and Adorno's analysis of post-

Baconian science, in which "there is no specific representation," merely "universal interchangeability" (10). At this point the rhetoric of the *Odyssey* and the rhetoric of modern science coalesce. Indeed, Bacon himself views the epistemological project of his science as an essentially "matrimonial" affair, in which it is important to isolate and do away with "the things which have forbidden the happy match between the mind of man and the nature of things; and in place thereof have married it to vain notions and blind experiments: and what the posterity and issue of so honorable a match may be, it is not hard to consider" (3). Bacon reinscribes himself within the discourse of the wife—and the problem of scientific knowledge is presented as a marital drama. Lack of progress, the absence of "posterity and issue," can be traced back to this unfortunate *mésalliance* between "the mind of man" and "vain notions and blind experience." Bacon is a marriage-broker, no less, whose greatest wish is to bring about the "happy match between the mind of man and the [presumably feminine] nature of things." Marriage—the return home to Penelope, so to speak—would seem to be the ideal, the completion of the scientific project.

But the situation is rather more complicated. For there is another woman on the scene, as Horkheimer and Adorno observe: "For Bacon as for Luther, "knowledge that tendeth but to satisfaction, is but as a courtesan, which is for pleasure, and not for fruit or generation" (5). On the one hand we have the fruitful wife (nature, married to the mind of man), on the other the courtesan, meant for pleasure, not procreation. And between them is that troublesome marriage of inconvenience with vain experiment. The opposition of wife and whore is not, then, a simple one. It is an epistemological love-triangle consisting of the false wife of "vain notions and blind experiments," the ideal wife of nature, and the courtesan of "mere satisfaction." Furthermore, the opposition of wife and whore is not represented—as one might have expected—as an opposition of truth and falsehood. It is not truth, but generation, which is on the side of the wife—in other words, productivity. Horkheimer and Adorno paraphrase Bacon's logic as follows: "Not 'satisfaction, which men call truth,' but 'operation,' 'to do the business,' is the 'right mark'" . . . (5). Truth is not, then, simply identified with the virtuous wife, for it is not truth in any abstract or absolute sense which is at stake for Bacon, but rather something more functional—a (pro)creativity for which he uses the term "business." And yet at the same time the "businesss" of the courtesan must be rejected. We seem to be caught between the epistemological and the economic consequences of the wife-whore opposition—caught, in brief, between patriarchy and science. "Truth" has become a luxury, mere satisfaction, the realm of the courtesan. In the equivocation of wife and whore what is being constructed—and, it seems, rejected—is nothing less than the Eros of knowledge. The function of the mother and wife—withdrawn from the business transactions of the courtesan—is, however, the type of business Bacon has in mind.

As critics of the Baconian tradition, Horkheimer and Adorno are, nevertheless, adamant that there can be no way out by means of a historical regression. This thesis is worked out specifically with reference to the category of the "symbolic," when they insist that: "The separation of sign and image is irremediable. Should unconscious self-satisfaction cause it once again to become hypostatized, then each of the two isolated principles tend toward the destruction of truth" (18). Could it be that, for all its critique, *Dialectic of Enlightenment* threatens to erect an equally repressive model, in which truth takes the place of Baconian efficacy? The "mere satisfaction" of Bacon's courtesan is replayed in the "unconscious self-satisfaction" which marks, in the *Dialectic of Enlightenment*, any attempt to rethink the relationship of sign and image. The similarity of terms obliges us, I think, to ask ourselves whether Horkheimer and Adorno are themselves implicated in precisely the terminological oppositions they oppose in Bacon, and if so what implications this has for both their analysis and for a feminist reading of that analysis. In pursuing the analysis of systems of representation, the feminist critic, by daring to pose any alternative, plays the courtesan.

What emerges from Horkheimer and Adorno's analysis in *Dialectic of Enlightenment*, then, is a consistent picture of the simultaneous hypostatization and repression of the notion of "woman" in the realms of political, economic, scientific, and religious discourse. To understand the totalizing value of the critique, it is necessary to follow the thread of argumentation back to the most fundamental level, to the critique of representation itself. *Dialectic of Enlightenment* is far from being a programmatic text—and it should not be surprising that on the issue of a potential liberation of "woman" it has little to offer by way of direct political proposals. Indeed, more worthy of note is precisely the way in which woman seems to function as a utopian figure, pointing—at least—the way beyond the aporetic constructions of the dominant philosophical discourse. The question remains, however, whether Horkheimer and Adorno move beyond the instrumentalization of woman within their own analysis, and whether they do not—as I have indicated at key points—replicate at a more sophisticated level that denial of the "honor of individualization" practiced both practically and theoretically upon women. As a *cipher* for the specific, woman is once again denied specificity.

It is not, then, a question of chastizing Horkheimer and Adorno for failing to articulate a coherent and practicable political project. By this criterion, *Dialectic of Enlightenment* would be a failure in almost every respect. Instead, the pressing concern is to recognize the ways in which it is in and through the figure of "woman" that this analysis both marks its difference from and asserts its complicity with the object of its critique. The problem lies in the perspective from which the dilemma of "woman" is presented in *Dialectic of Enlightenment*. Convinced that the repressed can be liberated only *as* the repressed, Horkheimer and Adorno had great difficulties in creating from the "repressed" a potential subject position not defined purely in terms of its objectification by the dominant discourse. The analysis of power—prompted by the experience of consensual domination in both fascism and capitalism—serves only to strengthen this critical tendency.

The daughter's experience of domination is a case in point; the privilege of "experience" itself—even if it is experience as pain, an experience of domination—is valorized only in so far as it is an experience closed to the directly socialized male. It is valorized, that is, from a male perspective. The "specificity" of the experience—its value *to* the woman—is secondary to its fantasmatic utopian value to the male theorist. Central to the analysis is not the experience of the womoan, but the patriarchal construct within which it becomes potentially subversive. In other words, an obsession with the structures of patriarchy actually serves to blind Horkheimer and Adorno to strategies of liberation which might escape the social parameters dictated by those structures. As Jessica Benjamin has pointed out in her sympathetic but thorough critique of Horkheimer and Adorno, the empirical decline of the family as an economic—and therefore ideological—determinant by no means results in the emergence of a "society without fathers."[8] A society characterized by what Horkheimer and Adorno would term "direct socialization" is by no means incompatible with the structure of patriarchy, even if patriarchy itself has had to yield to a more thoroughgoing rationalization on the basis of economic performativity. The very process of internalization whereby direct socialization becomes possible is itself structurally determined by the patriarchal or Oedipal family. The act of internalization is, in fact, an act of compensation through which the loss of a familial mediation is made good.

Such questions, however, would lead us to a fundamental critique of the psychoanalytic models underlying *Dialectic of Enlightenment;* such has not been our objective here. Instead, it is a question of understanding the ways in which the text—for all its awareness of the instrumentalization of women—cannot break out of that instrumental rationality. Women—as the bearers of specificity—are never considered as a potential social and political collective, and specificity of experience itself becomes a paradoxical panacea—a general solution to the totalizing tendencies of the dominant masculine discourse. Given Horkheimer and Adorno's pessimistic analysis of the dwindling possibilities for the subject, it becomes incumbent upon us to analyze not only the (potentially anachronistic) psychical structures—the languages of the subject—which serve to (dis)-locate women in the *Dialectic of Enlightenment,* but also to trace the social, linguistic, and symbolic structures within and by which the notion of "the feminine" can be articulated. The utopian communicative categories so often identified in the text with woman—magic, for example—must be examined not simply as subject-oriented psychoanalytic models, but as complex *textual* models, which demand a rethinking of the possibilities not only of a utopian experience, but of experience *and its representation.* Such would be the true challenge of a "feminine" dialectic of enlightenment.

Notes

1. Max Horkheimer and Theodor W. Adorno, *Dialectic of Enlightenment,* trans. John Cumming (New York: Continuum, 1987). Where the possibility for any terminological confusion arises in translation, I have chosen to insert (in brackets) the original German from *Dialektik der Aufklärung: Philosophische Fragmente* (Frankfurt/Main: Fischer, 1969).

2. See for example Wilhelm Reich, *The Mass-Psychology of Fascism,* trans. Vincent R. Carfagno (New York: Farrar, Straus, Giroux, 1970). Thus, the shift from an analysis of domination to an analysis of power can already be perceived in works like Wilhelm Reich's. At the same time, Reich's work also sought to legitimate methodologically a move beyond Marxist economism and into the realm of mass-psychology by examining the disparity between the emergence of a dominant petty bourgeois "character structure" unsupported by economic power.

3. Strategically, my position is not dissimilar from that of certain "postmodern" feminist artists, who, in the words of Craig Owens, "work with the existing repertory of cultural imagery—not because they either lack originality or criticize it—but because their subject, feminine sexuality, is always constituted in and as representation, a representation of difference. It must be emphasized

that these artists are not primarily interested in what representations say about women; rather, they investigate what representation *does* to women." "The Discourse of Others: Feminists and Postmodernism," *The Anti-Aesthetic: Essays on Postmodern Culture,* ed. Hal Foster (Port Townsend, Wash.: Bay Press, 1983), 71.

4. Space does not permit me to examine the broader ramifications of the implication of the idealist philosophical tradition in notions of sexual difference. Perhaps the most fascinating such analysis is to be found in Jean-Joseph Goux, *Symbolic Economies: After Marx and Freud* (Ithaca: Cornell University Press, 1990). In an analysis which parallels the more limited textual reading offered here, Goux argues that "[i]f the phylogenetic odyssey of libidinal positions of knowledge, through which social access to reality is gained, comprises a multiphased shift from inclusion in nature as mother, through a separation, and finally to an inclusive reciprocity with the *other* nature, human history through the present has been limited to the history of *man*: history is masculine" (241). It should be noted, however, that Horkheimer and Adorno are acutely aware of the social mediation of any such heterosexual historical phylogenesis in such institutions as marriage and remain skeptical of any real *social* reconciliation with nature, any return to Marxian "natural history."

5. At the level of psychology, such a position might lead toward the position of, for instance, Michèle Montrelay, namely that "[f]eminine eroticism is more censored, less repressed than that of a man." Repression here would be a collusive strategy of power, and censorship an *experience* of domination. "An Inquiry into Femininity," trans. Parveen Adams, *Semiotext(e)* 4, no. 1 (1981): 228.

6. The original German original makes clear what the translation only implies, namely that the girl's desire for freedom was *never* fulfilled: "erfüllte sie sich weder in der Ehe noch irgendwo draussen" (115). The point I wish to make here, however, concerns not the realization of desire, but the very possibility of its being experienced *as* desire.

7. Clearly, the category of mimesis is both crucial and eternally problematic in any consideration of Adorno's project of reconciliation. For this reason much has been written on the topic. For the purposes of the reading I propose here, however, the most pertinent analysis is found in Seyla Benhabib, "Autonomy as Mimetic Reconciliation," *Critique, Norm, and Utopia: A Study of the Foundations of Critical Theory* (New York: Columbia University Press, 1986), 186–223. In this book, Benhabib attempts to place Adorno within an Enlightenment continuum of theories of autonomy, which moves from the Kantian notion of self-legislation, through Hegelian and Marxist models of self-actualization, to Adorno's own mimetic project, which is "intended to anticipate a new non-dominating mode of relation to inner and external nature" (11). The ambiguities of mimesis are themselves a function of the dialectic of Enlightenment for Benhabib (who observes no real discontinuity in the mimetic project from *Dialectic of Enlightenment* to *Negative Dialectics*). She writes: "Under the conditions of civilization, mimesis does not reveal the affinity of the self with nature; the natural condition to which the self regresses is corrupted by civilization itself" (209). In other words, mimesis itself colludes in a system of domination—as in the case of Bacon. As Benhabib points out, "Adorno distinguishes between a relation to otherness that acknowledges otherness and a relation to otherness that imitates without acknowledgment" (219). Quoting Adorno, she locates the dialectic within the ambiguity of mimesis itself, which—by virtue of its very respect for otherness—potentially mutates either into a process of self-alienation, wherein even the self becomes other, or into a murderous attack upon the other as such:

> "If mimesis makes itself like the surrounding world, so false projection makes the surrounding world like itself. If for the former the exterior is the model which the interior has to approximate [*sich anschmiegen*], if for it the stranger becomes familiar, the latter transforms the tense inside reality to snap into exteriority and stamps even the familiar as the enemy" (*DE*, 167). Western reason, which originates in the mimetic act to master otherness by becoming like it, culminates in an act of projection which, via the technology of death, succeeds in making otherness disappear. (165)

8. Jessica Benjamin, "Authority and the Family Revisited: or, A World Without Fathers?" *New German Critique* 13 (Winter 1978): 35–37. See also Jessica Benjamin, "The End of Internalization: Adorno's Social Psychology," *Telos* 32 (Summer 1977): 42–64. Benjamin is building, of course, upon a long tradition of work addressing the question of the subject in its relation to both patriarchy and capitalism. Specifically, she is responding to Alexander Mitscherlich, *Society Without the Father: A Contribution to Social Psychology*, trans. Erich Mosbacher (London: Tavistock, 1969); and to Max Horkheimer, "Authority and the Family Today," *The Family: Its Function and Destiny*, ed. Ruth Nanda Anshen (New York: Harper, 1949), 359–74. See also Nancy Love, "Epistemology and Exchange: Marx, Nietzsche, and Critical Theory," *New German Critique* 41 (Spring–Summer 1987). Any comprehensive analysis of the psychoanalytic question as it relates specifically to questions of "the feminine" from within the problematic of the Frankfurt School would necessarily address the entire *oeuvre* of writers and thinkers such as Fromm, Reich, and Marcuse. The most recent contribution to this tradition would be Klaus Theweleit's *Männerphantasien*.

5

"No Happiness Without Fetishism"

Minima Moralia as *Ars Amandi*

Eva Geulen

Theodor Adorno's greatest success is a book on failure, in which he famously decreed that "there is no right life in the wrong one."[1] Numerous
formulations play on *Minima Moralia*'s pervasive theme of inevitable failure. "There is no way out of entanglement" (27), for example, although
perhaps less familiar, is certainly no less clear. However, *Minima Moralia*
is also Adorno's most intimate book. The dictate "no way out" discloses
a negative freedom in its own right; the categorical impossibility of any
"right life" brings to the surface those mundane details of daily life that
usually fall below the threshold of philosophical, or even literary, dignity.
In the light of world historical injustice, Adorno seems to be able to

afford a worldliness that is missing in most of his other writings.[2] As with any good vade mecum, among the entries of Minima Moralia readers may hope to find something appropriate for any occasion. But Adorno's concern with individual experience also increases the level of exposure; nowhere else is he more vulnerable to critique and ridicule.

On the pain and glory of love, Minima Moralia proves to be a particularly rich, and particularly embarrassing, source.[3] The somewhat dated slogan, according to which "the private is the political," can hardly legitimize prolonged indulgence in Adorno's rather ubiquitous romantic musings. Nevertheless (and, perhaps, even therefore) it is likely that many a line from Minima Moralia has found its way into lovers' discourse. A proposition such as "You are being loved only where you may show yourself weak without provoking strength" (192) strikes just the right balance between banality and profundity that is required of such tokens of love. In contradistinction to those few readers who are acutely in love, the majority of lucid professionals have long since unmasked Adorno's notoriously romanticizing speculations and banned them accordingly. Albrecht Wellmer, for example, stigmatized what he termed Adorno's "somatic" tendencies as remnants of dubious theologisms that ought to be surrendered.[4] Most recently, Clemens Pornschlegel heaped ridicule on the entry titled "Constanze," which portrays the loving couple as a dormant revolutionary cell: "Perhaps the secret of success of the young republic's best-selling author is nowhere more graspable than in his sentimental lines on love . . . 19th century through and through."[5] Indeed. Not much can be said in defense of Adorno's anachronistic sentimentality. Moreover, he so unabashedly assumes the point of view of a male heterosexual that this perspective tends to cloud even his once poignant insights into the dialectics of the women's movement, the pitfalls of the so-called sexual revolution, and other potentially redeeming features of his thoughts on love in particular and gender relations in general.[6]

Yet the reasonable suggestion to forego further examination of the "somatic" underpinnings of Adorno's thought runs the risk of castrating the entire oeuvre. For none of Adorno's theorems—neither those pertaining to art and aesthetic experience or to history and social relations, nor those addressing problems of literary or musical expression—can be sustained at all if their roots in erotic desire are severed, "because even thought's remotest objectifications are nourished by the drives" (122). Nietzsche's claim that "the degree and kind of a man's sexuality extends to the highest pinnacle of his spirit" figured among Adorno's deepest convictions (122). In particular, his scant, strained references to utopia tend to be modeled on sexual fulfillment: "Only he who could situate utopia in blind somatic pleasure, which, satisfying the ultimate intention, is intentionless, has a stable and valid idea of truth" (61). The very idea of happiness, Adorno suggests, is "sexual union" as "blissful tension" (217). Similarly, his most succinct formula for the specific quality of aesthetic experience unequivocally recalls the peculiarities of "la petite mort": "If anywhere, then in this respect, aesthetic experience resembles sexual experience, in particular its culmination. As the beloved image transforms itself, as petrification is united with the most vivacious, it is as if culmination were the incarnation of the original idea of aesthetic experience."[7] The succession of mutually canceling terms in this sentence—"as if" (*gleichsam*) but "incarnate" (*leibhaft*), yet inaccessible and unverifiable as a platonic idea (*Urbild*) at the same time—underwrite Adorno's determined refusal to let anyone decide whether this "culmination" should be understood literally or figuratively. In fact, the momentary equilibrium of opposites is precisely at issue here. Adorno's description of the successful artwork as a fleeting instance of *Einstand,* or "balance," between utmost tension and complete relaxation also borrows its evidence from the same phenomenon. (But it is worth pointing out that on Adorno's view, an orgasm is not privy to the pleasure he likens to aesthetic experience. It belongs to the onlooker, who observes the rare coincidence of tension with its opposite. Even ecstasy requires distance: "Contemplation without violence, the source of all the joy of truth, presupposes that he who contemplates does not absorb the object into himself: a distanced nearness" [89–90].)

The point of these and countless other examples is not that Adorno's theoretical constructions are, in the final instance, reducible to sexual desire or sexual fulfillment, respectively.[8] Equally crude would be an interpretation that casts sexual pleasure as the last bastion of resistance within the "totally administered world." Yet dismissing Adorno's persistent allusions as mere flourishes on hard-core theory obviously sells short what is overrated in the other scenario. And mapping Adorno's obstinate references onto a grand theory of desire (Lacanian, for example) clearly misses the point as well. The problem is that the sphere of sexuality has been so greatly expanded as to become an enveloping presence; it has become so diffuse as to saturate virtually everything. Sexuality's impotent omnipotence in *Minima Moralia* is intriguing enough to tempt one to experiment with a more systematic reconstruction of its theoretical significance.

Recourse to Freudian psychoanalysis proves to be of limited help in this endeavor—for Adorno himself drew the line that separates his work from psychological interpretation. Where Freud hovers, hesitating, on the border, Adorno plants himself firmly on "*this* side of the pleasure principle," not because Freud underrated rationality, but "rather because he rejects the end, remote from meaning, pervious to reason, which alone could prove the means, reason, to be reasonable: pleasure [*Lust*]" (61). Since occasional references to Nietzsche cannot adequately explain the idiosyncratic privilege *Minima Moralia* accords to sexual experience, it seems heuristically sound to assume that in matters of love and sex Adorno went his own way.[9] From this follows the method: to pursue Adorno's obsessions with comparable determination. Rather than exhaustively cataloging all references to sexuality—and who is to say what qualifies in this respect?—one should understand that eclecticism is key. One best proceeds *as if* Adorno had left us with a fully developed theory of love. Against the backdrop of that hypothetical premise it becomes possible to measure the familiar against the unfamiliar. One must isolate those instances in which Adorno's claims in matters of love extend beyond, run up against, or even clash with the accustomed theoretical paradigms of his thought: Nietzschean, Freudian, Marxian.[10]

Mimetic Desire

"Love is the power to see similarity in the dissimilar" (191). Not surprisingly, love in Adorno tends to appear in the context of mimesis, one of the thorniest theorems in his aesthetic theory, a quasi-anthropological constant in all his reflections, and, above all, a site of great ambivalence. For, on the one hand, mimesis belongs to an archaic level of experience that reason and abstraction have long overcome—at least this is how the story of mimesis is told in the *Dialectic of Enlightenment*, where the Jewish imposition of the taboo on images thwarts the regressive tendencies of mimetic impulses.[11] On the other hand, all that has been lost, was abandoned, or remains, for either historical or structural reasons, inaccessible, exerts irresistible attraction over Adorno's intellectual imagination. This latter aspect helps to account for the fact that a passage in *Minima Moralia* joins mimetic heritage and love in the name of humanity: "The human is indissolubly linked with imitation: a human being only becomes human at all by imitating other human beings. In such behaviour, the primal form of love, the priests of authenticity scent traces of utopia which could shake the structure of domination" (154). Adorno is ostensibly concerned here with the fate of the concept of authenticity; the chastised "priests of authenticity" include Kierkegaard, Schopenhauer, Heidegger, and anyone else smacking of the existentialism Adorno abhorred, and which he treated in the *Jargon of Authenticity*. In the preceding passage, mimesis functions as antithetical corrective to claiming authenticity for one's self and one's identity. Mimetic remainders remind those who speak in the name of the self that no relationship to the self can ever be authentic. Even childhood, Adorno suggests, already teaches us about the inauthenticity of all attempts at self-relation: "They always contain an element of imitation, play, wanting to be different" (153). As a relationship between at least two, love supposedly articulates the dialectical truth of the one: an individual or subject is not itself but other than itself, and it is not available to itself except through the other whom it imitates. Any self always owes itself to an other. But only in love is this truth acknowledged. While strictly dialectical, this logic is by no means Hegelian in any straightforward sense.[12]

On account of the subject's dependency on the beloved other, love attains the status of a model. For the experience of the self in love has some bearing on the relationship between society and individual. Vis-à-vis society, individuals conceive of themselves in ways analogous to those in which the existentialist conceptions of the self are formulated. They also imagine themselves as originary biological units opposed to and separated from the social totality—Adorno argues, however, that society is in fact prior, and "not only is the self entwined with society, it owes [*verdankt*] it its existence in the most literal sense. All its content comes from society, or at any rate from its relation to the object. It grows richer the more freely it develops and reflects this relation, while it is limited, impoverished and reduced by separation and hardening that it lays claim to as an origin" (154). As the imitation of an other, love can serve as a model for what the relationship between self and society should be in Adorno's eyes. Rather than claiming distance from the other, love revels in imitation. The individual thus no longer claims a self but gains itself as another by mimetically laying claim to the other, by claiming the other in the act of imitation. If individuals could achieve that same affirmative relation with society, if they could mimetically emulate the mimesis operative in love, then—so runs the quasi-platonic logic of Adorno's argument—the political and moral pitfalls of the discourse of authenticity could be avoided and the presumed antagonism between self and society would turn into something like a love affair. His argument hinges on one essential premise: imitation somehow redeems the other as well as self, and it even redeems the banned practice of mimesis.[13] Following Adorno's seductive suggestions on this point would yield the conclusion that love relationships are a role model for how individuals should relate to the social whole—and this in turn would entail the rather absurd and justly ridiculed concession that as role models, loving couples harbor revolutionary potential.

Yet it is precisely up to mimesis to mediate and mitigate such claims. Given that the mimesis presumably at work in love is itself still in need of being mimetically emulated, significant differences separate loving another person from loving society. To begin with, lovers are (at least) two, but society is one—because the many that make up society appear here only as the totality of society; and a totality is neither human nor easily imitated. Therefore, it can only be a question of imitating the *type of relation to mimesis* that Adorno attributes to lovers. This relation to mimesis alone can become the subject of mimetic practice.[14] Lovers are in the unusual position to freely assert, even revel in, mimetic bonding, but such freedom is by definition lacking in the relationship between self and the social, where the individual is unwillingly and unknowingly mirroring the social whole. There is nothing particularly humane in this second type of mimesis. It would have to be substituted by imitating the type of mimetic behavior presumably familiar to lovers. Its strong humanistic overtones notwithstanding, Adorno's concept of mimesis proves to be more complicated even where it plays the relatively unambiguous role of a corrective to the discourse of authenticity. The unity of the concept of mimesis is jeopardized by the fact that imitating an other is not the same as imitating a relationship to imitation.

The *Urgeschichte* of Pleasure

The reign of ambivalence over the concept of mimesis manifests itself in other respects. Adorno's allusion to childhood experiments in self-reflexivity—"they always contain an element of imitation, play, wanting to be different" (153)—suggests an idealist trajectory in the tradition of

Schiller's dictum that man is human only where he plays. However, at other points in *Minima Moralia* the purportedly humane features of mimesis reveal rather violent underpinnings. Those passages suggest that the loving mimetic impulse is already a secondary formation, responding to the structurally and historically earlier experience of the encounter with a "recalcitrant object" (109). At this juncture, the positively accentuated concept of mimesis borders on Adorno's understanding of narcissism—that other highly problematic and fundamentally ambivalent theorem, which frequently figures as both a parallel and a competing model to mimesis.[15] As such, it emerges in, among other places, section 72, titled "Second Harvest," in which Adorno denies the psychoanalytic idea of sublimated sexual drives and argues instead for the primacy of another affect: "Talent is perhaps nothing other than successfully sublimated *rage*, the capacity to convert energies once intensified beyond measure to destroy recalcitrant objects into the concentration of patient observation, so keeping as tight a hold on the secret of things, as one had earlier when finding no peace until the quavering voice had been wrenched from the mutilated toy" (109). For those unfamiliar with this scenario from their own childhood, Gottfried Keller has described it emblematically in the opening pages of one of his novellas, where he depicts two children mutilating a doll. In this kind of "primal scene," the relationship to the object is not yet mimetic but is ruled by destructive curiosity. Before mimesis can even enter as a human and humane, civilized and civilizing practice that foregoes destruction in favor of imitation, "aggression" (109) reigns supreme. Adorno's quasi-Nietzschean question at the end of that passage leaves no doubt about the origins of mimesis in destruction: "Might not everything conciliatory been bullied out of that which destroys?" (109). Anger and aggression are thus prior; and mimetic behavior already constitutes a step toward liberation, because it is a freer, "sublimated" relationship to the object, just as contemplation is the concentrated sublimation of the archaic cult of the fetish (see 224). In the final instance, which is to say in the beginning, it is "violence, on which civilization is based" (163). If Adorno knows a primary desire, it is not love or sex but rage.

Whatever one might think of Adorno's quasi-anthropological theorizations, the latent fiction of a quasi-Hobbesian state of unrestrained destructive impulses in *Minima Moralia* serves a very specific purpose: it allows for the historicization of seemingly primary affects, in particular the affect of pleasure (*Lust*). Along with mimesis, pleasure is "a late ac-

quisition, scarcely older than consciousness. Observing how compul-
sively, as if spell-bound, animals couple, one recognizes the saying that
'bliss' [*Wollust*] was given to the worm as a piece of idealistic lying, at least
as regards the females, who undergo love in unfreedom, as objects of
violence" (90). Pleasure, *Lust*, is mediated, deflected, and foregone violence, just as mimesis is mediated and deflected destruction.[16] The gendering according to which men rape their "recalcitrant objects" and to
which victimized women suffer from "archaic frigidity, the female animal's fear of copulation, which brings her nothing but pain" (90), is
certainly stereotypical, but at the very least, neither (male) aggression
nor (female) fear have their equal share in primordial violence. Fear of
the object corresponds to the impulse to destroy the object: "[i]s not
indeed the simplest perception shaped by fear of the thing perceived?"
(122). And, impervious to the difference, Adorno adds, "or by desire for
it?" (122). Even the mere perception of an object is ruled by impulses
that defy the distinction between fear and desire, just as the distinction
between destruction and desire must remain obscure because they co-
originate in the very same dialectic of losing oneself to gain oneself that
is operative in mimesis: "The capacity for fear and for happiness are the
same, the unrestricted openness to experience amounting to self-abandonment in which the vanquished rediscovers himself" (200).[17]

What disrupts the tendency of all differences to dissolve in the murky
Urgeschichte of pleasure as a constitutively "mixed feeling" is nothing
other than social deformation, sometimes apostrophized as "pathological
narcissism." It intervenes regularly to guard against any unreflected identification with the powers of pleasure. Almost sternly, Adorno reminds
his readers that in this world nobody is actually capable of losing him- or
herself. "The yearning into unformed joy, into the pool of salamanders
and storks" (178) remains just that, desire without satisfaction: "[t]he
experience of pleasure presupposes a limitless readiness to throw oneself
away, which is as much beyond women in their fear as men in their
arrogance. Not merely the objective possibility but also the subjective
capacity for happiness, can only be achieved in freedom" (91). So much
for pleasure; it is delayed, withheld, and postponed until some impossible
utopian state: "Pleasure in this world is none" (175). But *Minima Moralia*'s imperative of failure is sufficiently reliable to ensure that abstinence
and asceticism are no alternative either. "The transience of pleasure, the
mainstay of asceticism, attests that except in the *minutes heureuses,* when
the lover's forgotten life shines forth from the knees of the beloved, there

is, as yet, no pleasure at all" (176). The sentence significantly modifies the categorical impossibility of pleasure. From the "mainstay of asceticism" Adorno wrests a notion that allows him to reinstate the very prerogative of pleasure he had just negated. What saves pleasure is ultimately not that it is not (yet) "pleasure," but that *Lust* does not last.

Love and Death

Why (and how) could pleasure's transience underwrite its antiascetic affirmation? Initially, a pseudotheological logic seems at work. It suggests that pleasure's fleetingness holds out the promise of a type of pleasure that would never end. If that were so, the transient experience of love would function as the placeholder for infinity or, as Adorno would have it, transience would allegorically prefigure "reconciliation" or utopia. By the same token, but in stark contrast to the tradition of ennobling carnal love by imbuing it with transcendental significance, one could also argue that pleasure's transience alone sustains the life of pleasure. Pleasure's transience would then not stand in for something else but would signify an emphasis on finitude pure and simple. Since there is insufficient evidence to rule out one interpretive possibility in favor of the other, the question needs to be left open at this point.

But this indicates a good juncture at which to introduce two additional systemic features of Adorno's thoughts on love and desire that might help to further contextualize the issue. One of those dimensions—the power of fantasy—is well known beyond the limits of the present topic and recognized as a significant theorem in Adorno in general.[18] The other, much less acknowledged, trait of his intellectual universe is an obsession with death and mortality, whose intensity rivals that of sexual experience in the widest sense.[19]

If "love is the ability to perceive similarities in the dissimilar," then in the extreme, love would be the ability to perceive similarities where there are none whatsoever. (A case in point is the ability of the lover to recognize his forgotten life in the reflection of a pair of knees.) Indeed, the very absence of any defining traits and marks of individuality can incite love, according to Adorno. Where there is nothing to imitate, fantasy steps in and makes plenty out of nothing. In a passage strongly indebted to the Romantic phantasma of heartless female beauty, Adorno writes:

"Imagination is inflamed by women who lack, precisely, imagination. . . . Their attraction stems from their lack of awareness of themselves, indeed of a self at all: Oscar Wilde coined the name unenigmatic Sphinxes for them" (169). While *Minima Moralia* contains many peculiar and, for a female reader, frequently irritating and occasionally enraging propositions about women, this remark deviates so little from the well-known stereotypes of female beauty that one might be inclined to write it off as just that: the unreflected reproduction of a stereotype.[20] However, Adorno immediately launches into a self-corrective maneuver by adding that such perception of women "does no justice to their needy empirical existence" (169). His proof comes by way of a novella by Theodor Storm in which the young Friesian boy's infatuation with the poor Bavarian girl from the traveling players is ignited not only by her relative exoticism, but also, and above all, by her poverty. Adorno comments: "Imagination gives offence to poverty. For shabbiness has charm only for the onlooker" (170). But in the same breath he asserts, conversely: "And yet imagination needs poverty, to which it does violence: the happiness it pursues is inscribed in the features of suffering" (170). While this is somewhat enigmatic, the remaining lines suggest that Adorno seeks to critically expose what he terms the "cycle of bourgeois longing for naïveté," the logic organizing the cultural fascination with exotic phenomena such as the North's stereotypes about the South or the bourgeoisie's investment in nomadic cultures. But under the cover, as it were, of this well-meaning enlightenment and critique, Adorno doggedly pursues his initial point about the erotic fascination with beauty that lacks a soul. The closing paragraph returns full circle to the beginning: "Love falls for the soulless as a cipher of living spirit, because the living are the theatre of its desperate desire to save, which can exercise itself only on the lost: soul dawns on love only in its absence. So the expression called human is precisely that of the eyes close to those of the animal, the creaturely ones, remote from the reflection of the self. At the last, soul itself is the longing of the soulless for redemption" (170). Love's attraction to the soulless reveals the lover as akin to Walter Benjamin's allegorist, who entertains a similar relationship to the dead objects of his learned fascination. In both, the soulless and lifeless advance to a cipher of something other than itself. No doubt, for Adorno, love attends to and tends toward not just the creaturely but, eventually, also the nonliving. And one should pause before subsuming the sex appeal of the dead under the Platonic-Christian dogma that love begets life. For it is dubious whether awakening the dead to life is the point of Adorno's remark. His disdain for the cult of life is as deep-seated as his fascination with death.

Like Benjamin (in his 1921 essay "Critique of Violence"), Adorno voiced strong suspicions about the dogma of the sanctity of life. In a passage criticizing in no uncertain terms the vitalist tradition of philosophy, Adorno calls upon beauty to halt the course of life. Beauty "arrests life and therefore its decay" (77). The impression that beauty thus renders the transitoriness permanent is misleading: life needs to be arrested not because of its transience but because of its destructive furor. Life is violence: "[t]o hate destructiveness one must hate life as well" (78). The subsequent sentence elevates death to the utopian image of a nondestructive life: "[O]nly death is an image of undistorted life" (78). At issue here is not the religious doctrine that mortality guarantees eternal life, nor is it a matter of rendering fleeting life permanent. For Adorno, death (and beauty, which is akin to it) amounts to nothing less than a recovery from the sickness that is life. Adorno's inversion of Kierkegaard becomes explicit in the title of another entry: "The Health unto Death" (58). The same technique of symmetrical inversion makes it possible to expose "healthy" individuals as walking corpses: "[u]nderlying the prevalent health is death" (59). The Kürnberger motto of Minima Moralia's "Life does not live" (19) points in the same direction. But Adorno's erotic interest in death is not exhausted by its dialectical constellation with the cult of life.

Adorno's reading of one of the most famous fairy tales tells a somewhat different story. Lovingly, he lingers on the image of Snow White in the glass coffin. "For deeper knowledge cannot believe that she was awakened who lies as if asleep in the glass coffin" (121). The poisoned apple lodged in her throat is not a "means of murder" but, rather, "the rest of her unlived, banished life, from which only now she truly recovers, since she is lured by no more false messengers" (121). Only death grants recovery from the sickness of life. Moreover, Snow White's death also restores and recovers "her unlived, banished life." This "unlived life" is not eternal life but the life not lived because living one life excludes other possibilities and other, potential lives. Life, any life, is destructive above all because it produces, at every moment, countless other possibilities of life, all of which are sacrificed to the one lived life.[21] In death, when no life whatsoever is possible any longer, a sort of justice has been done to the possible lives that were not lived at the expense of the lived life. For now this lived life has also become what the other lives were from the beginning: nothing but a past possibility. The past as it was lived and the past possibilities that were not lived now share the same plane. This is Adorno's version of the affinity between pleasure and death. Incidentally, it also answers the question of why the lover can recognize his "forgotten life in the knees" of the beloved. The experience and the observation of pleasure afford the unique spectacle of death in life. Adorno has a very specific reason to privilege this phenomenon: in this experience the sequential order of time has been dissolved, the mutual exclusion between the facticity of lived life and the unlived possibilities it produces, only to abandon them, momentarily disappears.

In the particular case of "Snow White," the unlived life is not an abstract possibility but a very specific life that remained quite literally unlived: that of the Queen, who had been "wishing for her daughter, after the lifelessly living beauty of the flakes, the black mourning of the window-frame, the stab of bleeding; and then dying in childbirth" (121). The actual love between the reawakened Snow White and the Prince fails to redeem that original loss: "The happy end takes away nothing from this" (121). Like the Prince in the fairy tale, who fell in love with the beauty behind glass and only accidentally dislodged the apple when lifting the coffin lid, Adorno's own theorizations of love are, in the final instance, inspired by the eroticism of that which no longer lives. As a memento mori, the transience of pleasure is, then, not the placeholder for a life that would have escaped mortality, but a form of fidelity to the transitoriness of life. According to Adorno, the "minutes heureuses" of self-abandonment momentarily restore unlived possibilities.

1-800-Flowers

Flowers must be among the oldest symbols of love. The gendered symbolic value of breaking flowers, familiar from medieval poetry down to Goethe, still resonates in the term *defloration*. If one believes Adorno, a certain usage of the flower metaphor betrays the truth of female castration: "The woman who feels herself a wound when she bleeds knows more about herself than the one who imagines herself a flower because that suits her husband" (95).

But plucking flowers for the purpose of adorning the beloved was origi-

nally a different matter altogether: decoration, sacrifice, and reconciliation all at once. "Now that we can no longer pluck flowers to adorn our
beloved—a sacrifice that adoration for the one atones for by freely taking on
itself the wrong it does all others—picking flowers has become something
evil" (112). The logic of this passage is complicated and ambivalent.
Who exactly is being sacrificed? The flower or the beloved? Given the
intricate symbolic potential of flowers, probably both. Plucking flowers
(rather than lovers) is a deflected substitute; primary violence has been
displaced from a person to the adorning flower. However, as in any sacrifice, it not only deflects but also recalls and reenacts the original violence.
This is why even this harmless sacrifice is in need of reconciliation or
atonement. According to Adorno, this is achieved by acknowledging the
injustice done to all those other possible relations by the adoration of
this person and none other. Once again, the unlived, possible relationships, the unlived, possible lives, demand a justice that no court, human
or otherwise, can extend, as Adorno's reflections on the betrayed or refused lover show. It is an "inalienable and unindictable human right to
be loved by the beloved" (164) but no court can enforce this right because what the lover "desires can only be given freely" (164). In a dis-
tinctly theological vein, Adorno concludes that "the secret of justice in
love is the annulment of all rights to which love mutely points" (165).
In the passage on flowers, reconciliation consists quasi-Christologically
in assuming guilt incurred by loving someone particular. While this
might all seem dangerously close to a theology of love—although one
may wonder whether there is any sustained reflection on love that would
not be theological in some way—Adorno makes abundantly clear that
plucking flowers will no longer do. "It serves only to perpetuate the transient by fixing it" (112). Despite the stern rejections, Adorno leaves one
option open: "But someone in rapture who sends flowers will reach in-
stinctively for the ones that look mortal" (112). Immortal memories turn
into memories of mortality. The section titled "All the Little Flowers"
makes explicit this very nontheological emphasis on transience for transience's sake. "The pronouncement, probably by Jean Paul, that memories are the only possessions which no-one can take from us, belongs in
the storehouse of impotently sentimental consolation that the subject,
resignedly withdrawing into inwardness, would like to be the very fulfilment he has given up" (166).

"Post Festum"

Adorno banned his final word on the matter of love and lust from the book proper. Whereas the official version of *Minima Moralia* concludes with the entry "Towards the End," the appendix contains a section aptly titled "Post Festum." Its subject is the inevitable decline of erotic relationships. Feared loss of love is not the only reason for the accompanying melancholy. Another factor at play is "fear of the transience of one's own feeling."[22] It is not hard to guess that the entire section amounts to the clearest possible rejection of passion's redemptive value—not because it does not last, not because this world knows no true passion, but because Adorno enters love unambiguously under the rubric of the "guilty cycle of all creaturely [*schuldhaften Kreis des Natürlichen*]," which has no way out. The only available option is "reflection on the closure [*Geschlossenheit*] of this cycle." This is the end of Adorno's love affair with love. It is as if he had sobered up, relinquished all quasi-theological passions, and dutifully subjugated his occasional excesses under the law of reflection. To be sure, the insight that every passion is relative in the big picture of reflection and hindsight is still considered "blasphemous," but Adorno adds: "Und doch ist der Passion selber es unausweichlich, in der Erfahrung der unabdingbaren Grenze zwischen zwei Menschen auf eben jenes Moment zu reflektieren und damit im gleichen Augenblick, da man von ihr überwältigt wird, die Nichtigkeit der Überwältigung einzusehen" (293). The power of passion, it turns out, is no power at all, or, better, it is a power that is *nichtig*. And this very knowledge dawns on the lovers already in the very moment of rapture. Like everything else, passion is doomed to fail.

Adorno had good reason to exclude this "post festum"; it reverses his other speculations on love in *Minima Moralia*. Their implicit theoretical significance has been severely restricted. Post festum, Adorno seems to take it all back. However, he holds on to the failure of love with the same exclusionary, blind passion as that of a lover clinging to the beloved. The fireworks of pleasure and passion might be over. But then, as Jean Paul knew, the point of fireworks never was to illuminate the night, but to use it.

Notes

1. Theodor Adorno, *Minima Moralia: Reflections from a Damaged Life*, trans. E. F. N. Jephcott (London: Verso, 1985), 3. All quotations in the present chapter are from this work; page numbers are cited parenthetically in the text. Occasionally, the translation has been slightly modified.

2. The pieces written for television and radio are an exception in this regard. See Theodor W. Adorno, *Critical Models: Interventions and Catchwords,* trans. Henry Pickford (New York: Columbia University Press, 1998). Yet, compared with *Minima Moralia*'s rich materials, even these works seem spare and ascetic.

3. On the topic of embarrassment and shame in *Minima Moralia,* see E. G., "Mega Melancholia: Adorno's Minima Moralia," in *Critical Theory: Current State and Future Prospects,* ed. Peter Uwe Hohendahl and Jaimey Fisher (New York: Berghahn Books, 2001), 49–68.

4. Albrecht Wellmer, "Wahrheit, Schein, Versöhnung: Adornos ästhetische Rettung der Modernität," in *Zur Dialektik von Moderne und Postmoderne: Vernunftkritik nach Adorno* (Frankfurt: Suhrkamp, 1985), 9–47.

5. Andreas Bernhard and Ulrich Raulff, eds., *Minima Moralia neu gelesen* (Frankfurt: Suhrkamp, 2003), 99.

6. The matter might look slightly different from a U.S. perspective, in that Adorno's reception skipped the formative political phase; in the United States, the very features disdained in Germany found a warm welcome in the 1990s. One of the few works offering a sustained engagement with problems on love is Tom Pepper's "Guilt by (Un)Free Association": Adorno on Romance et al.," in *Modern Language Notes* 109 (1994): 913–37. For an important discussion of homosexuality in *Minima Moralia,* see Andrew Hewitt, "A Feminine Dialectic of Enlightenment? Horkheimer and Adorno Revisited," *New German Critique* 56 (Spring–Summer 1992): 143–70.

7. Theodor W. Adorno, *Ästhetische Theorie,* in *Gesammelte Werke,* ed. Rolf Tiedemann et al. (Frankfurt: Suhrkamp, 1997), 263, translation my own.

8. In accordance with the logic of failure, fulfillment remains subordinate to longing. The fleeting experience actually seems primarily destined to renew longing. In that sense Adorno desires desire.

9. The biographical accuracy of this statement was amply underscored by the revelations that marked the recent centennial. They are obviously besides the point here.

10. In other words, Adorno's exaggerations on this point are not to be neutralized but, rather, engaged and exaggerated in turn. On the role of exaggeration in philosophy and in Adorno in particular, see Alexander García Düttmann, *Philosophie der Übertreibung* (Frankfurt: Suhrkamp, 2004).

11. See Anson Rabinbach's lucid analysis in "Why Were the Jews Sacrificed? The Place of Anti-Semitism in the 'Dialectic of Enlightenment,'" *New German Critique* 81 (Fall 200): 49–64.

12. Hegel, for one, had little sympathy for love's universal aspirations. In his eyes, all love stories are misguided from the start in their sad attempt to stake the claim of universality on the contingency of "this woman" or "that man." Adorno's insistence on the powers of love is, to some extent, understandable as a compensatory posture assumed in defiance of Hegel's presumed negligence of the individual at the expense of the universal. Among those likely to take issue with this admittedly rather crude differentiation between Hegel and Adorno on love is Judith Butler. Already in her first book, *Subjects of Desire: Hegelian Reflections in Twentieth-Century France* (New York: Columbia University Press, 1987), she was able to locate in Hegel a mechanism of desire. This reading was substantially refined in the chapter on the master/slave dialectic and its aftermath in her more recent book *The Psychic Life of Power: Theories in Subjection* (Stanford: Stanford University Press, 1997), esp. 31–62.

13. The redemptive potential of mimesis is best illustrated by an anecdote. When taking leave from a party in Hollywood, Adorno found himself shaking the hand of a guest who had no hand but a prosthesis instead. Charlie Chaplin had observed the incident from nearby and immediately proceeded to imitate Adorno's gesture of horrified recoiling. The comical imitation, Adorno comments, released him (and presumably the guest with the prosthesis as well), from the shock of their encounter. The story is told in the volume *Vierzig Jahre Flaschenpost.*

14. It is tempting to argue that Adorno's thoughts are prototypical for what has been called

"performativity" in the wake of Judith Butler's reflections. But since this particular concept has become so ubiquitous as to have lost much of its meaning, sober asceticism recommends itself.

15. This is why the typological distinction between "good" and "bad" narcissism does not hold. See Deborah Cook, *The Culture Industry Revised: Theodor W. Adorno on Mass Culture* (London: Rowman and Littlefield), 1996.

16. The logic organizing such transitions is the dialectic of sacrifice, together with mimesis and narcissism the concluding pillar of the theoretical edifice on which the narrative of the *Dialectic of Enlightenment* rests. In *Minima Moralia*, love is also called the "after-image" or "re-enactment" (*Nachbild*) of the sacrificial ritual (217).

17. The shadow of pleasure's violent *Urgeschichte* looms large enough to extend to other forms of pleasure as well, among them aesthetic production and experience. In *Minima Moralia* Adorno calls every artwork a "coerced malfeasance" [*eine abgedungene Untat*] (111). The expression is characteristically ambivalent, for *Untat* is the deed not done, but the prefix also connotes a particularly gruesome deed.

18. For a pertinent discussion of fantasy in Adorno, see Britta Scholze, *Kunst als Kritik: Adornos Weg aus der Dialektik* (Würzburg: Königshausen und Neumann, 2000).

19. One writer who has acknowledged this trait is Christoph Menke, who in *Die Souveränität der Kunst: Ästhetische Erfahrung nach Adorno und Derrida* (Frankfurt: Suhrkamp, 1988) remarks on Adorno's death-bound existentialism (214).

20. On representations of the feminine, see Maggie O'Neill, ed. *Adorno, Culture, and Feminism* (London: Sage, 1999).

21. That this is not an existentialist conviction is evident from Adorno's detailed discussion of the relationship between linear time and property relations in the entry titled "Morality and Temporal Sequence" (78ff.).

22. The appendix is not translated into English. All quotations in this section are from the German edition. *Minima Moralia: Reflexionen aus dem beschädigten Leben* in *Gesammelte Schriften*, ed. Rolf Tiedemann et al. (Frankfurt: Suhrkamp, 2003). All references are to page 293 of that edition; translations my own.

6

The Bared-Breasts Incident

Lisa Yun Lee

The philosophers have only interpreted the world, in various ways; the point is to change it.

—Karl Marx, *Theses on Feuerbach*

Thought itself is already a sign of resistance, the effort to keep oneself from being deceived any longer.

—Max Horkheimer, *Traditional and Critical Theory*

One of the myths circulating about Theodor Adorno is that he died of a heart attack from the shock of the "bared-breasts incident," otherwise referred to, in the German, as "der Busenaktion." In the spring of 1969 at the University of Frankfurt, leftist students were ardently fighting for long-overdue reforms at the university and attempting to ignite a dialogue about the Nazi past of a German society that had been lulled into complacency in the postwar years. Students were particularly disenchanted with the Frankfurt School thinkers and criticized them for failing to produce a viable response to Fascism and to the emerging monopoly capitalism. One afternoon, shortly after Adorno began his lecture in his class

Introduction to Dialectical Thinking, a student at the very back of the seminar room spoke out, interrupting him, as another student rushed to the blackboard and wrote, "Whomever allows the beloved Adorno to do what he pleases will remain under the spell of capitalism forever."[1] Adorno, clearly angered by the disruption, issued an ultimatum: "I'll give you five minutes. You decide if my lecture will take place or not."[2] A commotion broke out in the seminar room and three leather jacket–clad feminists from the SDS (German Socialist Students) barged up to the podium, surrounded Adorno, and bared their breasts to him, lavishing him with rose and tulip petals and erotic caresses. They also distributed fliers that contained the statement "Adorno as an institution is dead."[3] The women were frustrated with what they considered Adorno's manda-rin approach to the current political situation. They were disgruntled with the lack of support for their spontaneous demonstrations and tired of the subordination of their political and revolutionary goals to the in-tellectual demands of theory set out by the "fathers of the move-ment"—of whom Adorno was the patriarch.

Although the effects of this bizarre incident have been greatly over-stated, it touches on and illustrates the complexities of the issues I will discuss in this chapter: theory, praxis, and their relation to the body in Adorno's philosophy.[4] These students represented a part of the emerging criticism of the Frankfurt School that claimed that thinkers such as Adorno, Horkheimer, and others abandoned the working class and its economic struggles as the primary agents of social history and substituted in their place the power of critical thought. Dissident intellectuals re-placed the proletariat, and theory replaced praxis. Adorno continued to infuriate many activists in the German New Left when he criticized the "illusory character of the student's form of praxis," in an interview with *Die Süddeutsche Zeitung* a few days after the incident. Adorno naively asks, "I postulated a theoretical model for thought. How could I suspect that people want to realize it with Molotov cocktails?"[5] His statement further stressed the growing schism between critical theory and revolutionary action.

The fact that these students believed that baring their breasts would be the most appropriate course of action to demonstrate their discontent is revealing, because it exposes a series of classical dualistic oppositions at work in their critique: mind/body, theory/praxis, reason/passion, and masculine/feminine. The students' actions were undertaken to humiliate Adorno, not just as a thinker, but also as a *male* thinker and an icon of the institution that critical theory had come to represent. Baring their breasts was a direct challenge to his masculinity and aimed at exposing the impotence of theory. In this act, their bodies became the transcendental signifier of everything on the right side of the restrictive binaries listed above.

At the same time, Adorno's inability to directly confront the corporeal specificity of this situation is also revealing. The immediacy, materiality, and sensuality of the bodies forced him—speechless, ashamed, and flustered—to sheepishly leave the lecture hall. The body that Adorno champions in his theoretical prose is not the equivalent of the unruly bodies of those female students.

I will use this historical event as a point of departure for an examination of the profound importance of corporeality in Adorno's philosophy. My discussion will focus primarily on Adorno's most self-reflexive work, the quixotic book of aphorisms *Minima Moralia*. Adorno notes in the foreword to the book that he is writing "from the standpoint of subjective experience," and it is painfully obvious how his damaged experience of living in the United States shapes the somatic quality of his writing. "Every intellectual in emigration," writes Adorno in one poignant moment, "is, without exception, damaged, and does well to acknowledge it of himself. . . . He lives in an environment that must remain incomprehensible to him . . . he is always astray."[6] This mutilation is experienced in the body, as both a lack of voice, resulting from the expropriation of language, and as a form of disembodiment, caused by the physical displacement. Adorno refashions the pain of his experience by employing metaphors of corporeality in order to viscerally critique the discipline of philosophy that bifurcates mind and body. In my discussion, I will show how he recasts this tenacious dualism as a constellation of contradictions that illuminates the body in a new and insightful way for feminists. Adorno's nuanced discussion exposes the rupture of mind and body as a nested set of problems that includes the division of mental and physical labor, the troubled relationship between theory and praxis, and the oppressive relationship between subject and object—all of which have played a role in the subjugation of women.

I will also look at Adorno's short essay "Marginalia on Theory and Praxis," which he wrote under great duress, after he had returned to Germany and was compelled to respond to the student revolts at the end of the 1960s. Both texts were written during tumultuous periods in which the effectiveness and usefulness of theory was being questioned in the face of social upheaval and unrest.[7] In this chapter, I am particularly interested in the contradictions between Adorno's evocation of the body in theory and his description of the practice of the body as an agent of political change. Instead of trying to resolve these moments of tension, I will argue that it is precisely within this dialectic of the body that Adorno's philosophy is most illuminating.

It is important to immediately emphasize that there is no single unified theory of the body in Adorno's writings. In fact, although I will be arguing for its significance in Adorno's thought, there is only one short, sustained piece of writing directly concerning the body; it is located in a text appended to the *Dialectic of Enlightenment* titled "The Importance of the Body." However, the body persistently appears in heterogeneous fragments throughout Adorno's oeuvre as the specifically corporeal (*Leib*), the more general body (*Körper*), and what he refers to as "metaphors of the body." As I will discuss below, the absence of a sustained, systematic analysis of the body in Adorno's thought is entirely consistent with his commitment to the formative nature of style, dialectical thought, and immanent critique. This manner of criticism confronts a particular mode of thinking with its own logic, using the strength of its own arguments against its own conclusions. Adorno adopts this mode of critique from Hegel, who claimed that genuine refutation is not achieved "by defeating the opponent where he is not." Immanent critique remains within what it criticizes, using the internal contradictions of a work to criticize the work itself. Adorno's style can be understood as a kind of strategic asceticism and critique of forms of thought that would deny pleasure and desire in an effort to repress the body. "Dialectic thought," Adorno insists, "is an attempt to break out of the coercion of logic through its own means."[8] The scattered references to the body should be read as an attempt to formally evade the homogenizing impetus of identity logic, one of the key leitmotifs of his thought.

It is compelling that the text that contains the most startling revelations about the tension between theory and praxis and the relationship between philosophy, lived experience, and social change is Adorno's most personal work, *Minima Moralia*. Its subtitle—*Reflections from a Damaged Life*—expresses the degree to which Adorno felt wounded and maimed by his American experience. "An emancipated society," Adorno writes in one of his few prophetic statements, "would conceive the better state as one in which people could be different without fear."[9] Adorno's experience of the United States was characterized by his difference—his identity as a German-Jewish intellectual—which thrice marked him as an outsider. The United States did not produce or regard intellectuals in the same way that Europe did, and there was no established social niche to accommodate the artists and thinkers who had migrated during the Fascist period. When this motley group of intellectuals introduced their work to the general public in the United States, the American people did not know how to respond. In addition, anti-Semitism was still very much a part of the American landscape, and the war with Germany created an understandable if not excusable suspicion toward all Germans—natives or descendents—in the United States. Instead of repressing the characteristics that marked his "otherness," and rather than attempting to blend into the American landscape, Adorno accentuated his differences. He refused to write in English, leaving his wife, Gretel Karplus Adorno, to translate most of his work. Adorno was the very model of the absentminded (German) professor for his entire tenure in the United States. As Jamie Owen Daniel has provocatively argued, "Theodor Adorno actively held on to and even accentuated all the markers of his cultural difference precisely because he recognized that the pressure being brought against him to stop behaving 'so foreign' . . . and dissolve into the melting pot was tantamount to a demand that he acquiesce to a form of self-annihilation."[10] Adorno insisted on his otherness so that he would not easily become consumed by the American culture industry. This was a matter of living his philosophy. I am reminded here of bell hooks's description of marginality and outsider status as something that can be more than a site of deprivation and pain. She beautifully argues that it can, in fact, become the opposite. Living in the margins can be fostered as a site of radical possibility. Rather than seeing it simply as a place of exclusion and a status that one wishes to lose, we can cultivate it as "a site one stays in, clings to even, because it nourishes one's capacity to resist. It offers to one the possibility of radical perspective from which to see and create, to imagine alternatives, new worlds."[11] hooks describes this as a form of "choosing the margin as a space of radical openness." One can imagine that Adorno, who clearly suffered because of his exile, also managed to derive a strange pleasure from the assertion of his otherness and his outsider status. Marginality can be understood here as a sort of defiant political gesture, or an oppositional aesthetic act. hooks argues that one should "maintain that marginality even as one works, produces, lives, if you will, at the center."[12] Adorno's philosophy is entirely consistent with this acknowledgment of the fact that the work is never done, that one never reaches utopia, and that change is precisely that, a constant movement toward a better human condition. This is an underpinning of Adorno's works, and the project of critical theory is precisely that effort to maintain marginality.

Minima Moralia deals self-reflexively with Adorno's role as an intellectual in general and with his work as a philosopher in particular. There is a persistent examination of philosophy's "original sin"—the division of mental and physical labor. The structure of the book shapes Adorno's discussion. The work consists of 153 aphorisms that reflect Adorno's plea for "micrological" thinking and a "philosophy of the fragment." The trivial pursuits that Adorno writes about here fly in the face of the philosophical tradition that attempts to create "theories of everything" and considers only "enduring" issues and "timeless" concerns while masking its own historicity. Drawing on Walter Benjamin's formulation of the fragment, the aphorisms formally assault the supposedly seamless totality of capitalism by revealing the discontinuous nature of experience.

Living in Los Angeles—with its artifice, the heart of the culture industry—with the bodybuilders of Venice Beach only a few miles from his bungalow in Holly Hills, Adorno perceived the Californian obsession with the perfect body as an ersatz version of the Nazi preoccupation with the perfect form. In his fascinating work *The Case of California*, Laurence Rickels profoundly names California the "unconscious of Europe."[13] Rickels astutely draws connections between the experience of California and the critique of Fascism by the Frankfurt School thinkers and argues that exile from Nazi Germany forced them to read the rise of National Socialism through the lens of California coastal culture. Although Rickels tends to view this as a form of unintentional slippage and a shortcoming in the Frankfurt School's critique of Fascism, I would argue that Adorno was aware of this juxtaposition of the proliferation of the culture industry in the United States and the rise of National Socialism in Germany. Adorno wrote about both as a set of twin phenomena that are both products of the processes of reification. This understanding informs both the particular *and* the universal aspects of Adorno's material historical analyses.

In the dedication of *Minima Moralia*, Adorno reflects with melancholy on the paradox of his earlier experience and that from which he writes: "The major part of this book was written during the war, under conditions enforcing contemplation. The violence that expelled me thereby denied me full knowledge of it."[14] This contradiction—the fact that he is denied a full knowledge of Fascism because of the exile imposed on him by Fascism—motivates and propels this work. *Minima Moralia* must be read, therefore, as a text that is about both Fascism and Adorno's reflections on his experience of practicing philosophy in exile because of Fascism. In order to fully comprehend the complex issues that help shape Adorno's critical attention to the body, it is useful to make a brief detour here and sketch out some of the fundamental aspects of the perverse fascination with the body in Nazi ideology. This effort will allow me to historically situate Adorno's understanding of the body and to give a sense of the complex dynamics to which he is responding.

Nazi culture was enchanted by the human form. The body was, however, more a "phantasmagoric" ideal than a living, breathing, material reality. The appeal of and to the body did not encourage sensuousness, or a revolt from traditional morals, but rather was propagated to encourage a puerile longing for the genuine and the natural. George Mosse, in his seminal work, *Nationalism and Sexuality*, shows how the "rediscovery of the body" during the Nazi period drew on existing German literary and cultural trends, from Johann Joachim Winckelmann's notion of beauty to Stefan George's poetic plea to return to the purity of nature in his cult of genius.[15] Favoring a more austere and puritan model of the body, the Nazis rejected the sensuousness that had prevailed in the preceding generation of fin de siècle decadents. Artistic and literary renderings of the body that inspired heightened sensibility and stimulation, such as expressionist art or the works of Thomas Mann, were labeled decadent and unworthy of the pure political body that the Nazis were attempting to fashion. The invocations of ancient Greece in paintings, memorials, and films expressed a physical beauty stripped of sexuality and uncontrolled passion. Numerous marble statues for public spaces were commissioned by the Nazis, fulfilling their cool, controlled, restrained ideal of perfection. The art promoted an aestheticized, repressive sexual society based on the containment of vital forces. The Lebensreform movements that promoted gymnastics and bodily awareness were exercises in disciplining the individual's body and also a rehearsal for the creation of a submissive polity. The movements of the gymnasts in rigid patterns performed as mass athletic demonstrations evoke what Susan Sontag describes in "Fascinating Fascism" as "the holding in or confining of force: military precision."[16]

The body, as celebrated in proto-Fascist and right-wing groups such as the German Youth Movement and the Nacktkultur, led by Richard

Ungewitter, was purified of contamination through diet and exercise in the name of the regeneration of the race. Bodies were ranked according to character and physique. Popular books such as *Der Sieg der Körperfreude*, published in 1940, and the widely distributed series *Die Schönheit* focused on the body but operated under strict censure. Nudism in print media was banned during the Nazi period with the exception of bodies depicted as engaged in motion or sport. Discussions of sexuality in the media were also banned, except in "public service" announcements, which consisted of warnings to the reader about the dire consequences of masturbation and sex for pleasure rather than procreation. These imperatives about the body were manifest in virtually all cultural artifacts from this period, whether they were from the visual arts, literature, films, or public events and spectacles.

The point of this digression is to suggest that the Nazi fascination with and fear of the body provided the historical context for Adorno's own investigation and critical attention to the body. Klaus Theweleit, the thinker most associated with an interpretation of Fascism revolving around the centrality of the body, has accused the Frankfurt School intellectuals, and particularly Adorno, for ignoring the body. In his fascinating and influential psychoanalytic study, *Male Fantasies*, Theweleit draws connections between history and fantasy. Theweleit uncovers an exterminating rage against female sexual power and a fear of the female body behind the masculine constructions of bands of German paramilitary groups during World War II. At the beginning of his book, Theweleit attacks the Frankfurt School for their "historical-materialist" approach, which he claims is a means by which "rational men have at once attempted to account for fascism and protect themselves from what it means."[17] He goes on to argue: "All of the lines of scientific research based purely on ideological criticism, or *Ideologiekritik* (headed by the Frankfurt School), and all of the theoretical approaches that practice historical-materialist-philosophical-metapsychological manipulations . . . ignore the same basic area: the things that happen in, and to, human bodies."[18] The Frankfurt School, Theweleit further suggests, is guilty of ignoring feelings and emotions and repressing desire in favor of the "intellectual," who, he argues, is incapable of grasping the somatic origins of Fascism. Although it is impossible to thoroughly debate Theweleit's overreaching contentions here, my discussion of *Minima Moralia* will show that the body is not absent from Adorno's work, but, contrary to Theweleit's assertions, is absolutely central to Adorno's investigations. The difficulty in locating the body in Adorno's work is a result of his theoretical insistence on mediation, the inner coherence of his style, and the logical structure of his critique, rather than of a lack of attention.

In Adorno's writings, philosophy is the enterprise that is most guilty of perpetuating the division of mental and physical labor and performing what Adorno graphically describes as a "vivisection of the body." He cleverly integrates the body into his critique of philosophy. He criticizes philosophy for conspiring with the dominant mode of production to bifurcate the human subject into mind and body. He exposes what he considers to be the "forces of production" behind the work of philosophy. "The official philosophy ministers to science in the following way. It is expected, as a sort of Taylorism of the mind, to help improve its production methods, to rationalize the storage of knowledge, and to prevent and wastage of intellectual energy."[19] In 1911, in his influential book, *The Principles of Scientific Management*, F. W. Taylor introduced a new system of production. In the name of promoting worker productivity, Taylor devised a system of ordering labor that transformed work structures and labor relations. In his book, Taylor suggested the separation of skilled workers, who performed mental labor, from unskilled, manual workers. This fracturing of the workplace ensured that a division of labor would be built into the very structure of the workplace. In Taylorism, the worker's body becomes increasingly regarded as purely functional and composed of elements that can be divided into discrete parts and employed mechanistically to perform alienating tasks. In addition, Taylor, replacing the old rule-of-thumb approach, suggested these improvements in the name of "scientific" management, thus giving authenticity and immutability to his ideas about how to run a place of work. In other words, Taylorism "reified" the division of labor and made this way of managing the workplace appear inevitable and "natural."

Adorno accuses philosophy of following the principles of Taylorism. In the name of promoting "productivity of thought," philosophy attempts to disunite the physical, sensual aspects of human existence from sentient being. A simple example of this is the standard philosophical notion of "separating emotions from reason." In the effort to promote "pure reason," emotions are discounted and marginalized. In contrast, Adorno attempts to realize philosophy in his own efforts as a form of work that is not just cerebral, but also corporeal and grounded in sensual experience.

In one of the longer fragments in *Minima Moralia*, titled "Intellectus Sacrificium Intellectus," Adorno examines the ways in which the intellect sacrifices itself to a concept of itself that it worships self-destructively as a false god.[20] This false understanding of intellect is one that is sanitized, purified of emotions, instincts, impulses, and desires. Adorno writes: "The assumption that thought profits from the decay of the emotions, or even that it remains unaffected, is itself an expression of the process of stupefaction. The social division of labour recoils on man, however much it may expedite the task exacted from him. The faculties, having developed through interaction, atrophy once they are severed from each other."[21] This division of work—allocating thought to one task and emotions to another, under the false presumption that thought can be more productive once it is disentangled from emotions—is yet another rendition of the "dialectic of enlightenment." Adorno argues that the more "efficient" thought becomes, the less capable it is of actually thinking. "Sanitized thinking" is condemned to reiterate the known and reproduce that which already exists. "Once the last trace of emotion has been eradicated, nothing remains of thought but absolute tautology. The utterly pure reason of those who have divested themselves entirely of the ability 'to conceive of an object even in its absence,' converges with pure unconsciousness" (123). Reason, when purged of emotions, tends to reproduce and numbly accept the world without challenging it. Sentient beings are no longer able to think and act imaginatively or creatively, but are instead reduced to a set of truisms and a series of neurotic repetitions. Thought itself becomes banal.

In another aphorism, titled "Wishful Thinking," Adorno, astoundingly, suggests that there is a moral imperative to make emotions and feelings an integral part of the thinking process. He writes, "Intelligence is a moral category. The separation of feeling and understanding, that makes it possible to absolve and beautify the blockhead, hypostasizes the dismemberment of man into functions" (127). In this quote, Adorno attacks the kind of thinking that hypostatizes the dualistic division of human beings. In other words, Adorno wants to unmask what appears to be a "natural condition" in order to reveal its historical specificity. He viscerally describes this division of human beings into mind and body as a form of dismemberment. Even more explicitly, he calls this "the castration of perception by a court of control that denies thought any anticipatory desire" (123). In philosophy's pursuit of epistemic objectivity, forms of perception—seeing, hearing, touching, tasting, smelling—are cut off, which dams the wellsprings of desire and splits human beings into separate functions: thinking versus feeling. A breach occurs between body and world that leaves human beings "castrated," impotent when it comes to thinking meaningfully about the surrounding world.

The preceding quotes reflect a way of conveying thoughts that is characteristic of Adorno. In his critique of philosophy, he often makes use of images or metaphors related to the mutilation of the body. *Castration, vivisection, evisceration,* and *dismemberment* are words that Adorno uses to remove his critique from an abstract mode of intellectual jargon and to place it into a material and physical mode of communication. For example, he repeatedly uses metaphors of the body in order to illustrate his most central points: "Someone who has been offended, slighted has an illumination as vivid as when agonizing pain lights up one's own body" (164). In another instance, Adorno refers back to the body to viscerally evoke a critical stance: "The splinter in your eye is the best magnifying glass" (50). This manner of discourse shocks intellectually engaged readers into acknowledging their own corporeality. Elsewhere, Adorno insists, revealingly, that "only in the metaphor of the body can the concept of pure spirit be grasped at all, and is at the same time cancelled" (242). Adorno wryly describes how the dream of "pure spirit" of Hegel and other philosophers, who fantasize about the transcendence of the knowing subject, can only be understood through the body—the feeling, emotional body that I have described. The irony being, of course, that this very process of knowing through the body annuls the notion of pure spirit. At one point, Adorno accuses Hegel of turning "belly into pure spirit." Adorno reverses Hegel and, in a manner of speaking, returns spirit to the belly. Adorno uses these metaphors and images of the body to create a new philosophical language that moves toward a philosophy that has not excised emotion, sensitivity, practicality, and curiosity precisely because it emerges from, not at the expense of, the sentient body.

Since Adorno never directly names the body or writes about it in a sustained fashion, it is through the mediating role of language that one finds the specifically corporal. One of the reasons that it is so difficult to locate the body in Adorno's work is lies in the oft-noted "subterranean influence of a Jewish religious theme on the materialism of the Frankfurt School."[22] Susan Buck-Morss, among others, has documented Adorno's adherence to "the Jewish *Bilderverbot*," seen in his refusal "to delineate the nature of utopia."[23] In Adorno's thought, this refusal to describe the body in positive, substantive terms can also be ascribed to Adorno's fundamental distrust of immediacy and his reliance on dialectical mediation. Such wariness stems from his familiar critique of identity thinking and what he describes as the "fanatical intolerance" of epistemological systems that transform the particular into abstract repetitions of the universal in their attempt to render objects unmediated and immediate.[24] One of the central claims of Adorno's polemic against philosophy—the "peddler of identity thinking"—is that the language of philosophy yearns to get closer to the prelinguistic realm, using conceptual language in an attempt to capture the object. The problem, Adorno points out, is that this attempt does violence to the object, which is nonconceptual (*begriffslos*). Philosophical/conceptual language represses, marginalizes, and eliminates the nonconceptual and asserts its identity. Mediation (*Vermittlung*) is the epistemological key to alleviating this problem. Mediation operates in various ways in Adorno's thought. Often it is used in the traditional sense, to mean that a third term is required to make a connection between two ideas. In other instances, however, and in relation to language, the concept of mediation becomes more complex. When language mediates, it does not merely act as an agent between two things, but, more important, points to the *absence* of, and nonidentity inherent in, the object. Language plays a mediating role by making the negative obvious. It is this communication of negativity that acts as the critique of the failures of philosophy. This is one way to understand the contradiction between the difficulty in precisely locating the body in Adorno's writing, and the curious, unshakable sense of its omnipresence. In Adorno's typical dialectical fashion, the body's presence is articulated only through its absence. Rather than writing directly about the body, Adorno uses metaphors and visceral language to underscore its negativity, and it is from here that he is able to launch his critique of philosophy.

It is Friedrich Nietzsche—who reintroduces the body into the discourse of the social, scientific, and cultural production of knowledge and who Adorno himself invokes in the foreword to *Minima Moralia*—who invites comparison with Adorno in the latter's understanding of the body and playful use of metaphor. "The history of philosophy up to now," Nietzsche contends at the opening of *The Gay Science*, "has been the history of the repression of the body."[25] Like Adorno, Nietzsche locates the malaise and sadism of reason in philosophy's misguided approach. He conveys this tartly in his pithy fragment "Why Philosophers Are Slanderers."

> The treacherous and blind hostility of philosophers towards the senses—how much of mob and middle class there is in this ha-

tred! . . . if one wants a proof of how profoundly and thoroughly the actually barbarous needs of man seek satisfaction, even when he is tamed and "civilized." One should take a look here at the "leitmotifs" of the entire evolution of philosophy:—a sort of revenge on reality, a malicious destruction of the valuations by which men live, an unsatisfied soul that feels the tamed state as torture and finds a voluptuous pleasure in a morbid unraveling of all the bonds that tie it to such a state.[26]

Mistrusting the senses, which seductively lead rational thought astray, philosophers are engaged in a self-destructive "dialectic of enlightenment," repressing with barbarity the very nature upon which civilization depends. Nietzsche contrasts and distinguishes his own philosophy by describing it as following the "guiding thread of the body" (*am Leitfaden des Leibes*). Nietzsche is writing against a Platonic, Christian tradition that believes that man is a noble being by nature of his spirit, but unfortunately afflicted by one flaw: the body. For Nietzsche, it is man's animalism, his sureness of instinct, that is weakened by the precariousness of his spirit and conscious thought. According to Adorno, Nietzsche's "liberating act, a true turning point of Western thought," is that he "refuses homage to the speculative concept, the hypostasis of the mind."[27] Adorno's critique of philosophy, as discussed earlier, is directed precisely at the attempts of philosophy to make mind the immutable and autonomous foundation of thought. Adorno's thought parallels Nietzsche's in certain respects, especially in regard to Nietzsche's characterization of mass psychology and the masochistic elements of bourgeois rationality. Both Nietzsche and Adorno can be understood as engaged in a project of attempting to jar human beings from a life of self-surrender.

Like Adorno, Nietzsche does not have a coherent theory of the body, but instead relies on abundant metaphors of the body in order to emphasize its important role in the production of truth and knowledge. Adorno owes much to Nietzsche's antisystematic form of philosophy and his use of the essay form to cultivate a fragmentary and aphoristic syntax and style. Literary conventions such as parallax, parataxis, chiasm, and tautology are employed by both thinkers to stylistically avoid complicity with prevailing philosophical systems of discourse.[28] This can be understood as effecting a linguistic "transvaluation of values." In Nietzsche's writings, his style is intimately connected with the body, and he artfully uses physiological metaphors, especially those related to smell and digestion, to criticize the "lie" about the autonomy of mind in epistemology. Nietzsche writes, for example, "What we experience and digest psychologically does not, in the stage of gestation, emerge into consciousness any more than what we ingest physically does."[29] The gastric terms *digest, live', 'absorb,* and *incorporate* (*verdauen, erleben, hineinnehmen, einverleiben*) are often used by Nietzsche to describe human interactions. The body becomes the foundation for virtually all his metaphors and especially for thought itself. He asserts: "Consciousness is an organ like the stomach."[30] And: "Our intellect is only the blind instrument of another drive."[31] Consciousness and intellect are for him a passion or a bodily state like hunger or thirst.

Nietzsche describes his philosophy as a genealogy, which is a process suffused with bodily implications and intimately associated with sexuality. The etymological root of the word—*genea*—is defined as race or family. Genealogy is therefore a history of the descent of a person or group from a common blood relation. Genealogy traces the history of sexuality and bodies to reconstruct its particular account. Privileging the body in such a way emphasizes the notion that history is not simply a neutral record of an established reality, but rather an account that is the result of sexual desire, psychological needs, and social ends.[32] Nietzsche's genealogical philosophy traces the "origin" and process by means of which something becomes legitimized by culture. In this way, genealogy can be understood as a problem of legitimization (*Legitimitätsproblem*). By radically interrogating the validity of origins and evaluating how mere "things" become entrenched in society's values and norms and become "facts," it is acts as a critique of ideology. The genealogical imperative—to unmask the "natural" as a result of historical human intervention bears a striking similarity to the critique of reification—to show how relations between things that appear immutable and timeless began as relations between humans. Nietzsche, of course, does not specifically place his arguments within the critique of capital, but instead uses the umbrella term *bourgeois society*.

For Nietzsche, the results of the body's activities—passions, instincts, the struggle to survive, to mature, to overcome itself—are the source of the will to power. Consciousness is a direct effect of reactive forces attempting to regulate the body. From the turmoil of bodily forces comes consciousness, a force of domination that orders, commands, and imposes perspectives that help the body interact with other bodies. In this respect, consciousness is a kind of necessary illusion: on the one hand, a convenient fiction that helps to organize the chaos of bodily organic material and forces and, on the other hand, an effect of the deflected will to power that instead of subduing other bodies and outside forces has turned inward and subdues itself. Nietzsche despises the efforts of thinkers to look inward and examine consciousness through introspection, psychology, or self-reflection. This is a mistake because the psychical interior, what is called consciousness or mind, is in fact a product of the body. Philosophers are the most guilty of this. They are filled with what Nietzsche disparagingly calls a *ressentiment*, a fear of the body's activity and its vicissitudes and a fleeing from the reality of life into the world of illusion. Philosophy should not be simply an intellectual system of inquiry, Nietzsche argues, but a struggle and a battle.

I do not want to overstate the similarities between Adorno and Nietzsche here. Paradoxically, the convergence of their styles of writing is also the location in which they are most divergent. While Nietzsche's thought continually *evades* the codes and systems of civilization that he criticizes, Adorno's passion for immanent criticism *invades* the object of his critique.[33] While Nietzsche philosophizes with a hammer, and forcefully attacks and criticizes, Adorno's labors are more somber and work from the inside out, attempting to explode, rather than break apart. Most important, while both thinkers contest the duality of body and spirit, Nietzsche tends to reduce the human being to body, in the attempt to tap into some sort of "immediacy." Adorno, in contrast, is attempting to dialectically reconfigure the relationship between the two, continually stressing the importance of mediation. Nietzsche's influence on Adorno is best understood as what Adorno calls a "philosophy of retrieval." Adorno understood intellectual history as a practice of retrieving those thinkers and thoughts, and more crucially in this case, modes of thinking, that have been systematically suppressed and repressed by the dominant modes of philosophy and forgotten by society. Philosophy, Adorno argues in *Minima Moralia*, should be suffused with "impulses," "memory," "fantasy," and "curiosity." These constitute what Adorno describes as "the Pleasure Principle of thought." They counteract Western culture's antagonism to pleasure (*Glücksfeindschaft*). Adorno retrieves this particular way of writing and thinking through the body from Nietzsche. Rather than lifting any particular ideas or concepts from Nietzsche's philosophy, Adorno mimics Nietzsche's use of language to evoke the body in order to formally and stylistically critique the autonomy of thought.

Gilles Deleuze once wrote of Nietzsche, "Those who read Nietzsche without laughing—without laughing often, richly, even hilariously—

have, in a sense not read Nietzsche at all."[34] This concisely sums up the difference between Nietzsche's "gay" and Adorno's "melancholy" science. This is, of course, a result of not only philosophical differences, but also historical contexts. Adorno is writing "after Auschwitz," and Nietzsche's admonitions to give up guilt and bad conscience are fundamentally unthinkable for someone who feels "guilty solely by being alive." The feeling that Adorno's language evokes is an immeasurable sense of sorrow and loss. The plaintive object of language is "the need to lend a voice to suffering." When language does not function in this way, it becomes, to quote Adorno's chilling formulation, "more incidental music such as that with which the SS had tried to drown out the screams of its victims."[35]

Returning now to *Minima Moralia*, the question that begs to be asked is, Which body is Adorno talking about? Bodies are not abstract, but formed, shaped, and marked by difference, most notably sexual difference, and what does Adorno have to say about this? Although I would not claim that Adorno was a protofeminist by any means, there is a remarkable collection of eight fragments at the beginning of the second part of the work beginning with "Where the stork brings babies from" to "Since I set eyes on him," that all address the question of sex and gender and the subordination of women. There are no other Adorno texts that offers such a detailed and sustained investigation of patriarchal bourgeois society and its repercussions. Adorno reflects on "the feminine character," sexuality, marriage, and Ibsen's Hedda Gabler and offers astute observations about the reproduction of domination in the "masculine liberal competitive economy."

Adorno suggests that allowing women to participate equally in such a society merely "levels the playing field" to the point that both women and men can successfully achieve equal-opportunity dehumanization. "The admittance of women to every conceivable supervised activity conceals continuing dehumanization. In big business they remain what they were in the family, objects."[36] This act of admitting women into social activities to which they have previously been excluded is not a step toward emancipation, but rather an ill-fated gesture that weakens the ability of women to recognize the true extent of their oppression.

While acknowledging that women have a different experience in bourgeois society, Adorno is careful when describing the uniqueness of feminine experience. He does not want to reify a particular definition of femaleness and fall into a discourse of identity. Femininity is not innate or natural, but a result of the inscription of women's oppression. "The Femininity which appeals to instinct, is always exactly what every woman has to force herself by violence—masculine violence—to be: a she man."[37] Adorno comes startling close to naming Woman as the "second sex." Simone de Beauvoir, of course, does so in her work *The Second Sex* where she describes the ontological process whereby "man" defines himself through the hierarchical contrast with an "Other" that is "woman." Mapping the Hegelian master/slave dialectic onto male-female relations, de Beauvoir shows how "man" assumes a universalistic position in this formulation, whereas "woman" is doomed to the contingent and subordinate status of the "second sex." Clinging to the notion that transcendence in general is equal to transcendence of the body, de Beauvoir goes on to claim that the price men pay for representing the universal is a kind of loss of embodiment. Whereas the price women pay is an immanent existence defined by her confinement to the body. Men are disembodied and gain their entitlement to transcendence, and women are embodied and consigned to immanence. These are two asymmetrical corporeal situations that Adorno recognizes. Adorno acknowledges that the disembodied, affect-free epistemological systems privilege the "wholly autonomous, narcissistic, *male* ego" and that Woman represents the "other" to this masculine-gendered way of knowing. However, he also insists that "the concept of gender can never be fully adequate to its masculine object." In other words, while Adorno does interpret the feminine as the "other" to the masculine, he does not suggest that the feminine is a binary or polar opposite of the masculine as is typically the case in postmodern theories of alterity. The feminine in Adorno's reading is of an otherness that consistently disrupts the totalizing concept of masculinity, which pathologically asserts itself over bourgeois society. Kate Soper concisely sums it up this way: "The whole is not masculine, and feminine negativity surfaces as the immanent refusal and critique of this supposed 'truth.'"[38] This is what Adorno means when he describes the "feminine character" as "a negative imprint of domination." No longer shackled to the subject as defined in the Master-Slave relationship, Otherness is reevaluated and recast by Adorno as a form of negativity that is so charged that it jars us from passively accepting claims of totality by reminding us that the so-called totality is actually incomplete, or in other words, "the whole is the false."

A variety of theorists, both feminists and nonfeminists, have identified negativity as the feminine. Adorno differentiates himself from these thinkers in a crucial way. For Adorno, negativity is not simply the opposite of some affirmative state.[39] He eschews binary opposition when he describes the subject-object relation between male and female in favor of negative dialectics. As he insists, "Total contradiction is nothing but the manifested untruth of total identification."[40] Liberation, therefore, is not conceived as making woman equal to man, which, as I have discussed, would merely give her equal access to dehumanization in a reified society. Liberation also does not include the obliteration of any differences that might exist between the two. Liberation must be examined as a reconcilement of the antagonism between the two that preserves difference. The difference between the feminine and the masculine would still be relational but without being hierarchical. As Adorno describes it: "The reconciled condition would not be the philosophical imperialism of annexing the alien. Instead its happiness would lie in the fact that the alien, in the proximity it is granted, remains what is distant and different, beyond the heterogeneous and beyond that which is one's own."[41] Healing the severed relationship means placing them back into a dialectical relationship.

This finally brings me to Adorno's most sustained reflection on the dialectical relationship of theory and praxis, in "Marginalia to Theory and Praxis." Adorno wrote this essay during the period of student protest, and it is addressed to the critics of his unrelenting belief in the transformative potential and power of critical theory. His tone is uncharacteristically agitated, and one senses how besieged he must have felt. The essay is usually regarded as a strong attack against student activism, which he calls a "delusional" form of "mystified praxis" (*Scheinpraxis*). But even as he caricatures students and their hostility toward theory as selfish, demanding, and "snotty nosed," the true object of his criticism is, once again, the philosophical tradition that has privileged thinking and reflection over action. His defense of theory, therefore, is really an offensive against forms of thinking that bifurcate the mind and body through the fetishization of intellectual labor over physical labor. In this way, Adorno refuses to align himself with those who express an aversion to praxis, which is another form of belittling manual labor, or with those who express enmity toward theory (*Theoriefeindschaft*), which Adorno characterizes as a manifestation of the fear of reason and autonomy. Adorno unpacks the long history of tension between theory and praxis to reveal how deeply entangled their division is with emotional, epistemological, and ideological motives.

In typical Adorno fashion, he complicates things in order to make them more transparent. He insists that the theory-and-praxis relationship needs to be understood as a rupture between mind and body, intellectual and physical labor, and subject and object. Like a set of Russian dolls in which each small figurine rests within another larger version of itself, the complex relationship between theory and praxis is necessarily understood when nested within these other questions. Adorno writes, "At the same time as the Cartesian doctrine of two substances ratified the dichotomy of subject and object, literature for the first time portrayed praxis as a dubious undertaking on account of its tension with reflection."[42] In the general imagination, the division of the human being into a mind-body dualism, in the context of Western civilization, had its beginnings in the seventeenth century, when René Descartes uttered his famous "Cogito ergo sum." Descartes's meditations became the wellspring of classical rationalism, which privileged the conceptual or mental over the corporeal, thereby extracting the body from the production of knowledge. This hierarchy of mind over body, referred to as Cartesian dualism, has become so calcified in contemporary culture and society that its rigid structure defines virtually all modern and postmodern philosophical thought.[43] Furthermore, Descartes's cogito—*I* think, therefore, *I* am—places the emphasis on the subject, shifting the focus in science and philosophy from the object of knowledge to the knowing subject.[44] Although Descartes is widely given the dubious credit of being the first modern philosopher to articulate and canonize the dualism of mind and body, he is by no means its "originator"; rather, he represents yet another historical instance that makes evident something that was always already a part of the dialectic of enlightenment. In the oft-quoted passage on the encounter between Odysseus and the Sirens, Adorno and Horkheimer describe how the division of mind and body devolves from the division of labor, a trope that will be repeated throughout history. In the myth of Odysseus, the Hegelian master/slave dialect is reinterpreted as a narrative about both self-preservation and the division of mental and physical labor. While Odysseus restrains his body by chaining himself to the mast in order to contemplate and experience the Siren song, the sailors are bound to physical work by rowing the boat. The division of mind and body asserts itself here in its primordial form—as a division of labor.

In Adorno's essay on theory and praxis, he suggests how this tenuous relationship to work influences how we regard the contemplative art of thinking and the act of doing. "Praxis arose from labor. It attained its concept when labor no longer wanted to merely reproduce life directly but to produce its conditions: and this clashed with the already existing conditions. Its descent from labor is a heavy burden for all of praxis. . . . Contemporary actionism also represses the fact that the longing for freedom is closely related to the aversion to praxis."[45] The aversion towards praxis results from its association with physical work, which has been historically constituted as a form of unfreedom. In other words, praxis, like Adorno's understanding of negativity, is a result of "the wrong state of things." In a compassionate and just society, praxis would be unnecessary.

Adorno describes the dialectical relationship between theory and praxis by describing what it is not. Above all, Adorno argues against the notion that theory must lead to concrete action and answer the question, What do we do now? He vehemently rejects the position that theory should be beholden to pragmatic questions. "If in the end," Adorno argues, "theory, which bears upon the totality if it does not want to be futile, is tied down to its effectiveness here and now, then the same thing befalls it despite its belief that it escapes the immanence of the system. Theory steals itself back from the system's immanence only where it shirks its pragmatic fetters, no matter how modified they may be" (260). It is not possible, nor is it desirable, for theory to prescribe praxis. This distinction Adorno makes is directed towards the misrepresentation of the theory and praxis relationship as a temporal continuity. In other words, Adorno is arguing against the "first theory and then action" mentality. Adorno explains: "The relationship between theory and practice after both have once distanced themselves from each other is that of qualitative reversal, not transition, and surely not subordination" (277). Once we begin to think about the relationship between theory and praxis as discontinuous, it allows us to also get away from the notion that one must necessarily lead to the other, which also no longer lends itself to a process of valorization.

Rejecting the characterization of theory as a flight away from action, Adorno suggests that theory is yet another form of emancipatory practice. "Thinking is a doing, theory a form of praxis" (261). Thought should not be considered to be passive, but proactive. Thinking and critique are inalienable and real modes of behavior in oppressive times. "Despite all of its unfreedom, theory is the guarantor of freedom in the midst of unfreedom" (265). Or as Horkheimer put it, "[T]hought itself is already a sign of resistance, the effort to keep oneself from being deceived any longer."[46] At the same time, theory and praxis are not entirely identical. Conflating the two is just as problematic as separating them. It is the tension of the contradiction and interplay of their relationship to each other that productively generates any possibility of movement and change. It is important to stress that Adorno is not arguing that theory should ignore concrete social realities or withdraw into an isolated ivory tower. Instead it should throw itself into the art of compelling change through dialectical critique, thereby unleashing a radical imagination that allows us to simultaneously give voice to suffering and preserve hope. "Every meditation upon freedom extends into the conception of its possible realization," Adorno writes with faith but then adds with caution, "so long as the meditation is not taken in hand by praxis and tailored to fit the results it enjoins."[47]

In the essay, Adorno also defends theory against the so-called ivory-tower argument, namely, the accusation that theory is a traitor to socialism (*Verräter am Sozialismus*) because it is obscure, isolationist, and incomprehensible to the mass majority of people, the proletariat, for whom it claims to speak. Adorno's tone becomes impatient when addressing this argument. He suggests that the very notion of a traitor implies that there is a repressive collective identity at work attempting to liquidate any inkling of autonomy. This is, once again, an extension of his argument against identity thinking. Adorno reveals here his fear and suspicion of mass movements of any kind. This is something about which he consistently disagreed and clashed with Walter Benjamin, who believed in the great potential of a revolutionary collective consciousness. Adorno laments the loss of the possibility of real praxis (*richtige Praxis*), which is a form of self-determined activity that springs from human spontaneity. This type of actionism, Adorno argues, presupposes a free and autonomous agent that could not possibly exist in an administered society. The actionism of the time was under the spell of illusory or mystified praxis (*Scheinpraxis*), a repressive collective act that liquidates voluntarism and individuality. When one participates in Scheinpraxis, one derives a sense of security from acting as a group, sheltered from true individuality. This is the predominant form of praxis that Adorno saw at work when he was writing the essay. The student revolts were viewed by Adorno as a form of Scheinpraxis, which he described as "jumping into the melting pot of action."

At one point, Adorno writes, "The requirement that theory should kowtow to praxis dissolves theory's truth content and condemns praxis to delusion; in practical terms, it is high time to voice this. A modicum of madness furnishes collective movements—. . . with their sinister power of attraction."[48] Adorno often uses words such as *madness* (*Wahnsinn*) and *mania* (*Wahn*) when describing mass action. Even Marcuse, who became the malcontent of the Frankfurt School because of his vociferous support and participation in social-protest movements, never abandoned his un-failing belief in the principal role of critical theory. "Theory will preserve the truth," Marcuse insisted, "even if revolutionary practice deviates from its proper path."[49] Theory and thought have the ability to maintain a critical focus, whereas practice is susceptible to delusion.

Adorno's harshest criticism of praxis is that it masks the reality of the situation, in that "if praxis obscures its own present impossibility with the opiate of collectivity, it becomes in its turn ideology."[50] Praxis quickly becomes yet another form of ideology, because it acts as an opiate that alters consciousness, intoxicating and numbing the actor to the true ex-tent of his or her oppression and the misery of his or her circumstances. It becomes easier to accept one's situation when empowered by the false sense that one is actually doing something. I know I myself have fallen under this collective enchantment, most recently at the March for Wom-en's Lives in Washington, D.C., on 22 April 2004, where the pleasure, strength, and empowerment I felt while collectively marching and shout-ing until my voice was raw did not completely dispel my bewilderment at the unproductive, nonsensical nature of screaming, "Choice! Choice! Choice!" at antichoice, antiabortion activists who were on the sidelines screaming back "What about the baby's choice? What about the baby's choice?" Adorno recognized this tendency when he wrote: "Instead of arguments one meets standardized slogans, which apparently are distrib-uted by leaders and their acolytes."[51] At the same time, my desire to join the march was compelled by a sense of urgency and the necessity of the times. The dizzying pleasure of collective unity was also tinged with the critical perspective of women and men who have been fighting for a wom-en's right to choice for a very long time, and the unpalatable and exasper-ated feeling that we needed to do it yet once again.

It is important to note that Adorno does not completely disparage praxis, because he understands it as a reflex of necessity (*Lebensnotwendig-keit*—literally, "resourcefulness of life") that acts as a defense mechanism. People protect themselves from resignation and hopelessness with praxis. And he would, of course, not begrudge a march on Washington or an antiwar rally. As long as it was acknowledged on some level that "[t]he goal of real praxis would be its own abolition."[52] Instead of being a form of "crisis management" that simply reinforces conformity, real praxis works toward the moment of its own dispensability—the utopian state in which there would be no real need for such praxis. This is one of Adorno's valuable insights. Praxis works toward its own abolition: a utopian point at which praxis becomes obsolete.

How does any of this illuminate the wacky event of the bared breasts, my initial point of departure? The central tension that prompted the students to act out against Adorno arises from a fissure situated between theory and praxis. The students' action that day was directed toward theory as it is understood as a sort of "male fantasy." The delusion of an autonomous intellect—whether conceived of as pure reason, spirit, or intention—freed from material constraints is radically challenged by the negativity of the body, a negativity or absence that is made obvious only in its uncomfortable presence in the intellectual space of the seminar room that day.

It is troubling in a way that the body seems to always play a central role in feminist theory. Feminist struggles have hovered over issues related to the body—contraception, the right to abortion, maternity rights, rape, self-defense, body image, pornography . . . However, there has also been a lingering ambivalence about casting women's oppression and liberation in corporeal terms. The body conjures up allegations of ahistoricity, essentialism, and biologism—loaded terms that feminists might rather avoid. Essentialism, as it is commonly understood, is the belief in a real and true essence of things, and signals the accompanying notion that there are invariable and fixed properties that define the "whatness" of a given entity.[53] For women, the body has been the locus of essence. Women have been linked with, reduced to, and projected as the body. The humbling, contaminating, threatening, and tempting characteristics of the flesh have been culturally encoded as female. This is, of course, only one side of the dualist axis, the characteristics of nobility, pureness, and transcendence being the other. Woman's liberation seems to be predicated precisely on women being freed from this identity with the body, freeing her from an essential notion of herself.

Liberation and freedom, however, cannot be predicated on a separation from the body. Adorno's critique of epistemology is an effort to reconcile mind and body through a process that does not reify or collapse difference, but instead moves toward placing them back into a dialectical relation. The body is, to borrow Adorno's formulation, both the "splinter in the eye" and the "best magnifying glass." Adorno's important insight about the various incarnations of this dualism—mental/physical labor, theory/praxis and subject/object—gives expression to the ideological, emotional, and epistemological forces that are invested in these ruptures. While the students challenged this mode of identity thinking with the immediacy of the body, the solution, for Adorno, is found in the reconciliation of mind and body through mediation. Difference between the two is preserved without doing violence to the object by liquidating its otherness. In recent discourse, the notion of incommensurability has gathered steam as a way of discussing the object without giving in to the compulsion of the self-identity of the subject. "Incommensurability is the only way," one critic writes, "to resist the powerful sway of the subject and preserve any semblance of difference in the object."[54] For Adorno, this state of total disjunction and alienation is undesirable. Even as he wants to retain the moment of nonidentity between subject and object and avoid granting priority to either, he also wants to place them within a relationship of reciprocity. Adorno evocatively describes this process: "Approaching knowledge of the object is the act in which the subject rends the veil it is weaving around the object. It can do this only where, fearlessly passive, it entrusts itself to its own experience. . . . The subject is the object's agent, not its constituent; this fact has consequences for the relation of theory and practice."[55] Adorno's use of language here is highly suggestive—an experience that verges on erotic surrender. Critical in the preceding quote is the emphasis on the passivity of the subject and of thought itself. This kind of reciprocal relationship between subject and object maintains a fidelity to the object, or what Adorno calls the "preponderance of the object." Reconciliation is therefore understood as the moment of nonidentity, in which neither is granted priority over one or the other. Ultimately, however, in the current reified society, this reconciliation remains a utopian promise, and whether it is the troubled relationship between mind and body, the tension between theory and praxis, the division of intellectual and manual labor or of subject and object, these dualisms remain examples of "torn halves of an integral freedom, to which they do not add up."[56]

Notes

1. Quoted by Wolfgang Kraushaar, *Frankfurter Schule und Studentenbewegung: Von der Flaschenpost zum Molotowcocktail* (Hamburg: Rogner and Bernhard, 1998), 418. (My translation.)

2. Quoted by A. B. Rosen in *Münchner Merkur*, 26 April 1969, 23.

3. *Die Süddeutsche Zeitung*, 26–27 April 1969, 10.

4. Adorno immediately left the lecture hall, flustered and humiliated, and he canceled the seminar until further notice. He died unexpectedly of a heart attack in Switzerland about four months later. For a more in-depth description of the event and the sensationalized press coverage the following day, see Rolf Wiggershaus, *Die Frankfurter Schule: Geschichte, theoretische Entwicklung, politische Bedeutung* (Frankfurt: C. Hanser, 1986), 635.

5. *Die Süddeutsche Zeitung*, 26–27 April 1969, 10.

6. Theodor W. Adorno, *Minima Moralia: Reflections from a Damaged Life*, trans. E. F. N. Jephcott (New York: Verso, 1978), 33.

7. Constraints of space do not allow me to offer an in-depth analysis of one other essay that bears mentioning. "Resignation," which originated as a radio lecture, also deals with the troubled relationship between theory and praxis. It recapitulates many points of another essay that I will examine at length in this chapter, "Marginalia to Theory and Praxis."

8. Adorno, *Minima Moralia*, 150.

9. Adorno, *Minima Moralia*, 102.

10. Jamie Owen Daniel, "Temporary Shelter: Adorno's Exile and the Language of Home," *New Frontiers* 17 (Summer 1992): 26.

11. bell hooks, "Choosing the Margin as a Space of Radical Openness," in *The Feminist Standpoint Theory Reader: Intellectual and Political Controversies*, ed. Sandra Harding (New York: Routledge, 2004), 157.

12. hooks, "Choosing the Margin," 157.

13. Laurence A. Rickels, *The Case of California* (Baltimore: Johns Hopkins University Press, 1991).

14. Adorno, *Minima Moralia*, 18.

15. George L. Mosse, *Nationalism and Sexuality: Middle Class Morality and Sexual Norms in Modern Europe* (Madison: University of Wisconsin Press, 1985), 48–66.

16. See Susan Sontag, "Fascinating Fascism," in *A Susan Sontag Reader* (New York: Farrer, Strauss and Giroux, 1982), 317. Sontag further argues that the repressed sexual energy could then be transformed and channeled into the orgiastic worship of the leader.

17. For Theweleit, "what it means" is the psychic roots of violence, which he locates in middle-class men, who, faced with the psychic trauma of absent Fathers, enact a perverse Oedipal drama and direct their rage against mothers and obliterate them. Klaus Theweleit, *Male Fantasies*, vol. 1, *Women, Floods, Bodies, History* (Minneapolis: University of Minnesota Press, 1987), 12.

18. Theweleit, *Women, Floods, Bodies, History*, 416.

19. Theodor Adorno and Max Horkheimer, *Dialectic of Enlightenment*, trans. John Cummings (New York: Continuum, 1972), 242.

20. The title is a play on a Jesuit maxim expressed by Loyola: "Dei sacrificium intellectus" (To subordinate the intellect to obedience is to offer the highest sacrifice to God).

21. Adorno, *Minima Moralia*, 122. Further page numbers are cited parenthetically in the text.

22. Martin Jay, *The Dialectical Imagination: A History of the Frankfurt School and the Institute of Social Research, 1923–1950* (Berkeley and Los Angeles: University of California Press, 1973), 56.

23. Susan Buck-Morss, *The Origin of Negative Dialectics: Theodor Adorno, Walter Benjamin, and the Frankfurt Institute* (Hassocks, U.K.: Harvester, 1977), 24.

24. Theodor Adorno, *Against Epistemology—a Metacritique: Studies in Husserl and the Phenomenological Antinomies*, trans. Willis Domingo (Oxford: Basil Blackwell, 1982), 13.

25. Friedrich Nietzsche, *The Gay Science*, trans. Walter Kaufmann (New York: Vintage, 1974), 32.

26. Friedrich Nietzsche, *The Will to Power*, trans. Walter Kaufmann (New York: Vintage, 1968), 253.

27. Theodor Adorno, *Negative Dialectics*, trans. E. B. Ashton. (New York: Continuum, 1983), 23.

28. Gillian Rose's work remains the best argument for Adorno's engagement with Nietzsche in reference to methodology and style. See Rose, *The Melancholy Science: An Introduction to the Thought of Theodor Adorno* (New York: Columbia University Press). See also Sabine Wilke, *Zur Dialektik von Exposition und Darstellung: Ansätze zu einer Kritik der Arbeiten Martin Heideggers, Theodor W. Adornos und Jacques Derrida* (New York: Peter Lang, 1988); Rainer Hoffmann, *Figuren des Scheins: Studien zum Sprachbild und zur Denkform Theodor W. Adornos* (Bonn: Bouvier, 1984); Alexander Nehamas, *Nietzsche: Life as Literature* (Cambridge, Mass.: Harvard University Press, 1985).

29. Friedrich Nietzsche, *The Genealogy of Morals*, trans. Walter Kaufmann (New York: Random House, 1967), 57.

30. Friedrich Nietzsche, *The Dawn*, trans. Walter Kaufmann (New York: Random House, 1967), 276.

31. Nietzsche, *The Dawn*, 290.

32. For a good study of Nietzsche's thought and the body, see Eric Blondel, *Nietzsche: The Body and Culture* (Stanford: Stanford University Press, 1991).

33. For this distinction, see Karin Bauer, *Adorno's Nietzschean Narratives* (New York: State University of New York Press, 1999), 190.

34. Gilles Deleuze, "Nomad Thought," in *The New Nietzsche*, ed. David B. Allison (Cambridge, Mass: MIT Press, 1985), 147.

35. Adorno, *Negative Dialectics*, 358.

36. Adorno, *Minima Moralia*, 92.

37. Adorno, *Minima Moralia*, 95.

38. Kate Soper, *Troubled Pleasures: Writings on Gender and Hedonism* (London: Verso, 1990), 216.

39. Kristeva develops her influential theory of the negativity of woman. Briefly stated, according to Lacan, Woman is absence. She does not exist, except as the Other of a discourse grounded in Her radical exclusion. Kristeva displaces this notion to suggest that this sort of negativity of "the feminine" acts as a force to shake up the foundations of the linguistic order. Woman's absence acts as a blind spot and weakness to the masculine order. "For Kristeva, feminine negativity is the unrepresentable, nonviolent disruptor of all fixed linguistic and social codes." See Drucilla Cornell and Adam Thurschwell, "Feminism, Negativity, Subjectivity," in *Feminism as Critique*, ed. Seyla Benhabib and Drucilla Cornell (Minneapolis: University of Minnesota Press, 1987), 143–62.

40. Adorno, *Negative Dialectics*, 18.

41. Adorno, *Negative Dialectics*, 142.

42. Adorno, "Marginalia to Theory and Praxis," in *Critical Models: Interventions and Catchwords*, trans. Henry W. Pickford (New York: Columbia, 1998), 259.

43. This has been effectively argued by thinkers such as Seyla Benhabib, Jane Flax, and Rita Felski, who have all shown that postmodern theories tend to reinscribe the very binaries that they claim to deconstruct. See Seyla Benhabib and Drucilla Cornell, eds., *Feminism as Critique* (Minneapolis: University of Minnesota Press, 1987). Kate Soper also has a useful discussion of this performative contradiction in postmodernism in her essay "Constructo ergo Sum," in *Troubled Pleasures: Writings on Gender and Hedonism* (London: Verso, 1990), 146–65.

44. Husserl would later describe this as the crisis between "transcendental subjectivism" and "physicalist objectivism." Heidegger, Habermas, Lyotard, Rorty, and Jameson, among others, have displaced the mind/body distinction and broadly reformulated it in similar terms as the conflict between "objectivity" and "subjectivity," within discussions of identity, modernity, capitalism, morality, and science.

45. Adorno, "Marginalia to Theory and Praxis," 262. Further page references are cited parenthetically in the text.

46. Max Horkheimer, "Traditional and Critical Theory," in *The Essential Frankfurt School Reader*, ed. Andrew Arato and Eike Gebhardt (New York: Urizen, 1990), 116.

47. Adorno, "Marginalia to Theory and Praxis," 265.

48. Adorno, "Marginalia to Theory and Praxis," 265.

49. Herbert Marcuse, *Reason and Revolution: Hegel and the Rise of Social Theory* (Cambridge, Mass.: Harvard University Press, 1960), 322.

50. Adorno, "Marginalia to Theory and Praxis," 276.

51. Adorno, "Marginalia to Theory and Praxis," 268.

52. Adorno, "Marginalia to Theory and Praxis," 267.

53. See Diana Fuss, *Essentially Speaking: Feminism, Nature, and Difference* (New York: Routledge, 1990).

54. Hauke Brunkhorst, "Irreconcilable Modernity: Adorno's Esthetic Experimentalism and the Transgression Theorem," in *The Actuality of Adorno: Critical Essays on Adorno and the Postmodern* (Albany: State University of New York Press, 1997), 47.

55. Theodor Adorno, "Subject and Object," *The Essential Frankfurt School Reader*, ed. Andrew Arato and Eike Gebhardt (New York: Urizen, 1990), 505.

56. In letters from Adorno to Benjamin, 18 March 1936, in *Aesthetics and Politics*, ed. Frederic Jameson (London: New Left Books, 1977), 123.

7

Mimetic Moments

Adorno and Ecofeminism

D. Bruce Martin

Mimesis has played a variety of roles in the history of philosophy, but can it direct a revolution? From Plato to the deconstructionists it has been treated primarily as aesthetic representation, while science emphasizes its power to explain adaptive and evolutionary behavior. The early Frankfurt School critical theorists used mimesis from the beginning, in key passages of *Dialectic of Enlightenment*. Adorno continued to use the term throughout his career, and may have gone furthest in combining the multiple aspects of mimesis, including the aesthetic, biological, and anthropological. Mimesis in its various manifestations has had both repressive and emancipatory implications, which, as Adorno emphasized, may simultaneously exist side by side philosophically and culturally, both in texts and in the world generally.

In their use of mimesis, feminists and ecofeminists have tended to emphasize aesthetic representation, except for those heavily influenced by ecological science and the environmental movement who have often asserted that their biological interpretations of the term have immediate, transparent implications for social and political theory. In addition, important psychological or psychoanalytic uses of mimesis have functioned for both feminists and critical theorists as a crucial support for broader philosophical claims with political implications.

Following is an excursion first into the beginnings of the use of mimesis in philosophy, and critical theory more specifically, then into the problems and potentials of the scientific meanings of the term, before a final arrival at Luce Irigaray's mimetic critique of philosophy, sometimes labeled a form of ecofeminism. Finally, Adorno's understanding of the relationship of mimesis to "natural beauty" will be visited for his perspective on possibilities for moving beyond situations of social-political domination and ecological destruction.

Mimesis and Political Thought

In the key essay "The Concept of Enlightenment," contained in the pivotal text of Frankfurt School critical theory, the *Dialectic of Enlightenment*, Horkheimer and Adorno focus on myth and philosophy, and magic and science, to establish the long-standing relationship between reason and domination. The critical theorists draw important distinctions in how domination is manifested in these various modes of representation and how mimesis provides the crucial link and difference between them. From Hitler's Fascism to Homer's *Odyssey*, connections between representation and repression are revealed to the extent that the claim can be made that "[t]he universality of ideas as developed by discursive logic, domination in the conceptual sphere, is raised up on the basis of actual domination. . . . The individuality that learned order and subordination in the subjection of the world, soon wholly equated truth with the regulative thought without whose fixed distinctions universal truth cannot exits. Together with mimetic magic, it tabooed the knowledge which really concerned the object."[1]

In the same originating text of critical theory, Horkheimer and Adorno turned to the workings of repressive mimesis expressed in anti-Semitism, the fundamental argument depending on a complex understanding of the transformations of mimesis. Early mimesis in magic and sacrifice have "developed" into ever more elaborate forms of domination, including those of science and psychological projection. In their discussion of biological adaptation, magic ritual, and conceptual domination, they conclude: "Science is repetition, refined into observed regularity, and preserved in stereotypes. The mathematical formula is regression handled consciously, just as magic ritual used to be; it is the most sublimated manifestation of mimicry."[2] The relationship between the repressive and emancipatory moments of mimesis in Adorno's subsequent philosophical and "aesthetic" work will continue to resemble the early critical theorists' treatment of science and technology.

In his last, nearly completed work, Adorno returned to mimesis and its potential to resist the history of domination and its actuality in the present. His focus is finally on the relationship of mimesis and art, and the emancipatory moment of the mimetic:

> Mimetic behaviour is a receptacle for all that has been violently lopped off from and repressed in man by centuries of civilization. . . . What the stubborn persistence of aesthetic mimesis proves is . . . that to this day rationality has never been fully realized, rationality understood in the sense of an agency in the service of mankind and of human potentials, perhaps even of "humanized nature" (Marx). . . . Art keeps alive the memory of ends-oriented reason. . . . Aesthetic behaviour is the ability to see more in things than they are. Its is the gaze that transforms empirical being into imagery.[3]

Several commentators and critics have noted that even though mimesis has been most closely linked to aesthetic philosophy, beginning with Plato and Aristotle, the critical theorists used it to travel a much more anthropological and sociohistorical path. However, before we move to its other forms, it may be helpful first to retrace one of the earliest uses of mimesis in the construction of social and political theory, in its philosophical and aesthetic beginnings, in order to set the background for viewing the relationship of mimesis to ecological politics, philosophical representation, and (eco)feminism.

In Plato's *Republic*, mimesis plays a central role in the constitution of the just political system. Although there are technical arguments over how many types of mimesis exist in Plato, it is unarguable that Plato does use mimesis as a principle of exclusion.[4] In book 10 of the *Republic*, Plato explains that the poets and similar artists must be excluded from the just state because their representations excite the emotions and encourage irrationality, thus undermining the basis of the just state: Reason. The poet, painter, and others who evoke an emotional response set a bad example for those who love truth, who must rely solely on reason to gain access to the true knowledge necessary for the properly run *polis*. So the poets must be banned, not for mimesis itself, but for specifically what is represented: suffering, irrationality, and the instinctual desires that lead those of good character away from knowledge and truth.

It is for this "aesthetic" sense of mimesis in philosophy that Adorno's work, especially his *Aesthetic Theory*, is most frequently criticized, but the basis for its earliest use came as much from anthropology or biology as from the tradition of aesthetic philosophy. Adorno's inclusions of mimesis frequently commence with reference to Walter Benjamin, whose short essay "On the Mimetic Faculty" begins not with an appeal to Greek discussions of literature but to Nature: nature itself produces similarities. For Benjamin the mimetic faculty is a subterranean force within even the most developed forms of human activity, including language. The very ability to perceive similarities or resemblances is a manifestation of "the powerful compulsion in former times to become and behave like something else."[5] This compulsion to imitate, to be like the other, is exhibited in human behavior in the earliest years, including in child's play, whereby the child not only imitates adults, in learning language, for example, and in attempting to assume social roles such as that of a doctor or a teacher, but also imitates objects, such as making the motions of a train or a windmill. The mimetic faculty is one of the most basic of human activities and is present generally in nature. According to Benjamin, this "gift" of recognizing and producing similarities has changed historically, initially being found in dance and magic, more recently in language and technological reproduction. He asks whether the mimetic faculty has continued to decay from its ubiquitous place in the magic and enchantment of ancient peoples, or if it merely has been transformed. He answers by discussing the historical transformation of the mimetic faculty and its ability to recognize and produce "nonsensuous similarity," connecting mimetic magic's flash of recognition of our similarity to the "other" to its now central manifestation in language.

A number of commentators, in addition to Adorno and Horkheimer, have expanded on Benjamin's insight. Michael Taussig, exploring the context of the colonizer and colonized, understands the mimetic faculty as "the nature that culture uses to create second nature, the faculty to copy, imitate, make models, explore difference, yield into and become Other." This capacity, of course, has both repressive and emancipatory potentials and is to be understood, in its more "shamanistic" uses, as a form of "sympathetic magic" in which "the wonder of mimesis lies in the copy drawing on the character and power of the original to the point whereby the representation may even assume that character and that power."[6] Taussig probes the history of mimesis and the "mimesis of history," the telling of the story of possibility of social transformation:

> If I am correct in invoking a certain magic of the signifier and what Walter Benjamin took the mimetic faculty to be—namely, the compulsion to become the Other—and if, thanks to new social conditions and new techniques of reproduction (such as cinema and mass production of imagery), modernity has ushered in a veritable rebirth, a recharging and retooling (of) the mimetic faculty, then it seems to me that we are forthwith invited if not forced into the inner sanctum of mimetic mysteries where, in imitating, we will find distance from the imitated.[7]

(This invitation to "release through imitative distance" is also a theme of Irigaray's work, as will become clear below.)

From its earliest uses by the critical theorists to its more recent recognition by those who have drawn on their insights, mimesis provides both a critique of the positivist understanding of knowledge and the potential for an alternative philosophical writing. This alternative writing would have implications for political practice, especially the relationship between ecofeminism and ecological science. Marcuse foresaw the potential of the women's and ecology movements for pursuing transformative politics and also called for a "New Science" and "New Technology." The new social movements had the potential, he argued, to create a new set of social and economic influences that could reshape the actual practice of science and technology; that is, these new influences could restructure the fundamental determinants of the objects and purposes of science and technology. Natural evolution has not come to an end, but takes on new forms in the dialectic of history and nature.[8] A clearer understanding of our present predicament comes from understanding that evolution has become primarily a regressive and repressive devolution, through the destruction of species and the potential destruction of entire ecosystems, including the irrevocable disintegration of planetary ecology. As some radical ecologists and ecofeminists now argue, it is even possible that this devolution may culminate in a final catastrophic global ecological collapse, destroying human "civilization" if not the species itself. From a radical ecological perspective, scientific-technological development is best viewed as closely approximating Adorno's view of history: modern ecological history is the history of catastrophe.

A question that is key for radical ecology and ecofeminism, as it was for the early critical theorists, is whether a new science and new technology can be brought into existence. One of the central efforts of ecofeminism has been combining the insights of feminism with those of science, while recognizing the limits of existing conventions of science and its product—technology. As Mary Mellor explains this central dilemma for ecofeminism, "While feminism has historically sought to explain and overcome women's association with the natural, ecology is attempting to re-embed humanity in its natural framework."[9] Feminists and others have developed alternative understandings of objectivity and have shown that "reliable knowledge of nature" can be produced without limiting science to the role of "shop foreman" in the full extension of the domination of nature through instrumental rationality. Nontraditional methods and theories of science producing reliable knowledge of nature could be encouraged with a fundamental transformation of society.

The insights of critical theory support the ecofeminist and generally radical ecological perspective that nature is best viewed not as a collection of objects for manipulation and control, but as a profound process that develops in not entirely predictable directions, and that always exceeds existing conceptualization. The categories and concepts that guide radical ecologists' interaction with nature tend to develop differently from those of a science and technology harnessed to the ideology of industrial production and continuous growth, of an instrumental rationality whereby means become the ends of reason.

Taussig explains how Adorno shows in various contexts that "the sensuous moment of knowing includes a yielding and mirroring of the knower in the unknown, of thought in its object. This is clearly what

Adorno often has in mind with his many references to mimesis, the obscure operator, so it seems to me, of his entire system."[10] This "dialectical" way of knowing involves a "yielding" to the other, the immersion
of the self in the other, a loosening of boundaries of identity. In the
context of the philosophy of *Negative Dialectics*, Adorno claims:

> The changed philosophy itself would be infinite in the sense of
> scorning solidification in a body of enumerable theorems. Its sub-
> stance would lie in the diversity of objects that impinge upon it
> and of the objects it seeks, a diversity not wrought by any schema;
> to those objects, philosophy would truly give itself rather than use
> them as a mirror in which to reread itself, mistaking its own image
> for concretion. It would be nothing but full, unreduced experi-
> ence in the medium of conceptual reflection, whereas even the
> "science of empirical consciousness" reduced the contents of such
> experience to cases of categories.[11]

Adorno, in a complex and "dialectical" manner, also connects mimesis
to science and psychology, to the fundamental difficulties and promises
of conceptualization. As Taussig indicates, "This strange mixture of activity and passivity involved in yielding-knowing, this bodily mirroring
of otherness and even ideas, is in the center of much of Horkheimer
and Adorno's elusive discussion of mimesis, and precisely in the activist
possibilities within such yielding lie serious issues of mimesis and science,
mimesis as an alternative science."[12]

Evelyn Keller uses a different language, one without the term *mimesis*,
to show that science as a social institution tends to select those individuals whose emotional needs are met by the rhetoric of domination and
aggression. This produces certain types of knowledge and power relative
to the objects of knowledge and to the new and unknown.[13] Like the
critical theorists, Keller contends that science does not have to put itself
in the service of "instrumentalism," that there is an alternative understanding of the methods of science that still produces reliable knowledge
about the world but does so by respecting the integrity of that which it
studies. "The need to dominate nature is, in this view, a projection of
the need to dominate other human beings; it arises not so much out of
empowerment as out of anxiety about impotence."[14]

Keller cites several scientists, both male and female, who claim to have
recognized an alternative method of acquiring reliable knowledge.[15] She

writes extensively about Barbara McClintock as an exemplar of this alternative understanding and possibility for science. McClintock received
the Nobel Prize for discovering "genetic transposition," that is, she established that genetic elements can move in large organisms (greater than
single cell) in an apparently coordinated way from one part of a chromo-
some to another, thus challenging the orthodoxy of modern genetics.[16]
What Keller finds most interesting about McClintock, besides that the
latter does not view herself as fighting for a "feminist science," is how
McClintock's alternative vision of science translates into differences in
methodology, concepts, and theory development. Keller views this alternative vision of science as based in a "respect for difference."[17] In Mc-
Clintock's case, the respect for difference meant focusing attention on
an "aberrant pattern of pigmentation on a few kernels of a single corn
plant" and the subsequent six years of research to explain the observation.[18] In this science the unique or exceptional is not seen simply as an
example that proves or disproves a general law, but as an opportunity to
make those exceptions or differences meaningful "in and of themselves."

For the critical theorists, science attempts to demythologize or disen-
chant the world, but it does so at the expense of the uniqueness of each
individual. Science in its repressive forms is extended into a means for
the control of human nature as well, and it thus acquires the characteristics of the very nature it first wanted to control. Science, in the hands of
a society dominated by the exchange principle as broadly understood,
transforms the individual into a mere instance of universal processes, a
specimen available for control and manipulation. The history of "development" from magic to science, from myth to enlightenment, is also a
story of the return into the mythic, of renewed confrontation with fateful
necessity. "Mythology itself set off the unending process of enlightenment in which ever and again, with the inevitability of necessity, every
specific theoretic view succumbs to the destructive criticism that it is
only a belief—until even the very notions of spirit, of truth and, indeed,
enlightenment itself, have become animistic magic."[19]

The tendency toward ever increasing domination is not confined to
science or only directed toward external nature, but is also the tendency
of philosophy, with its confinement of subjectivity to rational calcula-
tion, what Adorno understands as "identity thinking." If philosophy is to
break the hold of the logic of domination, then it must become aware of
the alternative possibilities of thought lodged in the repressed fragments
of mimesis that remain.

> While doing violence to the object of its syntheses, our thinking heeds a potential that waits in the object, and it unconsciously obeys the idea of making amends to the pieces for what it has done. In philosophy, this unconscious tendency becomes conscious. Accompanying irreconcilable thoughts is the hope for reconcilement, because the resistance of thought to mere things in being, the commanding freedom of the subject, intends in the object even that which the object was deprived by objectification.[20]

A repeated concern of critics of some versions of radical ecology has been the tendency to use ecological science in a sociobiologistic way that has all the overtones of a new racism, if not Fascism. The parallels with Fascist arguments of the 1930s are too close to be ignored and can be very fruitfully subjected to the same criticism that the early Frankfurt School applied to the German situation. Some of the most egregious uses of science and technology have come at the hands of Fascists, and the link between technoscientific logic and the Holocaust was a constant theme of the early critical theorists. The most often cited demonstration of the repressive power of mimesis is that of anti-Semitism, as Horkheimer and Adorno repeatedly emphasize. Racism is infused with the mimetic, whereby stereotypical imitation becomes a means of domination and repression, an indispensable element in the formation of the racist consciousness. Anti-Semitism and racism share with Fascism the use of mimesis to direct the mimetic faculty, analyzed by the critical theorists as the "organized control of mimesis." As nature rebels against its repression it is channeled in ever new, ever old directions useful for domination.[21]

A basic question for a critical radical ecology, or ecofeminism, then, is, Can mimesis escape its fate in the "administered society" of late capitalism wherein commodity fetishism takes on ever greater dimension, becoming truly global, threatening the existence of complex life on the planet, as the heat of exchange "warms" the earth? How might Adorno's development and transformation of Benjamin's understanding of mimesis stimulate new thought about the problem of the domination of nature, especially those conjunctions of dominations that include women? Can the nature that is used by culture to create second nature be transformed once more to become the "culture used by nature to rescue nature," to end its unnecessary destruction and pointless suffering? Is it possible to fully develop a new science that produces useful knowledge and an alternative mode of representation and conceptualization with the capacity for emancipatory political agency without implication in domination? Does a new or old mimesis offer access to an alternative to the various forms of "identity thinking" manifested as racism, sexism, class conflict, and ecological destruction? Some answers may be found in the themes of Adorno's critical theory where it intersects in reflections on science, psychoanalysis, and possible visions of a future free of domination.

Mimesis and Psychology

Freudian psychoanalysis was a major influence on the early Frankfurt critical theorists and is clearly present, along with the critique of capitalism, in the *Dialectic of Enlightenment* and other early works, and therefore, any examination of the potentials of Adorno's critical thought should reflect on the implications of the influence of psychoanalysis. In addition to addressing the potential to transform thought through mimetic representation, Horkheimer and Adorno repeatedly emphasized the contradictory potentials of mimetic identification:

> The system of things, the fixed universal order of which science is merely an abstract expression, is . . . the unconscious product of the animal organ in the struggle for existence, of automatic projection. But in human society, where affective and intellectual life are differentiated with the formation of the individual, the latter requires an increasingly firm control over projection; he must learn at one and the same time to refine and inhibit it. By learning to distinguish between his own and extraneous thoughts and feelings under the force of economic necessity, a distinction is made between without and within, the possibility of distancing and identifying, self-awareness and the conscience. Further consideration is necessary to understand the controlled projection, and the way in which it is deformed into false projection—which is part of the essence of anti-Semitism.[22]

One challenge for a critical theory mindful of its past is to incorporate post-Freudian psychoanalytics, including its feminist critiques and perspectives. Before we move to feminist encounters with psychoanalysis and mimesis, it is important to note a problem in recent attempts to develop a "post-Freudian" and "post-Lacanian" theory of psychoanalysis, and therefore a problem in developing alternative theories and practices of women's subjectivity or consciousness. This problem occurs at the intersection of mimesis and psychoanalysis.

An important reason for the turn to Lacanian psychoanalysis by many feminists and deconstructionists has been Lacan's development of an understanding of subjectivity that addresses problems he saw with Freud's notion of the Ego.[23] Lacan developed the idea of the "mirror stage" (or mirror phase) of development to help explain the formation of the Ego or the "I." One important interpreter of Lacan has even observed, "Some critics have called the concept of the mirror stage Lacan's myth (just as the instinct was Freud's, or the collective unconscious was Carl Jung's). Other commentators have described the mirror stage as Lacan's only piece of 'empirical' data."[24]

It is in the relation between "empirical" data and mimesis that a fundamental problem may exist. As Elizabeth Grosz has demonstrated, Lacan's understanding of the mirror stage is indebted to an article on mimicry and psychology written by Roger Caillois. In Lacan's "Mirror Stage" article he develops his idea of the organization of an I by the infant, an organization that occurs even before the child has the ability to use language. This "primordial form" of the I is based on the image (or *imago*) the infant forms of itself, an image that is "fictional" but that will have enduring effects on the subsequent "social determination" of the agency of the ego. Lacan's claim that this prelinguistic self-image has determinate effects on the human organism is supported by reference to effects of visual identification in other species, specifically female pigeons and migratory locusts. This observation about the effects of psychic organization reverses the usual understanding that asserts that organismic development *precedes* the psychological. (Adorno reviewed the Caillois essay and concluded, "The attempt to trace back psychological tendencies to real somatic factual findings rather than to the conscious life of the autonomous individual, offers a truly materialistic aspect." The connections between these observations and Benjamin's writing have been explored by Jeneen Hobby.)[25]

Lacan mentions that the female pigeon must see another member of its species at the appropriate time as "a necessary condition for the maturation of the gonad of the female pigeon."[26] The same effect may be induced, he notes, by simply placing the pigeon before a mirror. Lacan generalizes from this empirical observation to make larger claims for the phenomenon: "Such facts are inscribed in an order of homeomorphic identification that would itself fall within the larger question of the meaning of beauty as both formative and erogenic."[27] When this observation is broadened further to include identifications in a larger field, it raises other issues and questions circulating around the ideas of self and other: "But the facts of mimicry are no less instructive when conceived as cases of heteromorphic identification, in as much as they raise the problem of the signification of space for the living organism—psychological concepts hardly seem less appropriate for shedding light on these matters than ridiculous attempts to reduce them to the supposedly supreme law of adaptation."[28] Lacan seems to be saying that the whole representation of the not-I, of all of space and its occupants, is bound up in this mimetic process, but with an emphasis on the psychological rather than the Darwinian.

Grosz's further observations uncritically follow Lacan's subsequent citation of Caillois on mimicry and psychology. As Grosz interprets it, Caillois's exploration of the relationship of mimicry and spatiality was a "powerful influence on Lacan's notions of the mirror stage, the order of the imaginary, and psychosis."[29] In the original essay, Caillois examined the behavior of insects, specifically the way they "mimic" other insects and their natural environment. This exploration of mimesis then provided a model or "analogue" for the understanding of forms of psychosis. The analysis results from what he claims mimesis reveals about the relationship of an organism to the space it occupies: "Mimesis is particularly significant in outlining the ways in which the relations between an organism and its environment are blurred and confused—the way in which its environment is not distinct from the organism but is an active internal component of its identity."

However, it is the additional statements by Caillois that are problematic and that Grosz does not challenge. As Grosz explains:

> Caillois claims that mimicry does not serve any adaptive function. Its purpose is not to ensure the survival of the species through disguising the insect, hiding it from its predators. Mimicry does not have survival value, for most predators rely on the sense of smell rather than of vision. Mimicry has no value in the dark. Caillois considers mimicry a "luxury" or excess over natural sur-

vival, inexplicable in terms of self-protection or species survival. He abandons naturalistic explanations to seek some kind of answer in psychology. The mimesis characteristic of certain species of insects has to do with distinctions it establishes between itself and its environment, including other species. Mimicry is a consequence not of space but of the *representation* of and captivation by space.[30]

Grosz cites in a footnote the basis for Caillois's determination that mimesis has no adaptive value, that the ability to camouflage itself does not further the survival of the individual and the species. The passage from the article on mimicry and psychosis provides empirical observations as evidence for its conclusions. Caillois is quoted directly: "Generally speaking, one finds many remains of mimetic insects in the stomachs of predators. So it should come as no surprise that such insects sometimes have other and more effective ways to protect themselves. And conversely, some species that are inedible and would thus have nothing to fear, are also mimetic. It therefore seems that one ought to conclude with Cunot that this is an 'epiphenomenon' whose 'defensive utility appears to be null.'"[31] However, the conclusions derived from these empirical observations are illogical and are better explained by more current ecological understandings of mimesis and its relation to evolution.

There are a variety of ways to understand mimesis and its role in adaptation for both individual and species survival. One form of mimesis is Batesian mimicry, involving the false warning coloration of a species, which works to its advantage against predators. A distasteful or poisonous model is mimicked by a species that a predator would otherwise find edible and therefore seek out. Examples include viceroy butterflies, which mimic distasteful monarch butterflies; clearwing moth mimics of bees and wasps; and so on. The mimic gains advantage as the predator learns to avoid the distasteful or poisonous model; however, the model is disadvantaged because the predators' encounters with the edible and harmless mimics increases the time required for the predator to learn of the model's potential harmfulness, thus resulting in the consumption of the less-than-desirable model. The learning time for predators depends largely on the ratio of mimics to models; indeed, if mimics outnumber models at a specific time, predators may not learn to avoid the models. This explains why the mimics are usually less numerous than the inedible model. It also helps explain why mimics frequently mimic several model species.

There are other types of adaptive mimicry, including "Mullerian mimicry," which occurs when two species that are both distasteful or dangerous mimic each other, such as happens with bees and wasps, which both have characteristic black-and-yellow banding. Predators will encounter both species more frequently than they would one species alone, therefore reducing the learning time necessary for the predator to avoid harm.[32]

The presence of mimetic insects in the stomachs of predators is not scientific proof or even a reasonable argument against the adaptive function of mimesis. Contrary to its being an epiphenomenon with a "null defensive utility," mimesis has a very broad explanatory power in species evolution. The question, then, for Lacanian psychoanalysts and those who develop a metapsychology from his observations is how this changes the status of mimesis and identification in "the mirror stage, the order of the imaginary and in psychosis." How does an alternative understanding of mimesis, one that recognizes its "natural" adaptive function, affect the possibilities of new subjectivities and a new relationship to nature?

Additionally, it should be noted, the focus by Caillois on the visual as the site of mimesis fails to adequately account for other mimetic adaptations such as the calls of birds and other auditory imitative behavior, for example, bull snakes' mimicry of the rattler. Vision and image are only one, although important, aspect of mimesis in evolutionary adaptation.[33]

The relationship between psychoanalysis and identity as conceptualized by Lacan and others is challenged when the basis for the assertions is traced to their ecological roots. The concept of mimesis as used in ecological science, and implicitly consistent with an ecofeminist reliance on the importance of understanding ecosystems in both their human and nonhuman aspects, shifts the meaning of key psychoanalytic concepts from those centered on idealistic issues of representation to those of material conceptions of adaptation. However, this shift also places us back on the terrain of concerns of the early critical theorists about the possibilities of both regressive-repressive mimesis and its emancipatory counterpart, and it also brings us back to feminist uses of mimesis.

Feminist Mimesis

The use of mimesis by women for the development of feminist theory has varied greatly, but two general perspectives stand out. The first consists of those who retain the largely aesthetic understanding of mimesis; the second goes beyond this to link the body or materiality to mimetic behavior and therefore comes closer to the strategy of Adorno, who combines the aesthetic with the material, natural, or anthropological understandings of the term. Even when the category remains largely aesthetic, it still has considerable critical power to reveal the usually hidden or unconscious processes of exclusion, marginalizing, or "othering" characteristic of patriarchal and dominating society. For example, Julia Kristeva achieves significant insights into the workings of language and the possibility of the "speaking subject" by examining "mimesis and the poetic language inseparable from it."[34]

Luce Irigaray has followed a "strategy of mimesis" to challenge the current order, aiming to "effect a shift in the position of the subject of enunciation."[35] In other words, Irigaray's project is to help make it possible for women to speak for themselves as themselves, when throughout social, political, and philosophical history women have been silenced, spoken for, and spoken about. Central to the conceptual apparatus Irigaray uses and opposes is Lacanian psychoanalytics. Resembling Adorno, Irigaray is notorious for the difficulty involved in unpacking her language and style. Instead of making this a too simple summary of her concerns, for our present needs we can focus on her understanding of mimesis in relation to the possibility of female subjectivity and do this through the elaborations of her writings by both sympathetic and critical commentators.

The necessity for the mimetic strategy can be seen as a consequence of the Lacanian understanding of the place of the subject in language and the resulting impossibility for "woman" to speak at all. Irigaray (like Derrida) interrogates the history of philosophy and the philosophy of history to show what has been excluded or marginalized. The excluded other is found to have the uncanny function of serving as the pivot or hinge of philosophy; that is, philosophy's "coherence" depends on that which it excludes. Irigaray takes this practice of following the trail of the marginalized and excluded further than Derrida by refusing to halt at the recognition of the aporetic gaps in philosophical and literary texts, refusing to accept the silences and exclusions as a functioning of "the feminine," as the mark of the possibility of masculine or phallic philosophy. Irigaray attempts to further interrogate this abyssal center of philosophy, seeking to liberate the excluded other from its servitude. Irigaray's project does not end with the recognition of the functioning of "the feminine";

of "woman"; and of women in philosophy, literature, and politics, but attempts to establish the possibilities for a truly female subject who can speak for herself. She recognizes that subjects are formed in a complex system of "structuring effects" through "variables" such as "sexual morphology," cultural identity, age, religion, and so on. However, for Irigaray, as for most feminists, sexuality has a privileged place in the history of these structuring effects.

Feminist analyses of Western civilization, and especially society under capitalism and continuing patriarchy, have shown how women have been systematically denied a voice in their own self-becoming. In the analyses that rely on the structural linguistics that influenced understanding of Lacanian psychoanalytics, "woman" has been found to serve as the condition of possibility of language itself, yet cannot itself be truly represented. For Irigaray, then, the mimetic strategy involves occupying the masculine position in order to disrupt its claims and open a space for what is supposedly unrepresentable, the female subject. It is an attempt to raise a voice for those who cannot speak for themselves—yet.

The strategy of mimetic repetition is rooted in the psychoanalytic understanding of how to treat the disturbance of a patient or analysand that has resulted in the inability of the individual to fully experience what life has to offer. Freud's "talking cure" is an attempt to raise to consciousness what has been repressed in the unconscious but that still manifests itself in a symptomology that makes it impossible for the patient to adequately function. For the analyst, then, the process of relieving the patient from the burden expressed by dysfunctional symptoms is centered around allowing the repressed contents of the unconscious to resurface to the level of language.

In the story of psychoanalysis, the current symbolic order is based on the male's acquisition of language, which occurs with the development of the individual male Ego. This process is fundamentally dependent on the child's relationship to its parents. Without going into the details of the psychoanalytic account of the process, it can be said that under existing sociohistorical conditions the process of identity formation for the male child involves the exclusion and separation of the mother from the child's "imagined" or fantasized identity. Irigaray suggests that this has led to the apotheosis of rationality—modern technology—and to apparently unstoppable processes of destruction.[36] The strategy of mimesis, then, involves occupying the male position in order to disrupt it, thus making a space for possible other, female subjects. Simple opposition would merely amount to women's returning to their place in the male order of exclusion. To simply proclaim a female rationality incommensurable to male rationality would be to reenact the dominant symbolic order based on the process of exclusion. As Margaret Whitford states in her interpretation of Irigaray, mimesis also serves an "ecological" function: "We might note also that of the terms Irigaray uses: mimesis, mimetisme, masque, etc., one of them, mimetisme, usually translated mimeticism, comes from the domain of animal ethology and means 'camouflage' or 'protective colouring.' I think this may be relevant too. Irigaray may be arguing, I think, that women also need to protect themselves against (re)assimilation and destruction by the masculine economy."[37] Even more clearly, Whitford believes that Irigaray understands the feminine as receptacle for the natural world, the male psyche's attempt to distance itself from nature: "It is significant that Irigaray stresses that nature (the natural world) is not respected. This is not simply a version of ecofeminism (though it is that too), but part of her argument about the symbolic distribution, and the allocation of the 'lower functions' to women. The symbolic distribution is hierarchical. What is being disrespected is those parts of himself that the male imaginary has split off and projected—into the world, on to women."[38]

Irigaray's strategy, then, is to inhabit the language of the philosopher in order to reveal what remains as the condition of its own possibility even as it is excluded from representation. The strategy is to mime the passages that operate to exclude the feminine and present woman as an inferior copy. The point is to show how what is excluded as unrepresentable is already within the system of representation. Mimetic representation will be repeated, reproduced, copied until "this emergence of the outside within the system calls into question its systematic closure and its pretension to be self-grounding."[39] In miming the philosophers and psychoanalysts, including Plato and Lacan, Irigaray both violates the "prohibition against resemblance" and the "notion of resemblance as copy."[40] The system of representation is shown to be an effect of power, "Insofar as the Platonic account of the origin is itself a displacement of a maternal origin, Irigaray merely mimes that very act of displacement, displacing the displacement, showing that origin to be an 'effect' of a certain ruse of phallogocentric power."[41] Irigaray is playing with representation, using mimesis to disrupt the prevailing order and to make a space for an alternative representation from which women are not excluded: "To play with mimesis is thus, for a woman, to try to recover the place of

her exploitation by discourse, without allowing herself to be simply reduced to it . . . so as to make 'visible,' by an effect of playful repetition,
what was supposed to remain invisible: the cover up of a possible operation of the feminine in language."[42]

However, Judith Butler is not satisfied with the strategy, for it seems in
its miming to reenact the logic of identity it seeks to challenge. Why
should "the feminine" be identified with the space of unrepresentability?
Butler insistently recalls the consequences of Plato's exclusions that go
beyond the feminine:

> Plato's scenography of intelligibility depends on the exclusion of
> women, slaves, children, and animals, where slaves are character-
> ized as those who do not speak his language, and who, in not
> speaking his language, are considered diminished in their capacity
> for reason. This xenophobic exclusion operates through the pro-
> duction of racialized Others, and those whose "natures" are con-
> sidered less rational by virtue of their appointed task in the
> process of laboring to reproduce the conditions of private life.[43]

Butler wonders if Irigaray's strategy, which tends to keep in place a heterosexual economy, might present the possibility of not only the feminine "penetrating" the masculine order of representation, but also the
feminine the feminine, and the masculine the masculine, to the point
where the status of the terms *feminine* and *masculine* begins to destabilize.
The destabilization of reason's claim to represent itself would then come
from a variety of directions. "To the extent that a set of reverse mimes
emerge from those quarters, they will not be the same as each other; if
there is an occupation and reversal of the master's discourse, it will come
from many quarters, and those resignifying practices will converge in ways
that scramble the self-replicating presumptions of reason's mastery. For
if the copies speak, or if what is merely material begins to signify, the
scenography of reason is rocked by the crisis on which it was always
built."[44]

These observations by Irigaray and other "feminist" theorists of representation and female subjectivity, along with feminist challenges to the
dominant ideology of science, come together to address the concerns and
claims of ecofeminism. At the very least, strategies of mimetic representation may have "survival" value, encouraging the process of creation of
new subjectivities and of a newly mimetic world.

Mimetic Possibilities

The strength of feminism has been its ability, based on its recognition of the unfreedom and suffering of actual women in their day-to-day lives, to generate a variety of analyses revealing the depth and breadth of the domination of women under social systems controlled by and for the benefit of men. Further, women with feminist commitments have been able to show that an adequate answer to the problem of domination does not consist in a "liberal" solution of equal inclusion in the existing system. The problem goes to the very structure of language and beyond; to the unconscious imaginings of both men and women; to how we become gendered subjects capable of speech; and to the question of how the images, concepts, and practices of society can be changed. Central to this desired change, then, is the "impossible image" of the new world of the future to be formed in the present. What image(s) will spark the imaginations, open the unconscious, and provide the energy to motivate other individuals and new generations to continue hoping and struggling for a changed world, a world where suffering recedes and the ideas of freedom and happiness can truly fulfill themselves in concrete reality?

In asking these questions one might seem to have already surrendered to an optimism contradicting so many representations of critical theory as the "melancholy science."[45] Or the question might be raised that this talk of freedom and happiness is itself a collapse into the discredited rhetoric of "the modern." These questions aside, what I want to examine here is the similarity between Adorno's concerns and many of those voiced by feminism and ecofeminism. This is not an attempt to claim that the concerns or the concepts and terms used are the same, that there is a shared identity between them, but it does seem correct to claim that the similarities are not fortuitous but result instead from the fact that they are related through the objects of their studies. This would be perfectly in keeping with Adorno's temperament and his belief that "[t]ruth is objective, not plausible."[46] As Susan Buck-Morss has indicated, "The uniquely individual experiences of critical subjectivity ran parallel because they focused on particulars which reflected the same objective reality, and it followed that collaboration was possible among intellectuals even when they worked alone. Nothing pleased Adorno more than when a friend came to similar insights independently, for he considered it a validation of their correctness."[47]

Adorno's understanding of mimesis helps illuminate an understanding of aesthetic phenomenon, including the relationship of aesthetics to the domination of nature, subjectivity, and new possibilities (the not-yet). As earlier indicated, however, mimesis often seems to be equated with aesthetic behavior, in poetry, painting, or music, for example, and contrary to so many cursory readings that are now prevalent, Adorno does not collapse mimesis into aesthetics: "Aesthetic behaviour is neither mimesis pure and simple nor the repression of mimesis. It is a process set in motion by mimesis, a process also in which mimesis itself survives through adaptation. This process shapes both the relation of the individual to art and the historical macrocosm."[48]

Mimesis "survives" in aesthetic behavior, but it is not unchanged, raising the question of the possibility of recuperation of the mimetic impulse, and the forms a recovered mimesis might take in a world freed of domination. Negatively, the triumph of one transformation of mimesis, "instrumental rationality," is the death of reason more broadly understood:

> Thinking begins to turn around in circles when it shrinks back from the task of sublimating mimetic behaviour. The deadly dichotomization of emotion and thought is a historical result that can be undone. *Ratio* devoid of mimesis negates itself. (Ends, the *raison d'être* of *raison*, are qualitative and the mimetic faculty is a qualitative faculty.) This self-negation of reason, it should be added, is historically necessary: as the world objectively loses its openness, it tends to have less and less need for spirit, which is defined by its openness; indeed, the world has become quite intolerant of spirit.[49]

Intolerance for openness to otherness or the nonidentical is a manifestation of "reified consciousness." Fredric Jameson has helpfully located within negative dialectics the place of the critique of capitalism that Adorno borrows from Marx and shown that it is intimately connected to a certain understanding of the psychology of the individual and to the figure of mimesis.[50] Capitalism as it consolidated itself, especially from 1945 to the 1960s, was also gaining increased control over subjectivity. As Jameson argues, Adorno's writing moves between figures of private property and personal identity:

> The figures of the tendential restriction of the individual subject, and its increasing penetration by the social division of labor, re-

join the language of Capital itself, and Adorno can speak of an "organic composition of capital" within the psychic subject: that is to say, an increasingly higher percentage of mental machinery and instrumental operations as opposed to living human labor, to the free subjectivity whose role is ever more diminished. Now human creativity shrinks to machine-minding and reason to a fitful organic impulse.[51]

Reification for Adorno, however, again, should not be viewed as identical to the crude or orthodox Marxist understanding of "alienated objectification of subjectivity" exemplified in the factory setting alone, although it is that too. As Martin Jay makes clear, Adorno's understanding of reification owes as much to Nietzsche as Marx, in that reification is also to be understood throughout Adorno's writings as "the suppression of heterogeneity in the name of identity."[52] Mimesis provides an avenue of resistance to reification, resistance to the near-total suppression of otherness, which still assumes the name of reason, but which has become a reason turned against itself, reduced to mere means.

How can mimesis resist the logic of identity, the collapse of the unique characteristics of the particular or the individual into a positivistically manipulable variable? As Adorno explains, mimesis must become an ally of the new: "Now, it is only through the new that mimesis can be so firmly wedded to rationality that it will not regress, for *ratio* itself becomes mimetic through the thrill of the new."[53] Of course "the new" has also become an integral part of capitalism, especially "late capitalism," with its increasing reliance on fashion—change of style. "In its original economic setting, novelty is that characteristic of consumer goods through which they are supposed to set themselves off from the self-same aggregate supply, stimulating consumer decisions subject to the needs of capital. . . . Art has appropriated this economic category. The new in art is the aesthetic counterpart to the expanding reproduction of capital in society. Both hold out the promise of undiminished plenitude" (31). The ever recurring image of the advertiser is the appearance of the new product, which in its fantastic representation quenches the ideal consumer's never ending thirst for more. Capitalism portrays the answer to the end of suffering as the latest consumer item; art offers an alternative reality. Of course nothing would ever be so simple for Adorno as to say that the realization of the new would be Utopia, for "[t]he new is the longing for the new, not the new itself. This is the curse of everything new. Being a negative of the old, the new is subservient to the old while considering itself to be Utopian" (47). How, then, is the time after suffering to be represented? Here is the problem of representing the unrepresentable again, but this is an unrepresentable future, not the unrepresentable before the (male) subject. What light is shed by mimesis on the problem of the unrepresentability of the Utopian future?

The utopia of undiminished plenitude is the image art offers against the repetition of the same and suffering within the logic of identity and the domination of nature, but freedom through mimesis, as Adorno presents it, is at the core of art's mission. Adorno attempts to explain the freeing of the substance of the artist (which is not the same as subjective expression as usually understood in aesthetic philosophy) in the artwork: "As for those vases, their similarity to language seems to say something like 'this is me' or 'here I come,' asserting a selfhood which is not carved out of the interdependent totality of being by identifying thought but stands on its own. In the same way, a speechless animal, say a rhinoceros, seems to be saying 'I am a rhino'" (164). This declaration on the part of the artwork (like that of the individual animal) is an assertion of its uniqueness and of its participation in "spirit." What is being imitated in the artwork is the process that brings into being the unique and therefore inimitable.

Art enables its "consumer" to experience the uniqueness otherwise repressed in existing situations of domination. In addition, in Adorno's theory of aesthetics, mimesis has an ambivalent relationship within art (as it does in science, and in philosophy). It is the basis for the critical subjectivity made possible by "authentic" art, but it also participates in that adaptive function imposed by society's domination of the individual.

> This modification of mimesis is the constitutive act of spiritualization in art, prior to any reflection upon spirit which develops spiritualization further. Spirit is already posited in this modified mimesis by the work; perhaps spirit even occurs in the original form of mimesis itself, which would make mimesis the physiological progenitor, as it were, of spirit. On the other hand, modified mimesis has to bear some of the blame for art's affirmative essence because it mitigates pain, making it controllable within a spiritual totality without really changing it. (165)

For Adorno, then, art remains within the sphere of "universal alienation," but it is at least partially less alienated to the extent that "in art everything passes through spirit" so that it is "humanized in a non-repressive, non-violent way." Art is forced to use the means of domination of nature to some extent in order to express the possibility of an alternative existence without domination, alienation, or suffering. Expression in art, then, is part of the attempt to create a new subjectivity. "The emancipation of society from the predominance of material, economic conditions aims at creating a true subject which has been stymied so far. Seen from this point of view, expression reflects not only the subject's hubris but also its just complaint about the failure of subjectivity, expression being the cipher for the possibility of that subjectivity" (171).

This cipher or hieroglyph of subjectivity is an image of a future possibility in which suffering is absent and pleasure and happiness reign. The moment of joy in art has a certain playfulness to it that, although it does not indicate that art can be reduced to a form of play, implies for Adorno that freedom from repression will have certain childlike and "clownish" aspects:

> The attraction clowns have for children is the same as the attraction art has for them. Both kinds of attraction are rooted out by the world of adults, along with a third attraction: that to animals. Likeness to animals, however, is a human characteristic which is never entirely repressed by consciousness. There are instances of a sudden rediscovery of that likeness, instances which spell happiness for the individual. The language of little children and of animals seems to be the same. (175)

What can be taken from these observations by Adorno and feminists who are trying to find alternatives to the present order of dominating subjectivity? First, mimesis plays a fundamental role in the emergence of subjectivity. When combined with the discussion of mimesis in *Dialectic of Enlightenment*, passages on mimesis in *Aesthetic Theory* and elsewhere reveal a consistent concern with mimesis as a primordial influence on, if not foundation for, subjectivity. Mimesis has evolved through human history, and also natural history, in various directions, from magic to science, philosophy, art, and elsewhere. In its metamorphoses, however, it retains a moment that challenges the overwhelmingly repressive uses to which it has been put. Examples of this moment can be found in areas of life that resist assimilation into the logic of identity and domination. Adorno focused on art and critical philosophy as two of these areas in mutual need of each other; however, he always emphasized the negative aspects of mimesis, its uses in a society of increasing domination and repression.

Critical philosophy and art formed the basis of Adorno's understanding of negative dialectics that, while focusing on the continuous extension of domination, retains the hope of an alternative future, one freed of unnecessary suffering and open to the possibility of true happiness. If there is hope of a better future, is it possible to elucidate the more politically specific ramifications of "mimetic subjectivity" for (eco)feminism and democratic politics?

Adorno's discussion of natural beauty and its historical relation to the domination of nature contributes to an understanding of the alternative to domination. Adorno's turn to aesthetics, to art and the critical evaluation of art, is an attempt to articulate a critical philosophy that puts into concepts the process by which works of art attempt to speak of an alternative world. "The restitution of nature hinges on the emergence of something that has escaped the fatefulness of nature. . . . [M]ankind becomes aware through art of what rationality has erased from memory. Second reflection serves to remind us of this. The vanishing point of this development is the insight—incorporated as a partial aspect in modern art—that the beauty of nature cannot be copied" (98–99).

Beauty in nature becomes a point for "second reflection" about the direction of reason. Although a moment in the process of self-reflection, the beautiful in nature does not then become the principle of aesthetics. "The beautiful in nature is different from both the notion of a ruling principle and the denial of any principle whatsoever. It is like a state of reconciliation" (110).[61] For Adorno the "essence of natural beauty" is the "anamnesis" of "something that is more than just for-other" (110).[62] What natural beauty suggests is an independent moment of nature irreducible to an object for human use or conceptual captivation. It does not mean that critical reflection on art and its relationship to the beautiful in nature involves some "pointing" to a metaphysical transcendence of material life. Rather, art may provide a glimpse of a possibility that also appears in the beautiful in nature. It is a glimpse of the possibility of being more than just for-other. Art provides an image that is denied in a society reduced to instrumental rationality, to a world become means.

> Every act of making in art is an endless endeavour to articulate what is not makeable, namely spirit. This is where the function

of art as a restorer of historically repressed nature becomes important. Nature does not yet exist. To the degree to which art pines
after an image of nature, it represents the truth of non-being. Art
becomes conscious of it in a non-identical other (which instrumental, identity-positing reason reduces to a material and which
is called nature). This other is not some unifying concept but a
manifold, for truth content in art is a manifold and not an abstract or generic concept. . . . This corresponds to the plurality of
things in general: they too defy identification. (191)

But then how does art function to provide images for imitation? What is
the process of mimesis released in this understanding of aesthetics? What
is the relationship between mimetic acts in the present, and the future
"utopia?" Adorno argues against any aesthetics that attempts to assert
that art should function to represent the world as it is. Artworks are
constellations of existing elements, but not simple reproductions of existing relationships. The mimetic moment in the new constellation of elements is not an act of simply copying or mirroring reality but results in a
displacement of current relationships. Artworks are indicators of possibility, of the not-yet.

Art illuminates the possibility of a nature that does not yet exist and
has never existed, a nature made possible through the mediation of subjectivity. However, this subjectivity is also not of the present, at least not
in its dominant forms, not in any form that can be simply copied. The
transformation of subjectivity will involve a complex relationship of creation and destruction, of life and death, just as works of art destroy as
they create. Works of art succeed to the extent that they betray mimesis.
"They kill what they objectify, tearing it away from its context of immediacy and real life. They survive because they bring death. This is particularly true of modern art, where we notice a general mimetic abandonment
to reification, which is the principle of death. Illusion in art is the attempt to escape from this principle" (193). The "escape" from the principle of death, from reification, that reduction of life into a mere object, a
thing, the reduction of the other into yet another example, depends on
some possibility of humans' acting otherwise. This is what is meant when
Adorno speaks of the possibility of reconciliation.

Spirit tones down its antagonistic essence and becomes conciliatory. This differs from what classicism meant by reconciliation.

> Reconciliation here refers to the mode of conduct of works of art
> in so far as they become conscious of the non-identical in their
> midst. By following the dynamic of self-sameness to the end, art
> works assimilate themselves to the non-identical. This is the stage
> of development mimesis has reached today. . . . The utopia antici-
> pated by artistic form is the idea that things at long last ought to
> come into their own. (194–95)

The question for feminism and radical ecology, for ecofeminism, is
whether the alternative knowledge and ethics that they offer can serve
as models of a mode of behavior that is mimetic without reverting or
regressing to mere repetition of the existing system of domination, the
mere continuation of instrumental rationality and reification behind a
new mask.

Ecofeminism

Ecofeminists do not have a common unified position or methodology, or
even a common analysis of the ecology crisis, but they do tend to make
use of the central radical ecological categories of nature and subjectivity,
while attempting to include the concept of gender in their analyses.[54]
The examination of the concept of "the feminine" by feminists and ecofeminists has revealed the historical association of women with nature,
and the historical devaluation of women's subjectivity with respect to
male subjectivity. One "goal" of feminism has become the redefinition or
resymbolization of the relation of women's experience to the concept of
subjectivity.

Ecofeminism frequently details the lives of women and their relationship to nonhuman nature to reveal how both are systematically dominated and repressed.[55] Those who attempt to recover a prior or "pre-his-
toric" subjectivity often turn to cultural anthropology for empirical and
philosophic support. This ecofeminism hypothesizes a prepatriarchal culture that honored women; included goddess worship; and was organized
through matriarchal, or at least matrilineal, relationships. One of the
most problematic developments in this area is that of "spiritual ecofeminism," which has failed to address the problems of hierarchy that result
from political interpretation by a single "spiritual" authority. In this ver-

sion of ecofeminism, political authority is derived from spiritual authority, resulting in a premodern rather than a postmodern political agency.
This understanding of the relationship of politics to spirituality collapses
the political back into the spiritual or religious. This produces a fundamentally hierarchical and antidemocratic politics, reducing the political
consciousness of individual subjects and making them subservient to a
higher interpretive authority. Instead of representing feminine sensitivity
and spirituality it reproduces the typical structures of power, only in ecofeminist disguise.[56]

However, when traditional philosophical categories and concepts are
retained, rather than those of spirituality or religion being used, ecofeminism's ecological and political practices tend to be guided by Enlightenment or rationalist impulses. "Rationalist" ecofeminism attempts to
provide enlightened guidance of social development, thereby very closely
paralleling mainstream feminism, which insists that women's reason is
equally human reason and therefore entitles women to equal access to
all rational democratic institutions and the legitimate exercise of power.
Unfortunately, this form of feminism seems to be largely content with
acquiring for women the same powers over the domination of nature that
have for so long been uniformly controlled by men.

Much of recent feminism's concerns with subjectivity and identity re-
volves around the status of "the feminine" and its critical potential for
restructuring symbolic and political orders, and may help to address the
shortcomings of "spiritual" and "rationalist" versions of ecofeminism. Efforts in this area, including those of Irigaray, have attempted to transform
the relations of women to society and politics by transforming the categories and concepts of Western philosophy and political thought; however,
these approaches to feminism and ecofeminism, while challenging the
entire framework of philosophy and political thought, have yet to establish other than a negating practice. This means that radical forms of
feminism and ecofeminism are forced to face the same charges Habermas
has made against Adorno concerning the relation of philosophy to itself
and political practice. Does the negativity of the critique preclude political action other than that based on mystical or metaphysical notions of
peace, reconciliation, or freedom?[57]

One interpretation of critical or "negative" thought asserts that participation in politics in the present liberal, parliamentary framework only
serves to strengthen the bindings of oppression and domination. Those
who oppose the atomistic individualism typical of liberal politics contend

that political practice should instead be conceived as an attempt to con-struct alternative subjectivities and identities. However, efforts at (re)-constructing identities have also had unexpected consequences, as feminism generally has found, when attempts to analyze women's experi-ences begin to include other categories such as race and class. It is now widely acknowledged that "women's experience" cannot be collapsed into a single descriptive category, but can only be adequately approached through the recognition of the uniqueness of individuals' experiences in specific situations, while avoiding philosophical or political "nominal-ism" by including social and historical context in the analysis. Interpreta-tion of these experiences is further complicated by the frequent occupation by women of multiple categories of oppression and domina-tion. Radical ecological insights additionally force these analyses to rec-ognize that under conditions of unfreedom "subject positions" of individuals or groups are established through a symbolic order in which social identities are at least partially constructed from categories of na-ture, dominated nature.

Adorno also questioned the dominant conceptual process and its rela-tionship to subjectivity, including the conceptual operations by which the nonidentical is reduced to the identical, incorporating it into the system of domination, and thus extending instrumental rationality to the point of its culmination in a "false totality." In efforts echoing those of the critical theorists, feminists and ecofeminists have attempted, in their philosophical examinations and political actions, to challenge imposed identities. As was indicated earlier, Luce Irigaray, using her strategy of mimesis, attempts to resymbolize "the feminine" and so create new possi-bilities for women's subjectivity. Others, such as Judith Butler, have ques-tioned why *women* should solely occupy the space of the "other" in this analysis, suggesting that other others, including nonhuman others, must also be resymbolized, creating multiple strategies of mimesis that might disrupt the current system of domination. The problem for ecofeminists, radical ecologists, and feminists generally is to find the links both theo-retically and practically that can tie politics to the insights generated in relation to mimesis.

Radical ecological and ecofeminist reliance on ecological science pro-vides empirical information and practical orientation that are lacking in the tradition of critical theory. Ecological insight is an historical and empirical corrective, or developmental supplement, to those of early criti-cal theory. Mimesis may be of crucial importance in the development of an adequate philosophical and practical approach to the problems of ecological destruction and catastrophe. Development of a nondestructive mode of ecological interaction with nature can only be fully achieved by human beings who are capable of individually interpreting their everyday life activities from the perspective of ecological subjects and then representing that experience in a radically democratic manner.

There have been important developments in cultural and ecological understanding since the feminist and ecology movements' "rebirths" in the 1960s, including an increase in the awareness of the world about the impact of systems of domination on the lives of women, and about the destruction of nature. However, it is still unclear whether these changes in consciousness will be long-lasting enough and deep enough to prevent future catastrophes of a wholly new scale. Changed consciousness in part of or even most of the population, of course, does not mean that it actually will be translated into better conditions on the planet. As Adorno said in the context of Fascism, "Its horror lies in the fact that the lie is obvious but persists."[58] Even in the most "enlightened" age, there remains the potential for mimetic regression. The holocaust against other species continues essentially unabated, and foreseeable global ecological disruptions could result in a rapid destruction of human populations to such an extent, and in a brief enough time period, that it would dwarf the destruction of human populations of any previous historical epochs.

For Adorno, the imagining of a reconciled future took the form of an "exact fantasy." This is an image of a future possibility, one in which the "reconciliation" of humans with nature will have taken place. This exact fantasy is accomplished through a mimetic transformation, not to be understood as a mere copying of the given, but as its metamorphosis, accomplished through the translation of existing elements into an image of the desired future. The idea of an ecological society is an anticipation of a situation of reconciliation, an anticipation of the development of possibilities and potentials existing latently in the present damaged life, an anticipation of the elimination of reification, and the flowering of otherness. The ecological subject will not be an absolute subject, for it recognizes what is nonidentical to itself. It will not attempt to reduce the other to its own concepts, or to the needs of a production apparatus. The ecological subject's attitude toward the other is a willingness to let it be and become. The future ecological society assists the development of the other, occurring through its own impulses, in its own time. This will bring into being a different world, one where the blossoming of what-we-are-not will reveal who we truly are.

Notes

1. Max Horkheimer and Theodor W. Adorno, *Dialectic of Enlightenment* (New York: Continuum, 1987), 14.

2. Horkheimer and Adorno, *Dialectic of Enlightenment*, 181.

3. Theodor W. Adorno, *Aesthetic Theory*, ed. Gretel Adorno and Rolf Tiedemann, trans. C. Lenhardt (London: Routledge, 1984), 453.

4. Amelie Oksenberg Rorty, ed., *Essays on Aristotle's Poetics* (Princeton: Princeton University Press, 1992).

5. Walter Benjamin, "On the Mimetic Faculty," in *Reflections*, ed. Peter Demetz, trans. Edmund Jephcott (New York: Schocken Books, 1978).

6. Michael Taussig, *Mimesis and Alterity* (New York: Routledge, 1993).

7. Taussig, *Mimesis and Alterity*, xviii–xix.

8. Herbert Marcuse, *One-Dimensional Man* (Boston: Beacon Press, 1964), 225ff.

9. Mary Mellor, *Feminism and Ecology* (New York: New York University Press, 1987), 180.

10. Taussig, *Mimesis and Alterity*, 45.

11. Horkheimer and Adorno, *Dialectic of Enlightenment*, 13.

12. Taussig, *Mimesis and Alterity*, 46.

13. Evelyn Fox Keller, *Reflections on Gender and Science* (New Haven: Yale University Press, 1985).

14. Keller, *Reflections*, 124.

15. Keller, *Reflections*, 125.

16. Evelyn Fox Keller, *A Feeling for the Organism: The Life and Work of Barbara McClintock* (New York: Freeman, 1983).

17. Keller, *Reflections*, 161.

18. Keller, *Reflections*, 163.

19. Horkheimer and Adorno, *Dialectic of Enlightenment*, 11.

20. Theodor W. Adorno, *Negative Dialectics* (New York: Continuum, 1987), 19.

21. Horkheimer and Adorno, *Dialectic of Enlightenment*.

22. Horkheimer and Adorno, *Dialectic of Enlightenment*, 188.

23. Jacques Lacan, *Écrits* (New York: W. W. Norton, 1977), 1.

24. Ellie Ragland-Sullivan, *Jacques Lacan and the Philosophy of Psychoanalysis* (Urbana: University of Illinois Press, 1987), 16.

25. Jeneen Hobby, "Benjamin and the Faculty of Mimesis," *Cardozo Law Review* 16, nos. 3–4 (1995).

26. Lacan, *Écrits*, 3.

27. Lacan, *Écrits*, 3.

28. Lacan, *Écrits*, 3.

29. Elizabeth Grosz, *Volatile Bodies: Toward a Corporeal Feminism* (Bloomington: Indiana University Press, 1994), 46.

30. Groz, *Volatile Bodies*, 46.

31. Groz, *Volatile Bodies*, 24–25.

32. Eric R. Pianka, *Evolutionary Ecology*, 4th ed. (New York: HarperCollins, 1988), 295.

33. Pianka, *Evolutionary Ecology*, 290.

34. Julia Kristeva, "Revolution in Poetic Language," in *The Kristeva Reader*, ed. Toril Moi (New York: Columbia University Press, 1986), 110.

35. Margaret Whitford, *Luce Irigaray: Philosophy in the Feminine* (New York: Routledge, 1991), 7.

36. Whitford, *Luce Irigaray*, 73.

37. Whitford, *Luce Irigaray*, 73.

38. Whitford, *Luce Irigaray*, 95.

39. Judith Butler and Joan W. Scott, eds., *Feminists Theorize the Political* (New York: Routledge, 1992), 157.

40. Butler and Scott, *Feminists Theorize the Political*, 157–58.

41. Butler and Scott, *Feminists Theorize the Political*, 158.

42. Luce Irigaray, "The Power of Discourse," in *This Sex Which Is Not One* (Ithaca, N.Y.: Cornell University Press, 1985), 76.

43. Butler and Scott, *Feminists Theorize the Political*, 161.

44. Butler and Scott, *Feminists Theorize the Political*, 164.

45. Gillian Rose, *The Melancholy Science: An Introduction to the Thought of Theodor W. Adorno* (London: Macmillan, 1978).

46. Adorno, *Negative Dialectics*, 41.

47. Susan Buck-Morss, *Origins of Negative Dialectics* (New York: Free Press, 1977), 85.

48. Adorno, *Aesthetic Theory*, 455.

49. Adorno, *Aesthetic Theory*, 455.

50. Fredric Jameson, *Late Marxism: Adorno; or, the Persistence of the Dialectic* (London: Verso, 1990), 70ff.

51. Jameson, *Late Marxism*, 71.

52. Martin Jay, *Adorno* (Cambridge, Mass.: Harvard University Press, 1984), 68.

53. Adorno, *Aesthetic Theory*, 30. Further page references are cited parenthetically in the text.

54. Karen Warren, ed., *Ecological Feminism* (New York: Routledge, 1994).

55. Karen Warren, ed., *Ecofeminism: Women, Culture, Nature* (Bloomington: Indiana University Press, 1997).

56. Carol Adams, *Ecofeminism and the Sacred* (New York: Continuum, 1994).

57. Jürgen Habermas, *The Philosophical Discourse of Modernity*, trans. Frederick G. Lawerence (Cambridge, Mass.: MIT Press, 1987), 106ff.

58. Horkheimer and Adorno, *Dialectic of Enlightenment*, 208.

8

Intersectional Sensibility and the Shudder

Sora Y. Han

But then what would art be, as the writing of history, if it shook off the memory of accumulated suffering?

—Theodor Adorno, *Aesthetic Theory*

Kimberlé Williams Crenshaw's momentous "Mapping the Margins: Intersectionality, Identity Politics, and Violence Against Women of Color," was republished in *Critical Race Theory: The Key Writings That Formed the Movement*, the first major anthology of law review articles gathered under that by now well-known banner.[1] As one of the articles that heavily influenced the emergence of the field of critical race theory (CRT), a progressive body of knowledge about race and the law produced mostly by legal academics, "Mapping" is read widely today across academic disciplines in the humanities and social sciences.

In the article, Crenshaw offers a structural analysis of contemporary identity politics and how such politics, grounded on limited experiences of race and gender, have relegated Black women and other women of color to the margins of racial and gender liberation movements. Attempting to locate Black women and other women of color on the social landscape through a critique of national antiracist and antisexist discourses, Crenshaw argues that Black and other women of color's experiences of racial and gender oppression have been erased. This erasure is elaborately mapped according to the intersectional locations of Black women and other women of color at structural, representational, and political scales of social life. The article outlines these multidimensional scales—structural, representational, and political—from which the concept of intersectionality is derived.

In this chapter I am most concerned with submitting Crenshaw's article to an ethic of reading guided by certain aesthetic principles put forth by the critical theorist Theodor Adorno. In doing so, I discern two levels of literacy enabled by the concept of intersectionality. In addition, an ethical reading provides us with an opportunity to better understand the concept of "women of color." "Women of color," as the illusion that gives rise to the concept of intersectionality, is the experience of a certain critical attitude. Crenshaw implicitly calls this attitude an "intersectional sensibility"—and one we might understand further as a human-looking metaphor, an "apparition." We will find under the guidance of Adorno's work in aesthetic theory that the concept is aesthetically figured in the text, and that the figuration produces what Adorno has called the experience of the "shudder."

The first section of this chapter situates the two bodies of knowledge—critical race theory and critical theory—alongside each other for purposes of this ethical reading of intersectionality. In the second section we return to the actual text of Crenshaw's article, in which the ethic of reading is embedded in the formal construction of the concept of intersectionality. The third section draws out the social significance of such a reading of intersectionality through Adorno's concept of the shudder. The final section demonstrates how this ethic of reading is performed outside the parameters of the text, through a reading of Angela Davis's application of intersectionality in formulating a radical feminist agenda at the 2000 Incite! Women of Color Against Violence Conference.

These sections taken together suggest the impossibility, as well as the undesirability, of a "postintersectionality" CRT.[2] Even if postintersectionality purports to develop an analytical framework that is more inclusive and egalitarian than is intersectionality, this actually misses the theoretical work of intersectionality altogether. For where intersectionality brings us to the limit of knowledge, beyond which is not more objective social reality subject to rational thought, we find that the justification for intersectionality is its ability to retain a negative moment in the dialectical relation between politics, on the one hand, and imagination and desire, on the other, toward a more radical transformation of the future.

Critical (Race) Theory

Within CRT there is some amount of confusion about whether intersectionality is an analytical framework or a concept, with the additional complexity of how the concept of "women of color" figures upon this confusion. For the moment, we will grant that intersectionality can be interpreted as both an analytical framework and a concept; however, the distinction between each will hopefully become clearer through the discussion offered below.

Indeed, the concept of intersectionality has a complex and troubled intellectual history.[3] Such an observation bears repeating at a time when a faction of those working within the field of CRT are calling for the transcendence of intersectionality,[4] naming such a movement "postintersectionality." While the debate around this call has generated much discussion in the published literature and the classroom alike, I broach the basic question underlying this debate: How does one do this? While I do not attempt to answer this initial question here, I leave it as background, a question requiring a rereading to figure out what exactly "intersectionality" is in the first instance. To that end, I return to Crenshaw's article as the most widely cited work on the concept. Further, to represent what I feel is essential to understanding the theoretical work of intersectionality—that is, the text in which the concept and analysis take form—I refer to Crenshaw's article as *Intersectionality* to capture the textuality of the concept.

I suspect that in his position as a public philosopher and cultural critic, Theodor Adorno would have approved of accepting the text's invitation for such a rereading. Granting that the exercise of critical thought always involves a gesture of return, I believe that Adorno may have recognized this project as such an exercise when he observed in his essay "Sexual Taboos and Law Today":

> The theorist who intervenes in practical controversies nowadays discovers on a regular basis and to his shame that whatever ideas he might contribute were expressed long ago—and usually better the first time around. Not only has the mass of writings and publications grown beyond measure: society itself, despite all its tendencies to expand, in many cases seems to be regressing to earlier stages, even in its superstructure, in law and politics. Embarrassingly enough, this means that time-honored arguments must once again be trotted out. Even critical thought risks becoming infected by what it criticizes. Critical thought must let itself be guided by the concrete forms of consciousness it opposes and must go over once again what they have forgotten.[5]

Intersectionality has perhaps been buried under scholarship that has indeed "grown beyond measure" in our time of professionalized academic research. I do not mean to use Adorno as an excuse to "trot out" the "time-honored arguments" articulated by Crenshaw through the concept of intersectionality. To do this would be to take Adorno literally and miss the value of his work completely. Rather, I want to include Adorno as a guide in reading the language of those concepts instantiated by intersectionality as a theoretical text. My point is to bring out the concept in and of *Intersectionality*, but through the language and metaphorical acts instantiated by the form taken by the concept in the text. Following the form of the concept as it appears in the theoretical text, I believe the text itself reflects *how* it is that those engaged in the field of CRT, and other like-minded bodies of legal theory more generally, should go about the project of critical thought. In other words, because the concept of intersectionality is itself an attempt to recover what has been forgotten by critical thought, the concept also suggests how to go about this recovery.

Additionally, underlying Adorno's implicit suggestion that this rereading of Crenshaw is both necessary and appropriate for theory and politics, there is a practical affinity between Crenshaw and Adorno that should not be understated. Their affinity is based upon the historicity of the social impulses from which their respective fields of thought garnered their "critical" edge. While CRT organized knowledge against the hegemony of post–civil rights racism, the Frankfurt School undertook similar intellectual work against the emergence of Fascism on the world scene.[6] Indeed, CRT and critical theory clearly are intellectual movements for social justice. And constituted in part by those writing within, the two might be seen in solidarity with each other, as both organize against the oppressive institutions and structures of an administered society. Both CRT and the Frankfurt School are best characterized by their critical attitudes toward Enlightenment ideals—including the rule of law as a technical system of social norms and philosophy as a universal system of human truths—which have historically gone hand in hand with mass human suffering and domination. These preliminary avenues of communication between CRT and critical theory having been laid out, what follows is the return.

Reading Intersectionality

The critical analytical gesture through which the concept of intersectionality takes figure targets two historically disparate social movements—feminist and antiracist. Crenshaw argues that these movements' legal reforms and discursive productions continue to reproduce the very structures of domination that they resist.[7] At the same time, motivating Crenshaw's concern with the history of these movements is a mighty effort to deconstruct the opposition between margin and center; identity and heterogeneity; and, no less, race and gender.[8] Specifically, in *Intersectionality* the attention to the texture of antiracist and feminist discourse illuminates how the correspondence between object (woman or Black) and subject (women and Blacks) represented by those discourses could not actually correspond if a certain mode of critical thought were applied.

This critical analytical framework demonstrated in *Intersectionality* recognizes that in every discursive production, in the social and cultural consolidation of every political identity, there is what Gayatri Spivak has described as "an itinerary of a constantly thwarted desire to make the text explain."[9] Discerning this itinerary requires a "trick of rereading." Accordingly, Spivak poses the deconstructive method by which such an itinerary can be read as a question: "What is this explanation as it is constituted by and as it effects a desire to conserve the explanation itself . . . ?"[10] For the purposes of *Intersectionality*, Crenshaw implicitly poses an analogous question: What is this politics (antiracist or feminist) as it is constituted by and as it effects a desire to conserve (racial or gender) identity itself?

Before I flesh out the precise significance of an intersectional sensibility, I want to reiterate the preceding point. That is, as the text itself anticipates its failed explanation; the politic itself contains the potential for its failed strategies. Both text and politic contain their margins to the extent that neither could exist as each historically has without such "marginalia." Crenshaw mines the value of this deconstructive principle by naming this particular critical gesture "intersectionality," which both figures and exhibits the incommensurability of conflicting identity-based movements. Additionally, Crenshaw would call the frustration imposed on the desire for identity politics "intersectional sensibility."[11]

Crenshaw's engagement with each movements' discursive effects on the production of identity politics maps a profoundly inward-moving, introspective path. In the conclusion of her analysis of structural, political, and representational violence against women of color, Crenshaw argues that intersectionality makes it "easier to understand the need for and to summon the courage to challenge groups that are after all, in one sense, 'home' to us, in the name of the parts of us that are not made at home. This takes a great deal of energy and arouses intense anxiety. The most one could expect is that we will dare to speak against *internal exclusions and marginalizations*, that we might call attention to how the identity of 'the group' has been *centered on the intersectional identities of a few*."[12]

In other words, the tension imposed by the exclusion and marginalization of social movements premised on the ideals of egalitarianism and democracy is generated from within. The imposed tension is a privileged process engendered not so much by the pressure of multiply subordinated identities on and outside singularly subordinated identities, but by the proscription of marginality as such.

At the same time that this imposed tension directs a considerable amount of analytical attention to the center in understanding the opposition between identity and heterogeneity, we are able to reread the significance of the margin nonetheless. Spivak reminds us that "although the prohibition of marginality that is crucial in the production of any explanation is politics as such, what inhabits the prohibited margin of a particular explanation specifies its particular politics."[13]

About the inhabitance of this prohibited margin, Crenshaw makes two key observations. First, if antiracist discourse prohibits the explanation of violence against women of color, then antiracist discourse relies on a sexist politics. Moreover, if feminist discourse prohibits the explanation of violence against women of color, then feminist discourse relies on a racist politics. Most of those who have taken up *Intersectionality* have been able to extrapolate this first observation, thereby allowing the reader to specify the particular politics of certain historical political movements.[14]

The first figure of deconstruction in *Intersectionality* is "identity politics" and the metaphorical act that instantiates this figure of deconstruction are the concepts "antiracism" and "feminism" brought together with the unstable meanings of "social justice" and "internal exclusions and marginalizations." The text in bold in Chart 1 depicts this metaphorical act.[15]

Chart 1

1st Figure	Concepts	Meanings	Illusions
Identity politics (*Intersectionality*)	**Antiracism** **Feminism**	~~Social Justice~~ **Internal exclusion marginalizations**	**Intersectionality** **"Women of color"** **(version 1)**

The bold in Chart 1, in other words, represents the first metaphorical act under the deconstruction performed by the text. The phenomena of "internal exclusion and marginalizations" destabilizes the pure correspondence between the concepts "antiracism" and "feminism" and the meaning "social justice," (thus '~~social justice~~'). This destabilization enacts a deconstruction of the figure "identity politics." (My inclusion of *Intersectionality* in parenthesis becomes clear immediately below).

Earlier I referred to an "intersectional sensibility" as that which poses a frustration of the desire for an identity politic. Intersectional sensibility as that which interrupts this desire actually allows for more clarity about the functional gap between "antiracism" or "feminism" and "social justice."[16] We will note, then, that the primary deconstructive narrative of *Intersectionality* has less to do with narrating the location or experiences of women of color than with understanding the limitations of identity politics. In addition, *Intersectionality* emerges as one of the most important illusions, or images, from this first metaphoric act.

At the same time, this metaphorical act, posited as a deconstructive analytical framework, is also named *Intersectionality*. *Intersectionality* not only contains this metaphorical act, but also calls this metaphorical act an intersectional analytical framework. We might understand this first deconstructive narrative as "tropological," in that the text gives it a name and positive representation as intersectionality. This positive naming has caused considerable confusion in the literature on intersectionality where the positive naming of the metaphor as an intersectional analytical framework hides the original metaphorical act.[17]

Flawed readings of this first metaphorical act do not lie in failures to recognize both the metaphorical act and literal meaning, as that is the precise function of metaphor. Readings that only recognize the literal meaning are simply reductive ones. Rather, flawed readings lie in the tendency to conflate the various illusions emerging from the metaphoric act in and as the figure under deconstruction. They return the illusions back to the place of the first figure of deconstruction to subject it to a "tropological" deconstructive narrative[18] (hence, the renaming in CRT of *Intersectionality ad nauseum*). In Chart 1, the *Intersectionality* in parenthesis then denotes the result of these flawed readings, which replace or conflate the first figure of deconstruction with the illusion that arises from that very deconstruction.

However, if the reader recognizes that *Intersectionality* is the product of the initial critical gesture of reading (which is decidedly *not* the case for identity politics), then the conflation of *Intersectionality* with identity politics becomes impossible. Nonetheless, Crenshaw's second critical comment, attendant to this proper recognition of *Intersectionality* as it relates to the problem of knowing through language, remains relatively untouched by CRT. More to the point, by grasping the significance of inhabiting the prohibited margin as that experience of existing outside the realm of sociality, discourse, and cultural representation, Crenshaw's second observation recognizes the unknowability of the illusions (*Intersectionality*, "women of color") *except through structures of metaphorical acts, or language in general*. This second observation is made clear by Crenshaw's introductory remarks about the main objective of *Intersectionality*. "When [feminist and antiracist] practices expound identity as woman or person of color as an either/or proposition, they relegate the *identity of women of color to a location that resists telling*. My objective in this article is to *advance the telling of that location* by exploring the race and gender dimensions of violence against women of color."[19] Put simply, the intersectional location cannot be spoken from. What Crenshaw's writing takes as its goal is not, then, to speak from that untellable location, but rather to create a discursive shift so that that location might become somehow tellable—a shift to make it known, to reveal it, account for it. But this shift commences from the very real, and originary, problem of language that precludes that location as a site of enunciation. The reader finds that the presentation of this second observation is actually underwritten with a subtle, intricate, and imaginative thought that distinguishes *Intersectionality* from all its succeeding applications and various appropriations in CRT.

Certainly, marginalized existence does not make identitarian existence for such inhabitants impossible. For this reason, it remains possible throughout *Intersectionality* to write of a detailed but necessarily unspecified kind of identity through references to "women of color" that function only to describe a location—structural, political, and representational—in history. However, distinguishing this identitarian existence is precisely *not* the motivational issue of *Intersectionality*. Instead, the "who" of *Intersectionality* is only ever textually figured as "the location of women of color," and there is a key *absence* of a positive type to which "women of color" refers. *Intersectionality* appears, therefore, as a play on the non-correspondence of "*woman* of color" with "*women* of color" in order to preserve the tension between object and subject, center and margin, identity and heterogeneity. In fact, *Intersectionality*'s single mention of "*woman* of color" is introduced, not by way of that woman of color's own description of her experiences, but by way of a prosecutor's and witness's descriptions of that woman of color's experience of violence. This because the lethal nature of said violence silenced that woman of color by sentence of death. Further, in *Intersectionality*, "*woman* of color," as a referent, takes as its meaning the "forgotten" rapes (on the week the national public began its prosecution to vindicate the Central Park jogger in 1989), the "devaluation of Black women and the marginalizations of their sexual victimizations."[20] That is all to say that the "*woman* of color" referent finds meaning in the actual experiences of "Black women," and not "women of color." Actual experiences are not fleshed out by "women of color." "Women of color" only remains in the text as a referent that must be fleshed out with history and actual experiences. Thus, we have the position of illusion "women of color" (version 1) takes in Chart 1.

At the same time, the precise significance of "women of color" in the text cannot be seen unless we analyze the supplementary—allegorical— deconstructive narrative of *Intersectionality*.[21] Where the text facilitates the flawed reading I mentioned above, a repaired reading is attempted here, and depicted below in Chart 2.[22]

Chart 2

2d Figure	Concepts	Meanings	Illusions
Intersectionality	Race	~~Violence~~	"women of color"
as Chart 1	Gender	Structural IS*	(version 2)
		Political IS	
		Representational IS	

* IS = Intersectionality

Having done the first reading, the deconstructive meaning "marginalization and internal exclusions" is given the supplemental meaning "Violence." And "Structural IS/Political IS/Representational IS" is the deconstructive force in this particular metaphorical act that attempts to create a pure correspondence between "Race/Gender" and "Violence." The metaphorical form of *Intersectionality* together with the gap between concepts and meanings in Chart 2 give rise to a supplemented illusion of "women of color" (version 2).

Chart 2 differs from Chart 1 in that *Intersectionality* is both the *figure* under deconstruction and the *force* of deconstruction: *Intersectionality* (*as* Chart 1) and "Structural IS/Political IS/Representational IS." This dual role of *Intersectionality* makes this second deconstructive moment allegorical because it does not provide a new positive figure of deconstruction, and, further, does not provide a new force of deconstruction. Rather, it builds, supplements, Chart 1 with the recognition of having passed through the first deconstructive moment. It recognizes that there is no other name for Chart 1 other than the illusion that arises from the first metaphorical act, and that the recognition of this illusion is recognition of the failure of reading.

The illusion "women of color" (version 2), as a supplement to version 1, deserves special attention because it provides the reader with two relationships to illusion. First, as mentioned above, is the problem of knowing and the attitude of skepticism, or "intersectional sensibility," the illusion issues. Second, made evident in the way version 2 arises in Chart 2, is the problem of history and its effect on the reader. To elaborate the two relationships established between the illusion and the reading subject, we will first note that the deconstructive force in Charts 1 and 2 arise from the historicity of the experiences of women of color, and not any actual "women of color" experience. Thus, while marginal existence cannot be spoken out of, the historicity of that existence "speaks" by and through this deconstructive force. It is the historical accuracy of the structural, political, and representational intersections of race and gender described in *Intersectionality* that interrupts the process of metaphorization, and subsequently interrupts the tropological process of deconstruction. Indeed, the text seems to implicitly recognize this where *Intersectionality* intends only to "advance the telling," and not to speak about or from the location of "women of color,"[23] and yet proceeds with its historical work (largely centered about the legal institution). In positing the problem of "a location that resists telling," *Intersectionality* commits thought to the problem of what it means to be an identity without history and, through this commitment to the object, illuminates this history.

Adorno's Aesthetics

Shierry Weber Nicholsen, in her excellent study of Adorno's aesthetics, has described a common relationship between art and theory and their respective objects. This common relationship is premised on the "productive imagination" of the subject encountering the object for the creation of either art or theory. "Hence Adorno . . . speaks of a 'productive' imagination . . . to evoke the associative activity of the subject that accompanies or alternates with contemplative immersion in the details of the object. The experiencing subject fantasizes and speculates, producing associations from the subject's own experience, which are then matched against what is perceived of the object. The process is as crucial to intellectual experience as it is to aesthetic experience."[24] Nicholsen's observation of this particular commitment to the object that both art and theory possess is part of the general Adornian insight that gives twentieth-century aesthetic theory its critical edge. Thus, in order to better understand the larger significance of my appreciation for the commitment in *Intersectionality* to the object and the intersectional sensibility it creates, I turn to one of Adorno's important theoretical contributions to aesthetic theory below.

Adorno references "apparitions" in artwork as we have been discussing illusions in metaphor.[25] More specifically, he writes, "The linguistic habitus of 'the world is as it is' is the medium through which the social spell becomes aesthetic appearance [or an apparition]."[26] We might take this linguistic habitus as analogous to the structure of metaphor in language, and the "social spell [that] becomes aesthetic appearance" as analogous to the collection of illusions we have been discussing thus far. For Adorno, this aesthetic appearance, or illusion, is captured in the text as an apparition and is felt by the reader through what he calls the "shudder." In one place, he notes, "The shudder is a response, colored by fear of the overwhelming" (245). He adds in another place that the shudder is a type of experience that is "radically opposed to the conventional idea of experience. . . . [The shudder] provides no particular satisfaction for the I; it bears no similarity to desire. Rather, it is a memento of the liquidation of the I, which, shaken, perceives its own limitedness and finitude" (245).

Adorno's conceptualization of the shudder aptly captures the experience of reading that *Intersectionality* enables.

> Experiences are not "as if." The disappearance of the I in the moment of the shudder is not real. . . . For a few moments the I becomes aware, in real terms, of the possibility of letting self-preservation fall away, though it does not actually succeed in realizing this possibility. It is not the aesthetic shudder that is semblance but rather its attitude to objectivity: In its immediacy the shudder feels the potential as if it were actual. The I is seized by the unmetaphorical, semblance-shattering consciousness: that it itself is not ultimate, but semblance. (245–46)

Despite the fact that the aesthetic shudder results in a rejection of any semblance of the I, it is through the aesthetic shudder that the reading subject is provided with an unmetaphorical and immediate sense of actuality. It is through the aesthetic shudder that the subject realizes that there is only the metaphorical, and yet it is this realization that allows the subject to experience something that is not "as if." Thus, the possibility of this experience enabled by the aesthetic shudder echoes the complete dissatisfaction on the part of *Intersectionality* with the fact that the particular historical experiences of women of color can only ever be metaphorical.

If an artwork successfully creates this apparition that can effect the shudder in its readings, then Adorno calls this a "social-ethical accomplishment" (260). However, we should note that the divide between the apparition in the text and the shudder as an effect is somewhat artificial to the extent that both occur and exist through the reader's encounter with the text. Thus, while it might be possible to call *Intersectionality* a "social-ethical accomplishment," this is true insofar as the encounter— between the reading subject and the text of *Intersectionality*—gives rise to the aesthetic shudder in the reader, the experience by the reader of something that is not "as if."

At this point, I think it is possible to grasp a clearer understanding of "women of color" (version 2) in *Intersectionality* as this apparition that, when encountered by the reader, effects a shudder. As we have now been able to see (Charts 1 and 2), the process of reading metaphor entails an acute and self-conscious sense of history, not as events of the past, but as past events that are instantiated by the work of a text and the reader's desire to work with the text. Perhaps most important, this desire is premised on an "intersectional sensibility" and the openness of readers to subject themselves to the experience of the shudder.

Marginality reread as the concept of intersectionality—*Intersectionality*—imagines the possibility of identity that is unspeakable, unknowable, unrepresentable, uncategorical, and yet illusory, suggestive, descriptive, conceptual, and most of all, historical. Thus, *Intersectionality* operates in more than three dimensions; it is the form of illusions that provides us with the space to exercise what Nicholsen has called " 'exact imagination' . . . [as] the experiencing subject's ability to follow the quasi-logical relationships in the artwork with accuracy and precision."[27] It teaches us to read.

Ethic of Reading

In April 2000, more than fifteen hundred women of color attended the "Color of Violence: Violence Against Women of Color" conference, held at the University of California at Santa Cruz, in an effort to redefine antiviolence politics. Angela Davis marked the event as one offering up both the contradictions and possibilities of the moment. The gathering would help to "imagine ways of attending to the ubiquitous violence in the lives of women of color that also radically subvert the institutions and discourses within which we are compelled by necessity to think and work."[28]

The contradiction of the moment: the institutions and discourses inhabited by the women of color caused the violence they desired to abate. The possibility of the moment: that same violence would drive the imaginations of women of color to depose these institutions and discourses. In other words, if violence is engendered by our participation in institutions and discourses out of necessity, then a challenge to that violence would have to make recourse to something other than necessity. We might take the political desire of the conference, expressed in the event's primary motivating question, as the materialization of that "something else":

> One of the major questions facing this conference is how to develop an analysis that furthers neither the conservative project of sequestering millions of men of color in accordance with the contemporary dictates of global capital and its prison industrial complex, nor the equally conservative project of abandoning poor women of color to a continuum of violence that extends from the sweatshops through the prisons, to shelters, and into bedrooms at home. How do we develop analyses and organizing strategies against violence against women that acknowledge the race of gender and the gender of race? . . . Can we, for example, link a strong demand for remedies for women of color who are targets of rape and domestic violence with a strategy that calls for the abolition of the prison system?[29]

For many of the women in attendance, this primary question represented their first encounter with the historical attempt by feminists of color to articulate an intersectional analytical framework.

I offer Davis's keynote address as an exemplary articulation of intersectionality as an analytical framework because of her substantive application of the framework in positing a "women of color" political agenda against violence, which at the same time demonstrates the form of the concept as an ethics of reading. As the preceding passage demonstrates, the questions Davis poses to encourage substantive analysis of state and interpersonal violence simultaneously demonstrate the questions themselves to be the product of her reading of the current political condition. Further, the excerpt is self-conscious of the limits of rational analysis, as the formation of political demands is bracketed by the desires for relief from interpersonal violence and reversal of mass incarceration. We might say that we get a sense of the passage not only through what Davis says or asks, but also, how she asks and says those things. Thus, following Davis's example, I would conclude by suggesting that the value of inter-sectionality as an analytical framework for critical approaches to race and gender studies, among which CRT is located, is lost if one element (the substantive) is privileged over the other (the formal) or vice versa.[30]

In the same speech Davis delivered at the opening of the conference, she cites Crenshaw's analysis of violence against women of color. This reference then allows Davis to extend and elaborate on the way in which the specific location of Native American women furthers the event's po-litical desire.

> Gina Dent has observed that one of the most important accom-plishments of this conference is to *foreground Native American women* within the category "women of color." As Kimberlé Cren-shaw's germinal study on violence against women *suggests, the situ-ation of Native American women* shows that we must also *include within our analytical framework the persisting colonial domination of indigenous nations* and national formations within and outside the presumed territorial boundaries of the U.S. The U.S. colonial state's racist, sexist, and homophobic brutality in dealing with *Native Americans* once again shows the futility of relying upon the juridical or legislative processes of the state to resolve these problems.[31]

At once, this passage demonstrates various modes of reading on several different levels: First, reading as generative. Crenshaw's study is taken as "suggestive." Expanding this adjective, we might think of the study as possessing a certain ability to evoke something beyond itself, of hinting at some future meaning, and most important, of stimulating further thought in those encountering it. The preceding passage expresses this impact on the speaker as a reader, an identification of the speaker as a reader, and thus, producer of meaning.

Second, reading as feminist. The category "women of color" is main-tained in an abstract but materially situated form. While placing into relationship the category and the study, the passage remarks the study's commitment to representing the heterogeneity of women's experiences ("women"), while at the same time demonstrating the usefulness of the concept ("'women of color'") developed out of historical experiences. The subsequent discussion of Native American women's situation seems less about a concern for identitarian inclusiveness then a concern for historically and politically situating the relationship of distinction between the heterogeneity of women's experiences and the concept of "women of color." The nuance with which the relationship of distinction is given form in the language of this passage reflects the feminist concern with negotiating the imperialism of language to subsume women as woman; moreover, it reflects a feminist practice of negotiation involved in reading itself.[32]

Third, reading as social act. The inclusion of colonial domination within the study's analytical framework is accompanied by a demonstration of how the analytical framework, by way of the repetition it enables, broadens the social sphere in which Native American women bear influence. The repetition of "Native American women," "the situation of Native American women," and "Native American" through the analytical framework's attention to colonial domination—or by underscoring the category "women of color"—reforms the language of the conference's political motivation. This amounts to the reform of a discursive space in which Native Americans can be spoken about. The challenge of tracking this repetition contained in the analysis of this passage encourages its readers to understand reading as a social act.

Fourth, reading as ethical. The naming of the analytical framework as "our" analytical framework presents the ethical question the concept demands as the product of a set of social practices working with and from a history of domination. Naming it as such is an ethical gesture that recognizes both the epistemological limits of the concept and the alterity of the Other that exists beyond this limit.[33]

I believe that these observations, taken together, are an example of an "ethic of reading" that is perhaps the best way to approach intersectionality. We can see through Davis's ethic of reading that intersectionality, as an analytical framework, and its corresponding concept of "women of color," are not based on unified identities or locations, precisely because any such unity is defied by the fact that the reader is structured into the framework and concept. If they appear unified, then the ethic of reading performed by Davis reveals such an effect as nothing less than the problem of language to impose this unity. At the same time, this ethic allows for the most generous and productive approach to intersectionality be-

cause of the different types of acts that reading becomes in the process—
generative, feminist, social, and ethical.

Finally, I close this reading with an acute sense of wariness in our
present historical moment. To the extent that legal scholars and activists
continue to undermine the development of intersectionality theory, this
contemporary incitement by women of color—a demand for remedies to
domestic violence *and* strategies for the abolition of the prison system—
will remain a question still, ever posed but not pursued. Proposing em-
phatically that CRT reaffirm its commitment to "the critical," which is to
say an ethics of reading, I look forward to productive debate. However,
such can only proceed if we accept the insistence of *Intersectionality* on
engaging, with increased diligence, our intimate relationship with the
ubiquity, the globality, of violence instantiated by the intersection of
race and gender in the United States. For this intimate relationship is,
simply, the condition of possibility for social transformation and cultural
life as such.

Notes

1. The term *intersectionality* is popularly attributed to the work of, the legal scholar Crenshaw,
and specifically as it appears in "Mapping the Margins." However, a genealogy of Crenshaw's
thought, offered by her explicitly and implicitly, locates the concept specifically within the tradition
of black feminist thought in the United States. "Mapping the Margins: Intersectionality, Identity
Politics, and Violence Against Women of Color," *Stanford Law Review* 43 (1991): 1241; reprinted in
Critical Race Theory: The Key Writings That Formed the Movement, ed. Kimberlé Williams Crenshaw,
Neil Gotanda, Gary Peller, and Kendall Thomas (New York: New Press, 1995).

2. For an intellectual history of the postintersectionality camp of CRT, see Robert S. Chang and
Jerrome McCristal Culp Jr., "After Intersectionality," *UMKC Law Review* 71 (2002): 485; and Nancy
Levit, "Introduction: Theorizing the Connections Among Systems of Subordination," *UMKC Law
Review* 71 (2002): 227.

3. However, along with Crenshaw, several critical race theorists have productively popularized
the term *intersectionality*. See Kimberlé Williams Crenshaw, "Demarginalizing the Intersection of
Race and Sex: A Black Feminist Critique of Antidiscrimination Doctrine, Feminist Theory, and
Antiracist Politics," *U. Chi. Legal F.* (1989): 139; Trina Grillo, "Anti-essentialism and Intersectiona-
lity: Tools to Dismantle the Master's House," *Berkeley Women's L.J.* 10 (1995) 16; and Angela P.
Harris, "Race and Essentialism in Feminist Legal Theory," *Stanford Law Review* 42 (1990): 581.

In addition, intersectionality has evoked a broad range of topics. See Beverly I. Moran, "Key-
note Address Delivered for the Journal of Contemporary Legal Issues Conference on the Future of
Intersectionality and Critical Race Feminism," *J. Contemp. Legal Issues* 11 (2001): 691. Radhika
Coomaraswamy, United Nations special rapporteur on violence against women, has emphasized
ethnicity, class, and caste in the construction of women's issues. See, e.g., Radhika Coomaraswamy,
"To Bellow Like a Cow: Women, Ethnicity, and the Discourse of Rights," in *Human Rights of*

Women: National and International Perspectives, ed. Rebecca Cook (Philadelphia: University of Pennsylvania Press, 1994), 39.

4. Peter Kwan, "Intersections of Race, Ethnicity, Class, Gender, and Sexual Orientation: Jeffrey Dahmer and the Cosynthesis of Categories," *Hastings L. J.* 48 (1997): 1257.

5. Theodor W. Adorno, "Sexual Taboos and the Law Today," in *Critical Models: Interventions and Catchwords,* trans. Henry W. Pickford (New York: Columbia University Press, 1998), 71. According to the preface, by Pickford, the essay was presented in *Critical Models* as an expression of Adorno's "practical motive . . . to promote political maturity by bringing reified consciousness to self-awareness" (vii).

6. For an excellent history of CRT as an intellectual movement, see Kimberlé Williams Crenshaw, Neil Gotanda, Gary Peller, and Kendall Thomas, eds., *Critical Race Theory: The Key Writings That Formed the Movement* (New York: New Press, 1995), xiii–xxxii. For an excellent history of the Frankfurt School and critical theory, see Martin Jay, *Dialectical Imagination: A History of the Frankfurt School and the Institute of Social Research, 1923–1950* (Boston: Little, Brown, 1973).

7. Crenshaw, "Mapping the Margins," 1265–82.

8. Crenshaw, "Mapping the Margins," 1296–99.

9. Gayatri Spivak, "Explanation and Culture, Marginalia," in *In Other Worlds: Essays in Cultural Politics* (New York: Routledge, 1987), 105.

10. Spivak, "Explanation and Culture," 105.

11. Crenshaw, "Mapping the Margins," n. 4.

12. Crenshaw, "Mapping the Margins," n. 4, my emphasis.

13. Spivak, "Explanation and Culture," 106. In an earlier passage, which alludes to who such inhabitants might be, we find that they are those whose radically different experiences render the universe unexplainable and incapacitate the subject from explaining. "The will to explain [is] a symptom of the desire to have a self and a world. In other words, on the general level, the possibility of explanation carries the presupposition of an explainable (even if not fully) universe and an explaining (even if imperfectly) subject. These presuppositions assure our being. Explaining, we exclude the possibility of the *radically* heterogeneous" (105, emphasis in original).

14. See, for example, Karen Wang, "Battered Asian American Women: Community Responses from the Battered Women's Movement and the Asian American Community," *Asian L. J.* 3 (1996): 151.

15. Charts 1 and 2 are based on Fredric Jameson's general discussion of Paul DeMan and his theory of deconstruction as reading. Frederic Jameson, *Postmodernism, or the Cultural Logic of Late Capitalism* (Durham: Duke University Press, 1991), 205–42.

16. According to Paul DeMan's theory of reading, this intersectional sensibility would be akin to the attitude of skepticism towards metaphor that marks the first moment of deconstruction in the act of reading. Jameson, *Postmodernism,* 205.

17. Jameson observes this more generally when writing, "The metaphoric act constitutively involves the forgetting or repression of itself: concepts generated by metaphor at once conceal their origins and stage themselves as true or referential. . . . That process, then, generates a variety of illusions." Jameson, *Postmodernism,* 242.

18. Jameson, *Postmodernism,* 205.

19. Crenshaw, "Mapping the Margins," 1242, my emphasis.

20. Crenshaw, "Mapping the Margins," 1267.

21. Jameson, *Postmodernism,* 205–42.

22. See note 15 above.

23. Indeed, such advance is made by Crenshaw's rereading of race and gender dimensions of violence against women of color, not as a "woman of color," but as a black feminist constituted by her intervention. Crenshaw, "Mapping the Margins," n. 8.

24. Shierry Weber Nicholsen, *Exact Imagination, Late Work: On Adorno's Aesthetics* (Cambridge, Mass.: MIT Press, 1997), 20.

25. Theodor Adorno, *Aesthetic Theory*, trans. Robert Hullot-Kentor (Minneapolis: University of Minnesota Press, 1990), 95.

26. Adorno, *Aesthetic Theory*, 230. Further page references are cited parenthetically in the text.

27. Nicholsen, *Exact Imagination*, 19.

28. Angela Y. Davis, transcription of keynote speech on file with author. See also <www.national-incite.org>.

29. Davis, keynote speech.

30. Few, if any, references to the concept in CRT have demonstrated an understanding that the concept is constituted by both its substantive and formal elements. In fact, the appropriation of the concept in CRT has largely taken up the concept's formal elements to leave to the wayside its substantive elements. Here, I am only noting the problem of CRT's noncritique of intersectionality, about which a more comprehensive review will follow in the future. However, a lack of such a review does not preclude what the present chapter attempts to illuminate, i.e., the pedagogical impulses of intersectionality to teach us to read.

31. Davis, keynote speech, my emphases.

32. Teresa de Lauretis, *Alice Doesn't: Feminism, Semiotics, Cinema* (Bloomington: Indiana University Press, 1984), 36.

33. See, generally, Emmanuel Levinas, "Ethics and the Face," in *Totality and Infinity: An Essay on Exteriority*, trans. Alfonso Lingis (Hingham, Mass.: Kluwer Boston, 1979).

9

An-aesthetic Theory

Adorno, Sexuality, and Memory

Mary Anne Franks

I still cannot decide to agree to the use of chloroform in general surgical practice. . . . My scruples are founded on the simple fact that operations with chloroform, and presumably also with the other forms of narcosis, have an illusory success. . . . Under the influence of chloroform, the nervous substance loses a considerable part of its ability to absorb traces of impressions, but it does not lose the power of sensation as such. On the contrary . . . pain is experienced even more strongly than in the normal condition. The public is misled by the fact that after an operation the patient is unable to remember what he has undergone. If we told our patients the truth, it is probably that not one of them would wish to have an operation performed under chloroform, where they all insist on its use now because we shroud the truth in silence.

. . . It is possible that the painful stimuli which because of their specific nature may well exceed all known sensations of this kind, may lead to permanent mental damage in the patient or even to an undescribably painful death under narcosis; and the exact features of this death will be hidden for ever from the relatives of the patient and the world at large. Would this not be too high a price to pay for progress?

—Pierre Flourens, nineteenth-century French physiologist,
quoted in Theodor Adorno and Max Horkheimer, *Dialectic of Enlightenment*

If Flourens had been right here . . . the suspicion would then arise that our relationship with men and creation in general was like our relationship with ourself after an operation—oblivion for suffering. For cognition the gap between us and others was the same as the time between our own present and past suffering; an insurmountable barrier. But perennial domination over nature, medical and non-medical techniques, are made possible only by the process of oblivion. . . . All objectification is a forgetting.

—Adorno and Horkheimer, *Dialectic of Enlightenment*

In the notes to the *Dialectic of Enlightenment*, Adorno and Horkheimer cite Pierre Flourens's reservations about medical anesthesia to suggest that they can be read as a larger statement on the condition of the modern social order. Adorno and Horkheimer argue that the physical "process of oblivion"—forgetting suffering—involved in medical anesthesia is psychologically replicated in our ethical relationships. This *an-aesthetic* process is at work in our relationship both to the suffering of others and to our own suffering. This process of oblivion, this psychosocial anesthesia, is accomplished not only through increasing technological domination of our bodies by but also through the diversionary trappings of the culture industry (and these two intersect significantly in modern times).

In Adorno's view, the culture industry—which includes television, film, and advertising—erodes the human capacity to recognize and resist suffering. This degradation of sensibility is the degradation of the aesthetic in Adorno's mind—the aesthetic whose purpose is not diversion or amusement, but awareness of the wrongs perpetrated against human beings. The culture industry domesticates people through an endless supply of products, aimed at reconciling them with a consumption-driven, stupefied existence that actively represses the consideration of human suffering through mindless diversions and "entertainment."

It is my claim in this chapter that Adorno's critique of what could be called the "an-aesthetic" administered by the culture industry, which actively seeks to erase the sensitivity to and memory of suffering, is especially appropriate to contemporary cultural representations of sexual violence. The deadening effect of the compulsive and consumptive representation of female sexuality in popular culture depoliticizes and naturalizes sexual violence against women. Adorno's visionary aesthetic goal—of true aesthetic representation that radically decenters the viewer and compels him or her to resist the world as it is—can disrupt the stagnant ideological field of universally accepted sexual violence. Adorno's aesthetic position of *Betroffenheit* (concern) can serve as a powerful weapon against the accommodation of sexual violence hegemonic in the world today.

According to Adorno's political aesthetics, art's duty is to oppose itself to the suffering that takes place in reality. This cannot be accomplished if suffering is presented as an object of consumption. The culture industry makes a commodity of every emotion and experience, offering a sensuous immediacy that reinforces the distance between the subject that consumes and the object that suffers: Adorno writes "while the artwork's sensual appeal seemingly brings it close to the consumer, it is alienated from him by being a commodity that he possesses and the loss of which he must constantly fear."[1]

Adorno's critique of "sensual appeal" demonstrates his suspicion of the pleasure that the culture industry so insistently promises to deliver. For Adorno, pleasure "always means not to think about anything, to forget suffering even when it is shown. It is basic helplessness. It is flight; not, as is asserted, flight from a wretched reality, but from the last remaining thought of resistance. The liberation which amusement promises is freedom from thought and from negation."[2] The culture industry's promise of pleasure is a promise to depoliticize suffering, to neutralize and negotiate with it. It is the exact opposite of the aesthetic sensibility Adorno proposes: the posture of radical openness to the other's suffering. Adorno's invocation of Pierre Flourens is thus clear: the culture industry offers (imposes) an anti-aesthetic—an an-aesthetic—an imposed loss of feeling that does not actually prevent suffering but only the active remembering of it.

By contrast, the genuine aesthetic moment for Adorno involves a sense of concern (*Betroffenheit*) that goes beyond mere sensuous feeling (*Gefühl*); it is an experience of being touched by the other's suffering and, significantly, refusing to appropriate it. There must be something finally "unassimilable" about the true work of art, something that moves the viewer out of him- or herself. As Adorno writes, "[T]he spectator must not project what transpires in himself on to the artwork in order to find himself confirmed, uplifted, and satisfied in it, but must, on the contrary, relinquish himself to the artwork, assimilate himself to it, fulfill the work in its own terms. . . . [H]e must submit to the discipline of the work rather than demand that the artwork give him something."[3]

This feeling-beyond-oneself, this aesthetic concern, is for Adorno significantly bound up with the artwork's aura, its unique situation in time and space. Adorno's conception of the aura differed in many ways from Walter Benjamin's, whose essay "The Work of Art in the Age of Mechanical Reproduction" (1968) outlined potentially positive consequences of technological reproducibility. In that essay Benjamin proposed that the loss of an artwork's aura, accomplished through mechanical reproduction, could have a liberating effect. According to Benjamin, mechanical reproduction has the potential to liberate art from ritual, and as Shierry Nicholsen writes, his enthusiasm for this potential is understandable against the background of Fascist monumentalism.[4] Although Benjamin himself by no means embraced mechanical reproduction unreservedly, Adorno was even less optimistic than Benjamin regarding the loss of the aura, especially in photography and film.[5] "The world of imagery, itself thoroughly historical, is done an injustice by the fiction of a world of images that effaces the relations in which people live."[6] Adorno felt that Benjamin seriously underestimated the possibility of "the misuse of aesthetic rationality for mass exploitation and mass domination," especially regarding photography and cinema.[7] Kafka's claim that "we photograph things in order to drive them out of our minds" is expressive of this point.[8] Adorno's sensitivity to this tendency to drive out of mind—to forget—must be read in the context of "the darkest moments of culture, moments where precisely through recourse to sensual experience and the aestheticization of culture millions were murdered."[9] The reproduced photographic image both affirms and invites the "promiscuous acceptance of the world," to use Susan Sontag's phrase. Such images, by destroying suffering's particular presence in time and space—its aura—become an ideological support of that suffering. When an image is reproduced and commodified, the very pathos that it might invite ultimately "justifies the world which makes it necessary."[10] Terrence des Pres echoes this sentiment when he notes that "thanks to the technological expansion of consciousness, we cannot not know the extent of political torment; and in truth it may be said that what others suffer, we behold. The triumph of technology has created two classes which can coexist in the same person: those who suffer, and those who observe that suffering."[11] This observation of suffering leads us not to intervene or resist it, but rather to become indifferent to it, or worse, to obtain pleasure in viewing it.

Thus when Adorno comments that "aura is not only—as Benjamin claimed—the here and now of the artwork, it is whatever goes beyond its factual givenness, its content; one cannot abolish it and still want art," he seems to suggest that, contrary to Benjamin, one should decry the loss of aura in mechanical reproduction and maintain the aesthetic position of preserving that aura.[12] However, Adorno at the same time agreed with Benjamin that the culture industry itself can manipulate aura and turn it into "cult value." "Entertainment art adulterates on the one hand the real layer of the aesthetic, which is divested of its mediation and reduced to mere facticity, to information and reportage; on the other hand, it rips the auratic element out of the nexus of the work, cultivates it as such, and makes it consumable. Every close-up in every commercial film mocks aura by contriving to exploit the contrived nearness of the distant, cut off from the work as a whole. Aura is gulped down along with the sensual stimuli; it is the uniform sauce that the culture industry pours over the whole of its manufacture."[13] Even or especially aura, then, can become a support of the "logic of familiar things," even as the expulsion of that aura also serves this logic.[14]

Despite this danger, Adorno argues that the aura's potential to evade and thus go beyond "ideological superficies" is too important to disregard the way Benjamin seems to.[15] Benjamin himself, Adorno points out, credited early photography for presenting an aura that demonstrated the viewed object's ability to "look back." Adorno suggests that we should concentrate on this potential of the aura, the peculiar combination of closeness and distance, that brings us to the genuine aesthetic and to the truly ethical moment. If art and culture's task in a brutalized and brutalizing world is to expose suffering and encourage resistance, it can only do so by refusing to reproduce and commodify it: it has to preserve that suffering's fundamental unassimilability. The image of suffering should not gratify sensuous feeling or evoke a sense of possession. Although one must be in some way "close" to the image, this closeness cannot be maintained without the acknowledgment of the distance that finally exists between viewer and viewed; and as Kaja Silverman writes, mere closeness "signifies possession, that 'belong-to-me' quality which is such a notable feature of certain contemporary images. It implies not only the substitution of the subject's own frame of reference for that specific to the object, but the possibility of 'getting hold' of it at 'very short range,' i.e., of appropriating it."[16] An auratic work, by contrast, resists becoming subject to the viewer's pleasure, or jouissance. The aesthetic "shudder" of which Adorno speaks "does not provide a satisfaction to the ego and is removed from desire."[17] When Adorno writes that the true aesthetic response involves concern, this concern means "the moment in which recipients forget themselves and disappear into the work; it is the moment of being shaken."[18]

My contention, then, is that the an-aesthetic of the culture industry specifically targets the aura of objects. It refuses to encourage or even allow auratic representations of certain kinds of suffering, particularly those related to sexuality. The use of *auratic* here should be distinguished from Benjamin's pejorative use of the word, and Adorno's concurring critical remarks about the commodified aura, to indicate the complex nearness/distance that grounds the possibility of real ethical feeling, of "concern." The culture industry's an-aesthetic disrespects the specific presence in time and space of suffering or sensuously commodifies that specificity (creating cultic value for that suffering), or does both. An authentically auratic representation of suffering would exclude any accommodation, acceptance, or redemption of the causes of that suffering, while maintaining a certain respectful (but not ritualizing) distance from that suffering. The feeling—the literal aesthetic—that auratic suffering should inspire must be a full shock of the other's pain that is yet not appropriated by one's own desire or made consumable in any way. As

López writes, "[A]esthetic comportment assimilates itself to that other rather than subordinating it."[19]

The culture industry largely devotes the administration of its anesthetic against the perception of sexual violence. As des Pres points out, in the contemporary world one can no longer not know of the suffering of others—including that of millions of women and female children around the world. In our technologically advanced society we now hear and see accounts of rape warfare in the former Yugoslavia, Chechnya, Rwanda, the Congo; sexual trafficking of Eastern European women; girls sold into sex tourism in Thailand; the unsolved and largely unremarked (by official governmental and criminal institutions) murders of young women in Juárez, Mexico. The world knows that sexual inequality and the oppression of women by men, both explicitly and in more subtle ways, goes on even in our "liberal" day: "honor" killings in Muslim countries; female genital mutilation in African, Middle Eastern and Far Eastern countries; domestic violence in every part of the world. And yet in the West, we continue to have great difficulty identifying sexual violence as one of "our" real problems—unlike tax cuts or terrorism, sexual violence has yet to even make its way into being a significant part of any major political platform in the United States. But the statistics speak volumes: in the United States, approximately one out of every six women has been raped in her lifetime[20] and between 3 and 4 million women experience domestic violence (including rape) every year.[21]

What explains how a phenomenon that is so widespread, so common, and so (at least recently) reported still persists? No American would publicly condone rape warfare, the oppression of women under the Taliban, or the practice of throwing acid in the faces of Indian women who have rejected suitors. But violence against women keeps happening both "over there" and "over here." In our "enlightened," liberal society, many women are raped, tortured, and murdered. Western resignation to this phenomenon seems inexplicable. Some explanation for the West's lack of resistance lies in our very representation of sexual violence, or rather the preemptive representation of sexuality that portrays every imaginable sexual atrocity within the range of legitimate "visual pleasure."

This is perhaps made most apparent by the fact that the most disturbing images from some of the worst crimes in history have been appropriated by pornography with no public censure or outcry.[22] Naked women wearing gas masks or pressed against barbed wire are a staple in Israeli pornography; African American women shackled at the hands and feet being beaten with whips appear regularly in American pornography. More recently, some of the images depicting American soldiers raping Iraqi women at the Abu Ghraib prison were dismissed as "only" pornography—while such acts have reportedly taken place in reality, the pictures in question were "bogus," allegedly taken from an Internet porn site.[23] The very same images that were condemned as "atrocities" when they were believed to have taken place at Abu Ghraib were celebrated or dismissed when discovered to have been staged for entertainment. As Susan J. Brison pointedly asked regarding the American response to the "real" torture that took place at Abu Ghraib, "Given our tolerant, even self-congratulatory, attitude toward pornography, why should we be so shocked when torture takes this form? Why should it be cause for international alarm when sexually degrading, dehumanizing things are done to Iraqi prisoners (and photographed) if doing the same things to women around the world (and photographing them) for a multibillion-dollar pornography industry is considered entertainment?"[24] When images that bear testament to the worst excesses of racism and cruelty are ripped from their context of suffering and transposed into a context of "entertainment" and "pleasure," this effect is to suggest that the subjects involved enjoy or deserve the pain inflicted upon them—in reality as well.

Several survivors of the "rape camps" in the former Yugoslavia reported the presence of video cameras during the rapes, and there are numerous reports of these videos being distributed and sold, among them claims that these tapes have found their way into the Los Angeles pornography market. In September 1992, the films of at least two of these rapes were broadcast on Serb-controlled television.[25] A few years ago, when I gave a presentation about these events and asked if we should not be extremely disturbed that what is being consumed as "pornography" could be in fact, unknown to us, the depiction of a brutal rape, a woman responded that perhaps it is more disturbing to think that even if the violence were known, it either would not matter to the viewer or it would increase his pleasure in viewing it. Confirmation of this is all too easily found: a quick Internet search using the keyword *rape* yields, among Web sites offering research tools and resources on the topic of sexual violence, countless sites advertising "100% real rape," "hard-core non-consensual sex," "the most violent rape pix ever." These sites offer pictures of "raped Chechen women," "young girl brutally raped by three men," "tiny teen gang-raped." Some of the sites run disclaimers in extremely small print that the women portrayed are in fact eighteen or older and consenting, and that no real images of rape are published on the site; some do not. It is at this extreme end of the pornographic spectrum that one confronts the truth of all pornography: a woman's consent to sex is at best a matter of indifference in pornography and very often seen as irrelevant, and in the worst case, the violent imposition of sex on a nonconsenting woman is itself presented as an arousing spectacle.

The objections are not difficult to imagine: the liberal response would be to condemn these extreme images (though most likely not to argue, as is argued with child pornography, that such pornography warrants police investigations and crackdowns on purveyors and consumers) and to argue that mainstream pornography is a very different case altogether. The women are of legal age and clearly consent to the activity depicted. Unfortunately, even this is not true: porn star Traci Lords made more than a hundred hard-core films before she turned eighteen and was a *Penthouse* centerfold at the age of fifteen. Until her age was made known to the authorities and the tapes and magazine banned, the image of Traci Lords's body—her child's body—was consumed as a sexual object. The fact that this was not explicitly known only testifies to the deep ambiguity of the pornographic image. A few years after *Deep Throat* (the first mainstream porn film) was released, its star, Linda Marchiano, claimed that she was raped on the set. Although she fought to have videos of the film recalled, she was unsuccessful and rental sales actually went up once her allegations were made public. Those who cast doubt on Marchiano's credibility can do so (but should perhaps acknowledge that in their efforts to insist that pornography is actually an empowering industry, they have to revile, belittle, and throw the worst clichés of misogyny at women to do so—in effect saying, The whore lied), but whether her claims were true or not is ultimately irrelevant to the fact that viewers who thought is was true found the movie even more appealing for this fact.

There are numerous examples of such troubling ambiguity. The controversial documentary *Raw Deal: A Question of Consent* tells the story of the stripper Lisa Gier King, whose performance at a frat party ended, she claimed, in rape.[26] The entire evening was filmed by one of the men at the party, and this videotape was the evidence that police viewed to decide that King was lying and to charge her with making a false report. The state attorney released this videotape to the general public (purportedly to demonstrate the reasoning behind the controversial decision) over King's protests, and local men scrambled to get copies of it. The tape made for common viewing at subsequent fraternity parties. One of the most revealing objections against treating both Marchiano's and King's claims seriously takes the form of "but she doesn't look like she's being forced"—but this is precisely the question: how could she? In a video or an Internet image, how could one tell if a woman was being raped or not, unless the caption said so? Film critics who watched *Raw Deal* seemed surprised by the fact that the videotaped footage does not answer the question of whether rape occurred or not—it is impossible to tell. What is beyond dispute is that many people who believe it is a recording of a rape are able to watch the videotape for entertainment.

It is telling that many of the images displayed on "rape" sites are identical to images one finds on "mainstream" Web sites, where the women supposedly do consent. In fact, often the only thing that changes is the caption—the very same image is "blonde whore taken anally and loving it" on one site and "young blonde Chechen viciously raped" on another. The viewer looking for depictions of "consensual" sex and the viewer looking for images of rape are looking at the same image. It is this indifference of the image, and not the supposedly disproved causal relationship between rape and pornography, that should be addressed and conceptualized in the discussion of sexual violence. The photographic image in itself cannot demonstrate consent. The illusion that it can is used to shield consumers of pornography from any association with "real" sexual violence. If mainstream pornography by its very nature asserts that all the women depicted "want it," then no one has to engage the difficult question of, How could I tell if they didn't? (and further, Would I care if they didn't?). One can condemn violent pornography and child pornography and real sexual violence without ever feeling implicated; and then one can throw out the word *consent* like a rhetorical hand grenade and run away. But mainstream pornography is an ideology. It is based on the photographic, "real" image, which is in itself ideological. As Adorno writes, "[I]deology is split into the photograph of stubborn life and the naked lie about its meaning—which is not suggested and yet drummed in."[27] The mechanically reproduced pornographic image is ideological because it takes what is unique in time and space—whether a genuinely consenting sexual act or an act of sexual violence—and projects it across all time and space. In that gesture the image "rips the auratic element out" of the portrayed act and turns it into a commodity; recall Adorno's claim that "every close-up in every commercial film mocks aura by contriving to exploit the contrived nearness of the distant, cut off from the work as a whole"—is the pornographic film not the clearest exponent of this?

In Lisa Gier King's case, she voluntarily agreed to strip for the party, and be filmed doing it, but was unaware that this tape would be reproduced and made available to the public. She claims furthermore that the videotape shows her being raped; whether she is telling the truth or not—and are fraternity boys to decide, especially considering that one of them declared at the beginning of the videotape that the proceedings would include "the raping of a white trash, crack whore bitch"?—she certainly had no control over the fate of her sexual image. We know of Benjamin's unease regarding the mechanical reproduction of the face: "people no longer have faces when the face itself becomes a fetishized commodity"[28]—but what of the fate of the body? In pornography, mainstream and otherwise, a woman's body is endlessly reproduced, out of context and very often against her will.

Linda Marchiano is only one of several women who have claimed that they were forced to take part in a pornographic scenario under threatening circumstances. Whether one decides to believe women who claim that they have been raped on set, there is no way to guarantee that it did not occur. A raped woman will also lose any control over her image, which can make its way to a "consensual" Web site with a caption announcing both to her and anyone who wants to take a look that she did consent. Her consent in this case is a fabrication, and yet looking at the image no one can discern this.

Moreover, as uncomfortable as it may be for a liberal viewpoint, sexual violence and pornography often do share the same ideological space. The rape camps in the former Yugoslavia were reportedly steeped in pornographic images, on the walls, on tanks, in the soldiers' rooms. According to the Yugoslavian critic Bogdan Tirnamic, the former Yugoslavia has the "freest pornography market in the world." Serbian tanks were reportedly "plastered with pornography" according to witnesses, and rape victims have testified to the pervasive presence of pornographic materials in the camps.[29] Several survivors have reported that the walls of the rooms in which they were raped as well as the officers' chambers were covered with pornographic pictures. The soldiers reportedly showed pornography to their victims to illustrate what they were going to do to them. Survivors also report that in some cases the soldiers reenacted scenes from the pornographic materials when raping the women. Serbian soldiers themselves have confirmed that pornography was frequently used during the rapes, to assist those who were having difficulty getting an erection.

It is not difficult to see how one can progress from indifference to a woman's consent to arousal at her refusal, or see how the two at least intersect. The mainstream Web site and the rape Web site present the same images for a reason: indifference to a woman's consent, lack of any evidence or concern for her consent, belongs to the logic of rape just as much as explicitly forcing a woman against her will. A consent merely stipulated across time and space, irrespective of circumstances or context, lies at the core of rapist logic. It is the same mindset behind laws still in existence in many countries today that allow men who rape their wives and girlfriends to argue, "once consented, always consented."

But even if one concedes all this, one could protest that the average consumer of pornography is just looking, after all; he's a consumer, not a rapist. Of course all or almost all sex offenders use pornography (a fact that is not mentioned very often), but this doesn't make every man who uses pornography a sex offender. The average pornography consumer is just a passive viewer who has nothing to do with the actual execution of sexual violence. He may be a repugnant person who gets off on images of terrified girls forced into sex, or images of guns inserted in the blood-spattered crotches of headless women, and maybe these images are not faked, but nonetheless he doesn't commit any actual crimes himself. As repulsive as this might be, our free society protects the right of men to have violent, misogynist fantasies and indulge in them as long as they do not act them out (such was the message of the highly popular film *The People vs. Larry Flynt*).

But someone is acting them out (including, according to his daughter, Larry Flynt himself).[30] And even though pornography consumers know this, they do not think about it when they get their newest issue of *Playboy*.[31] The ethical question to ask is why some men do it; how some men are able to do it. To override a woman's protests. To rape a young girl repeatedly and bash her head in with a brick. To get together with their fellow soldiers and gang-rape a female Iraqi prisoner who has no possible means of escape or resistance. As Katharine Viner writes apropos the abuse at Abu Ghraib, there is a connection between what we look at for pleasure and entertainment and what we are capable of doing to another human being.

> It is hard not to see links between the culturally unacceptable behaviour of the soldiers in Abu Ghraib and the culturally ac-

cepted actions of what happens in porn. Of course there is a gulf between them, and it is insulting to suggest that all porn actors are in the same situation as Iraqis, confined and brutalised in terrifying conditions. And yet, the images in both are the same. The pornographic culture has clearly influenced the soldiers; at the very least, in their exhibitionism, their enthusiasm to photograph their handiwork. And the victims in both don't have feelings: to the abusers, they didn't in Abu Ghraib; to the punter they don't in pornography. Both point to just how degraded sex has become in western culture. Porn hasn't even pretended to show loving sex for decades; in films and TV most sex is violent, joyless. The Abu Ghraib torturers are merely acting out their culture: the sexual humiliation of the weak. So Charles Graner and his colleagues can humiliate Iraqi prisoners because the prisoners are dirt; they can humiliate women, forcing them to bare their bodies and raping them, because that way they can show their power.[32]

How it is that there can be so many men, in this day and age, in our neighborhoods and our cities and in every neighborhood and every city, who cannot see a woman as a human being? As an other who feels pain or suffering that shocks us in its intensity instead of exciting or arousing us? "Our relationship with men and creation in general [is] like our relationship with ourselves after an operation—oblivion for suffering."[33] Pornography—from the smiling *Playboy* centerfold to the struggling "Chechen woman"—is a social an-aesthetic, administered to keep us from conceptualizing and resisting the reality of sexual violence. It reassures us that it doesn't really hurt, that since everyone is smiling nothing bad could really have happened. And even if they're not smiling we know that, on some level, they either wanted or deserved it. Pornography reinforces the idea that one can commodify consent and buy it like a cheap magazine. The question must be asked: How can we then behold the literal images of rape—the videotape of the woman raped and beaten by Serbian soldiers? Or the picture of Iraqi women gang-raped by U.S. soldiers? How will we see it, this image that without a headline or an accompanying story is indistinguishable from the images on the Internet, in newsstands, even in so-called political journals in Yugoslavia and Israel? How will we see her suffering? The pornographic an-aesthetic has not only obliterated the context of suffering but has imposed onto its image the compulsion for viewers to enjoy it, and the stipulation that the woman herself enjoys it. The woman gang-raped by Serbian soldiers or by U.S. soldiers is any nameless woman held down by any nameless men and we have already configured our response—to enjoy her suffering—to that image. The pornographic an-aesthetic prevents us from seeing or feeling a depiction of rape as the suffering of the other.

Adorno and Horkheimer were keenly aware of the role that visual representations play in forming murderous prejudices. In "Man and Animal," Adorno and Horkheimer discuss caricature, and note the darkness that lurks behind the seemingly innocuous, seemingly humorous exaggeration of the Jewish caricature: "An over-accentuated human face, an embarrassing reminder of its origin in and degeneration from nature, now arouses only an irresistible urge to indulge in efficient manslaughter."[34] The capacity to caricature is linked to the capacity to murder and to ignore murder. The Jew was depicted as a kind of monster, with grotesquely lengthened or enlarged limbs, a glint in his eye suggesting that he more than deserves the punishment he will ultimately experience. Adorno and Horkheimer also noted the connection between anti-Semitism and misogyny: "The justification of hatred for woman that represents her as intellectually and physically inferior, and bearing the brand of domination on her forehead, is equally that of hatred for Jews. Women and Jews can be seen not to have ruled for thousands of years. They live, although they could be exterminated; and their fear and weakness, the greater affinity to nature which perennial oppression produces in them, is the very element which gives them life. This enrages the strong, who must always suppress their fear. They identify themselves with nature when they hear their victims utter over and over again the cry that they dare not themselves emit."[35] The caricature that pornography offers is a woman with gigantic, artificial breasts, shaved pubes, excessive makeup, and a "naughty look." The alleged sexual appeal of her broken-into body is the kind of beauty Adorno and Horkheimer are referring to when they write that "mutilation is an added luster to female beauty," beauty that is itself "that display of the wound in which subjugated nature recognizes itself."[36] To ensure that neither the givers nor the bearers of that wound recognize it as such, the culture industry deploys a vast number of images that pass off carefully structured violence as spontaneous beauty.

However, one can object, it is ridiculous to suggest that most women who appear in pornography are forced to have plastic surgery and herded onto porn sets at gunpoint (although it should perhaps be noted that women have claimed that this does happen, and even if it does not characterize the "majority" of experiences, one is tempted to ask how many times it would need to happen before it became relevant). One cannot blame the huge success of the porn industry solely on men; after all, it couldn't function without willing volunteers, and women can often make quite a lot of money in it. How does one explain this—should we not after all consider that regardless of how men may or may not view pornography, many women argue that their work in the porn industry is empowering, lucrative, sometimes even as feminist practice? Surely there is some legitimate motivation for their decision. If men's enjoyment is problematic, what about women's?

The first response to this is that sexual consent in the sex industry is a treacherously complex issue. The fact that a woman is not threatened at gunpoint to perform in a porn film or become a prostitute does not meant that she was not coerced in some other way—whether by economic circumstance, threats to loved ones, cultural pressure, or some other source of intimidation. Anyone wishing to argue that women by and large make autonomous decisions to enter the sex trade should inform themselves of the hundreds, if not thousands, of reports of exploitation, abuse, and financial despair that is the background story of so many "consenting adults."[37] The financial incentive to enter the sex industry is yet another point to reflect upon: the majority of jobs traditionally associated with women (cooking, cleaning, and so forth) hardly pay enough to live on. The grand exception to this is when women sell their bodies for sexual consumption. A society characterized by a genuine sense of concern for all its members must surely address this tragic valuation of women and the social contribution they are allowed or encouraged to make.

The second response must be to more closely examine what is meant by enjoyment. In her essay on Adorno, Juliet MacCannell writes that for Adorno, "preservation of the object against a culturally calculated desire is necessary to preserve the subject. . . . Adorno sees the defence against enjoyment as crucial to the subject, and makes it truer of his aesthetic than of Kant's because Adorno saw through, as did the later Lacan, to a secret enjoyment hidden in its 'disinterestedness.'"[38] Enjoyment, then, is a darker affair than the culture industry would have us believe. Slavoj Žižek's insights into "jouissance" in the context of the Holocaust are enlightening here. In his critique of her "banality of evil" theory, Žižek argues that Hannah Arendt overlooks one crucial factor in her analysis of the Nazis: the enjoyment, the jouissance that many of the Nazi officers experienced in torturing and killing Jews.[39] What else accounts for the behavior of Nazi commandants ordering prisoners to dance, sing, or play music even as they were forced to dig mass graves? Although psychoanalysis usually focuses on a subject's jouissance in terms of pleasure-in-pain, or pleasure-beyond-pleasure in regard to that subject's relationship to him- or herself, jouissance has historically often manifested itself as pleasure in the other's pain. This is what is blocked out by the culture industry's insistence that enjoyment, particularly sexual enjoyment, is always positive. As we have seen, Adorno suggests that the culture industry deploys pleasure to undermine the resistance to existing wrongs. We recall also that for Adorno, the an-aesthetizing effect of the culture industry does not only affect our ability to recognize the suffering of others; it numbs us to our own suffering as well.

To explore this further, we continue with MacCannell's reading of Lacan-with-Adorno: for Lacan, the structure of oppression is precisely "la jouissance de l'Autre," of being made an instrument of the other's jouissance. Particularly relevant to our discussion is that this instrumentalization extracts pleasure from the other's pain, turns the other's suffering into jouissance—with devastating consequences. As MacCannell writes in a particularly brilliant passage, "For Lacan, a subject traumatized by being made the imaginary object of the Other's enjoyment will repeatedly restage their horror as that enjoyment in a fantasy adjusted to grant them relief from that abuse, and to return to them some of the enjoyment they lost to the Other."[40] When one considers reports that more than 70 percent of the women involved in the porn industry were sexually abused as children, a picture of that industry as a massive restaging and appropriation of unbearable pain emerges. But even if this figure is wrong or if there is no way to reliably prove that this is the case, one must respond that there is more than one way to be made into the instrument of the other's jouissance. Let us consider the following:

- An estimated $8–10 billion is spent annually by Americans for pornography. This exceeds the combined gross of ABC, CBS, and NBC, which is approximately $6.2 billion.
- Two hundred million copies of *Hustler*, *Penthouse*, and *Playboy* are distributed in U.S. homes every year.
- The combined circulation of *Playboy* and *Penthouse* exceeds that of *Time* and *Newsweek*.
- The average age at which men first see *Playboy* or a similar magazine is eleven years.[41]

- In any major U.S. city and almost every major European city, magazine kiosks display pornographic magazines on street corners and
subway stops. In the United Kingdom, post offices are often housed
in magazine stores where customers buying stamps are faced with
shelves of pornographic magazines; "candy stores" often display
hard-core porn alongside lollipops and jelly beans. In Vienna, to-
bacco stores line their walls with hard-core pornography. In Italy,
newspaper stands sell bus tickets, Barbie magazines, and hard-core
porn. After 10:00 PM several Italian channels begin nightlong adver-
tisements for pornography. In Japan, images of women being tied up
and sexually tortured are common in mainstream films and magazines. In every major airport porn magazines are sold alongside aspi-
rin and souvenirs. In the United Kingdom, and Germany, Austria,
and other European countries, "page 3 girls"—appearing on pages
that feature topless women—or similar phenomena are commonly
found in "respectable" newspapers.

Adorno summarizes the degradation of pleasure in the culture industry
as "to be pleased means to say Yes."[42] Pleasure in the culture industry,
moreover, "means not to think about anything, to forget suffering even
when it is shown."[43] For the ideology of pleasure to survive, it must never
"leave the customer alone, not for a moment to allow him any suspicion
that resistance is possible."[44] The pornographic ideology will not let
women imagine a different kind of sexuality for themselves, surrounding
them even when they are walking down the street or buying stamps. As
Drucilla Cornell notes,

> To strip someone forcibly of her self-image, particularly when that
> image is as basic as that of bodily integrity, is a violation. . . . It is
> the confrontation with the images in their inevitability, because
> they are allowed to pervade our public space so thoroughly, that
> itself constitutes the violation. . . . [T]he images are those that
> have been encoded as the truth of our "sex" in a heterosexual
> masculine symbolic. . . . [I]t is the encoding of these images,
> through their domination of public space, that makes them seem
> as if they were the truth of sex and not just one particular imagi-
> nary.[45]

For a while, perhaps, if a woman has been fortunate enough to have love
and respect in her life, she will resist; she will be disturbed by the inces-

sant bombardment of the monotonous, dead-eyed images of what her sexual enjoyment should look like, but the culture industry will strive to make her capitulate and thus be forced to salvage the only happiness left to her: the happiness of those resigned to their fate. Adorno writes that "everyone can be happy, if only [s]he will capitulate fully and sacrifice his [her] claim to happiness."[46] The images that women confront are all alike and all untrue: "wrenched from all context, detached from thought, [objects] are made instantly accessible to an infantile grasp. They may never be broadened out in any way but like favourite dishes they must obey the rule of identity if they are not to be rejected as false or alien."[47] It will become easier to go numb and keep smiling as the magazine and Internet women do: "the face becomes a dead letter by freezing the most living thing about it, namely its laughter." The culture industry intends, finally, for women to "assimilate themselves to what is dead,"[48] to wrench enjoyment out of every sexual situation no matter how ambiguous, no matter how sadistically motivated.[49]

In an interview with an Oxford student newspaper, Hugh Hefner (founder of *Playboy*) stated that "sex is the most civilizing force on the planet."[50] Presumably the planet that Hefner lives on is the same one in which rape warfare has been used against women in countless conflicts, in which in many countries marital rape is still not considered a crime, in a world where good American men rape an average of 1.5 million women a year. But Hugh Hefner believes in the "civilizing" force of "sex" (by which he means pornography—already a revealing metonymy) because he is an exponent of the culture industry. He and those like him are the technicians of social anesthesia, the modern counterparts of the doctors Pierre Flourens criticized for lying to patients about the pain of an operation, the manipulators of memory who make butchery seem a blissful dream.

In his essay "Sexual Taboos and the Law Today," Adorno mocks the particularly American conception of the "healthy sex life"—the kind of ideological stance that Hefner typifies—regarding it as a "fun morality" that actually hides an ever-increasing repression of sexuality. According to Adorno, "[S]exual liberation in contemporary society is mere illusion," despite that society's obsession with sexual images and discourse.[51] Sexuality is not so much embraced by contemporary Western society as it is administered by it: "sexuality, turned on and off, channeled and exploited in countless forms by the material and cultural industry, cooperates with this process of manipulation insofar as it is absorbed, institutionalized, and administered by society. As long as sexuality is bridled, it is tolerated."[52] Sexuality has been "desexualized" and "neutralized" even as it seems to be everywhere endorsed and exposed.[53] Adorno's sentiment here is very close to that expressed in Roland Barthes's essay on striptease, where Barthes writes that public displays of sexuality can function as a kind of inoculation against the real, threatening power of undisciplined sexuality.[54] Particularly relevant to our discussion is Adorno's assertion that "socialized voyeurism" stands in for genuine sexuality today: "Contemplation by many replaces union with one and thereby expresses the tendency to socialize sexuality that itself constitutes an aspect of sexuality's fatal integration."[55] Adorno further identifies the specific feature upon which this sexual ideology hinges when he writes that "the desexualization of sexuality is strengthened by the premium patriarchal society places upon the female character, her passive docility, weaned from all personal affect, if possible from all aspiration to her own pleasure."[56]

These two sentiments sound like the preamble to a dialectical critique of the contemporary sex industry, but "Sexual Taboos and the Law Today" surprisingly offers nothing of the sort. In fact, Adorno goes so far in this essay as to defend the consumption of pornography and to suggest that the only real danger posed by prostitution stems from the hypocrisy of those who condemn it.

Adorno's first point in "Sexual Taboos" is a Foucauldian one, that modern society has taken what is disruptive and threatening about sexuality and domesticated it. Adorno's belief that there is something in sexuality that resists disciplining, something trivialized and demeaned by the crude machinations of the culture industry, is entirely in keeping with a feminist social critique. His contention that this undisciplined value of sexuality can somehow be found in practices considered sexually taboo by contemporary society, by contrast, reveals a dishearteningly simplistic take on both the nature of taboo and the "nature" of sexuality. Adorno maintains that a few sexual taboos are aggressively enforced even in—or rather, especially in—supposedly sex-positive (indeed, sex-driven) contemporary society. These taboos include pornography, prostitution, homosexuality, and sexual activity involving minors, and Adorno argues that these taboos are maintained by repressed people with authoritarian tendencies. The first of these is most relevant to our discussion here.

Adorno writes that "the allegedly dangerous effects of reading and viewing pornography are hypothetical. It is both foolish and an infringement upon personal liberty to withhold pornography from adults who enjoy it."[57] Adorno's claim that "unmutilated, unrepressed sex in itself does not do harm to anyone" is problematic for many reasons, not the least of which is the suggestion that pornography offers any such thing. The idea that the fragmented, artificial slices of female flesh showcased by pornography somehow represent sex at all, to say nothing of "unmutilated, unrepressed sex" is the kind of simplistic, misogynist statement one expects from Hugh Hefner—and in fact, the *Playboy* founder expressed a similar sentiment when he stated that "the major problems we have on this planet have nothing to do with pictures of people fucking." Second, the argument that pornography is justifiable simply because some people take pleasure in it sits uneasily with Adorno's contention, cited earlier, that pleasure "always means not to think about anything, to forget suffering even when it is shown." Adorno demonstrates his awareness of sexual violence when he writes of the persecution and murder of prostitutes, and yet accepts and defends a discourse that promotes women's passivity and eternal sexual availability.

Adorno paints a picture of contemporary society in which select sexual taboos truly have the force of law, so that transgressing these taboos means challenging social repression and opening oneself to the risks of undisciplined, authentic sexual pleasure. But it was Adorno himself who recognized in *Dialectic of Enlightenment* that pleasure is a helpless "flight; not, as is asserted, flight from a wretched reality, but from the last remaining thought of resistance. The liberation which amusement promises is freedom from thought and from negation."[58] The easiest way to justify the flight into mindless pleasure is to insist that one is actually attempting to escape a terrible reality of repression—and though Adorno well knows how false this insistence is, in "Sexual Taboos" he tries to portray the contemporary world as truly sexually repressed. But, as in an observation that he made apropos of striptease and one that is equally applicable to pornography, Barthes stated that "a few particles of eroticism . . . are absorbed in a reassuring ritual which negates the flesh as surely as the vaccine or the taboo circumscribe and control the illness or the crime."[59] The taboo is not a genuine prohibition; breaking it does not place one on the other side of a repressive law—it places one squarely within the law itself.

As Žižek has often pointed out, supposed violations of or exceptions to the law (crime, illegal institutions, and so on) often constitute an "underworld of unwritten rituals" in which we are libidinally invested but which also allow us to believe—insofar as we insist on their exceptional status—that we are in the main good, decent, law-abiding individuals.[60] This "obscene underside" functions as an inherent transgression that binds a community together: "what 'holds together' a community most deeply is not so much identification with the Law that regulates the community's 'normal' everyday circuit, but rather identification with a specific form of transgression of the Law, of the Law's suspension (in psychoanalytic terms, with a specific form of enjoyment)."[61] This unacknowledged law is the law of the (obscene) superego insofar as it pertains to enjoyment: "symbolic Law guarantees meaning, whereas superego provides enjoyment which serves as the unacknowledged support of meaning."[62] In the case of sexual taboos, such as the one against pornography, the taboo is inherently false and serves only to justify the transgression: its ideological argument is that in a world saturated by pictures of cut-up female bodies, we are nonetheless sexually repressed and need an outlet for all the wild, natural desires we have—an outlet characterized by pictures of cut-up female bodies. As Žižek describes it, there are always two sides to the Law: the law itself and the law's "obscene superego underside," its built-in contradiction, the inherent transgression that paradoxically ensures its existence.[63] On one side of the law, a taboo against pornography—on its underside, the sanction of breaking this taboo.

The theorist who so eloquently attacked the valuation of empty pleasure seems to have fallen prey in this instance to the very illusion of "real," "unmutilated" sexual pleasure falsely positioned as a counterpoint to the repressive, sexually stunted world of the law. The two are one and the same, and Adorno's failure to recognize this indicates a certain limit to his vigilance against the "logic of familiar things."[64]

Jennifer Rycenga, who expresses similar disappointment with Adorno's discussion of homosexuality in the same essay, writes that Adorno's constant critique of bourgeois moralism and his "passionate stance against all oppression provide ample openings to rescue what is liberatory from his thought, and to overlook or minimize his heterosexism."[65] Adorno's insistent demand for critical reflection of the culture industry that goes beyond merely legalistic discussions is a valuable one, especially if one does not wish to remain within a merely legalistic position. One can take from Adorno's work the urgency and value of dialectical reflection and critical debate of sedimented, simplified narratives of sexuality. However, in his essay on sexual taboos, Adorno fails precisely to accomplish this and stumbles over his own investment in a certain aspect of cultural ideology. It is nonetheless possible to draw from Adorno's theory a critique of the culture industry's anesthetic representations of female sexuality, and perhaps even to develop an aesthetic of female sexuality that might counter it.[66] There is much work to be done to expand Adorno's brilliant aesthetic vision in a direction that he himself could not or was not willing to take.

Notes

1. Theodor Adorno, *Aesthetic Theory*, trans. Robert Hullot-Kentor (New York: Continuum, 1997), 13.

2. Theodor Adorno and Max Horkheimer, *Dialectic of Enlightenment*, trans. John Cumming (New York: Continuum, 1995), 144.

3. Adorno, *Aesthetic Theory*, 218.

4. Shierry Nicholsen, "Adorno, Benjamin, and the Aura: An Aesthetics for Photography," in *Adorno, Culture, Feminism*, ed. Maggie O'Neill (London: Sage, 1999).

5. Benjamin was particularly concerned about its potential to reinstate a kind of degraded aura, a cultic value—see the work of Susan Buck-Morss, especially *The Dialectics of Seeing: Walter Benjamin and the Arcades Project* (Cambridge, Mass.: MIT Press).

6. Adorno, *Aesthetic Theory*, 218.

7. Silvia López, "The Encoding of History: Thinking Art in Constellations," in *Adorno, Culture, and Feminism*, ed. Maggie O'Neill (London: Sage, 1999), 70.

8. Quoted in Nicholsen, "Adorno, Benjamin, and the Aura," 57.

9. López, "Encoding," 69.

10. Adorno and Horkheimer, *Dialectic of Enlightenment*, 151

11. Quoted in Geoffrey Hartmann, *The Longest Shadow: In the Aftermath of the Holocaust* (Bloomington: Indiana University Press, 1996), 103.

12. Adorno and Horkheimer, *Dialectic of Enlightenment*, 45.

13. Adorno and Horkheimer, *Dialectic of Enlightenment*, 311.

14. Adorno, *Aesthetic Theory*, 56.

15. Adorno, *Aesthetic Theory*, 56.

16. Kaja Silverman, *At the Threshold of the Visible World* (New York: Routledge, 1996), 99.

17. Adorno, *Aesthetic Theory*, cited in López, "Encoding," 69.

18. Adorno, *Aesthetic Theory*, cited in López, "Encoding," 68.

19. López, "Encoding," 69.

20. National Institute of Justice and Centers for Disease Control and Prevention, *Prevalence, Incidence, and Consequences of Violence Against Women Survey: Findings from the National Violence Against Women Survey*, NIJ and CDC, November 1998. Available at http://endabuse.org/resources/facts.

21. American Institute on Domestic Violence, "Domestic Violence Statistics," American Institute on Domestic Violence, http://www.aidv-usa.com/Statistics.htm (accessed 14 August 2004).

22. I use the word *pornography* throughout this chapter to designate mainstream heterosexist visual pornography, exemplified by magazines such as *Hustler*, *Playboy*, and *Penthouse*. I do not address here homosexual pornography or so-called feminist pornography, a term I have always found misleading. Graphic depictions of sexuality are not in themselves pornographic, and if such depic-

tions are truly "feminist," and attempt to subvert or challenge the commodification of women's bodies and the mythification of her supposed "pleasure," I fail to see the accuracy or usefulness of calling them pornographic.

23. Sherrie Gossett, "Bogus GI Rape Photos Used as Arab Propaganda," Worldnet Daily, http://www.worldnetdaily.com/news/article.asp?ARTICLE_ID=38335 (accessed 15 August 2004).

24. Susan J. Brison, "The Torture Connection," San Francisco Chronicle, http://sfgate.com/cgi-bin/article.cgi?f=/c/a/2004/07/25/CMGF77DFKC1.DTL (accessed 14 August 2004).

25. Catharine A. MacKinnon, "Turning Rape into Pornography: Postmodern Genocide," in Mass Rape: The War Against Women in Bosnia-Herzegovina, ed. Alexandra Stiglmayer (Lincoln: University of Nebraska Press, 1994), 73–81.

26. Billy Corben, director, Raw Deal: A Question of Consent (Spellman/Corben Productions, 2001).

27. Adorno, and Horkheimer, Dialectic of Enlightenment, 147.

28. Nicholsen, "Adorno, Benjamin, and the Aura," 57.

29. See MacKinnon, "Turning Rape into Pornography."

30. Larry Flynt's daughter, Tonya Flynt-Vega, has alleged that her father sexually abused her as a child. See her book Hustled: My Journey from Fear to Faith (Louisville, Ky.: Westminster John Knox Press, 1998).

31. And this is perhaps the key to understanding why one of the only instances of America's explicit condemnation of violence against women concerned the Taliban's regime, and not that of the warring factions in power in Afghanistan before and after it: prior to the Taliban takeover, the jehadin were notorious for their campaigns of rape and torture. These were the same jehadin with whom the United States allied itself to oust the Taliban, and who continue to practice sexual violence against women today. While I in no way wish to downplay the Taliban's oppression of women, I suggest that the way it could be condensed into a specific image—that of women covered head to foot by burkas—affected American sensibilities in way that the mental image of rape and torture of women could and did not.

32. Katharine Viner, "The Sexual Sadism of Our Culture, in Peace and in War," Guardian Unlimited, http://www.guardian.co.uk/comment/story/0,,1222354,00.html (accessed 15 August 2004).

33. Adorno and Horkheimer, Dialectic of Enlightenment, 230.

34. Adorno and Horkheimer, Dialectic of Enlightenment, 252.

35. Adorno and Horkheimer, Dialectic of Enlightenment, 112.

36. Adorno and Horkheimer, Dialectic of Enlightenment, 251.

37. See, for example, reports by Human Rights Watch, Amnesty International, the United Nations, and the U.S. Department of Justice.

38. Juliet Flower MacCannell, "Adorno: The Riddle of Femininity," in Adorno, Culture, and Feminism, ed. Maggie O'Neill (London: Sage, 1999), 151.

39. Slavoj Žižek, The Plague of Fantasies (London: Verso, 1997), 55–56.

40. MacCannell, "Adorno," 153.

41. "Pornography Facts," http://www.womenofsubstance.org/por.htm (accessed 15 August 2004).

42. Adorno and Horkheimer, Dialectic of Enlightenment, 144.

43. Adorno and Horkheimer, Dialectic of Enlightenment, 144.

44. Adorno and Horkheimer, Dialectic of Enlightenment, 141.

45. Drucilla Cornell, The Imaginary Domain: Abortion, Pornography, and Sexual Harassment (New York, Routledge, 1995), 148.

46. Adorno and Horkheimer, Dialectic of Enlightenment, 153.

47. Adorno, The Culture Industry: Selected Essays on Mass Culture, ed. J. M. Bernstein (London: Routledge 1991), 74.

48. Adorno, *Culture Industry*, 82.

49. It is interesting to note how the practice of female genital mutilation (FGM) in African and Middle Eastern countries, performed without anesthesia and using primitive tools such as glass and razors, is seen by the liberal West as a barbaric, patriarchal intervention in women's bodies to force them to conform to male standards of beauty and sexuality, while the practice of breast-enlargement surgery and "genital landscaping," performed under anesthetic in modern hospitals, is commonly accepted as women's natural attempts to "improve" themselves.

50. Hugh Hefner interview with Andrew Morris, "Oldest Swinger in Town," *Cherwell*, 18 May 2001, 16–17.

51. Adorno, "Sexual Taboos and Law Today," in *Critical Models: Interventions and Catchwords*, trans. Henry Pickford (New York: Columbia University Press, 1998), 72.

52. Adorno, *Critical Models*, 73.

53. Adorno, *Critical Models*, 73.

54. Roland Barthes, "Striptease," in *A Barthes Reader*, ed. Susan Sontag (New York: Hill and Wang, 1998).

55. Adorno, *Critical Models*, 75.

56. Adorno, *Critical Models*, 75.

57. Adorno, *Critical Models*, 81.

58. Adorno and Horkheimer, *Dialectic of Enlightenment*, 144, emphasis added.

59. Barthes, 85–86, emphasis added.

60. Slavoj Žižek, "'I Hear You with My Eyes'; or, The Invisible Master," in *Gaze and Voice as Love Objects*, ed. Slavoj Žižek and Renata Salecl (Durham: Duke University Press, 1996), 101.

61. Slavoj Žižek, *Metastases of Enjoyment: Six Essays on Women and Causality* (London: Verso, 1994) 55.

62. Žižek, *Metastases*, 56.

63. Žižek, "'I Hear You with My Eyes,'" 101.

64. For a further critique of Adorno's conception of the "authoritarian personality," see Slavoj Žižek, *For They Know Not What They Do: Enjoyment as Political Factor* (London: Verso, 2002).

65. Jennifer Rycenga, "Queerly Amiss: Sexuality and the Logic of Adorno's Dialectics," in *Adorno: A Critical Reader*, ed. Nigel Gibson and Andrew Rubin (Oxford: Blackwell, 2002), 36.

66. In my view, one of the most exciting approaches to the possibility of this aesthetic can be found in Kaja Silverman's *At the Threshold of the Visible World* (New York: Routledge, 1996).

10

Living with Negative Dialectics

Feminism and the Politics of Suffering

Renée Heberle

Feminism encourages the public expression of gendered and sexual oppression and suffering to accomplish the ends of recognition and justice.
There has been a very visible backlash in the United States against what
some identify as "victim feminism," much of which focuses on those
feminist efforts that attend to sexual violence.[1] I am not interested in
engaging with these arguments, as they trivialize, dismiss, and delimit the
terms on which pain and suffering are real to the women who experience
them and suggest a limited responsibility on the part of the social world.
I am quite convinced that it is only through public struggles over the
terms on which sexuality will be lived in private that women can become

free from gendered and sexual coercion and violence. Rather than engage the current status of the discourse and activism about feminism and suffering on these terms, I take it up in the spirit in which I think Theodor Adorno would encourage us to take up the entanglements and complexities of seeking recognition and justice in conditions of late modernity.

Informed by a strong Nietzschean impulse, Adorno was profoundly concerned that we remember suffering in such a way that does not render justice (or the struggle for justice) contingent upon the ownership of suffering, attachments to suffering, or static meanings of suffering. Adorno argues that resistance to domination and oppression is not in itself a moment of freedom, autonomy, or agency. Nor does the accomplishment of recognition through collectivizing experience necessarily signal progress. It is this that has led to his reputation as a pessimist with respect to the potential for constructing a better future.

Adorno articulated as a categorical imperative of the post-Auschwitz world that we must live in such a way as to never allow anything like the Holocaust to happen again. The difficulty is, of course, that Adorno, along with other critical thinkers, understands the Final Solution not as a mistake or barbaric regression to premodern reactions to perceived threats, but as an extension of the logic of modern instrumental reason and exchange relations naturalized through capitalist relations of production and distribution. These systems flourish, albeit in the context of political systems that can be loosely described as liberal democratic. The contradiction persists that within liberal democratic society, these systems insistently cultivate political, social, and cultural relations of domination that systematically obscure and deny the potential to create the conditions of freedom.

Creating a living, present memory of suffering as a means by which to prevent its repetition is, thus, treacherous. Thinking in modernity is inevitably circumscribed by identitarian categories and instrumental reason. Adorno never claimed to escape this form of thinking. He "lived with the guilt of what he was thinking." More to the point, he lived and thought through his awareness of his survivor guilt as a Jew for whom accident of birth and circumstances of life allowed escape from Hitler's ovens. He felt his complicity with and embeddedness in the lived realities that made the Holocaust possible in such a fashion that the very form and substance of his philosophy should be read as a response. Adorno (in)famously wrote that it is barbaric to write poetry after Auschwitz. He later softens this claim, but perhaps not really, when he writes at the end of *Negative Dialectics*: "Perennial suffering has as much right to expression as a tortured man has to scream; hence it may have been wrong to say that after Auschwitz you could no longer write poems. But it is not wrong to raise the less cultural question whether after Auschwitz you can go on living—especially whether one who escaped by accident, one who by rights should have been killed, may go on living."[2] Adorno said he was enmeshed in the guilt of what he was thinking as an intellectual in the post-Holocaust age. He recognized his embeddedness as a subject in the very form of thinking that he argued made the Holocaust possible. To survive after Auschwitz calls for the "coldness, the basic principle of bourgeois subjectivity, without which there could have been no Auschwitz; this is the drastic guilt of him who was spared. By way of atonement he will be plagued by dreams such as that he is no longer living at all, that he was sent to the ovens in 1944 and his whole existence since has been imaginary, an emanation of the insane wish of a man killed twenty years earlier" (363). The vigilance this experience calls for and the form of critical theory such awareness adopts is negative dialectics.

Survivor guilt is not part of what women and feminists should experience, even in a world wherein sexual violence, predation, exploitation, and suffering is so common and apparently systematic. However, there are moments wherein a sensitivity to a kind of survivor guilt becomes clear, such as in the unwillingness to elaborate successful resistance to attempted rape in the context of speak-outs or public discourse about rape because of sensitivity toward women who did not "successfully resist." We also see the impulse in the self-consciousness within feminism and feminist movements about privilege among and difference between women. It signifies the lack of control the individual has over the objective world; the felt experience of that lack often translates as a productive form of guilt. It is this sensibility that Adorno's work often captures.

Adorno shares with feminism a desire to theorize from the concrete rather than deduce facts from general principles. Like many feminists, he is sensitive to the issues of difference, of embeddedness in one's historical context, and of the gradual erosion of the significance of the particular as abstract identitarian principles come to govern the most private, interior, subjective experiences.

However, Adorno says, "A question's urgency cannot compel an answer if no true answer is obtainable; even less can the fallible need, however desperate, point the direction of the answer" (212). Suffering does not speak easily in the public domain. It may be a prerequisite of knowing truth that we recognize and somehow find space for the need, but the conceptualization of suffering, which is what occurs when we lend it a voice that communicates in the public domain, is never adequate. The object never goes into its concept without remainder. There is always already something not heard, not rendered, in the conceptualization of suffering. "The power of the status quo puts up the facades into which our consciousness crashes. It must seek to crash through them. This alone would free the postulate of depth from ideology. Surviving in such resistance is the speculative moment: what will not have its law prescribed for it by given facts transcends them even in the closest contact with the objects, and in repudiating a sacrosanct transcendence. Where the thought transcends the bonds it tied in resistance—there is its freedom" (17). Adorno is thinking here about the articulation of suffering as a subversive moment. He goes on to say that "freedom follows the subject's urge to express itself. The need to lend a voice to suffering is a condition of all truth. For suffering is objectivity that weighs upon the subject; its most subjective experience, its expression, is objectively conveyed" (17–18).

Adorno understood that the quality of human experience is irreducible to concepts and categories, yet the human condition is nonetheless defined by concepts and categories. They are what we can know, while the excess that haunts all conceptualization makes it impossible to reach the truth through expression. This is precisely why politics is not about truth; though we may imagine a truth that haunts politics, we cannot speak it or know it without doing damage to a qualitative difference between experience and that which it is possible to communicate. Adorno writes: "Direct communication to everyone is not a criterion of truth. We must resist the all but universal compulsion to confuse the communication of knowledge with knowledge itself, and to rate it higher, if possible—whereas at present each communicative step is falsifying truth and selling it out. Meanwhile, whatever has to do with language suffers of this paradoxicality" (41).

As have some feminisms, Enlightenment epistemologies and social expectations demand that moments of suffering be transparently knowable. The irrational, desire—that which would not otherwise naturally have an identity in the social world—comes to be identified. It forces nonidentitarian moments into interchangeable relationships with other objects in the service of explanation and regulation. Modern ideologies of the individual and the authenticity of subjective knowledge deny or obscure the critical limits of the integrative forms of representation and communication available to the subject at any given time.

For Adorno, we are embedded in our social context through which our sense of self is continually being constructed. Relations of domination between the self and what is other never quite absorb the excess of what is other. His is a *limit* philosophy of knowledge. He argues in a lecture titled "The Experiential Content of Hegel's Philosophy" that Hegel understood "that the limits of knowledge to which its critical self-reflection leads are not something external to knowledge, not something to which it is merely condemned from the outside; rather, they are inherent in all moments of knowledge."[3] It is thus through immanent critique, through awareness of the inherent limits of knowledge, that we sustain critique in an as yet unreconciled world. Through critique, through the determinate negation of positive forms of knowing otherness, and without mapping out or presuming to plan the outcomes, we can suggest alternative ways of knowing otherness in the world. The dialectics of this process, the *negative* dialectics, leave a remainder, something not covered by the concept. This remainder sustains the possibility for critique and for change from a world whose dominant epistemologies and social forms encourage projects that privilege the subject as knower and thus a rigid separation between self and other. It is this that I find valuable for a feminism that privileges the concrete, the experiential, and the inarticulable not as "authentic" or prior to discourse and engagement in the political world, but rather as what haunts action, speech, and expression as we engage. Adorno argues for an approach to experience and the political through the elusive quality of experience. "Spontaneity of experience is neither continuously maintainable nor downright positive; the truth is not there. The most subjective, the immediate datum eludes subjectivity."[4] He set up the terms on which we may remember the historicity of experience and its link to memory, its increasingly mediated quality in modernity, and that our efforts to represent experience are always already political.

In his lecture, Adorno discusses the individual as constituted by the social world: "Not only does the bearer of personal consciousness owe his existence and the reproduction of his life to society. In fact, everything through which he is specifically constituted as a cognitive subject, hence, that is, the logical universality that governs his thinking, is, as the school of Durkheim in particular has shown, always also social in nature."[5] He goes on: "A mode of thinking that understands the individual as *zoon politikon* and the categories of subjective consciousness as implicitly social will no longer cling to a notion of experience that hypostatizes the individual, even involuntarily. Experience's advance to consciousness of its interdependence with the experience of all human beings acts as a retroactive correction to its starting point in mere individual experience."[6] Adhering to the tradition of materialist philosophy, Adorno believes that it is in the sensuous world that we create knowledge, that we become cognitive subjects. This relationship is our experience and in itself constitutes objects for interpretation by ourselves and others. Our relationship to otherness then becomes an object of interpretation. We can thus think of experience as a prism through which we interpret the world. The pattern of reflection is mediated by a dynamic totality and by parts of our lives and the lives of others to which we have no immediate cognitive access.

Adorno's discussion of experience is complicated by history; the quality of our experience changes over time, with the totalities that experience confronts. Walter Benjamin had a profound and lasting influence on Adorno's understanding of the changing quality of experience in late modernity. The notion of experience in the name of which Adorno mobilizes remembrance is not measurable or easily described. It refers back to Benjamin's ideas about experience.

Benjamin refers specifically to the quality of experience in modernity in two essays, "The Storyteller" and "Some Motifs on Baudelaire."[7] These essays articulate the difference between the knowledge of experience elicited through information, *Erlebnis,* and the experience that develops meaning through the remembrance and the passing on or communicating of experience over time, *Ehrfarung.* In storytelling, it is the latter that is elicited. Storytelling engages the audience in an active contemplation of the world.

The auratic quality of the experience related through the art of storytelling survives through the contemplative relationship the audience develops to the story. The story becomes embedded in their lives, as it has been in the life of the storyteller, rather than merely "jostling the consciousness" temporarily as pieces of information. It may be the simplicity of the story, the "dryness" of its terms and its lack of explanation that makes it live on historically, gathering meanings. As with painting, which entails the looking back and forth of the painter and the painted, which subsequently creates a living relationship between the audience and the painting, the storyteller and his or her audience interact. The reconstruction of experience as information eliminates that part of communication, making it instrumentally available to everyone while reducing its meaning to a brief shock effect. Information, that which attempts to bring experiences of others close to the listener or reader through explanation, destroys the auratic content of the experience, fails to enter it into the life of the listener as anything but a passing moment, easily replaced.

In "The Storyteller" Benjamin writes of the consuming flame of the story. Experience is only tellable in retrospect, never in its lived moments. As it is told, the life of the teller—he or she whose experience is being told—becomes remembered only through the terms of the story. "His gift is the ability to relate his life; his distinction, to be able to tell his entire life. The storyteller: he is the man who could let the wick of his life be consumed completely by the gentle flame of his story. This is the basis of the incomparable aura about the storyteller."[8] Experience evaporates upon contact with deliberative consciousness. For Benjamin it is the unapproachability of experience that sustains its nonidentity. As it is known it is consumed. Like the wick of the storyteller's life that is a source of wisdom, experience can only be known in retrospect; distance, in the sense not of objectivity or disinterestedness, but of time and attitude, is the key to understanding. The closer one is, the harder it is to see. This is why Benjamin, in this essay, privileges the storyteller and the flaneur over the man of the masses. These characters sustain a kind of relaxed, contemplative distance to the object that allows the experience of aura, of the witnessing of history "at a standstill" in the object. His thinking is reminiscent of that in Nietzsche's preface to the *Genealogy of Morals* (1967) wherein Nietzsche speaks of experience as a vanishing point to which we persistently refer while rubbing our ears after the bell tolls and wondering what it was that just happened.

Adorno sustained the argument about the quality of distance that Benjamin said offered access to the aura of the object, allowing it to live. However, Adorno's ideas about experience encourage an intensely political, though aesthetically styled, existence with the otherness of experience in the world. The dialectical images of Benjamin's theory of experience become still and then consumed as they are known in the contemplative life of the knower. History becomes a series of images seen only in retrospect, not in a dialectical movement in which subject and object are necessarily interactive. Benjamin's storyteller only knows experience as always already past. Adorno's theory allows for a sustained engagement with the world in experience.

Adorno, like Benjamin, found things immanent in the quality of individuality in the nineteenth century that sustained nonidentity. Adorno looks to the nineteenth century to show how the potential for nonidentity, immanent in historical movement, is continually extinguished by encroaching instrumental reason. He argues that nineteenth-century bourgeois individualism weakened the objectifying power of knowledge, contributing to the subversion of grandly oppressive systems theories of philosophy and science that privilege the objectification of the world in explanation as a path to knowledge. He said that the individual's capacity to be discriminating in his or her experience of the object rather than objectifying it through grand systems was present in early capitalism. In other words, individuality in the nineteenth century contained moments of resistance to the encroaching instrumental forces of enlightenment. It strengthened the individual's capacity to be discriminating in his or her experience of the object. Adorno explains the dialectical, negative effects of this discrimination: "Even in the conception of rational knowledge, devoid of all affinity, there survives a groping for the concordance which the magical delusion used to place beyond doubt. . . . If this moment were extinguished altogether, it would be flatly incomprehensible that a subject can know an object; the unleashed rationality would be irrational. In being secularized, however, the mimetic element in turn blends with the rational one. The word for this process is discrimination."[9] The concept of discrimination is a complex blending of a secularized mimetic element of intuition with the modern rational approach to knowing the object. This is not an affirmation or uncritical celebration of nineteenth-century individualism; it is an effort to redeem nonidentity, which never fully disappears, on terms immanent to historical experience in capitalist society. The longing for nonidentity, of the "groping for the concordance which the magical delusion used to place beyond doubt" continues, even in late capitalism.

Calvin Thomas persuasively argues that Adorno argues not for a "going back to," but rather for a resuscitation of, experience that is always already there, even in the age of organization. In "A Knowledge That Would Not Be Power: Adorno, Nostalgia, and the Musical Subject," Thomas argues that Adorno "mobilizes nostalgia." In other words, he engages it for purposes of critique rather than engaging himself in an empty yearning for times gone by. Thomas wonders how accusations that Adorno engaged in an elitist form of nostalgia for a protected bourgeois past could hold when Adorno's life work was consumed with critiquing the regression to or fetishization of *any* historical moment or theory of days gone by. Thomas argues: "Adorno's nostalgia . . . is not for a lost object but rather for a lost *possibility*, is not a conservation of the past but a move to redeem the hopes of the past. Adorno does not favor a regression but calls for the reactivation of a fundamental human capacity—a capacity without which the word 'human' in the sense not of 'humanist' but of 'humane' could hardly apply: the capacity to suffer and to recognize the suffering of others."[10] Thomas goes on to argue that Adorno was attempting to reactivate a capacity to hear, to experience, to be in a relation of mimesis to the suffering other and the suffering in ourselves; to know not through abstract concepts or totalizing knowledge, but through an elective affinity to otherness. It is through this relationship of elective affinity that we might know otherness in a manner that sustains connection without erasing difference.

Enlightenment knowledges deny the many-sidedness of any object and force the object into dimensions of total visibility. In denying many-sidedness, idealist philosophy creates abstract forms in the name of truth-telling. This affirms, prior to engagement, our access to the object. It signifies a will to identify first and engage only after the cognitive relationship is in place. This offers a sense of familiarity with the object, even if the familiarity is bred from our prior awareness that something is strange or alien as opposed to normal and close.

This process of constructing knowledge, or historical meaning, constitutes a political relationship with experience playing a critical role. In using the word *critical*, I am not referring to the sensibility with which most feminists approach experience, as ethically relevant or as truth-telling *in itself*. Rather, I am thinking of experience in its role as a critical check on Enlightenment forms of knowledge. Our experience is not transparent to us but always subject to interpretation; thus experiential cognition is itself an interpretive process. "Experience forbids the resolution in the unity of consciousness of whatever appears contradictory. For instance, a contradiction like the one between the definition which an individual knows as his own and his 'role,' the definition forced upon him by society when he would make his living—such a contradiction cannot be brought under any unity without manipulation, without the insertion of some wretched cover concepts that will make the crucial differences vanish."[11]

It is not through the totalizing and distancing effects of objectivism, or through knowledge stimulated by reliance on subjectivity and identity that we will come to live in peace with otherness. Rather, the subject must see its own power enough to yield to the object without fear of self-annihilation. It is through a complex process of recognition, one allowing for the constitutive nature of the object, that we might come to know ourselves and others. This "coming to know" implies an endless, iterative, and reflexive process of understanding that is receptive of the experience of otherness, including the otherness within ourselves.

Adorno limits the conception of the subject through theorizing the primacy of the object. He places the subject and object in an asymmetrical, nonhierarchical relationship that recognizes the constitutive nature of the object without eradicating the subject. It is asymmetrical because the subject is objectified in thought in a radically different way from how the subject knows the object. The subject cannot be without the object, without objectification, while the object can be (but not be known) without the subject or the subjective element.

If Adorno argues that the subject is a thing of the world and for the primacy of the object, how is the relationship nonhierarchical? "By primacy of the object is meant that the subject, for its part an object in a qualitatively different sense, in a sense more radical than the object, which is not known otherwise than through consciousness, is as an object also a subject."[12] The subject must see power in its object status, not weakness. It must see that a dominative relationship to the object is not necessary for it to exert itself in the world. He argues that it is in the cognitive relationship to experience as an object that the subject can do this. "The objective content of individual experience is not produced by the method of comparative generalization; it is produced by dissolving what keeps that experience, as being biased itself, from yielding to the object without reservation—as Hegel put it: with the freedom that would relax the cognitive subject until it truly fades into the object to which it is akin, on the strength of its own objective being."[13] This is Adorno's version of what others have called unity in diversity or the problem of sustaining autonomy within a community of solidarity. But his understanding is more complex than either of those familiar phrases imply. For Adorno, in experiencing the other one must yield to the other without losing one's sense of self. Only then can one know the other in such a way as to resist the dominative relationship that comes with positivist or idealist forms of knowledge that demand that the knowing subject wrap its mind around the known object or the other and assume total knowledge. For Adorno, this subject/knower is more powerful, not more resigned, in its contingency. In addition, this subject would recognize that it too is an object of knowledge to the other. We should always already be vulnerable to being seen and transformed in relationships to others. "Approaching knowledge of the object is the act in which the subject rends the veil it is weaving around the object. It can do this only where, fearlessly passive, it entrusts itself to its own experience. In places where subjective reason scents subjective contingency, the primacy of the object is shimmering through—whatever is in the object is not a subjective admixture. The subject is the object's agent, not its constituent; this fact has consequences for the relation of theory and practice."[14] For Adorno, the critical issue is not who or which social identity can know truth, but how truths that always already exist for us in the social world can be unlocked through constellations and how that interpretation can be transformed into new social meanings. "As for the privileged character which rancor holds against it, truth will lose that character when men stop pleading the experiences they owe it to—when they let it enter instead into configurations and causal contexts that help to make it evident or to convict it of its failings."[15]

Adorno makes clear that truths exist in the world and affect it materially but cannot represent it totally. "Yet the surplus over the subject, which a subjective metaphysical experience will not be talked out of, and the element of truth in reity—these two extremes touch in the idea of truth. For there could no more be truth without a subject freeing itself from delusions than there could be truth without that which is not the subject, that in which truth has its archetype."[16] Truths, as the cognitive relationship between the subject and the object, are in flux and are permeable.

Benjamin influences Adorno, encouraging him to see the importance of the idiosyncratic and the unexpected aspects of the object through the process of interpretation. The element of surprise, as if one were shocking oneself into a realization about an object, is critical to Benjamin's method of knowing within the conditions of modernity. Benjamin juxtaposes the constructed perspectives of many different, representative, historical figures such as the flaneur (made famous by Baudelaire) the whore and the street sweeper, to what he called dialectical images. "Benjamin's images functioned like switches, arresting the fleeting phenomena and starting thought in motion or, alternately, shocking through to a standstill and setting the reified objects in motion by causing them to lose their second-nature familiarity."[17] But remember that for Benjamin, the experiences elicited through this were consumed in the telling. They could not live in the present, but only as the past. They identify the experience being told through the process of the story, reconstituting it.

Adorno understands concepts as historical images, produced by human beings, which can be placed in relationship to an object in order to center it and illuminate its contradictory positioning in a world characterized by reification, the exchange principle, and identity thinking. "Authentic philosophic interpretation does not meet up with a fixed meaning which already lies behind the question, but lights it up suddenly and momentarily, and consumes it at the same time."[18]

Adorno argues that as cognitive subjects, we must live in the tension-filled spaces at the edges of our particular being in order to live in freedom with others. Persistent critique of the limits of one's own cognition may keep the moment of objectification temporary while sustaining the distance that defeats the smothering requirements of sameness. It will help us avoid the reification of difference as merely the flip side of identity or as a generic space between self-contained identities.

For Adorno, resistance to the integrative forces of the world requires distance between self and object or other. This is not a distance of disinterested objectivity, which implies that as subjects we can remove the moment of mediation from our relationship to others. It is a distance encouraged by the method of knowing in constellations that perpetually illuminate those sides of the object, of the other, that traditional means of knowing disregard as a burden or as insignificant to the conclusions the knower is obliged to reach. Adorno's thinking functions more like a cipher than a diagnosis: "He who interprets by searching behind the phenomenal world for a world-in-itself which forms its foundation and support, acts mistakenly like someone who wants to find in the riddle the reflection of a being which lies behind it, a being mirrored in the riddle, in which it is contained. Instead, the function of riddle-solving is to light up the riddle—Gestalt like lightning and to negate it (aufzuheben), not to persist behind the riddle and imitate it."[19]

What is it in Adorno's theory that I would argue contributes to a feminist politics? The relevance of Adorno's work, and much of critical theory, for feminism has been recognized with respect to concerns about the relationship between women's oppression and the domination of nature. Feminists have shown in many different ways how the repression of "woman" and the "feminine" represents the denial of nature and the catastrophe of historical progress. Modern Western thought consistently looks to woman as representative of what is necessarily private, natural, and prerational. The Hegelian-Marxian tradition has been shown to be no less biased in its perspectives on public and private lives and the contribution of each to history. In that tradition, women only become historical actors if and when they enter the sphere of public production; there is nothing specific to gendered lives having anything to do with historical change. Post-Marxist critical theory calls attention to the crises of modern subjectivity, challenging the concept of Reason as an emancipatory tool of conquest over necessity by a unified, self-knowing subject. Through these theoretical moves, it contributes to challenges to the notion of the unified Subject of history and examines the egocentric identity development of the individual as always interrupted by that which is inaccessible to instrumental reason.

Rather than assuming the suffering of nature as a residual effect of historical progress, as do many Hegelian-Marxian theories of history, Adorno argues that the persistence of the dialectic, the domination of nature in history, defies closure in identity. I attempt to advance these important insights with an inquiry into how Adorno might be relevant to urgent questions raised in contemporary feminist theory and politics about sexual identity and suffering. Adorno's work did not develop in a linear fashion; it is difficult to argue that any concept, including experience, is used consistently across his works. However, his critical theory of totality in modernity as legislated by Reason and identity logic is relevant to feminists concerned with politicizing sexuality in a world apparently fragmented and contingent, yet thoroughly suffused with relations of domination and power. For Adorno, I argue, totality is not final. It is not a self-contained apparatus operating out of the reach of individuals. It remains in a state of antagonism with its own terms of existence. It is nonidentical with its objects. Thus, while as subjects we cannot willfully step outside the terms of its logic, we can potentially subvert its terms where its limits become identified as such through interpretation of experience. There is always a constitutive outside to any system. The project of critique is to bear witness to its boundaries, to make them visible and thus to denaturalize the givenness or commonsense status of subject/object, human/nature, self/other relations of dominance. This is where experience and the constellatory quality of Adorno's thought precludes reductionist causal or structural analysis in interpreting the meaning of experience.

Feminist thought has been emerging and expands only through engagement with internal differences between women and constant and often conflictual self-questioning. Feminist theory remains critical because it is situationally grounded and contextual. We can take this imperative in a direction that does not lead us into the aporias of identity thinking through looking again at Adorno's theory of experience and negative dialectics. He prefers that a respectful distance, not a separation, be sustained between the truth and politics. Suffering does not speak easily and does not reveal truth in the public space of politics. Lending the experience of suffering a voice is a condition of truth and is an imperative if we are to aspire to live in a world free of suffering. However, that experience in itself is subject to interpretation and will take on life beyond the intention, will, or control of the teller as he or she moves on and the world moves on. This should not be thought about with dismay or resignation, but with an eye toward proliferating the possibilities of resistance that can be seen only simultaneously by keeping an eye on the horizon of freedom.

Notes

1. See, for example, Katie Roiphie, *Sex, Fear, and Feminism on Campus* (New York: Little, Brown, 1993); and Christina Hoff Summers, *Who Stole Feminism? How Women Have Betrayed Women* (New York: Simon and Schuster, 1994).

2. Theodor Adorno, *Negative Dialectics* (New York: Continuum Press, 1987), 363. Further page references are cited parenthetically in the text.

3. Theodor Adorno, *Hegel: Three Studies*, trans. Sherry Weber Nicholsen (Cambridge, Mass.: MIT Press, 1993), 76–77.

4. Adorno, *Negative Dialectics*, 39–40.

5. Adorno, *Hegel*, 63.

6. Adorno, *Hegel*, 94.

7. Walter Benjamin, *Illuminations*, ed. Hannah Arendt (New York: Random House, 164).

8. Benjamin, *Illuminations*, 109.

9. Adorno, *Negative Dialectics*, 45.

10. Calvin Thomas, "A Knowledge That Would Not Be Power: Adorno, Nostalgia, and the Musical Subject," *New German Critique* 48 (1989): 163.

11. Adorno, *Negative Dialectics*, 152.

12. Theodor Adorno, "Subject and Object," in *The Essential Frankfurt School Reader*, eds. Andrew Arato and Eike Gebhardt (New York: Continuum Press, 1988), 502.

13. Adorno, "Subject and Object," 506.

14. Adorno, "Subject and Object," 506.

15. Adorno, *Negative Dialectics*, 42.

16. Adorno, *Negative Dialectics*, 375.

17. Susan Buck-Morss, *The Origin Of Negative Dialectics: Theodor W. Adorno, Walter Benjamin, and the Frankfurt Institute* (New York: Free Press, 1977), 102.

18. Theodor Adorno, "The Actuality of Philosophy," in *The Adorno Reader*, ed. Brian O'Connor (London: Blackwell Press, 2000), 31–32.

19. Adorno, "The Actuality of Philosophy," 31.

11

Negative Dialectics and Inclusive Communication

Paul Apostolidis

The grim, foreboding vision of a seamlessly "administered world" haunts the critical theory of Theodor Adorno. "Something is provided for all, so that none may escape," he wrote concerning the culture industry. For Adorno, the ineluctability of incorporation into the self-perpetuating rituals of social domination was not only the modus operandi of the culture industry but also the hallmark of life as such under late capitalism. Adorno's meager hopes for political resistance were pinned, accordingly,

I am grateful to Renée Heberle, Lisa Disch, and Judith Grant for their generous and thoughtful comments on earlier drafts of this chapter.

on necessarily lonely acts of resistance by defiant intellectuals and inscrutable works of art. Solidarity with the victims of injustice could only be expressed indirectly, through aesthetic creation and criticism as such rather than through political communication and mobilization.

How contrary in ethos seem the concerns of feminist thinkers and activists who have waged battles attacking the systematic exclusion of women from positions of power in major political, economic, and cultural institutions, and mobilizing collective action to make society more inclusive. Preoccupied with the ways in which individuals' absorption into the "bad totality" of modern capitalism made a mockery of critical subjectivity, Adorno evinced little recognition of the injustices of exclusion. Nor was he particularly attuned to the varying patterns of inclusion within social processes that made women's experiences of domination different from those of men—for instance, the gender-specific modes of consumerism generated by the culture industry.

Yet a theory of democratic inclusion responsive to feminist concerns still can benefit from a reconsideration of Adorno. While not seeking to justify the gaps and crude overgeneralizations of Adorno's social theory, we can turn to Adorno for philosophical reinforcement in facing one of the main challenges for a democratic theory of deliberation: imagining how to expand the scope of meaningful and effective participation in democratic processes, without forcing individual idiosyncrasies and particular experiences into hiding. Adorno argued for a form of critical reason that prioritized the subject's unrelenting vigilance of its own tendency to assimilate the object's concrete, particular characteristics to abstract, general concepts. This theory of negative dialectics—extended beyond the realm of individual consciousness and considered as a criterion and practice of intersubjective relations—can illuminate certain vital features of a democratic communication that is inclusive without suppressing particularity.

Envisioning precisely this sort of communication is the core problematic of Iris Marion Young's theory of inclusive democracy. As we shall see, a retrospective glance at Adorno leads us to some important qualifications of Young's theory. It also takes us some distance toward a rapprochement between early critical theory, with its notorious blind spots regarding women, and contemporary critical theory that self-consciously bears the profound influence of feminist thought.

Young's Theory of Inclusive Communication

In *Inclusion and Democracy*, Young provides a critical alternative to theories of deliberative democracy, which, she argues, do not sufficiently account for the ways that democracy must enable people from an enormous range of different social locations to express their ideas and experiences. Young generally sympathizes with proponents of deliberative democracy in criticizing aggregative or adversary models of democracy. For Young, theories of democracy that make citizenship coextensive with voting, pressure-group activism, and other self-interested actions leave a number of tasks unfulfilled. These especially include inquiring into the origins of individual preferences rather than taking them as given, and conceptualizing a form of rationality that is carried out by a public and is able "to evaluate the moral legitimacy of the substance of decisions."[1] Young agrees with the theorists of deliberation that "democracy is a form of practical reason" wherein "participants arrive at a decision not by determining what preferences have greatest numerical support, but by determining which proposals the collective agrees are supported by the best reasons."[2] She faults other theories of deliberative democracy, however, for several specific biases, among which lies the tendency unduly to privilege argument over other forms of communication.[3]

Why should deliberation theorists not assign special primacy to argument, when, as Young agrees, democracy requires the public to determine which proposals "are supported by the best reasons"? Young answers this question by pointing to the problem of "internal exclusion," which she defines in this way: "Though formally included in a forum or process, people may find that their claims are not taken seriously and may believe that they are not treated with equal respect."[4] This can happen—and in fact tends to happen—because the dominant form of communication in official or mainstream public forums is not socially neutral. Rather, norms defining proper ways of communicating in venues ranging from federal judicial hearings to local school board meetings are grounded in historically specific social and cultural contexts. People who are familiar with those contexts and have been educated in how to follow those norms thus have a clear advantage in public deliberations. The dominant expectations in U.S. society are that a person worth listening to will speak dispassionately, avoid more than minimal bodily gestures, prefer literal language to metaphor and hyperbole (while still mobilizing abstract concepts with ease), and talk in a way indicating the superiority of written speech to other modes of communication. People in positions of authority and ordinary citizens alike attribute greater validity to remarks that exhibit "the construction of an orderly chain of reasoning from premises to conclusion," and to speakers who acknowledge that "there are some premises that all the discussants accept, and a generally accepted conceptual and normative framework for framing the issues." These norms, Young contends, thwart the ability of even those deliberations undertaken by the most radically diverse group of participants from being either truly inclusive or genuinely democratic. In concrete terms, the "speech culture of white, middle-class men" systematically dominates and deauthorizes the communicative endeavors of "women, racialized or ethnicized minorities, and working-class people" (37–40).

Democratic theory and practice, Young insists, must respond to this problem by expressly valuing forms of communication other than argument. Doing this allows communicative forums truly "to take all needs and interests into account," a necessary condition for formally democratic politics to lead to substantively just outcomes (30). Young identifies three kinds of expression to which communicative democracy should specifically attend: greeting, rhetoric, and narrative.

Greeting refers to "those moments in everyday communication where people acknowledge one another in their particularity"; when the speaker "announces 'here I am' for the other, and 'I see you'"; when she further "announces her distance from the others, their irreducible particularity." For Young, there is an *ineradicable*, crucially physical moment in greeting. In greeting someone, a person "responds to the other person's sensible presence," often with physical actions that complement speech, such as "handshakes, hugs, [and] the offering of food and drink." This physical interaction, in turn, expresses a sense of ethical obligation that seems to be of an exceptionally strong order: "the sensual, material proximity of the other person in his or her bodily need and possibility for suffering makes an unavoidable claim on me, to which I am hostage" (57–59). What is the nature of this claim, and what obligations ensue for the greeter? Young specifies that the one who greets another thereby declares, first, his or her commitment to engaging in a sustained discussion with that other person; second, his or her willingness to trust the other person enough to make the conversation work; and third, his or her acknowledgment that he or she and the other are in a relationship of mutual accountability. Such a relationship requires the greeter to seek to know the particular circumstances of the one being greeted, and to be especially attentive to the latter's vulnerability to suffering that inheres in his or her embodied status. In the course of a discussion in which there is disagreement, moreover, the act of greeting will have primed the greeter to forego references to what "all reasonable persons" should think in favor of "more particular" appeals based on that knowledge of the other (61).

Rhetoric and narrative, likewise, provide portals through which particularistic and socially situated experiences can enter into the conversation. Young takes *rhetoric* to refer to styles of speaking that reflect one's "attention to the particular audience of one's communication"—for instance, an emotional tone; the use of figures of speech; or the employment of visual media, including bodily expression (65). Theorists of deliberation (notably Jürgen Habermas) tend categorically to distinguish rational speech from rhetoric (in Habermas's case, attributing "communicative" intent to the former but only "strategic" intent to the latter). In contrast, Young argues that being "truly rational" should mean attending to rhetoric rather than attempting to "bracket" it. Besides concretely acknowledging the characteristics of the audience in its particularity, rhetoric "motivates the move from reason to judgment" and "from thinking to committed action" (64, 69). Without rhetoric, then, communication is shorn of its practical context. The point of democratic communication is to illuminate that context and proceed to address problems within it, rather than futilely attempting to transcend or avoid it.

Narrative, which Young also calls "situated knowledge," further helps bring that context to the fore. Ordinary argumentation "sometimes excludes the expression of some needs, interests, and suffering of injustice, because these cannot be voiced within the operative premises and frameworks. . . . Storytelling is often an important bridge in such cases between the mute experience of being wronged and political arguments about justice" (37, 72). Narrative, Young believes, can initially sensitize the hearer to the experiences of the storyteller, even when these experiences cannot yet be meaningfully articulated within the prevailing bounds of rational argument, or to the values and cultural meanings that lead the narrator to "normative starting-points" that differ from those that are dominant. Storytelling can further help "affinity groups" with shared experiences and exclusions find one another and begin to reflect collectively on how to define those experiences and how to secure space for themselves on the public agenda. For Young, consciousness-raising groups associated with the women's movement, in which women found safe places to tell stories of battering and sexual harassment, perfectly exemplify the contribution of narrative to communicative democracy (73–75).

Against critics who warn of the ease with which greeting, narrative, and rhetoric can be manipulated to derail their inclusive effects on democratic communication, Young emphasizes that these processes are "important additions to argument in an enlarged conception of democratic engagement," rather than alternatives to argument (79). The critics are right to be at least somewhat skeptical. How many times have commentators on the right resorted to anecdotes about "welfare queens" driving Cadillacs, supposedly paid for with fraudulently acquired welfare benefits, to justify cuts in public assistance to poor women? Why, despite President Bill Clinton's famous personal comfort in interacting physically and rhetorically with African Americans, did his administration ultimately help redefine affirmative action in terms of fighting "reverse discrimination" against whites? Nevertheless, Young rightly points out that sticking to what is commonly recognizable as rational argument does not necessarily prevent manipulation or deceit, either. Conservatives have eminently rational-sounding arguments, too, that welfare enforces a sense of personal failure and dependency in recipients, complete with objective-looking statistical data. When the Right claims to speak for and in the interests of poor women, Young gives us some new and potentially influential ways to evaluate the validity of these claims. We might consider, for example, whether conservative spokespersons have given a genuine greeting to those women's participation in public discussion, with all the ethical consequences that greeting entails. We could also assess whether, in their rhetoric, they demonstrate their willingness to fashion claims in ways that respond to the concrete particularity of the people most directly affected by their proposals.

Does Young, however, go far enough in developing her theory of the role of alternatives to argument within democratic communication? In the cases of greeting and narrative, these alternative forms seem mainly able to set the stage for rational argument in the dominant mode. Literally, in a temporal sense, they precede rational argument. They do not, however, seem to have much ongoing effect on the structure of rational argument itself. True, in discussing greeting, Young makes the potentially quite consequential assertion that speakers in a communicative interaction must avoid appeals to "all reasonable persons" and instead direct their persuasive comments to specific interlocutors in ways that recognize the interlocutors' particular social situations. This would be quite a strong criterion for inclusive communication indeed, if it were applied to the individual elements of an argumentative appeal. However, Young seems to conceive of this condition of communication in a more limited fashion, as simply a preliminary, explicit recognition that this other group is involved in the discussion, before going on to explicate an argument in the traditional sense. Hence she writes: "In practice in mass politics this means public acknowledgement by some groups of the inclusion of other social groups or social segments" (61).

The case of rhetoric is somewhat more complicated. Here, Young makes a positive plea to expand the notion of rationality itself to encompass the style and tone of speech, to view rhetoric as part of reason rather than auxiliary or hostile to it. She further contends that "any discursive content is embodied in a situated style and rhetoric," emphasizing the difficulty and limited utility of distinguishing between the rational and the rhetorical (64). Yet the process of argumentation, which is also still part of a more broadly conceived practice of rationality, seems to remain essentially the same. Rhetoric, like greeting and narrative, serves an instrumental function in orienting argument toward the particular experiences and values of a particular audience or individual. It does not, however, alter the practice of argument as such.

If argument indeed carries with it the sociocultural baggage Young identifies, then perhaps an even more effective way of ridding reason of this ballast would be to imagine a less mechanical and additive relationship—that is, a more interactive and mutually constitutive relationship—between argument and nonargumentative modes of communication, elevating the latter from mere instrumental value to being, in some sense, ends in themselves. In earlier writings on these issues, Young herself actually seems to have been thinking more along these lines than she does in *Inclusion and Democracy*. In a discussion of the traditional Western philosophical distinction between reason and affectivity, which received its classic formulation in Kant's conception of the good will and continues to influence deontological moral thought through to the present, Young endorses Adorno's critique (in *Negative Dialectics*) of the "logic of identity" that the notion of impartial moral reason presupposes. She describes this identitarian logic as the compulsion by which "thought seeks to have everything under control, to eliminate all uncertainty and unpredictability, to idealize the bodily fact of sensuous immersion in a world that outruns the subject, to eliminate otherness."[5] Anticipating her later work, she goes on to locate and criticize the persistence of this ideal of impartiality within Habermas's exclusion of "the concreteness of the body, the affective aspects of speech, the musical and figurative aspects of all utterances" from his model of ideal communication. The problem with Habermas, for Young, is his failure to acknowledge that "in the practical context of communication . . . such ambiguous and playful forms of expression usually weave in and out of assertive modes, together providing the communicative act."[6]

The challenge for an ethics of communication would thus seem to be to move toward a vision of a communicative practice incorporating a relation of mutual criticism and reconstitution between these two elements. Instead of pursuing this task, however, Young backpedals, both in this earlier piece and in *Inclusion and Democracy*. I would propose that Young set Adorno aside too soon and that a closer look at Adorno's theory of negative dialectics helps us make this move toward a more dynamically mediated, productive, and mutually transformative relationship between argument and nonargumentative forms of communication, and thereby toward a more capacious vision of democratic communication with respect to the inclusion of women and other historically subordinated groups.

Negative Dialectics and Inclusive Practices of Communication

As Adorno conceives it, negative dialectics is an *askesis* of the intellect in the age of late capitalism. It is a spiritual exercise or regimen by which thought seeks contact with the transcendent, defined in paradoxically materialist terms as the object in itself. It is a process, moreover, that requires thought to assume an attitude of self-denial toward the concepts that it incessantly produces out of its fecundity. For Adorno, finally, negative dialectics signifies a discipline of subjectivity and subjectivation that responds to what he views as the historically specific, mortal peril of critical thinking in an era of the giant corporation, mass culture, and the welfare-warfare state. The starting point of negative dialectics is the recognition of "nonidentity": the fact that concepts are not identical to their objects, and that objects always leave a "remainder" not contained by their concepts.[7] Concepts, therefore, always refer to nonconceptualities. And they do this more potently—and even *become* these nonconceptualities, though never totally—following upon the exertions of dialectical thought: "As the concept is experienced as nonidentical, as inwardly in motion, it is no longer purely itself; in Hegel's terminology, it leads to its otherness without absorbing that otherness. It is defined by that which is outside it, because on its own it does not exhaust itself. As itself it is not itself alone" (157). Dialectical thinking thus means making the relations between the concept and its nonconceptual otherness reflective, substantively altering and intensifying these relations. Such thinking offers "insight into the constitutive character of the nonconceptual in the concept" and invigorates the concept by reconstituting it as its otherness, to which, however, it never becomes wholly identical, even though every concept by its nature claims identity with its object. This generative act (reconstituting the concept as its otherness) thus depends on a stance of "unswerving negation" toward the concepts that thought yields, toward the "compulsive identification [between concept and object] which the concept brings" (12, 159).

Adorno's suggestion that truth arises from a voluntary effort by rational thought to "grant precedence" to the nonconceptual resonates with key aspects of Young's critique of deliberation, and allows us to pursue this critique further. First, there is a common sense that the truthfulness of rational processes depends crucially on their relation to a moment of physicality, a relation that at least temporarily inverts the traditional hierarchies of mind over body and subject over object. Dialectical thinking relies on a "moment" of thought that Adorno calls "immediate consciousness": "Whichever part of the object exceeds the definitions imposed on it by thinking will face the subject, first of all, as immediacy"(39–40). This "moment of spontaneity" is neither simply an active cogitation of the mind nor only a making-present of something to the mind, although it is in part both of these things—it also involves a "somatic" or bodily moment. It is a "sensation" that is both "part of consciousness" and "equally that which consciousness does not exhaust," "the not purely cognitive part of cognition" (193). This moment of thought enables thought to "transcend itself" in two ways: first, in the sense of "disintegrating" the false identities declared by its own concepts and moving closer to "the thing itself"; second, in the sense of presenting thought with an ethical-practical imperative: "The physical moment tells our knowledge that suffering ought not to be, that things should be different. Woe speaks: 'Go.' Hence the convergence of specific materialism with criticism, with social change in practice" (145, 203).

Young's emphasis on the physical aspect of greeting can be deepened and made more exacting with reference to this component of negative dialectics, in ways that make her conception of inclusive communicative practices better able to challenge the tendencies of rational argument to reproduce social domination. Accordingly, we might conceive this spontaneous welcoming of the other in her concrete physicality and particularity as involving an additional element that Young herself does not address: an element of negativity, expressing a recognition by the speaker of the necessary failure of her conception of the other to grasp the truth of the other's needs, concerns, and social situation. Further, physical sensation would not only have a role within the communicative interaction as a temporal "moment," a fleeting prelude to a conversation that would then proceed as an ordinary exchange of ideas. Beyond this, physicality would also become a "moment" within the interaction in a more rigorously dialectical sense, such that these sensations would repeatedly infuse the speaker's attempts to articulate rational claims and allow the speaker to gain a critical perspective on every such claim's constitutive inability to attend entirely to the other's experiences. Finally, this more dialectical relation between rational assertion and sensation would continually reintroduce a sense of the other's suffering physicality into the interaction, and of the speaker's ethical obligation not only to try to understand that suffering but also to transform the social forces that cause this suffering. Such a dialectic would substantialize—quite literally flesh out—the relationship of mutual accountability that Young provocatively contends is established by greeting.

Referring back to Adorno can further help us hone Young's argument on behalf of the inclusionary, democratizing implications of rhetoric. Adorno himself calls for "a critical rescue of the rhetorical element" for the good of philosophy, which he notes has traditionally striven to vouchsafe its own truth by establishing its otherness from rhetoric (56). "In philosophy," he writes, "rhetoric represents that which cannot be thought except in language. It holds a place among the postulates of contents already known and fixed. Rhetoric is in jeopardy, like any substitute, because it may easily come to usurp what the thought cannot obtain directly from the presentation" (55). Since philosophy aims to know the truth that lies behind such immediately accessible, "already known and fixed" contents, it has continually sought to "abolish language"—to get to the truth of its object by decisively getting beyond language as such. As an alternative and antidote, Adorno proposes "dialectics—literally: language as the organon of thought." Truth, Adorno argues, lies not in any definitive disjunction of reality from language but rather in "a mutual approximation of thing and expression, to the point where the difference fades. Dialectics appropriates for the power of thought what historically seemed to be a flaw in thinking: its link with language, which nothing can wholly break" (55–56).

Focusing on communication rather than (only) philosophical reflection, Young develops the notion of the practical import of rhetoric beyond the merely suggestive form it takes in Adorno's text. Adorno criticizes traditional philosophy for disdaining rhetoric because the latter "is incessantly corrupted by persuasive purposes." Absent these elements of persuasion, Adorno contends, "the thought act would no longer have a practical relation" (55). As we have seen, Young makes the related but more nuanced point that rhetoric situates a communicative intervention in a specific relation to a particular audience, enabling the speaker to express her sense of accountability to her listeners through a variety of linguistic and paralinguistic means that resonate in a familiar way with them. And for Young, rhetoric not only brings the practical context of speech to a higher level of self-reflection and explicitness—it further provides the motivation that enables the leap from critical-reflective thought to political and social action. Nevertheless, Adorno's conception of the dialectical relation between rhetoric and cognition offers a basis on which to enhance the dynamism and interactivity of the relation between rhetoric and argument in Young's theory, ameliorating the instrumentalism of this latter association. Young urges us to see argumentative discourse as "embodied" in rhetoric, and to appreciate both the content and style of argument as coequal elements of reason. Adorno, in turn, leads us to specify further that communication displays, enacts, and generates the most robust form of reason when truth-claims and the rhetorical aspects of argument continually refer back to each other, such that at every step of the argument the speaker's words are shaped by the practice of attending to the audience in its concrete, socially situated particularity. Such stringency would approach a guarantee that rhetoric would not wind up a mere auxiliary to argument, as it threatens to do in Young's theory, but rather would imbue and transform the structure of argument at its most minute levels, "to the point where the difference fades" between rhetoric and the logic of propositional truth-claims.

Young's argument on behalf of admitting narrative into democratic communication can also be adjusted by applying an Adornian perspective, in a way that enhances the prospects that allowing storytelling into the conversation will make the communicative interaction more substantially inclusive. Recall that Young defends narrative as a valid and necessary element of democratic deliberation because she recognizes that the logical structure of an argument, with its built-in and unavoidable basic premises, invariably excludes certain experiences and values that cannot find expression within this normative framework. Adorno, too, is preoccupied with the exclusionary operations of systematic thinking, criticizing the regimenting universalism of idealist logic as the quintessence of "rage" against the nonidentical (23). Rather than suggesting a total abandonment of systematizing thought, however, he advocates a more flexible, improvisatory, particularized practice for coming "to perceive the individual moment in its immanent connection with others" (26). Adorno thus proposes the construction of provisional "constellations" of concepts as an alternative to exclusive reliance on the "step-by-step progression from the concepts to a more general cover concept" (162).

The constellation, Adorno writes, "illuminates the specific side of the object, the side which to a classifying procedure is either a matter of indifference or a burden" (162). Constellation building requires a deliberate relaxation of systematic methodicism and a concomitant animation of thought with elements of "play," "clowning," and "mimesis" (14–15). The primary problem to be overcome, once more, is the concept's inevitable failure to achieve full identity with its object, even as it both falsely claims to do so and gestures toward the nonidentical. Yet it is not just concepts as such that create this problem, but more pointedly concepts as they are mobilized within logically structured discourse, within which the whole systematically imposes meaning on the parts. Hence the need for philosophy as the composition of constellations, since "constellations represent from without what the concept has cut away within: the 'more' which the concept is equally desirous and incapable of being. By gathering around the object of cognition, the concepts potentially determine the object's interior. They attain, in thinking, what was necessarily excised from thinking" (162).

For Young, the glimmer of understanding of women's normally unrepresented experiences that narrative provides can become the basis for a new normative ground, undergirding a new or revised, logically structured argument about the meaning and nature of justice. Adorno yet again prods us to imagine a less linear, less instrumental conception of the relation between rational argument and less normatively authoritative forms of communication. We might envision, that is, the playful and experimental juxtaposition of women's personal narratives to form constellations illuminating experiential particularity; and these thought-images would then furnish the necessary negativity for the continual revitalization of theories of justice, brought about through an ongoing negative-dialectical relation between theory and constellation. Negative dialectics, for Adorno, entails a "mobility . . . of consciousness," an "interactive" relation between "theory" and the immediate experiences of the object made possible by constellations, a "doubled mode of conduct" in which "both attitudes of consciousness are linked by criticizing one another" (31). Accordingly, narrative-constellations would not simply generate new starting points for arguments about justice conducted in the traditional mode. They would instead migrate into the interior of such arguments, re-creating their structures from within, producing a form of argument that involved a highly mobile attentiveness to both personal stories and abstract normative claims, and to the continuously unfolding critical implications of each for the other.

Rethinking Young's analyses of greeting, rhetoric, and storytelling in light of Adorno thus yields the following general point. In the interest of making communication more inclusive of women and other historically subordinated groups, and thus more conducive to justice, Young argues that elements of physicality, communicative style, and narrative must supplement traditionally conceived processes of deliberation. But these democratizing effects can become all the more pronounced if the relations between the traditional and nontraditional communicative practices Young discusses are set in dialectical relation to each other rather than merely instrumentally conjoined.

Preparing for Dialectics-in-Communication: Gender, Immigration, and Meatpacking

Admittedly, this praxis of communication sounds demanding in the extreme, an ideal that any number of practical constraints on actual communicative interactions could easily sabotage. Such constraints range from inevitable lapses of concentration to the predictable need to clarify or more thoroughly justify particular rational claims, which, precisely by forcing the speaker to spell out her logic more carefully and systematically, would necessarily distract from the effort to keep the dialectical moment of physical sensation alive. But of course, such circumstances also pose obstacles to individual critical reflection in the mode of negative dialectics; they make it more difficult, but not impossible. A more serious challenge, however, might be that we go astray by attempting to apply categories intended for a critical praxis of subject-object relations to intersubjective interactions, where the ability and responsibility for fostering dialectical reflection is shared rather than individual.

It is unnecessary to view this shift of categories as fundamentally suspect, nonetheless, because there are certainly moments of individual responsibility within intersubjective encounters that this model of negative-dialectical communication can help us theorize. I want to propose here that negative dialectics can be most readily incorporated into the inclusive communicative practices Young advocates as a praxis of *listening* to the Other across power-saturated divisions of class, race, gender, or a combination of these. This means that we need to turn the tables briefly and imagine not that the more privileged interlocutor is the speaker who is greeting and rhetorically addressing the one whose voice is usually muted or silenced, as Young does, but rather that the latter is speaking and the former is listening—though in a way that itself curiously involves aspects of greeting and rhetoric. It also implies a special attentiveness by the former to the thought-images that might arise through the constellational juxtaposition of the Other's stories. The point is for this more socially advantaged listener to take and demonstrate responsibility for becoming more capable of engaging in communication with the Other that continually reanimates rational formulations of ethical standards and political strategies by dialectically incorporating the particular experiences of the Other.

It is important to stress here that I mean to imply neither any essentialist, higher theoretical capacity of the socially privileged interlocutor, nor any special role of this individual to make dialectics or theory "happen" in a communicative context. Notwithstanding the truth of what Young writes about subaltern groups' historical lack of access to education and other benefits that interpellate subjects as rational agents, the main idea both for her and for me is to broaden the understanding of what "theory" is and to conceptualize new ways for members of dominant groups to think and act in response to the legitimate insistence by subaltern intellectuals that it is not *their* responsibility to teach the members of these privileged groups about their own racism and sexism, or to rid them of it. Innovative practices of listening seem a good place to start, and critically reworking Young's theory with the aid of Adorno helps us imagine how these might be defined.

The following example might help illustrate such an interactive context. In a small city near the place where I live in rural eastern Washington State, Teamsters Local 556, which represents the workers at several large meatpacking and food-processing plants, recently held a public event to denounce unsafe working conditions and to build community support for the workers' efforts to improve job-related health and safety and increase respect for workers' dignity.[8] Mexican immigrant women make up a majority of the workforce at the two frozen-food plants (Smith Frozen Foods and Lamb-Weston), and constitute roughly 40 percent of the workforce at the Tyson Fresh Meats beef-processing plant (which at that time was owned by Iowa Beef Producers [IBP]). More women than men spoke at the event, although there were more men than women in the audience, probably reflecting the somewhat greater reliance of Tyson on male labor. All the workers gave personal testimony (most of it in Spanish, with English translation provided) to the ways they had suffered physically and emotionally as a result of unsafe, unsanitary, and abusive practices on the part of their employers. The workers emphasized, moreover, that these practices were usually related to inordinately high speeds of production and called for these speeds to be diminished. Maria Chavez, a beef-processing worker at Tyson, described suffering infections in her hands because she had found it impossible to keep her gloves clean while keeping up with the line speed. Teresa Moreno, who also worked at Tyson in processing, recounted how what could have been a temporary disability had become permanent because the company had refused to send her to a doctor for an injury, which she had sustained because the speed of production left her too little time to sharpen her knife. Sandra Stewart, who worked on the line making frozen Hot Pockets at Lamb-Weston, told of how she had decided to challenge the verbally abusive behavior of supervisors out of consideration for the fact that "someday [her] children might have to work there" and that, as a single mother, she alone had fundamental responsibility for making her children's future as bright as possible.[9]

Besides other workers, the audience included students from an elite, private liberal arts college, professionals, and religious persons from the community. Most of the workers were Mexican, while most though not all the community members were Anglo/a. Our Adornian reworking of Young's theory enables us to conceptualize a particular way in which these audience members could receive the comments and physical presence of the speakers, a way conducive to facilitating subsequent communication among workers, and between workers and community members, to maximize genuine appreciation of the speakers' specific experiences and ideas. What is required is for these listeners to *prepare themselves* for articulating the kind of greeting and employing the sort of rhetoric Young has in mind and for engaging in some level of dialectical interaction between greeting and argument, and between rhetoric and argument, in actual communication. They would do this by receiving the workers' speeches in such a way that the listeners (1) had a constant reminder to themselves of their inevitable failure to understand wholly the speakers' experiences (or, as Young puts it elsewhere, to eschew the Habermasian fantasy of "symmetrical reciprocity" in communication, of ever exactly seeing things from the other's point of view);[10] (2) tried to the greatest extent possible to hang on to the moment of immediate sensation in encountering each of the speakers—in his or her self-manifested, injured, physical particularity—when reflecting on that person's rational demands for a reduced speed of production and for community involvement in disputes with management, and when contemplating courses of moral-practical action in response to the worker's statements; (3) attended to the speakers' attempts to use rhetoric to address community members in *their* concrete particularity, to invoke a sense of mutual accountability; and (4) listened and observed each speaker carefully to gain a sense of the forms of rhetoric that might eventually work to communicate back to that individual a confirming recognition that this relationship of mutual accountability existed. Engaging in such preparation for communication is, of course, not the same thing as carrying out the kinds of dialectics-in-communication that I sketched earlier in my initial attempt to elaborate and stretch Young's theory with reference to negative dialectics. But these preparatory *askeses* are easier to imagine in themselves, and they also help us envision a bit more clearly how such dialectics-in-communication could actually come into practice.

To conceive of what the dialectical incorporation of narrative constellations into deliberative contexts might look like, in turn, we need to examine the structure and agenda of the event as a whole. The forum involved three kinds of speeches. The workers' remarks came first and were followed by a keynote address, given by Eric Schlosser, author of *Fast Food Nation*, the popular exposé of food- and worker-safety hazards in the meatpacking industry. The final speakers were union officers and a community activist, who exhorted audience members to join in the workers' struggle for justice and reported on the steps that were being taken to challenge the companies, in particular a health and safety survey of the workers and plans to bring a reform proposal to management. Thus, the main point of the workers' speeches was to appeal to the audience in the mode of personal narrative, setting the stage for the more abstract, generalizing, and purposive-rational comments of Schlosser and the organizers. I want to avoid overstating the distinctions between these various speakers; as I have mentioned, the workers not only related their stories of suffering and mistreatment but also articulated causal claims to the effect that production-speed goals and management practices were to blame. In addition, both union officials had been workers in the meat-packing plant for many years, and both prefaced their more extended remarks about organizing tactics with references to their own work-related injuries. It is also worth noting that the agenda did not restrict women to the discursive mode of narrating direct personal and bodily experience, insofar as both the community activist and one of the two union officials—indeed, the union's principal officer and central leader— were women. Nonetheless, individual narrative furnished the dominant tone, form, and purpose for the current line-workers' speeches.

Now, it is undeniable that, from a purely instrumentalist perspective, the order and relative emphases of the speeches in the forum followed a well-worn formula for effective political organizing: sparking outrage and sympathy through personal stories that engender emotional responses, and then channeling that aroused sentiment into a prearranged path of action. Adorno would certainly have been attuned to these instrumentalist aspects of the situation and would likely have criticized them for reflecting a general societal tendency by which genuinely dialectical thought was increasingly giving way to a philosophically and politically barren vacillation between emotionalistic subjectivism and a technocratic obsession with action, a dynamic he saw as generated and easily controllable by big business and the bureaucratic state.[11] Nevertheless, unless we are prepared to endorse an extreme and monolithic view of the pall cast by "instrumental reason" over the late capitalist world, it seems unjustified simply to dismiss the forum as wholly manipulative in this manner and to disregard the prospects for critically reflective communication to which it may have given rise. Such a preemptory move seems especially unnecessary given that this forum was, after all, grounded in a spirit of resistance to the economic forces that, for Adorno, most sturdily underpinned the ascendancy of instrumental rationality. Local 556 is affiliated with the prodemocracy, dissident reform movement led by Teamsters for a Democratic Union, which is struggling against not only corporations but also the culture of "business unionism" favored by the Hoffa-allied "old guard," with its suppression of rank-and-file activism and routine cooperation with employers in exchange for secure positions and a steady flow of membership dues.

Besides serving to energize and mobilize a political coalition, then, the forum can also be viewed as an occasion at least potentially creating space for inclusive communication across lines of social difference that could involve elements of negative dialectics. We can begin to map this space by considering the workers' personal stories as a constellation of narratives. As was the case with rhetoric and greeting, so likewise here it is necessary to shift our perspective from that of the speakers to that of the listeners, to achieve some notion of how what could be called constellational communication might work in practice. The workers did not present their remarks deliberately in the form of a constellation of narratives. Instead, composing a constellation out of their stories required the agency of the listener, although the event planners facilitated this step by placing the workers' speeches all together in the first part of the program. What precisely did this constellation "represent" that the individual narratives themselves were not capable of making accessible to these audience members?

In part, this "more," as Adorno calls it, was the experience of mistreatment by supervisors as something held in common by Mexican and non-Mexican workers alike, since one of the speakers, Sandra Stewart, was neither a Mexican immigrant nor of Mexican origin. It was also partly the experience of being simultaneously a victim and a responsible agent, which became more vivid through the juxtaposition of Stewart's testimony with the other two women's stories than would have been possible through the former's narrative alone. And it was, in part, the irony and double bind faced by wage-earning women who labor for paychecks to contribute to their families' well-being, yet in doing so may expose their families to new rigors of disciplinary intervention by corporate institutions. This irony emerges when one considers Stewart's stalwart commitment to improving her children's future in relation to Chavez's disturbing account of how the company humiliated her and violated her family's privacy by blaming her family members for causing her infections and by proceeding to investigate the cleanliness of her home and the hygiene of her relatives. At the same time, the relation of contrast evoked by this constellation calls our attention to a particular experience of racism, inasmuch as it reminds us of the long and painful history of restrictive U.S. border-control policies that have reflected a stubborn suspicion that Mexican immigrants are unclean, likely diseased, and hence a threat to the "American" people.[12]

Constructing these constellations and discerning the insights they make available, as a mode of listening, is still just a preliminary step toward the dialectic between such immediacy and theory in a communicative context that I proposed above might be possible. How could community members and the male or white workers in the audience not only engage in constellational apprehension but further bring these narrative-based moments of "spontaneous experience" into a sustained, critical relation with social theory? What would the practical consequences be, were listeners to critically juxtapose these moments with general diagnoses of these workers' situation, with proposals for political action in response, and with feminist, Marxist, Chicano, and Latino social theories more broadly?

Doing this would mean listening to Schlosser's citations of the appalling national statistics on worker injuries in the meatpacking industry in a way that not only appreciates the magnitude of these figures but also questions how the hazards posed by elevated chain speeds differently affect men and women, and how they have distinct consequences for white and Mexican workers. Weaving an awareness of the thought-images composed through narrative constellations into mundane practices of communication could further lead to changes in political strategy. Above all, attending to these constellational moments could help spark a critical reconsideration of the union's hitherto commonsense position that the key to effective and inclusive mobilization of the rank and file is to organize based on the spatial distribution of work groups and the problems experienced by workers as "workers," rather than making special efforts to address the race- and gender-specific circumstances. Constellational communication further means finding in the workers' testimonies moments of critical illumination regarding social theory. These experiences of insight confirm, for instance, the efforts of some thinkers, including Young as well as Nancy Fraser and Carol Brown, to call attention to women's domination through corporate and government systems of "public patriarchy," and to characterize these power circuitries as just as crucial to understanding women's contemporary experiences as the intrafamilial relations that are emphasized by many feminist theorists.[13] Likewise, they resonate with attempts in the wake of the Chicano movement to rethink Mexican racial-ethnic solidarity in nonessentializing ways that enable communication with people of other racial positionings.[14] They also counsel the value of carrying forward the Gramscian project of analyzing how class is lived and contested not only through specific work processes but also through configurations of, and sorties against, hegemony, conceived in gendered national and transnational terms.

All these constructive endeavors, however, depend vitally on the persistence of negation. The logic of negative dialectics requires that the force of narrative constellations not simply be subsumed in a finalistic, linear way by giving rise to better-developed critical-social theory and plans for action. Instead, constellational thinking, with its special resources of negativity, should come into play with each stitch in the fabric of communicative—and listening—praxis.

Conclusion: On the Historical Grounds of Negative Dialectics

We should turn again to the relationship Adorno sees between social theory and philosophical method, before concluding this discussion of Adornian modifications of Young's suggested practices of inclusive communication. For Adorno does not see negative dialectics as a universally valid method of critical-reflective thought. Quite to the contrary, he insists that philosophical method in general should self-consciously respond to its sociohistorical situation and that negative dialectics in particular has a historical warrant. This historical imperative, theorized most extensively in *Dialectic of Enlightenment* and reinvoked in *Negative Dialectics*, is the near-total evaporation of the social bases for autonomous, critical subjectivity as a result of the epochal transitions from bourgeois-liberal to corporate capitalism, from the early liberal state to the national-security state, and from bourgeois culture to mass culture.

As I noted at the outset of this chapter, Adorno's theory of late capitalist society included only scattered reflections on conditions faced by women, and these had no structural influence on the shape of the theory as a whole. This certainly does not mean, however, that the justification for thinking in terms of negative dialectics vanishes once theorists start interpreting history from a feminist perspective. Rather, we can view Adorno's injunctions about the relationship between negative dialectics and late capitalism as one model of how to accomplish a more general and more flexible goal: formulating methods of critical reflection and communicative practice that do not seek a grounding in (or as) abstract, absolutist-universalist principles, but rather engage in a perpetual dialectic of mutual criticism with a historically attuned, theoretical account of social power relations.

Moreover, it is essential to remember that Adorno, with his lifelong emphasis on the crucial significance of culture for social-power relations, was anything but a proponent of vulgar economic determinism. Social theory was for him no "objective science" but rather a historically situated labor of reflective thought that itself was forever in need of determinate negation in light of the nonidentical that each of its successive renderings inevitably excluded.[15] Hence, by insisting that Marxist social theory had to break free from the solipsism of its traditional categories and concepts of analysis, by virtue of the critical force unleashed by dialectical reflection on historically specific experiences of nonidentity, Adorno can be seen as radically challenging the boundaries of received social theory in a manner not unlike that found in later, socialist feminist writings—as making a call for social theory to reinvent itself through rigorous engagement with concrete particularity in ways hitherto uncontemplated by historical materialists focused exclusively on the class struggle, and on those aspects of the class struggle in which (white) men have been the principal agents. On a more substantive level, additionally, there is more than a slight affinity between Adorno's exhortations to think the cultural, economic, and political dimensions of social power as a totality and Young's argument some years ago (against models of "separate spheres" of patriarchal and capitalist domination) that "we need not merely a synthesis of feminism with traditional Marxism, but also a thoroughly feminist historical materialism, which regards the social relations of a particular historical social formation as one system in which gender differentiation is a core attribute."[16]

Accordingly, insofar as a silencing or denial of women's experiences in their concrete particularity, and especially in their dimensions of physicality, constitutes an important element of women's subordination in contemporary society, the rhythms and rigors of negative dialectics can indeed enrich attempts by theorists such as Young to conceptualize those relations of power, along with practices that would alter them. To return a final time to our main example, Mexican immigrant working-class women have numerous experiences that are especially prone to being suppressed and misrepresented in mainstream discourses. Proponents of welfare and social-service restrictions for immigrant women, who are presumed to be nonworking, hyperfecund leeches on public budgets, routinely ignore these women's structural role in the U.S. labor force.[17] Even less attention is paid to these workers' vulnerability to the most extreme forms of labor commodification, bereft of any compensatory recognition by employers of their concrete, particular needs, concentrated as immigrant workers are in the lowest-paid, least secure jobs that are most difficult to unionize.[18] Finally, despite the fact that Mexican women are generally viewed as submissive and compliant, research on patterns of migration and union activism has shown that Mexican women usually make their own decisions about when and how to migrate north, in many instances use financial resources and social networks outside their husbands' control, and often take on more militant roles than men do in U.S. labor conflicts.[19] Stretching the bounds of ordinary communication to involve the alternative practices of greeting, rhetoric, and narrative that Young favors is necessary to enable the autonomous, responsible, and independent actions of these women, as well as their experiences of powerlessness, exploitation, and abuse, to be communicated in their concrete particularity and bodily immediacy. At the same time, precisely this demand for giving voice to the nonidentical furnishes the historical warrant, in this contemporary situation, for negative-dialectical thinking.[20]

Notes

1. Iris Marion Young, *Inclusion and Democracy* (Oxford: Oxford University Press, 2000), 21.
2. Young, *Inclusion and Democracy*, 22–23.

3. Young also criticizes deliberative democracy theorists for privileging unity, or the idea that "deliberative democracy must proceed on the basis of common understanding," over a notion of democratic engagement that is more focused on the mutual acknowledgment of differences and more attentive to the repressive potential of a hegemonic notion of the common good. She further contends that democratic theory needs to rid itself of the fetish of face-to-face discussion and endeavor to conceptualize meaningful democratic participation that occurs in multiple, networked contexts within mass-scale societies. Adorno has most to offer in elaborating and reworking elements of Young's critique of specific, argument-oriented practices of communication, which is my task in this chapter. There are certainly interesting resonances to explore, however, between negative dialectics and Young's emphases in other parts of *Inclusion and Democracy* on a stringent and perpetual questioning of representations of social objectivity (through the increasing inclusion of differentiated social positionalities in communicative contexts), and on a detotalized conception of social institutions.

4. Young, *Inclusion and Democracy*, 55. Further page references are cited in the text.

5. . Iris Marion Young, "Impartiality and the Civic Public: Some Implications of Feminist Critiques of Moral and Political Theory," in *Throwing Like a Girl and Other Essays in Feminist Philosophy and Social Theory* (Bloomington: Indiana University Press, 1990), 94–98.

6. Young, "Impartiality and the Civic Public," 106.

7. Theodor W. Adorno, *Negative Dialectics*, trans. E. B. Ashton (New York: Continuum, 1973), 5. Further page references are cited in the text.

8. The forum was sponsored by Teamsters Local 556 and was held at the Laborer's Union Hall in Pasco, Washington, on 20 January 2002.

9. My paraphrasing and quotation of the speakers' comments draws on my personal notes as an observer of and participant in the event.

10. Iris Marion Young, "Asymmetrical Reciprocity: On Moral Respect, Wonder, and Enlarged Thought," in *Intersecting Voices: Dilemmas of Gender, Political Philosophy, and Policy* (Princeton: Princeton University Press, 1997), 38–59.

11. For Adorno's development of these themes, see "The Psychological Technique of Martin Luther Thomas' Radio Addresses," in *Soziologische Schriften* II, *Gesammelte Schriften*, vol. 9, bk. 1, ed. Susan Buck-Morss and Rolf Tiedemann (Frankfurt: Suhrkamp, 1975), 7–141; Max Horkheimer and Theodor W. Adorno, *Dialectic of Enlightenment*, trans. John Cumming (New York: Continuum, 1972).

12. See Néstor P. Rodríguez, "The Social Construction of the U.S.-Mexico Border," in *Immigrants Out! The New Nativism and the Anti-immigrant Impulse in the United States*, ed. Juan F. Perea (New York: New York University Press, 1996), 223–43.

13. See Nancy Fraser and Linda Gordon, "A Genealogy of 'Dependency': Tracing a Keyword of the U.S. Welfare State," in Nancy Fraser, *Justice Interruptus: Critical Reflections on the "Postsocialist" Condition* (New York: Routledge, 1997); Nancy Fraser, "Women, Welfare, and the Politics of Need Interpretation," in *Unruly Practices: Power, Discourse, and Gender in Contemporary Social Theory* (Minneapolis: University of Minnesota Press, 1989); Iris Marion Young, "Humanism, Gynocentrism, and Feminist Politics," in *Throwing Like a Girl and Other Essays in Feminist Philosophy and Social Theory* (Bloomington: Indiana University Press, 1990), 73–91; Iris Marion Young, "Women and the Welfare State," in *Throwing Like a Girl*, 62–67.

14. On the race nationalism of the Chicano movement, see Ignacio M. García, *Chicanismo: The Forging of a Militant Ethos* (Tucson: University of Arizona Press, 1997). For attempts to imagine a more racially inclusive and alliance-based politics, see Elizabeth Martínez, *De Colores Means All of Us: Latina Views for a Multi-colored Century* (Cambridge, Mass.: South End Press, 1998); Cherríe L. Moraga and Gloria E. Anzaldúa, eds., *This Bridge Called My Back: Writings by Radical Women of Color*, 3d ed. (Berkeley, Calif.: Third Woman Press, 2002).

15. For an especially clear statement by Adorno of his critique of vulgar Marxist "economism"

and his vision of the need for a mutually transformative dialectic between cultural criticism and social theory, see Theodor Adorno, "Cultural Criticism and Society," in *Prisms*, trans. Shierry Weber and Samuel Weber (Cambridge, Mass.: MIT Press, 1983), 19–34.

16. Iris Marion Young, "Socialist Feminism and the Limits of Dual Systems Theory," in *Throwing Like a Girl and Other Essays in Feminist Philosophy and Social Theory* (Bloomington: Indiana University Press, 1990), 30.

17. See Pierrette Hondagneu-Sotelo, *Gendered Transitions: Mexican Experiences of Immigration* (Berkeley and Los Angeles: University of California Press, 1994), 28–33; Dorothy E. Roberts, "Who May Give Birth to Citizens? Reproduction, Eugenics, and Immigration," in *Immigrants Out! The New Nativism and the Anti-immigrant Impulse in the United States*, ed. Juan F. Perea (New York: New York University Press, 1996), 205–19.

18. See Edna Bonacich and Richard P. Appelbaum, *Behind the Label: Inequality in the Los Angeles Apparel Industry* (Berkeley and Los Angeles: University of California Press, 2000); David Lopez and Cynthia Feliciano, "Who Does What? California's Emerging Plural Labor Force," in *Organizing Immigrants: The Challenge for Unions in Contemporary California*, ed. Ruth Milkman (Ithaca, N.Y.: Cornell University Press, 2000), 25–48.

19. See Héctor Delgado, *New Immigrants, Old Unions: Organizing Undocumented Workers in Los Angeles* (Philadelphia: Temple University Press, 1993); Hondagneu-Sotelo, *Gendered Transitions*, 53–97.

20. Of course, the simple fact that a historical warrant for negative-dialectical thinking exists neither guarantees nor explains how it is that such a force of compulsion comes to be felt, acknowledged, and yielded to by historically situated subjects—in this case, for example, by the workers and community members who participated in the forum. Adorno's theory is of limited utility in addressing this pivotal question of cultural politics because this issue shifts the focus from the interplay of history and aesthetic or philosophical form to issues of political leadership. Here it would be beneficial to take recourse to Gramsci, and to theorists of "intellectual" activity in the Gramscian vein such as Stuart Hall and Andrew Ross, although such discussion is beyond the scope of this chapter.

12

Feminist Politics and the Culture Industry

Adorno's Critique Revisited

Lambert Zuidervaart

Theodor Adorno's critique of the culture industry is both highly relevant and historically dated, both theoretically provocative and politically problematic. Developed in the 1930s and 1940s before the rise of new social movements, Adorno's critique identifies crucial issues that contem-

Excerpts from this chapter were presented at a Critical Theory Roundtable in Hayward, California (October 2001), and in the panel "Socio-Political Issues in Feminism and Aesthetics" at the American Society for Aesthetics (ASA) meeting in Coral Gables, Florida (November 2002). I wish to thank the participants in these sessions for their comments, especially L. Ryan Musgrave, who organized the ASA panel. I also wish to thank Matt Klaassen for his research assistance and Renée Heberle for her instructive comments on an earlier version of this chapter.

porary feminism needs to address. Although his critique turns on an idea of aesthetic autonomy to which many feminists object, their objections make social-theoretical assumptions that Adorno's critique can challenge.

This chapter is an exercise in critical retrieval. I first identify a tension within feminism concerning the idea of aesthetic autonomy, then examine the role this idea plays in Adorno's critique of the culture industry. I conclude by proposing a reconfigured notion of aesthetic autonomy, one that aims to overcome the limitations of Adorno's critique and to support a feminist cultural politics.

Feminism and Aesthetic Autonomy

The idea of aesthetic autonomy emerged from the eighteenth-century Enlightenment in Europe.[1] It posits that the arts, and the sorts of experience that the arts afford, are properly independent from other types of human endeavor and need to follow their own rules. In the twentieth century modernist aesthetics made an emphasis on authentic works of art central to the idea of aesthetic autonomy. Not without criticism, however; as Peter Bürger has argued, the modernist attempt to anchor aesthetic autonomy in authentic artworks was challenged both by avant-garde movements such as Dada and surrealism and by a turn toward socially engaged art at both ends of the political spectrum. What I have described as the "paradoxical modernism" of Adorno's aesthetics took shape in this environment.[2] In debate with Walter Benjamin, Bertolt Brecht, and Georg Lukács in the 1930s, Adorno sided with other modernists against the avant-garde and against advocates of political "commitment" in the arts and scholarship.[3] As he puts it in his polemical statement from the 1960s, "This is not a time for political works of art; rather, politics has migrated into the autonomous work of art, and it has penetrated most deeply into works that present themselves as politically dead."[4]

Adorno's stance looks problematic from a feminist perspective. He seems to endorse the very notion that is resisted by feminist cultural politics: a Western notion of aesthetic autonomy that, in shoring up a patriarchal culture, excludes women or marginalizes their voices. As Mary Devereaux has shown, feminist resistance aims especially at an autonomist emphasis on formal qualities in art and on formal criteria for evaluating art.[5] The formalism of, say, Clive Bell and Clement Greenberg seems to sever art from its roots in embodied lives and to gut its role in politics and society. Moreover, formalist approaches to art history and art criticism not only misinterpret politically engaged art but also exclude women from the canon of artistic achievement. An autonomist stress on the formal side of art, which Adorno shares, has masculinist implications that feminists have persuasively criticized in the past several decades.

But the critique of aesthetic autonomy also has potential problems from a feminist perspective. While granting the legitimacy of the feminist critique, Devereaux raises concerns that resonate with Adorno's worries about politically engaged art. She says that an otherwise beneficial rejection of aesthetic autonomy runs two risks, one theoretical and the other practical. Theoretically, the feminist critique of aesthetic autonomy threatens to ignore or underestimate "the elements that make art *art*." Among such elements, Devereaux, like Adorno, would include formal matters, as distinct from content and context. Practically, the feminist critique of aesthetic autonomy might have the unintended consequence of "exposing art to political interference." Devereaux explains:

> Historically, the separation of the aesthetic and the political has provided an argument both against artistic censorship, narrowly defined, and what John Stuart Mill called "the tyranny of the majority." When threatened with interference, artists and their supporters simply appealed to the idea of the "autonomy" of art, claiming the illegitimacy of any evaluative criteria other than the purely aesthetic. But having abandoned strictly "aesthetic" (i.e., formal) criteria in favor of a wider set of political and social considerations, feminist critics of autonomy need a principled basis for distinguishing legitimate from nonlegitimate grounds of evaluation. If a work's misogyny may be relevant to its assessment as art, then why not its failure to promote the "family values" demanded by Senator Jesse Helms and others on the political right?[6]

In a similar vein, when Adorno criticized politically engaged art in the 1960s, one reason for doing so was that such art lent unintended support to a dangerous moral censoriousness that abetted Germany's postwar repression of guilt and suffering.

Indeed, Adorno would have recognized and refused the dilemma Devereaux poses for aesthetics: "*either* adopt a theory of autonomy that protects art from the exigencies of political fashion but isolates it from life, *or* opt for a political conception of art that integrates art with life at the price of compromising its independence." To avoid this dilemma, Devereaux proposes to redefine aesthetic autonomy as "the idea that works of art deserve a protected space, a special normative standing." By "protected space" she means that "works of art . . . remain under the control of artists and the institutions of the art world in which they work." Artworks deserve such protection for a political reason, she says, for "they often play an important social and political role: pushing beyond or challenging existing ways of seeing and thinking about the world."[7]

This formulation reminds one of Adorno's describing autonomous art as "the social antithesis of society" whose critical capacities depend on its relative independence from the rest of society.[8] But Adorno would have questioned Devereaux's emphasis on a "protected space." For he considers late capitalist society as a whole to be much more integrated and much more oppressive than Devereaux assumes. To think that existing practices and institutions of art could secure a "protected space" from "political interference," even if only in a symbolical fashion, would be politically naive and theoretically myopic. Naive, because the dominant institutions of government work hand in glove with an exploitative economy. Myopic, because the government-maintained capitalist system surrounds and permeates the very spaces that are supposed to be protected.

Despite Adorno's emphasis on aesthetic autonomy, then, the social theory informing his paradoxical modernism resembles the social theories of radical and socialist feminists who have a strong critique of aesthetic autonomy.[9] Both radical and socialist feminists launch their critiques of aesthetic autonomy out of opposition to the societal system as a whole— precisely that system to which autonomous art offers an important social antithesis, according to Adorno. Radical feminists think that the oppression of women stems from a patriarchal social system that has either biological or cultural roots. This patriarchal system thoroughly devalues women and their experience. Liberation would require breaking the grip of patriarchy on women's lives. The path to that lies in either subverting the patriarchal system or escaping it by developing a counterculture. Socialist feminists also think that the oppression of women is systemic. They differ, however, in understanding the system as an historical formation in which economic patterns are decisive. Socialist feminists claim that the liberation of women would require a fundamental transformation of the patriarchal capitalist order. For this neither subversion nor escape is sufficient.

Beyond their disagreement about the nature of oppression and liberation, however, radical and socialist feminists agree in regarding women's oppression as systemic. Like Adorno, they think the system's oppressive features permeate society as a whole, including the ways in which culture is produced and distributed. Where they differ from Adorno is in their understanding of which class is oppressed, how that oppression operates, and how it could be overcome—and how "the culture industry" figures in all this.[10] Because of those differences, radical and socialist feminists tend to reject the idea of aesthetic autonomy that Adorno seems to endorse.

Given both Adorno's proximity to radical and socialist feminist social theory and the risks of rejecting aesthetic autonomy, one wonders whether elements of Adorno's aesthetic autonomism are worth salvaging for a feminist cultural politics that is informed by a systemic critique of society as a whole. More specifically, would a critical retrieval of insights from Adorno's autonomist critique of the culture industry provide ways for feminists to address Devereaux's concerns without giving up legitimate criticisms of aesthetic autonomy's exclusionary content and consequences?

Adorno's Critique of the Culture Industry

A first step toward addressing this question is to show that Adorno's idea of aesthetic autonomy is more complex than the idea that radical and socialist feminists reject. His critique of the culture industry in *Dialectic of Enlightenment* uses Marx's dialectic of the commodity to rework eighteenth-century Enlightenment aesthetics.[11] Central to Adorno's critique, although barely thematized in the book itself, is the understanding of aesthetic autonomy captured in Kant's description of the beautiful as purposiveness without purpose (*Zweckmässigkeit ohne Zweck*). Adorno translates this description into a complex conception of autonomy with wide-ranging social implications. On Adorno's conception, purposiveness without purpose would both require and promote three forms of autonomy that are closely linked: (1) the internal and self-critical independence of the authentic work of art, (2) the relative independence of (some of) high culture from the political and economic system, and (3) the autonomy of the self as a political and moral agent. I shall label these three forms *internal, societal,* and *personal* autonomy, respectively. Adorno criticizes the culture industry for undermining all three types of autonomy. In subsequent writings he portrays authentic works of modern art as providing crucial resistance to pressures toward cultural commodification and social narcissism.

As this preliminary description suggests, although Adorno emphasizes "aesthetic autonomy," the version he emphasizes is more complex and dialectical than the idea many feminists reject. To begin with, Adorno's concept of the artwork's internal autonomy is substantial rather than merely formal. Authentic works of art have an internal dialectic of content and form, he says, and this dialectic expresses the contradictions of society as whole. Moreover, in carrying out a dialectic of content and form, authentic works challenge their own self-constitution and thereby challenge the society that makes them possible. They force people to confront society's unresolved tensions, and they point toward resolutions that artworks themselves cannot accomplish.

Adorno also links substantial internal autonomy to a societal autonomy that is itself dialectical. On his account, the relative independence some art has achieved in capitalist societies is itself dependent on political and economic developments that he strongly criticizes. So Adorno does not simply celebrate art's societal autonomy, nor does he regard it as ideologically neutral. Although societal autonomy makes possible a crucial mode of social criticism and utopian memory, it also reflects a class-based division of labor that Adorno rejects.

Where he goes wrong, as I have argued elsewhere, is in making internal and societal autonomy a precondition for art's social-critical capacities.[12] In effect this rules out most forms of folk art, popular art, mass art, and site-specific art as potential locations of social criticism. Such sites include many forms of art making that feminist historians have retrieved and feminist artists have promoted. The other problem with Adorno's dialectical autonomism is that it discounts the entwinement of autonomous art with other social institutions. As many feminists have shown, autonomous art is not as independent from the culture industry and other social institutions as Adorno's language sometimes suggests. Although a distinction can be made out between autonomous art and other forms of cultural production, this distinction is not fixed, nor is it the crucial one

for sorting out the social-critical capacities of specific cultural phenomena.

But this argument does not go sufficiently far to get at the problems in
Adorno's critique of the culture industry. It does not suffice to argue, as I
did, that autonomy is not a precondition for art's social-critical capacities. Nor does it suffice to argue, as Deborah Cook does, that some products of the culture industry might be capable of the sort of internal
autonomy that Adorno reserved for authentic works of modern art.[13] The
problems in Adorno's critique of the culture industry do not arise simply
from the way he reserves internal autonomy for certain works of high art.
Rather, they arise from how he connects such internal autonomy with
both the societal autonomy of art and the personal autonomy of political
and moral agents.[14] These connections must be reexamined, along with
the idea of autonomy that allows the connections to be posited in the
first place. Of particular importance for feminist criticisms of aesthetic
autonomy is the connection between internal and societal autonomy.

Let's consider, then, how Adorno's critique of the culture industry
accounts for art's societal autonomy and implicitly connects this with the
internal autonomy of certain artworks. *Dialectic of Enlightenment* lays this
out in two passages, which Cook also cites.[15] In the first passage Adorno
argues that the culture industry "proves to be the goal of . . . liberalism"
both culturally and politically (*DE*, 104–6; *DA*, 156–59). The argument
compares developments in the United States with ones in Germany.
Whereas the United States, with its more democratic culture and polity,
led the way toward "the monopoly of culture," the failure of democratic
"Kontrolle" to permeate life in Germany exempted leading universities,
theaters, and museums from market mechanisms: protection by local and
state governments gave them a measure of freedom from commercial
domination. At the same time, the market for literature and published
music could rely on the purchasing power of homage paid to an unfash-
ionable artistic quality. What really does contemporary artists in, says
Adorno, is the pressure to blend into commercial life as "aesthetic ex-
perts." They gain freedom from political domination only to become
slaves of a "private monopoly of culture" in which the imposed tastes of
the defrauded masses keep artists in their place. Pre-Fascist Europe, by
contrast, lagged behind the trend toward culture monopoly, and this lag
left "a remnant of autonomy" for intellectual activity (*Geist*). In other
words, whatever societal autonomy the arts enjoyed in pre-Fascist Europe
was a function of less-than-democratic political arrangements.

There are two obvious problems with this explanation. First, it does not explain the societal autonomy of the arts in the United States, where the development of democratic forms of polity coincides historically with the institutionalization of autonomous art. Although Adorno quotes Alexis de Tocqueville to negative effect in this passage, he never takes up Tocqueville's discussion of the voluntary associations that spawned intellectual activity in the United States when Germany still relied on state protection and control of culture. Yet one cannot simply ignore the prominence of voluntary associations in American culture, and their relative weakness in Germany, when one explains the social history of autonomous art and its relation to the culture industry. Local music societies, women's literary clubs, and philanthropically funded art museums did not disappear with the rise of mass media in the United States. Instead, they flourished and multiplied, even during the years when Nazis seized control of state-protected cultural organizations in Germany. To describe the American scene as a "culture monopoly," as Adorno does, is to ignore the crucial role played by such noncommercial and nongovernmental organizations.

The other problem with Adorno's account is that it fails to explain why Hitler and his henchmen would attack not only the state-protected institutions of education, scholarship, and art but also the commercial institutions of mass culture. Surely the Nazis found some threat and resistance there, and not simply the "conformism" Adorno associates with the culture industry. Apart from vague appeals to the fact that consumers are not completely duped by the culture industry, Adorno does not explore the critical and subversive tendencies inherent to culture-industrial production, as distinct from particular products of such production. Nor is this surprising, since Adorno's approach largely precludes the "truth potential" of art that does not fit his models of internal and societal autonomy.

The second passage occurs in a section on the "pseudoindividuality" said to prevail in the culture industry (DE, 124–31; DA, 181–89). Here Adorno argues that the culture industry involves a change in the commodity character of art, such that art's commodity character is deliberately acknowledged and art "abjures its autonomy" (DE, 127; DA, 184). Art's autonomy was always "essentially conditioned by the commodity economy," says Adorno, even when autonomy took the form of negating social utility (gesellschaftliche Zweckmässigkeit—literally, "societal purposiveness"). Internally autonomous works—works that "negated the commodity character of society by simply following their own inherent laws"—were still commodities. Adorno claims that their purposelessness was sustained by "the anonymity of the market," whose demands are so diversely mediated that the market partially frees the artist from specific requirements (*DE*, 127; *DA*, 184). He acknowledges, of course, that the artist's market-mediated freedom is also a "freedom to starve" (*DE*, 104; *DA*, 157) and contains an element of untruth. Yet the proper way for artists to counter this untruth, he says, is neither to deny nor to flaunt the commodity character of art, but to assimilate the contradiction between market and autonomy "into the consciousness of their own production" (*DE*, 127; *DA*, 185).

The culture industry, by contrast, dispenses entirely with the "purposelessness" that is central to art's autonomy. Once the demand that art be marketable (*Verwertbarkeit*) becomes total, the internal economic structure of cultural commodities shifts.[16] Instead of promising freedom from societally dictated uses, and thereby having a genuine use value that people can enjoy, the product mediated by the culture industry has its use value *replaced* by exchange value:

> [E]njoyment is giving way to being there and being in the know, connoisseurship by enhanced prestige. . . . Everything is perceived only from the point of view that it can serve as something else. . . . Everything has value only in so far as it can be exchanged, not in so far as it is something in itself. For consumers the use value of art, its essence, is a fetish, and the fetish—the social valuation [*gesellschaftliche Schätzung*] which they mistake for the merit [*Rang*] of works of art—becomes its only use value, the only quality they enjoy. (*DE*, 128; *DA*, 186)

Hence the culture industry dissolves the "genuine commodity character" that artworks once possessed when exchange value developed use value as its own precondition and did not drag use value along as a "mere appendage" (*DE*, 129–30; *DA*, 188).

In this second passage, then, the societal autonomy of art depends on the functioning of a capitalist market prior to the development of monopolistic tendencies. If Adorno were entirely consistent with this analysis, he should have concluded that economic preconditions for the societal autonomy of art had disappeared by the time he wrote his critique of the culture industry, and long before he began writing his *Aes-*

thetic Theory. But that conclusion would contradict the way in which he pits modern art against the culture industry, and it would make his critique of the culture industry reactionary and inconsistent with the progressive impulses of his social theory.[17]

Nevertheless, Adorno's critique has made an innovative and productive move, namely, to interpret Kant's notion of aesthetic autonomy through an updated reading of Marx's dialectic of the commodity, such that questions of internal and societal autonomy become inextricably linked. Too many of Adorno's Anglo-American critics, in their desire to secure legitimacy for "mass art" or "mass culture," overlook this move. They prefer instead to criticize Adorno for misconstruing "Kant's analysis of free beauty as a theory of art"[18] or for not understanding genre-specific characteristics such as the importance of individual performance in jazz and the salience of collaborative recordings in rock.[19] In effect, these critics suggest that Adorno did not really understand American "popular culture" and illicitly measured it by the standards of European bourgeois art. Such criticisms, while interesting in their own right, sidestep the challenge Adorno's idea of autonomy poses for politically inflected theories of contemporary culture.[20] The criticisms do not consider how culture and economy intersect, or what this intersection means for emancipatory politics. Feminists, however, cannot afford to ignore Adorno's challenge.

Autonomy Reconfigured

Earlier I mentioned Mary Devereaux's concern that feminist critiques of aesthetic autonomy might undermine the "protected space" required for feminist cultural politics. By itself, Adorno's critique of the culture industry would not help resolve this dilemma. His critique includes a concept of internal autonomy not unlike the notion of aesthetic autonomy that many feminists reject. Yet feminists need to take up the larger challenge of Adorno's complex idea of autonomy, namely, to develop a critical theory of the systemic roles fulfilled by culture in contemporary society.

A first step in that direction would be to revisit Adorno's claims concerning the internal economic structure of cultural commodities. On the one hand, his analysis illuminates the essential role of hypercommercialization in contemporary Western societies. Whether homespun or esoteric, whether radical or timid, no cultural good is protected from the juggernaut of consumer capitalism and the hegemony it secures. On the other hand, Adorno's analysis has an unfortunate consequence: it portrays many cultural goods as *no more than* hypercommodities whose exchange value has replaced their use value. This portrait is unfortunate because it inadvertently endorses the tendency toward hypercommercialization that Adorno opposes. He fails to acknowledge sufficiently that taking pleasure in exchange value is not the sole function of culture-industrial transactions—despite the "art is business" mentality of production and distribution companies, and despite the "I know what I like" self-understanding of culture "consumers."[21]

Of course, one can hardly deny that, under consumer capitalist conditions, cultural producers sell exchange values as use values and consumers buy them to be hip and fashionable. Simultaneously, however, and unavoidably, they also engage in cultural practices mediated by cultural goods. The "value" of these practices and goods cannot be subsumed under the economic categories of use value and exchange value. Accordingly, contemporary feminist social theory must ask how hypercommercialization either enhances or undermines such cultural practices, in which respects, and to what effect. One's answer would indicate what, beyond offering a critique of consumer capitalism, an appropriate cultural politics would be.

Because these matters are difficult to sort out, I cannot pretend to give satisfactory answers in a single chapter. But let me outline an approach that could prove fruitful for feminist cultural politics. Russell Keat has argued that cultural activities such as broadcasting, the arts, and academic research, and "the institutions within which they are conducted, should be 'protected' in various ways from the operation of the market."[22] Keat's argument is an economic counterpart to Mary Devereaux's political argument that the arts need a "protected space," by which she means, primarily, a space protected from censorship and other forms of "political interference." While acknowledging the point to both arguments, I would add that adequate political protection requires adequate economic protection, and vice versa. More important, I would also claim that protection is not enough: structural alternatives to the dominant economy and the dominant political system are required.

Why do such cultural activities need protection from both "political interference" and the "operation of the market"? The reason is that in contemporary Western societies a legitimate differentiation of cultural

and societal spheres has occurred in tandem with an illegitimate colonization of ordinary life and cultural institutions by both corporate and
governmental systems.[23] These systems mutually reinforce each other's
dominance and, in doing so, they reinforce patriarchal patterns in culture. That is why political protection without economic protection, or
vice versa, usually proves inadequate. Moreover, mere protection, accompanied perhaps by appeals to the intrinsic worth of education or research
or the arts or entertainment, is not sufficient to resist pressures toward
hypercommercialization and performance fetishism. Certainly, to thrive,
such cultural activities need to have economically and politically "protected spaces." If the spaces are themselves created by the corporate
economy or state agencies or are overly dependent on these entities, however, then the activities conducted within them remain subservient to
corporate or state dictates and ruled by the systemic logics of money and
power.

Hence, as radical feminists have seen more clearly than most, countereconomic and counterpolitical spaces need to emerge from cultural activities and cultural agents themselves. That means setting up and
strengthening organizations, media, and social networks whose economy
is noncommercial and whose public voice is not state sanctioned. Such
spaces are not simply a "counterculture" that would be noneconomic or
apolitical. A countereconomy is definitely an economy, but it operates
on noncommercial principles, whether nonprofit, cooperative, or communal. So too, a counterpolitics is definitely political, but it is not simply
caught up in lobbying, party politics, and occupying legislative, administrative, or judicial positions of power. Even if the long-term goal were to
break the dominance of corporate and state systems, as it seems to be in
the "antiglobalization" movement, fostering countereconomic and
counterpolitical spaces would still be internally important and externally
necessary; internally important because otherwise the colonization of
culture faces little resistance, externally necessary because there is hardly
any other way to mobilize economic and political opposition to systems
wielding enormous clout, with oppressive results.

As Adorno's linking of internal and societal autonomy suggests, countereconomic and counterpolitical spaces must foster intrinsically worthwhile cultural practices. This applies to the arts just as much as it applies
to education and research.[24] Perhaps a suitably expanded concept of "aesthetic value"[25] would provide a constructive alternative to Adorno's analysis and help resolve the dilemma within feminism concerning aesthetic

autonomy. By *suitably expanded* I mean two things. First, I mean a concept that does not restrict aesthetic merit to formal qualities of discrete art objects but encompasses the qualities of the practices in which people engage when they create and experience artistic products and events. Second, I mean a concept of aesthetic merit that does not restrict the relevant practices to those typical of high art but ranges over popular art, mass art, and site-specific art as well. I have described this concept elsewhere as "imaginative cogency."[26] Imaginative cogency is an horizon of expectations governing the intersubjective exploration, presentation, and interpretation of aesthetic signs. Within this horizon art products and art events are expected to elicit and sustain open-ended exploration, to present multiple and unexpected nuances of meaning, and to lend themselves to creative interpretation. And these processes are expected to occur with degrees of complexity, depth, and intensity that are both appropriate to the particular products and events and intrinsically worthwhile.

The concept of imaginative cogency helps articulate a notion of aesthetic autonomy that neither privileges authentic works of modern art nor construes aesthetic autonomy as a last bastion of social critique, à la Adorno. But it also resists either reducing aesthetic merit to the outcome of struggles for power or treating aesthetic autonomy as a merely strategic concern, in the manner of some feminists. On the approach I propose, the central normative question concerning aesthetic autonomy would be which contemporary art practices are better able, given a certain context and situation, to "generate creative and critical dialogue via production of and participation in events, products, and experiences that are multifaceted, innovative, and attuned to current needs." Accordingly, concerns about aesthetic autonomy would shift "from works as such to the quality of the practices in which artists and their collaborators and publics engage."[27] There is nothing in this notion of aesthetic autonomy to preclude its application to popular, mass, and site-specific art. Yet it retains a critical edge and does not simply become a classificatory category.[28] In fact, it derives in large part from collaborative and interventionist art practices pioneered by feminists artists such as Judy Chicago and Judith Baca.[29]

Given this critical hermeneutic notion of aesthetic autonomy, one can also ask which institutional patterns and societal structures are more likely to foster the sorts of practices in which imaginative cogency can be pursued. This question can be made more specific to feminist struggles for justice and recognition that include the creation and experience of art.[30] Since such questions are partly empirical, one cannot settle them in theory, no more than in theory Adorno could legitimately declare all products of the culture industry worthless, and no more than in theory a feminist can legitimately declare all aesthetic criteria to be simply ideological. Yet there is one respect in which a theoretical answer needs to be attempted. This has to do with the relationships between economy, polity, and culture that Adorno makes central to his own critique of the culture industry.

In the two passages I discussed, Adorno depicts the societal autonomy of the arts as the function, historically, of a paternalist state and premonopolistic capitalism. Although understandable both as a reflection of Adorno's own European experience and as an articulation of his background theory of state capitalism, such an account of societal autonomy misses a crucial feature of cultural politics and cultural economics in the United States. I mentioned earlier his failure to take up Tocqueville's discussion of voluntary associations in the United States. This is doubly unfortunate. Not only did these types of organizations resist the grid of the capitalist market in either its entrepreneurial or its monopolistic stages, but also they have provided alternative sites for the development of cultural practices outside the strict confines of church, state, and other institutions of control. Freestanding schools, music societies, libraries, and literary clubs, many of them founded or led by women, may have had as much impact as did the capitalist market on the development of culture in the United States. This is not to suggest that cultural organizations have a more decisive role in the development of culture than economic forces have. Nor is it to suggest that such sites were completely independent of class interests, patriarchal patterns, and a capitalist economy. Rather, the type of economy that helped give rise to twentieth-century American culture cannot be captured in either a simple market model or the model of state capitalism that informs *Dialectic of Enlightenment*. It is a three-sector economy, and it includes a voluntary component that mediates the development of cultural practices.[31]

If this series of hypotheses is on the right track, then the account to be given of the societal autonomy of art must go beyond Adorno's theses about the political backwardness of pre-Fascist Europe and the commodity character of artistic products. It needs to incorporate the role of civil society and public spheres, not only historically but also today. That, ironically, is the missing link both in the Kantian account of "fine art" (*schöne Kunst*) and in Adorno's Marx-inflected usage of Kantian notions to critique the culture industry—ironically, because, if Habermas is right in *The Structural Transformation of the Public Sphere*, the rise of fine art as an autonomous social institution in eighteenth-century Europe is itself intimately entwined with the development of a relatively independent bourgeois public sphere.[32]

As historians such as Joan Landes have shown, contemporary feminism must consider whether such institutionalizations are irreversibly bound to the masculinist structures in which they first emerged, or whether, through concerted counterhegemonic effort, they have become and can become sites of opposition and transformation.[33] For such effort to succeed, countereconomic forces are required. Habermas himself does not consider the alternative economic underpinnings of some public spheres, and in this he remains too close to Adorno's critique of the culture industry.[34] That has not escaped the attention of feminists who incorporate Habermas's emphasis on public spheres but who see that a feminist cultural politics might require countereconomic structures. Rita Felski, for example, partially recognizes the need for alternative economic support to a "feminist counter-public sphere." Yet she remains ambivalent about the prospects for developing such support, and she envisions the feminist counterpublic sphere as operating through "a series of cultural strategies" both internal and external to "existing institutional structures."[35] This raises a problem, it seems to me. Existing institutional structures such as "the educational system" are just as vulnerable to hypercommercialization and performance fetishism as are cultural strategies external to them. While I understand why Felski rejects Adorno's supposed "privileging of a modernist aesthetic as a site of freedom" and questions his apparent "diagnosis of the modern world as a totally administered society with no possibility of genuine opposition or dissent," I do not see how a feminist counterpublic sphere would escape Adorno's diagnosis if it did not actually have countereconomic support.[36]

So, although indebted to Felski's pioneering work, my response to Adorno's critique of the culture industry takes a different tack. I argue, against Adorno, that the societal autonomy of art depends on a number of interrelated social factors. While structural shifts in the dominant economy and polity have significant implications for the autonomy of art, they are linked to noncommercial and nongovernmental developments that also inform structural shifts in the dominant economy and polity. The twentieth-century shift from monopoly capitalism to consumer capitalism, for example, may well go hand in hand with the development of new public spheres where struggles for recognition and justice exceed the boundaries of state-sanctioned discourse, and with a proliferation of cultural organizations whose third-sector economy need not turn products into hypercommodities.

An account along these lines would not assume that "purposiveness without purpose" was definitive of fine art in Kant's own day, nor that the current prospects for autonomous art depend primarily upon aesthetic qualities internal to the work of art. Instead, the account would make more of the "communicability" and "sociability" that Kant links with aesthetic judgment.[37] It would also explore the matrix of civil society and third-sector economy that gives birth to diverse forms of cultural creation, not only in North America but also around the world.

Accordingly, my own alternative to Adorno's idea of autonomy involves three steps. First I replace the notion of a work's internal autonomy with a notion of the autonomy of certain cultural practices. Then I revise Adorno's political and economic account of art's societal autonomy. Finally, in other publications, I indicate how certain practices, as made possible by certain institutions, can foster a more dialogical type of personal autonomy characterized by creative coresponsibility.[38] This account would have three outcomes. First, the question of whether culture-industrial products can have emancipatory potential would turn into the question of whether cultural organizations can be fashioned where cultural products of many sorts can be taken up in autonomous cultural practices within organizations that, by virtue of their political and economic positioning, resist systemic colonization. Second, the blunt causal assumptions of Adorno's critique of the culture industry would give way to a more textured diagnostic model. And, third, the conflict in feminism between strategically appealing to aesthetic autonomy and theoretically rejecting it would dissolve. It would dissolve into the idea of autonomy as a multidimensional condition to be fashioned and won, ever anew, in struggles for recognition and justice.[39]

Notes

1. Here and throughout the chapter I use the term *aesthetic autonomy* loosely to cover what I have more carefully distinguished as *aesthetic autonomy* and *artistic autonomy* in Lambert Zuidervaart, "Autonomy, Negativity, and Illusory Transgression: Menke's Deconstruction of Adorno's Aesthetics," *Philosophy Today*, Society for Phenomenology and Existential Philosophy suppl. (1999):

154–68; reprinted in *Critical Theory*, ed. David Rasmussen and James Swindal, 4 vols. (London: Sage, 2004), 1:172–90.

2. See Lambert Zuidervaart, "Paradoxical Modernism," in *Adorno's Aesthetic Theory: The Redemption of Illusion* (Cambridge, Mass.: MIT Press, 1991), 150–77.

3. See Lambert Zuidervaart, "Aesthetic Debates," in *Adorno's Aesthetic Theory: The Redemption of Illusion* (Cambridge, Mass.: MIT Press, 1991), 28–43. Key documents in these debates are collected in *Aesthetics and Politics: Debates Between Bloch, Lukács, Brecht, Benjamin, Adorno*, ed. Ronald Taylor, afterword by Fredric Jameson (London: NLB, 1977; Verso, 1980). See also Eugene Lunn, *Marxism and Modernism: An Historical Study of Lukács, Brecht, Benjamin, and Adorno* (Berkeley and Los Angeles: University of California Press, 1982).

4. Theodor W. Adorno, "Commitment," in *Notes to Literature*, vol. 2, ed. Rolf Tiedemann, trans. Shierry Weber Nicholsen (New York: Columbia University Press, 1992), 93–94; "Engagement," in *Gesammelte Schriften*, ed. Rolf Tiedemann, vol. 11 (Frankfurt: Suhrkamp, 1974), 430. See also Lambert Zuidervaart, "Political Migration," in *Adorno's Aesthetic Theory: The Redemption of Illusion* (Cambridge, Mass.: MIT Press, 1991), 122–49.

5. Mary Devereaux, "The Philosophical and Political Implications of the Feminist Critique of Aesthetic Autonomy," in "Turning the Century: Feminist Criticism in the 1990s," ed. Glynis Carr, special issue, *Bucknell Review* 36, no. 2 (1992): 164–86. See also Devereaux's essays "Protected Space: Politics, Censorship, and the Arts," *Journal of Aesthetics and Art Criticism* 51 (Spring 1993): 207–15; and "Autonomy and Its Feminist Critics," in *Encyclopedia of Aesthetics*, ed. Michael Kelly, vol. 1 (New York: Oxford University Press, 1998), 178–82.

6. Devereaux, "Autonomy and Its Feminist Critics," 181–82.

7. Devereaux, "Autonomy and Its Feminist Critics," 182.

8. See Lambert Zuidervaart, "Society's Social Antithesis," in *Adorno's Aesthetic Theory: The Redemption of Illusion* (Cambridge, Mass.: MIT Press, 1991), 67–92.

9. I use the labels *radical feminism* and *socialist feminism* in the manner proposed by Alison Jaggar, *Feminist Politics and Human Nature* (Totowa, N.J.: Rowman and Allanheld, 1983) and recapitulated by Rosemarie Tong, *Feminist Thought: A More Comprehensive Introduction*, 2d ed. (Boulder, Colo.: Westview Press, 1998).

10. For an Adornian feminist critique of the "identitarian" logic at work in radical feminism, see Regina Becker-Schmidt, "Critical Theory as a Critique of Society: Theodor W. Adorno's Significance for a Feminist Sociology," in *Adorno, Culture, and Feminism*, ed. Maggie O'Neill (London: Sage, 1999), 104–18. Becker-Schmidt's diagnosis of women's oppression links the hegemony of specific societal spheres (primarily corporate and government sectors) with specific gender hierarchies.

11. Max Horkheimer and Theodor Adorno, *Dialectic of Enlightenment: Philosophical Fragments*, ed. Gunzelin Schmid Noerr, trans. Edmund Jephcott (Stanford: Stanford University Press, 2002), hereafter abbreviated as *DE*; *Dialektik der Aufklärung*, in Max Horkheimer, *Gesammelte Schriften*, vol. 5, *"Dialektik der Aufklärung" und Schriften 1940–1950*, ed. Gunzelin Schmid Noerr (Frankfurt: Fischer Taschenbuch, 1987), hereafter abbreviated as *DA*. I shall focus on Adorno's ideas, since he was the primary author of the culture industry chapter and elaborated its ideas in other writings.

12. See Lambert Zuidervaart, "Models of Mediation," in *Adorno's Aesthetic Theory: The Redemption of Illusion* (Cambridge, Mass.: MIT Press, 1991), 217–47. A shorter version of this chapter was published as "The Social Significance of Autonomous Art: Adorno and Bürger," *Journal of Aesthetics and Art Criticism* 48 (Winter 1990): 61–77. These writings focus on Adorno's notion of truth (*Wahrheitsgehalt*) in art, a notion that includes both social-critical and utopian elements. In the current context, I shall focus only on the question of social-critical capacity. I provide a systematic treatment of both elements in my *Artistic Truth: Aesthetics, Discourse, and Imaginative Disclosure* (Cambridge: Cambridge University Press, 2004).

13. Deborah Cook, *The Culture Industry Revisited: Theodor W. Adorno on Mass Culture* (Rowman

and Littlefield, 1996). Cook suggests that perhaps "some products of the culture industry already follow the model for cultural practice with political import which Adorno discovered in some works of high modern art" (129). Such products would have to achieve "a degree of autonomy" that allows them to "break the stranglehold of reification and . . . narcissism, holding out the promise of independent forms of communication between more rationally and instinctually robust individuals" (128). Here Cook is more faithful to Adorno than I consider warranted. For she adopts, without serious challenge, the concept of *internal* autonomy that underlies Adorno's critique.

14. In "Adorno on Mass Societies," *Journal of Social Philosophy* 32 (Spring 2001): 35–52, Deborah Cook demonstrates that Adorno's general critique of late capitalism links the development of a stratified mass society with the spread of narcissism. This casts doubt on a Habermasian "faith in [the] vitality of civil society or the lifeworld" (39), she argues. I am not sure whether there is an inconsistency between her embrace here of Adorno's general critique and her earlier attempt to rescue some culture-industrial products from Adornian dismissal. See also Deborah Cook, *Adorno, Habermas, and the Search for a Rational Society* (New York: Routledge, 2004).

15. Cook, *The Culture Industry Revisited*, 107.

16. Revisions introduced into the text before it was published in 1947 disguise the fact that Adorno and Horkheimer are employing the analysis of the commodity worked out by Karl Marx in *Das Kapital*. Where the 1947 and subsequent editions mention "eine Verschiebung in der inneren ökonomischen Zusammensetzung der Kulturwaren," the 1944 version more straightforwardly points to "eine Verschiebung in der Zusammensetzung der Kulturwaren nach Gebrauchswert und Tauschwert." In the English translation, then, the phrase "a shift in the inner economic composition of cultural commodities" substitutes for what would have been more clearly in line with Marx's analysis, namely, "a shift in the composition of cultural commodities in terms of use value and exchange value." See *DE*, 128 and the related note on *DE*, 271; *DA*, 185. A similar obscuring of Adorno's Marxian categories occurs in the revised version of his essay "On the Fetish-Character in Music and the Regression of Listening." It is this revised version which has been translated into English and widely anthologized. Such revisions have helped shield Adorno's Anglo-American readers from the economic claims that support his critique of the culture industry.

17. In *The Culture Industry Revisited*, Deborah Cook notes the problem here, but she does not seem to feel its full weight. She finds three "extrinsic conditions" for modern art's autonomy in Adorno's writings: (1) a cultural lag behind the culture industry, (2) the advancement of artistic techniques, and (3) the psychological dispositions of the artist. Of these, only the first is mildly economic, and it is hardly reassuring with regard to prospects for the societal autonomy of high art, much less the societal autonomy of popular culture. If one wants to argue as Cook does for the internal autonomy of artworks and of certain products of the culture industry, one must either abandon the notion that this internal autonomy is somehow linked to economic conditions or provide a different account of those economic conditions than Adorno himself provides. The first option requires one to give up Adorno's dialectical interpolations of culture and economy. The second option, although less problematic from a critical theory perspective, is also more difficult.

18. Noel Carroll, *A Philosophy of Fine Art* (Oxford: Clarendon Press, 1998), 105. It is curious that Carroll does not discuss Kant's own attempt to distinguish between "fine art" and "agreeable arts" where, it seems to me, Kant himself turns his analysis of free beauty into a theory of art. See sections 43–46 in Immanuel Kant, *Critique of the Power of Judgment*, ed. Paul Guyer, trans. Paul Guyer and Eric Matthews (Cambridge: Cambridge University Press, 2000), 182–87.

19. Theodore Gracyk, *Rhythm and Noise: An Aesthetics of Rock* (London: I. B. Tauris, 1996), 149–73.

20. The same avoidance occurs in Patrick Brantlinger's highly influential interpretation of Adorno's critique as an example of "negative classicism," in *Bread and Circuses: Theories of Mass Culture as Social Decay* (Ithaca, N.Y.: Cornell University Press, 1983).

21. Together with several colleagues in communications, film studies, history, and musicology, I

explore other functions of culture-industrial transactions in *Dancing in the Dark: Youth, Popular Culture, and the Electronic Media*, ed. Roy Anker (Grand Rapids, Mich.: Eerdmans, 1991).

22. Russell Keat, *Cultural Goods and the Limits of the Market* (London: Macmillan Press; New York: St. Martin's Press, 2000), ix.

23. The main lines of this answer stem from the diagnosis of modernization in Jürgen Habermas, *The Theory of Communicative Action*, 2 vols., trans. Thomas McCarthy (Boston: Beacon Press, 1984, 1987). I explore the relevance of this diagnosis for the arts in "Postmodern Arts and the Birth of a Democratic Culture," in *The Arts, Community and Cultural Democracy*, ed. Lambert Zuidervaart and Henry Luttikhuizen (London: Macmillan Press; New York: St. Martin's Press, 2000), 15–39, where I introduce the concepts of *hypercommercialization* and *performance fetishism*. By *hypercommercialization* I mean a tendency to make commercial potential the primary or sole reason for building and maintaining cultural organizations, as seen, for example, in moves to "privatize" state-funded schooling and to market the economic benefits of arts organizations. This tendency comes with a full-scale celebration of exchange value that makes it increasingly difficult to raise and address questions of cultural need and cultural norms. By *performance fetishism* I mean a tendency toward internal bureaucratization of cultural organizations in response to a government demand for administratively manageable certification of competence and output, with the result that strategic calculations take precedence over their cultural missions. Examples include moves to "retool" school curricula and pedagogies for the sake of competitiveness in the global economy and to "rationalize" arts organizations in accord with cost/benefit criteria.

24. Too many politically inflected theories of culture ignore just how meshed universities have become with the dominant economic and political systems and just how vulnerable this makes research and education to corporate and state dictates. The switch since the 1970s from mostly state funding to increasing amounts of corporate funding is simply a shift *within* a paradigm that hinders genuine academic freedom.

25. Here I take a cue from Peggy Zeglin Brand, "Revising the Aesthetic-Nonaesthetic Distinction: The Aesthetic Value of Activist Art," in *Feminism and Tradition in Aesthetics*, ed. Peggy Zeglin Brand and Carolyn Korsmeyer (University Park: Pennsylvania State University Press, 1995), 245–72. Brand argues that philosophical aesthetics needs to move away from "the rigidity of the traditional aesthetic-nonaesthetic distinction and toward a revised notion . . . of aesthetic value" (260). My proposal differs from Brand's in emphasizing cultural practices rather than artworks.

26. Lambert Zuidervaart, "Cultural Paths and Aesthetic Signs: A Critical Hermeneutics of Aesthetic Validity," *Philosophy and Social Criticism* 29 (2003): 315–40. In my book *Artistic Truth* I elaborate the implications of "imaginative cogency" for art's critical and utopian capacities.

27. Zuidervaart, "Autonomy, Negativity, and Illusory Transgression," 165.

28. This approach has affinities with Miriam Hansen's attempt to think through Adorno's writings on film and mass culture in "Mass Culture as Hieroglyphic Writing: Adorno, Derrida, Kracauer," *New German Critique*, no. 56 (Spring–Summer 1992): 43–73. Hansen tries to mobilize "the split between mass-cultural script and modernist *écriture*" into "a stereoscopic vision that spans the extremes of contemporary media culture," as both serving "the ever more effective simulation of presence" and birthing "a postmodern culture of difference" (73). But her essay does not address the connection of this vision to emancipatory politics.

29. See Lambert Zuidervaart, "Creative Border Crossing in New Public Culture," in *Literature and the Renewal of the Public Sphere*, ed. Susan VanZanten Gallagher and Mark D. Walhout (London: Macmillan Press; New York: St. Martin's Press, 2000), 206–24.

30. The relationship between struggles for economic justice and struggles for cultural recognition is especially crucial for the emancipation of what Nancy Fraser calls "bivalent collectivities," such as oppressed groups constituted along the lines of either race or gender. See Fraser, *Justice Interruptus: Critical Reflections on the 'Postsocialist' Condition* (New York: Routledge, 1997), 11–39.

31. The three sectors of the U.S. economy are the corporate, government, and "independent"

or "third" sectors. I have discussed the shortcomings of standard economic theories of the third sector in an unpublished paper titled "Short Circuits and Market Failure: Theories of the Civic Sector," presented at the Twentieth World Congress of Philosophy, Boston, August 1998.

32. Jürgen Habermas, *The Structural Transformation of the Public Sphere: An Inquiry into a Category of Bourgeois Society* (1962), trans. Thomas Burger and Frederick Lawrence (Cambridge, Mass.: MIT Press, 1989). For a brief summary, see Jürgen Habermas, "The Public Sphere: An Encyclopedia Article (1964)," trans. Sara Lennox and Frank Lennox, *New German Critique* 1 (Fall 1974): 49–55. Habermas revisits these topics in "Concluding Remarks" and "Further Reflections on the Public Sphere," in *Habermas and the Public Sphere*, ed. Craig Calhoun (Cambridge, Mass.: MIT Press, 1992), 462–79 and 421–61, respectively. See also the chapter "Civil Society and the Political Public Sphere" in Habermas's *Between Facts and Norms: Contributions to a Discourse Theory of Law and Democracy*, trans. William Rehg (Cambridge, Mass.: MIT Press, 1996), 329–87.

33. See especially Joan B. Landes, *Women and the Public Sphere in the Age of the French Revolution* (Ithaca, N.Y.: Cornell University Press, 1988).

34. Part of the problem is that Adorno's theses tend to be monocausal. It is always tricky to sort out causes from effects in social-theoretical and historical explanations, and even more tricky to include enough of the relevant factors. Did the arts achieve societal autonomy because market forces replaced court and church patronage? Or did market forces replace patronage in the arts because participants in the arts were seeking societal autonomy? Did the arts in pre-Fascist Europe retain a measure of autonomy because they enjoyed state protection from monopolistic market forces? Or did the state protect the arts in Europe in order to retain societal dominance over against monopolistic market forces? All these lines of inquiry are inadequate, since they assume a single direction of causality and leave out many other potentially relevant factors. At the same time, of course, theoretical simplification and abstraction can yield an account rich in explanatory potential.

35. Rita Felski, *Beyond Feminist Aesthetics: Feminist Literature and Social Change* (Cambridge, Mass.: Harvard University Press, 1989), 171.

36. Felski, *Beyond Feminist Aesthetics*, 163. For a shorter account of this attempt to go "beyond feminist aesthetics," see Rita Felski, "Why Feminism Doesn't Need an Aesthetic (and Why It Can't Ignore Aesthetics)," in *Feminism and Tradition in Aesthetics*, ed. Peggy Zeglin Brand and Carolyn Korsmeyer (University Park: Pennsylvania State University Press, 1995), 431–45.

37. See Kant, *Critique of the Power of Judgment*, sections 39–41, pp. 171–78.

38. I elaborate this alternative and explore its implications for public policy in a book manuscript provisionally titled "Art-in-Public: Politics, Economics, and a Democratic Culture."

39. Perhaps this idea of autonomy would be a social-philosophical counterpart to the attempt "to explore the possibilities of a post-structuralist aesthetics (hence, a postanalytic and a postfeminist aesthetics)" in Joseph Margolis, "Reconciling Analytic and Feminist Philosophy and Aesthetics," in *Feminism and Tradition in Aesthetics*, ed. Peggy Zeglin Brand and Carolyn Korsmeyer (University Park: Pennsylvania State University Press, 1995), 416–30. Margolis's essay responds to Joann B. Waugh's "Analytic Aesthetics and Feminist Aesthetics: Neither/Nor?" in the same volume, 399–415.

13

Unfreedom, Suffering, and the Culture Industry

What Adorno Can Contribute to a Feminist Ethics

Jennifer L. Eagan

A key problem in feminist ethics is how women can extricate themselves from the forces that have determined how they live their lives. These constraints, broadly characterized as the sex/gender system, take political, psychological, spiritual, and cultural forms. Taken together, these constraints constitute a matrix of perception and a limitation on thought that is nearly impossible to see beyond. However, if a feminist ethics is to be possible, there must be a way to act and think beyond the strictures of the sex/gender system. The philosophy of Theodor Adorno is an as yet untapped resource for thinking about such constraints on thought and possibilities. He describes the culture industry as a schema through which thought, imagination, and our capacity to critique is diminished. He advocates aesthetic expression as the last best hope for thinking beyond what is readily available. These themes are already present in feminist theory in the work of Judith Butler. Butler sees gender itself as such a cultural schema through which our thought and possibilities become limited. Her ethics advocates disruptive styles of living one's gender, while acknowledging that we never fully escape our gendered culture. Although some may want to posit wholesale freedom from constraint as a clear-cut goal of feminist ethics, Adorno and Butler address concrete social and cultural realties that show how difficult this goal is.

In this chapter, I examine the intersections of suffering and culture as these ideas appear in the works of Adorno and Butler.[1] First, I briefly define Adorno's concepts of culture, the culture industry, ideology, immanent critique, and art. Second, I examine the problem of freedom and unfreedom in Adorno's work and show how his perspective can inform questions important to feminist ethics and praxis. Next, I develop Adorno's notion of suffering as a mode of unfreedom and with Butler examine gender as a particular instantiation of suffering. Here, I argue that suffering is constituted by specific social contexts. Further exposing the contextual nature of suffering, I discuss cultural ideology as a schema, a necessary and fixed lens of perception that makes reality intelligible to us, and claim that gender is a part of that schema. Within this exploration, I argue that (1) all men and women experience unfreedom to varying degrees, (2) suffering always takes place within social and cultural contexts, (3) the experience of living one's gender is a particular example of suffering, and (4) art can give suffering meaning by revealing its social context, though its critical capacity is diminished by cultural ideology.

Culture and Ideology in Adorno

Adorno's reading of culture shows both the promise and pitfalls of cultural expression and production. *Culture* for Adorno can have many meanings. He writes, "Culture is the perennial claim of the particular over the general, as long as the latter remains unreconciled to the former."[2] In other words, culture, for Adorno, should express individuality in contrast to the status quo. Culture can be expressed through philosophy, art, music, and political thought, among other vehicles. However, because of the shared nature of culture, it contains the potential to become subsumed back into the general. "Culture as a common denominator already contains in embryo that schematization and process of cataloging and classification."[3] What is at one time an expression of individuality can become reified as a group perspective that shapes and homogenizes through the lens or schema of co-opted culture. Culture as a critique of the status quo is always in jeopardy of being subsumed into that status quo.

Culture can lapse into culture industry, the creation of cultural products for mass consumption. The culture industry violates the second condition of the claim of culture. The culture industry is the particular that has been reconciled to the general, laid out for the consumption for the general, while laying false claims to particularity, uniqueness, and individuality. J. M. Bernstein nicely encapsulates what Adorno means by *the culture industry*: "The culture industry, which involves the production of works for reproduction and mass consumption, thereby organizing 'free' time, the remnant domain of freedom under capital in accordance with the same principles of exchange and equivalence that reign in the sphere of production outside leisure, presents culture as the realization of the right of all to the gratification of desire while in reality continuing the negative integration of society."[4] The culture industry is not generated by the choices of a majority of people, but is generated by a few who shape these choices though the marketplace, the sphere of economic exchange where cultural products are bought and sold. Adorno is worried that the culture industry and the marketplace will become so totalizing as to altogether foreclose imaginative choices and possibilities beyond what is produced in this realm.

Part of the danger of culture's lapsing into the culture industry is that it creates a homogenizing schema whereby cultural products become ideology. *Ideology* for Adorno is the false story about what reality is that becomes reiterated until it is accepted as truth.[5] Ideology can be countered by *immanent critique,* a critique that appeals to social conditions and concrete experience while recognizing that any critique comes from within and is conditioned by that ideological perspective. However, Adorno claims that ideology no longer functions explicitly in the form of propaganda, but has become embedded in social practices that have been reiterated and reenacted in social practice. Here, as Adorno would say, ideology becomes part of "the overwhelming power of existing conditions."[6] Ideology tries to reduce the world to a series of brute facts that escape critique, reducing the power of culture to generate a counterpoint to the status quo. Adorno holds out the greatest hope for *art*, as something "that can speak for what is hidden by the veil" of ideology, to be able to best counter ideology by creating new possibilities beyond the world as it is.[7] Culture and art contain the power to counter the culture industry and ideology, but they also have the potential to lose their autonomy and be co-opted in the service of the status quo. If we have any hope for enacting our own freedom and creating change in the world, we will need enough distance to launch a critique. In the following section, I examine Adorno's view of freedom and how tenuous its potential is given certain social conditions.

The Puzzle of Freedom and Unfreedom

Serving as background to the possibility of any ethics, as well as any meaningful response to suffering, stands Adorno's dialectic of freedom and unfreedom that appears in *Negative Dialectics*. Responding to Kant's Third Antinomy on the unresolvability of the opposing possibilities of freedom and determinism, Adorno writes, "Each drastic thesis is false. In their inmost core, the theses of determinism and freedom coincide."[8] Adorno would claim that freedom (*Freiheit*) and unfreedom (*Unfreiheit*) stand in a dialectical relationship to each other. They are not antinomial, but interwoven, dependent upon each other and occurring simultaneously. We experience both (*ND*, 220). Adorno defines *freedom* as "a moment, rather, in a two-fold sense: it is entwined, not to be isolated; and for the time being it is never more than an instant of spontaneity, a historical node, the road to which is blocked under present conditions" (*ND*, 219). Unfreedom is what blocks this road to freedom. Although we might be tempted to conflate unfreedom and determinism, Adorno urges us to get beyond the abstract formulation of determinism by using the term *unfreedom*. He performs this switch in order to infuse both the concepts of freedom and unfreedom with social reality. Unfreedom is the conditioning of spontaneity by any social, cultural, or political factor. Therefore, unlike a wholesale determinism, unfreedom can occur in varying degrees.

Adorno elaborates his view of freedom by way of his critique of Kant. He claims that Kant mistakenly attacks this "pseudoproblem" in the

Third Antinomy and in his ethics (ND, 211–99). Kant's fundamental mistake is identifying the abstract, noumenal subject as the location of freedom. Adorno contrasts this view with a physicalist account of freedom; freedom is nothing more than the experiences and impulses stemming from an empirical subject. "Freedom would be the word for the possibility of those impulses" (ND, 212). If we are going to find freedom anywhere, beyond this signifying word, we will look to empirical conditions surrounding the interaction between subject and world. What we find when we look for freedom are the ways that social realities and psychological conditions create the empirical subject and constrain him or her in specific and predictable ways. Claiming it is more than a simple mistake, Adorno implicates Kant in his perpetuation of a bourgeois notion of freedom that reduces freedom to the interiority of the subject and therefore denies and forgives the real conditions that constitute unfreedom. Existentialism likewise serves this poisonous political project by convincing people that they are responsible for the conditions that they are subjected to, or that they are at least responsible for their ability to respond to such conditions (ND, n. 26).

This mistake of locating freedom within the subject stems from a misguided characterization of the subject. Kant presumes that the will is unified, that consciousness is transparent to itself, and that action can therefore always be guided by reason (ND, 239). To counter these notions, Adorno appeals to psychoanalysis as an obvious ally, but he also proposes another version of the will, one that is more compatible with an empirical subject.[9] Adorno's dialectical definition of the will would allow the subject to combat the forces of unfreedom by resisting any moral law that claims universality and serves as a socially imposed constraint. Such a will would appeal to real empirical conditions in addition to reason in order to determine action. In looking to real conditions, the will would not be determined by law or by a prefigured social narrative, but by a more genuine (though not perfect) judgment. An idealized will, such as Kant's, makes the mistake of presuming moral certainty. Adorno writes, "There is no moral certainty. Its mere assumption would be immoral, would falsely relieve the individual of anything that might be called morality" (ND, 243). Such moral certainty is beyond the ability of the empirical subject to discern, and it falsely presumes that morality and the subject are static and unchanging. Both morality and the self change as social conditions change. "By the concept of the self we should properly mean their potential, and this potential stands in polemical opposition to the reality of the self" (*ND*, 278). As opposed to substantiality, the empirical self is dynamic and alternating between the forces of freedom and unfreedom in a complex interplay of social and subjective forces, which cannot be thought of apart from each other.[10] Ultimately, Adorno is interested in the possibility for freedom for real empirical subjects once unfreedom has taken hold, and he is worried that specific social conditions, such as the effects of the culture industry, will foreclose the meaningful experience of freedom in the future.

This issue of freedom and unfreedom is obviously an important question for feminism. How is it possible for the oppressed to become liberated? How can women who are constructed in unfreedom attain a critical perspective from which to examine and possibly redefine their situation? To what extent is something like liberation even possible? I speculate that Adorno's dialectic between freedom and unfreedom can illustrate how feminists can move between these two poles, and show that we do not move in a simply linear direction from unfreedom to freedom. Adorno provides us with a way to take the suffering of the physical individual seriously, without mediating it or lessening it with a fictive freedom that is supposed to unify a transcendent subject-consciousness with a degraded body-object. As Drucilla Cornell explains, "The ethical significance of the disjuncture between meaning and being reminds us that reconciliation cannot be imposed. The oppressed thing—the object itself, the suffering, physical individual—bears witness to the failure of history to realize itself in the unity of subject and object."[11] Perfect freedom, in the form of liberation from oppressive social conditions, has never existed. Positing this ideal ignores these conditions; however, freedom from such conditions is still our goal. Next, I will examine suffering as a mode of unfreedom created by social conditions.

Suffering as a Mode of Unfreedom

Suffering is a particular variety of unfreedom, and one that reveals our condition of unfreedom to us. For Adorno, suffering is a physical event that runs counterfactually to ideal categories of being. In other words, suffering proves cultural ideology wrong. The specific cultural ideology that Adorno is attacking in *Negative Dialectics* is the ideology of identity thinking, or the metaphysics that attempts to subsume different things and ideas under unitary concepts.[12] This ideology has dominated Western philosophy and has been reiterated in different forms of idealism until particulars are degraded as unreal. This type of thinking tends toward subsuming all particulars under one giant universal; in Adorno's terminology, it is totalizing. To create an alternative to identity thinking in his discussion of suffering, Adorno distinguishes suffering from happiness, adopting a physicalist interpretation of both events. He remarks that "the smallest trace of senseless suffering in the empirical world belies all the identarian philosophy that would talk us out of that suffering" (*ND*, 203). Ultimately, what saves us from the totalizing power of ideology is our own immediate and subjective experience. The experience of suffering (our own or the observation of others) shakes us out of our acceptance of the status quo. Our experience informs immanent critique. Although one cannot escape the fact that ideology creates and frames the suffering that one experiences, that experience can give us enough distance from ideology to question it from within. The evidence against the ideology is not abstract, but comes from the empirical world and our own experience, with a healthy dose of skepticism, of course. "The physical moment tells our knowledge that suffering ought not to be, that things should be different" (*ND*, 203).

The problem with idealism is that it is unable to dwell with material reality, suffering, and death, and in this way it denies the human. As Adorno states, idealism "comes all too quickly to terms with suffering and death for the sake of a recollection occurring merely in reflection—in the last analysis, the bourgeois coldness that is only too willing to underwrite the inevitable."[13] This suffering, which is the result of cultural and political conditions for which we are collectively responsible, is repackaged and sold back to us as universal, natural, inevitable, and therefore beyond our control. For example, in *The Jargon of Authenticity*, Adorno takes on existentialism as an ideology, for its valorizing the suffering that particular people experience as a universal and permanent feature of the human condition when this suffering is actually produced by political and historical conditions such as gender, race, class, poverty, and war. This universalist position on suffering would seem to imply that all people suffer in the same way, thus reducing and trivializing particular instances of suffering. What Adorno calls "the pure positivity of jargon" (or ideology) causes us to overlook pain and suffering with an attitude of "trustful reliance."[14] This attitude reinforces attachment to the ideology of universality despite evidence to the contrary.

We cannot simply idealize concepts such as the ones Adorno critiques, (universality, authenticity, identity) without addressing the material. This is how concrete social, political, and cultural realities are ignored. The same is true in gender theory, although we will also need to examine how the material and biological are constructed through certain kinds of practices and discourse. I find that the work of Judith Butler addresses this best. Her philosophy is not the story of a simple discursive reading of the body as a text, as Nussbaum, Bordo, and others have claimed.[15] Butler's work, like Adorno's, addresses the disjuncture between an ideal subject and the real conditions that such a subject faces. She asks the question, "How can gender be both a matter of choice and cultural construction?"[16] In her response, she presents us with a version of Adorno's unfreedom as a kind of conditioned freedom, freedom within certain socially constructed parameters, which create the necessarily sexed and gendered subject, but do not wholly determine him or her. She explains that the choice about how to live one's body, gender, and sexuality is not made from a distance, but is an interpretation of what is already culturally available. This choice is conditioned by the culture that we find ourselves in. Butler's freedom, like Adorno's, is dependent on the conditions of unfreedom and always under threat of disappearance because of these same conditions. This choice is an ethical one that becomes instantiated in the materiality of the body and is consistently played out in the gendered actions of the subject.

Butler's work, like Adorno's, illustrates how ideology creates suffering, obscures pain, and works to construct subjects and their bodies in certain ways. She shows how the ideology that enforces rigid gender roles is not just a discourse, not the simple result of social conditioning, but a more subtle set of practices that subjects are compelled to enact under threat of unspoken sanction. The power of this ideology is so potent that the body-subjects who enact and submit to this ideology would be nothing (culturally intelligible) without it. But, I reiterate, this body is not literally nothing. The body is not a text for Butler. "There is no self that is prior to the convergence of who maintains 'integrity' prior to its entrance into this conflicted cultural field. There is only a taking up of tools where they lie, where the very 'taking up' is enabled by the tool lying there."[17] With Foucault, Butler sees the body as a culturally contested site where cultural contestations, identities, and events take place. However, in her taking up of particular instances of suffering and injustice of both real and fictional characters in her work, she remembers that the body is not just the abstract body. The body is a site of someone's specific suffering, and this cannot be cleverly avoided by abstracting completely from that site.[18] Although the body is given meaning through, partially constituted by, and often overly determined by, the discourse of gender ideology, this does not mean that the body is reducible to this text.

Butler recognizes the presence of suffering for those of us in "gender trouble" (which is all of us, to greater or lesser degrees) and, like Adorno, uses specific characters and examples. Butler, following Foucault, examines the study of the nineteenth-century French hermaphrodite Herculine, but unlike Foucault, Butler takes seriously Herculine's suffering as a result of this figure's ambiguity and cultural unintelligibility. Butler claims that Foucault "fails to recognize the concrete relations of power that both construct and condemn Herculine's sexuality" (*GT*, 94). Instead of dwelling in happy ambiguity as Foucault claims, Herculine suffers as a result of the concrete social conditions that demand that she choose to live as one sex that conforms to a heterosexual cultural norm. We see Herculine tell her own story through the lens of her own historical ideology. As Butler writes, "Romantic and sentimental narratives of impossible loves seem also to produce all manner of suffering in this text, and so do Christian legends about ill-fated saints, Greek myths about suicidal androgynes, and, obviously, the Christ figure itself" (*GT*, 99). In other words, Herculine tries to make sense of her suffering through the lens of the narratives available to her, but these seem to fail her in the end. There is no story that she could appeal to that fits with her experience. This is in part how suffering as a mode of unfreedom comes to our attention, through the chasm between ideology and our own experience. Foucault wants to romanticize this story as an example of how to live within and yet exceed gendered ideological borders. However, Butler reads Herculine's eventual suicide as a result of her unintelligibility. Herculine comes to realize that she cannot, and on some level does not, truly exist within her culture. In this sense, her suicide completes what her society has already accomplished.

From Adorno and Butler, I gather that suffering is a mode of living one's body that takes into account the ontic features that affect the body and what is created at the intersection of that body and its relationship to certain features in the world. Social and political events constitute the causes of suffering, even if the event is painted as natural (for example, famine or cancer, whose causes are environmental rather than just natural). Suffering can be distinguished from pain in this way as a natural event. Suffering obviously entails pain as a feature of subjective experience, but suffering is always situated and achieves meaning within a social context in which broader social and cultural forces are at work. However, I am skeptical about the existence of pure pain, so I am not sure that this distinction is very clear-cut. Suffering is often where the body and the social-linguistic order, in the form of discourse, meet such that the discourse constructs the sufferer in a particular way. Suffering is a part of a dialectic between the individual's experience of pain, injury, or disease and the social context that creates, conditions, and gives meaning to that pain. If we are talking about pain or discomfort as a subjectively posited reality, then we are only talking about half of that dialectical relationship. Next, I will show how this dialectic operates with two examples of suffering created and conditioned by social narratives about sexuality and gender.

Suffering in Context

In this discussion of suffering, I want to avoid what Adorno warns against, reducing the particular experiences of suffering to categories that are too theoretical and abstract to encompass them. Therefore, I want to discuss suffering within particular contexts in order to show how suffering comes from the social story or narrative about the pain, injury, or disease, not just the simple presence of these. These contexts will illustrate how social stories of certain kinds of pain and disease are more prominent and meaningful than others. These narratives construct the sufferer in certain specific and homogeneous ways that eradicate the particularity of individual experience. More specific forms of suffering often take place against the backdrop of sexualized, gendered, racialized, and classed identities, and these contexts are underwriters of the cultural narratives that create the suffering.[19] The following examples of suffering in context illustrate how gender and sexuality are suffered by most of us as a sort of low-grade fever, a cultural ideology that shapes us in ways of which we are only dimly aware, but our fever can burn higher within certain social conditions that amplify that suffering.

With the presence of AIDS, we are not just talking about the virus that eventually causes pain and then death; we are talking about the social climate that allows the virus to spread in certain ways, movements to find a cure, lack of governmental response, Reagan's not being able to say the word, fear of catching the virus, living with the virus in the presence of others to whom you will disclose your status or not, having a "status," and so on. All the items in this list contribute to the social context of the suffering, distinguishing AIDS from a simply natural experience of a disease. Randy Shilts shows us in his early history of the AIDS virus, *And the Band Played On*, how the social and political context fueled the suffering of particular individuals.[20] AIDS is not just a disease that *is*, but one that is experienced through the various changing social lenses with which we are all presented. In his work *At Odds with AIDS (Uneins mit AIDS): Thinking and Talking About a Virus*, Alexander García Düttmann views the virus from a particularized existential perspective, but also recognizes the unique ambivalence that this virus inspires, as indicated by the title. People with AIDS are simultaneously at odds with and at one with the virus; they are determined in part, but not wholly, by their status. He begins by commenting, "An expression of affliction and concern, the language used here always runs the risk of turning into jargon, a jargon of authenticity or interiority. But who will be surprised to read a book about AIDS that begins with these words? Words of resistance, of not wanting to occupy oneself with AIDS, of not being at one with AIDS; words that also express fear of AIDS, a fear heightened by AIDS."[21] Here, Düttmann is expressing his desire to maintain the ambivalence that sufferers of AIDS experience and to not lapse into a typical AIDS narrative, one that is infused with social mystification and fear or with the heroic overcoming that such narratives often lapse into. He wants to present something that displays genuine resistance and opposition, recognizing not only that AIDS entails guilt, fear, anxiety about "dying before one's time," and such seemingly necessary existential dimensions, but also that these dimensions cannot be thought of apart from the socially constructed story of AIDS, which in turn sets the conditions for the subjective experience of one's own death. These simply existential features of death and being-toward-death take place within the social framework of AIDS as a shameful disease, associated with sex, gay men, immigrants, fluid exchange, poverty, and drug use. In fact, Düttmann recognizes AIDS as a metaphor for the fear that we experience in relation to such social realities when we recognize that we are connected in ways that we do not want, choose, or intend.[22]

The social narratives that construct suffering often serve to reinforce fixed notions of identity and difference. They serve to dichotomize and

separate those who suffer from those who do not. Donna Haraway acknowledges the power of scientific immune system discourse as a metaphor for contestation, war, and difference.[23] Here she serves us "with a
reminder that science has been a travel discourse, intimately implicated
in the other great colonizing and liberatory readings and writings so basic
to modern constitutions and dissolutions of marked bodies of race, sex,
and class."[24] These social narratives, not just the sensational and hyper-
bolic ones but the scientific and educational ones as well, construct the
suffering person as a suffering person in a particular way. Social narratives
about AIDS both lump those with AIDS into one tainted category while
simultaneously acknowledging their difference from those not infected.
This dichotomy of pure and impure serves as an ideology that defies the
social realities of real practices, and the complicated and fragile identity
positions that each body occupies. This blinds us to the fact that AIDS as
virus crosses over from the impure/suffering to the pure/nonsuffering in
ways that social narratives discourage us from thinking out. This has particularly affected the narratives about AIDS and heterosexual women,
since the ideology of how such women have sex makes them appear to be
at low risk, when real practices may not warrant this judgment. As John
Nguyet Erni suggests, AIDS narratives do not dwell effectively with the
changing nature of the virus and the identities of those who become HIV
positive, in part because these differences defy our presumptions about
who suffers and who does not. "[H]ow do we make sense of the discourag-
ing news about the 'new' infection in populations not easily identified
along taken-for-granted sexual, gender, racial, or class lines (such as the
growing cases of infection among white middle-class heterosexual teenagers)?"[25] The answer to this question is that we may not make sense of
the blurring of the lines between the afflicted and the healthy, but insist
on such isolated cases being statistical outliers who are somehow culpable
for their own fate. Only if such groups remain distinct does the metaphor
have the power to explain the world and sustain current ideology.

Similarly, breast cancer for women serves as a metaphor for not only
for what cancer signifies generally, but also for the condition of being a
woman specifically. As Barbara Ehrenreich writes in her personal breast
cancer narrative, "There is a reason, it occurs to me, why cancer is our
metaphor for so many runaway social processes, like corruption and
'moral decay': we are no less out of control of ourselves."[26] However, she
also notes that she gets the message from the anxiety surrounding her
initial diagnosis that "femininity is death," that having a breast and being

a woman have already implicated her in her own mortality.[27] From her personal story and reaction to having the disease, Ehrenreich rightly points to the culture of breast cancer, the narrative of positive thinking, the ignorance of the environmental factors that are likely causes of the disease, and the presence of infantilizing, pink-ribboned products in the corporate-funded breast cancer marketplace. She finds that the scientific, social, and cultural story of her own breast cancer is "pretty well mapped out in advance," such that she has limited control over her treatment or her emotional response.[28] In the face of this overwhelming narrative, she finds that she can barely carve out a space for her own unique experience of the disease. This is the culture that creates her suffering, paints a picture of it in advance, a picture that she rebels against because, she insists, it does not speak to her experience. " 'Culture' is too weak a word to describe all this. What has grown up around breast cancer in just the last fifteen years more nearly resembles a cult. . . . The products—teddy bear, pink ribbon brooches, and so forth—serve as amulets and talismans, comforting the sufferer and providing visible evidence of faith."[29] But these comforts, symbols of faith, and displays of sisterhood deny the sentiment that this disease and its attendant suffering are not acceptable and that the social and environmental conditions that create the disease should be addressed. The jargon of breast cancer functions as does Adorno's jargon of authenticity, covering over suffering with that "trustful reliance" that this suffering is reasonable, justified, transcendent.

In the case of suffering a disease, not only can a particular situation serve as a metaphor for a powerless subject position, such as being gay or being a woman; in addition, disease can lead to a greater appreciation for the suffering caused by the subject position independent of that disease. In Margaret Atwood's *Bodily Harm*, we meet Rennie, a character who experiences suffering on several different levels throughout the course of the text. Initially we learn that Rennie is being treated for breast cancer and has recently undergone a mastectomy. We see her experiencing the suffering involved in her breast cancer in such a way that it not only forces her to face her own mortality as one might expect, but also changes her relationship to men. In particular, there is Jake, with whom she lived and with whom she has recently broken up as a result of the trauma of her breast cancer treatment. Although Rennie and Jake seem to try to stay together and remain interested in sex with each other, neither seems to be able to overcome the unsexy mark of mortality that Rennie's body now bears. This surprises Rennie, because she previously thought that sex with men was uncomplicated. "She used to think that sex wasn't an issue, it wasn't crucial, it was a pleasant form of exercise, better than jogging, a pleasant form of communication, like gossip. People who got too into sex were a little *outré*. . . . What mattered was the relationship. A good relationship: that's what she and Jake were supposed to have. People commented on it, at parties, as if they were admiring a newly renovated house."[30] She normalizes her relationship with Jake early in the novel, even as she periodically recounts his dominance over her and her loss of self in the relationship. Later in the novel she casually relays to us in a reminiscence that "Jake liked to pin her hands down, he liked to hold her so that she couldn't move. He liked that, he liked thinking of sex as something he could win at. Sometimes he really hurt her, once he put his arm across her throat and she really did stop breathing. Danger turns you on, he said. Admit it. It was a game, they both knew that. He would never do it if it was real, if she really was a beautiful stranger or a slave girl or whatever it was that he wanted her to pretend. So she didn't have to be afraid of him."[31] Or so she thinks, until a new experience of suffering causes her to reflect on her situation as a woman in a "real" situation of subjugation. This experience helps Rennie make the connection between all the levels of suffering that she experiences within the context of her being a woman.

Thinking about the pain, suffering, and meaning of her disease fills her consciousness until she finds herself no longer able to function in her capacity as a freelance writer. To avoid further treatment and other complications back home, Rennie embarks on an adventure. The adventure takes place under the auspices of her writing a travel piece. However, we find that through a heightened experience of her own and other people's suffering, which she experiences during the time she spends in prison after a revolutionary uprising on the island of Ste. Agathe, Rennie comes to change her position on what counts as suffering and what its source is. She realizes, through her more dramatic and immediate experience of suffering, that her gender makes her especially vulnerable and that aspects of her relationships with men that she did not used to find frightening actually were low-grade versions of the explicit modes of suffering that she is observing and on the verge of experiencing now. For example, Jake used to like to ask her to look and dress in certain sexy ways; Rennie had always taken this as a no-risk form of play, but play that mimicked her lack of agency within the relationship. Now, through the prison bars, she witnesses prisoners getting their hair cut via bayonet blade in the courtyard. At first, Rennie thinks that their throats will be cut. But they are just being forced to submit to prison policy.[32] From her intensified experience of suffering, and specifically the suffering of women, Rennie concludes that "[s]he's afraid of men and it's simple, it's rational, she's afraid of men because they are frightening."[33] Ultimately, Rennie's whiteness and nationality as a Canadian save her from the worst possibilities of her imprisonment. From this experience, Rennie reflects on how suffering is relative to her situation, which changed as she traveled. In order to realize that her relationship to these others was as a privileged Westerner, she had to witness the suffering of others. But she also experienced her gender as a liability and a heightened source of suffering when chaos erupted.

This example illuminates Adorno's definition of suffering. Suffering is not natural and is not a permanent feature of the human condition, but is primarily caused by social and political events and conditions. The justification for this definition lies in experience, not a subjective, but a dialectical one. As Cornell writes, "Suffering is not merely recognized by Adorno as historical or natural necessity. Rather suffering from the standpoint of the particular which endures it, is senseless."[34] However, I want to extend this definition of suffering to address the seemingly permanent features of this social-political landscape that causes human beings en masse to suffer in varying degrees. The pervasiveness and seeming naturalness of the social-political landscape comes from socially generated, not fixed or natural conditions. Just as individuals suffer from diseases partially within human control, political upheavals, and the like, so do whole classes of individuals suffer as a result of socially generated identity categories and the way in which they are rigidly constituted as a result. Even in moments when individuals are not actively experiencing the intense, high-pitched suffering of disease, fear, or imprisonment, there is a lower grade of suffering that comes from being overly determined by identity categories, such as gender; by social conditions; and by the culture industry. In the following section, I will explain how this lower grade of suffering occurs within the context of the culture industry and the promise of art to create ways of being that exceed such categories.

Suffering Gender in the Culture Industry

Often when reading Adorno, it is hard to distinguish the real from the ideal in his use of terms (of course, this is a problem of translation as well). There is pop music and music that challenges the status quo. There are the artifacts that other people call art (kitsch!) and there is autonomous art. And then, there is the culture industry and there is "real" culture. Adorno expresses what culture ought to be and how it ought to function in different ways in different texts. In each case he holds out some hope for culture to serve human freedom, even despite his most depressing critiques of the all-encompassing effects of the culture industry. Adorno's definition of culture in *Mimima Moralia* is not equated with ideology or lies, as it is for his two main influences, Marx and Nietzsche. Instead, he contrasts culture with exchange. He writes, "If material reality is called the world of exchange value, and culture whatever refuses to accept the domination of that world, then it is true that that such refusal is illusory as long as the existent exists."[35] Here culture is the refusal to accept the world of exchange that reduces the value of objects and subjects to their use values. However, as long as there is no cultural force that genuinely and fully contests the world of exchange, or the marketplace as Adorno sometimes calls it, there is no culture at all properly speaking. Even more broadly in his essay "Culture and Administration," he asserts this definition. "Culture—as that which goes beyond the system of self-preservation of the species—involves an irrevocably critical impulse towards the status quo and all institutions thereof."[36] This definition seems motivated by a hope that culture will always be there as a safeguard against injustices (particularly institutional ones) or at least to bear witness to the suffering caused by them. However, in this essay Adorno continues to decry the ability of culture to stand up in the face of a powerful and totalizing status quo.

Why is Adorno so skeptical about the power of culture? Because culture as it ought to operate is being consistently and increasingly co-opted by the culture industry. Throughout his various works, Adorno consistently discusses the limitations on the imagination that the culture industry imposes, and how our capacity for thought is reduced to repackaged images and words. The culture industry effectively eradicates freedom by prefiguring certain kinds of choices and in that sense limits the reality that we can receive. In his essay "The Schema of the Culture Industry," Adorno shows how the culture industry serves as a filter or matrix through which we perceive reality and points out that this schema functions like a Kantian schema, delimiting what is possible for our experience and imagination. "Imagination is replaced by a mechanically relentless control mechanism which determines whether the latest imago to be distributed really represents an exact, accurate and reliable reflection of the relevant item of reality."[37] If that reality is primarily a culturally constructed reality, as Adorno and Butler would claim, what we end up with is nothing but reification of the status quo recreated as an exact copy, and we become unable to even process anything that is not "realistic." But the idea that what is "realistic" is socially conditioned drops out of what is considered reality, so our capacity for critique is diminished, too. This is how Adorno links the capacity for our reception of art with our capacity for critique; it is really for political reasons that Adorno consistently tackles problems in aesthetics. Our inability to grapple with the truth content of art, insofar as it never corresponds to reality, is a barometer for our diminished status as political beings.

In "Schema," Adorno uses art as an example of how we "receive" reality, though this critique could be extended to how we perceive any object or idea. When we receive works of art, ideally we are looking to their conceptual content, not their status as object. Within the schema of the culture industry, "[t]he work of art becomes its own material and forms the technique of reproduction and presentation, actually a technique for the distribution of a real object" ("Schema," 64). The world becomes an inert field of objects to be taken as brute and natural facts; and ideas, such as they exist in the field, are likewise treated as though they were objects. Ideas, from the perspective of culture industry, either fit with that brute reality or else they are considered to be false. This forecloses the possibility of imagination, which is a necessary component of political, social, and cultural critique.

In his analysis, Adorno is talking about how ideas and works of art in recent history are being degraded by new junk that is being sold to us as the equivalent to high art, but is produced and treated by us as consumer products. However, taking a longer historical view, the alleged original, from which these cheap copies are supposed to come, the original simply becomes a myth and then disappears forever. This is what Judith Butler is talking about when she discusses the copy for which there is no original.[38] If there ever was an original, it has disappeared from view such that we cannot even reconstruct it. At best we can create myths about what that original might be (like Aristophanes' myth in The Symposium). These myths can be instructive, if we are allowed to think them, but they are reconstructions of something imaginary. Adorno's critique shows us how difficult it is to even posit the myth of autonomous art or autonomous styles of gender. We need art and myth to counter the empirical reality that we face, otherwise the "is" becomes the "ought" ("Schema," 65). Reality in this case becomes completely unproblematic.

Is gender such a schema that forecloses imaginative possibilities? The presence of gendered persons, treated objectively, forecloses the possibilities of other types of objects and ideas, such that they can scarcely be enacted or thought. Any gendered style that does not fit with a preestablished reality not only is not accepted, but in a sense is not real. Of course, it is there, but there like a Halloween costume, not taken seriously and under threat of annihilation. Butler writes that the situation of gender is socially constructed in a certain way, as a condition for the possibility, not the choice of a free subject who is already there. "Subjected to gender, but subjectivated by gender, the 'I' neither precedes nor follows the process of this gendering, but emerges only within and as the matrix of gender relations themselves . . . the matrix of gender relations is prior to the emergence of the 'human.'"[39] This is the story of gender according to Judith Butler, and it seems to serve as a schema, reified in new ways by the culture industry. As Adorno would phrase it, gender functions as an ideal that gets its worth from being continually instantiated into and onto objects. But ideals in the culture industry are not imaginative ideas to be aspired to, nor are they socially generated in the form of a common vision; they do not point to the world that is not yet. "They [ideals] are accepted as an ahistorical given along with others and the honour which they owe to their opposition to life becomes a means of vindicating them as legitimate and successful elements of real life" ("Schema," 65). In other words, we would rather take such ideals as givens than be bothered with interrogating them; ideals in this sense are ideological. As such ideals become reified over and over again in the same way, they become cemented as these ahistorical and natural givens. The potential for a critical standpoint continues to erode.[40]

"Certainly every finished work of art is already predetermined in some way, but art strives to overcome its own oppressive weight as an artefact through the force of its own construction. Mass culture on the other hand simply identifies with the curse of predetermination and joyfully fulfills it" ("Schema," 72). Ideally, identities also strive to overcome their inertia and weight. The alternative is to adopt the culturally designated correct identity as your own, assuming that you did make a free choice. Since the choice is preconscious and historically imbedded, there is no reason not to think of one's own gender as natural and inert, like a meaningless cultural product, devoid as a site of critique. In expressing the way in which cultural categories become naturalized, Adorno himself addresses gender. "Whatever is in the context of bourgeois delusion called nature, is merely the scar of social mutilation. If the psychoanalytical theory is correct that women experience their physical constitution as a consequence of castration, their neurosis gives them an inkling of truth. The woman who feels herself a wound when she bleeds knows more about herself than the one who imagines herself a flower because that suits her husband."[41] Granted, an odd quote, but I think that Adorno is recognizing that what is true for other cultural categories is also true for gender, that the origins of the natural can be traced to cultural roots.

These social and cultural sources of allegedly natural categories fit both gender and other forms of suffering. All are culturally posited and reified as universal, inevitable, and natural events, when as Adorno and Butler would argue, they are not. But the positing of these categories/events as natural allows us to receive them passively instead of actively engaging in critique or in constructing ourselves as distinct from this cultural ideology. "The viewer [of a cultural product] is supposed to be as incapable of looking suffering in the eye as he is of exercising thought" ("Schema," 69). Through the lens of the culture industry, if we are fortunate we treat ourselves as objects that do not experience suffering but observe the suffering of others as part of a natural process that somehow we have been saved from. Similarly, we may observe others' suffering as a result of their gender or sexuality, if we are traditionally gendered and heterosexual, as an aberrant problem that occurs only to the unfortunate upon whom nature does not smile favorably, or as brought on by those who just do not have the savvy to play by the sex/gender rules.

In both cases an appeal to naturalness or a deviation from it is used to cover over our collective responsibility for the suffering of others and a lack of recognition of the ways in which we all suffer from prepackaged acculturation. In a passage in which Adorno is talking about the pseudo-forms of happiness sold to us by psychoanalysis conjoined with the marketplace of junky pleasures, contrived, not genuine, he writes, "It is part of the mechanism of domination to forbid recognition of the suffering it produces, and there is a straight line of development between the gospel of happiness and the construction of camps of extermination so far off in Poland that each of our own countrymen can convince himself that he cannot hear the screams of pain" ("Schema," 63). This is how gendered systems and other oppressive systems that cause suffering maintain their existence. If the chain of events that led to the suffering were exposed, it could very well lead us to enact a plan to disrupt it.

So, I conclude with a note on what disruption, as a feminist ethics, might look like. My theoretical response to suffering gender would be something like Adorno's immanent critique of culture combined with Butler's notion of nonfixed performative identity—though both these strategies are not pure and each is unsure of what is possible within different configurations of power that create and situate us and that we cannot escape, whether the culture industry or a heterosexual matrix. A position like this would both complicate the sort of the stance we take toward culture, nature, and ourselves. Adorno's and Butler's projects expose ways in which an autonomous and aesthetic way of being and becoming is increasingly impossible in modern society. How can we ourselves enact something approximating freedom when ideology is foreclosing the possibility of existence itself? Adorno is worried that we will eventually operate in a world where art, creativity, and imagination are dead, and therefore the capacity for life will be, too. Butler is hopeful that new identities can emerge as a result of and despite the heterosexual matrix. Although the relationship between freedom, art, and life is complicated, they are potentially cofounding.

Notes

1. This chapter is a continuation of my work in Adorno's reading of Kant and an outgrowth of my concern with an appropriate philosophical response to suffering. I have argued in another work that Adorno's view of suffering that appears in *Negative Dialectics* has significance for a postmodern ethics in my article "Philosophers and the Holocaust: Mediating Public Disputes," *International Studies in Philosophy* 29 (Winter 1997). Now, I am curious what Adorno has to offer to a feminist ethics that can address suffering as well.

2. Theodor W. Adorno, "Culture and Administration," in *The Culture Industry: Selected Essays on Mass Culture*, trans. J. M. Bernstein (New York: Routledge, 1991), 113.

3. Max Horkheimer and Theodor W. Adorno, *The Dialectic of Enlightenment*, trans. John Cumming (New York: Continuum, 1993), 131.

4. J. M. Bernstein, introduction to Theodor W. Adorno, *The Culture Industry: Selected Essays on Mass Culture*, trans. J. M. Bernstein (New York: Routledge, 1991), 4.

5. See Martin Jay, *Adorno* (Cambridge, Mass.: Harvard University Press, 1984). Jay emphasizes Adorno's fear that ideology will be so totalizing as to annihilate ideology itself. Ideology requires an interplay between power relationships to take place and would not be possible if one totalizing power emerged with no resistance. Jay writes, "This transparency [of modern society] is itself masked by cultural practices that are unmediated reproductions of the status quo, practices which lack the necessary tension between justification and reality for immanent critique" (177).

6. The Frankfurt Institute of Social Research, *Aspects of Sociology*, trans. John Viertel (London: Heinemann, 1972), 202. Cited in Jay, *Adorno*, 117.

7. Theodor W. Adorno, *Aesthetic Theory*, ed. Gretel Adorno and Rolf Tiedeman, trans. C. Lenhardt (New York: Routledge and Kegan Paul, 1984), 27.

8. Theodor Adorno, *Negative Dialectics*, trans. E. B. Ashton (New York: Continuum, 1994), 264; hereafter abbreviated as *ND*.

9. For a critique of Adorno's use of psychoanalysis, see J. M. Bernstein, *Adorno: Disenchantment and Ethics* (Cambridge: Cambridge University Press, 2001), 250–62. Bernstein claims that Adorno's treatment of freedom in *Negative Dialectics* gives us a strange form of metacritique as immanent critique. Adorno continually fills in the material underpinning of any theory freedom, and one that the idealists leave out, the body behind the will. Also, freedom for Adorno is always conditioned by natural history, which Bernstein criticizes as Freudian in this case, or even as a historical genealogy. Adorno is interested in how ideas and defenses of them can be a necessary part of immanent critique.

10. For an interesting and deliberate misreading of Adorno's view of the subject from a postmodern perspective, see Wilhelm S. Wurzer, "Kantian Snapshot of Adorno: Modernity Standing Still," in *The Actuality of Adorno: Critical Essays on Adorno and the Postmodern*, ed. Max Pensky (Albany: State University of New York Press, 1997), 135–53.

11. Drucilla Cornell, *The Philosophy of the Limit* (New York: Routledge, 1992), 27.

12. See Deborah Cook, *The Culture Industry Revisited: Theodor W. Adorno on Mass Culture* (Lanham, Md.: Rowman and Littlefield, 1996). Although Adorno consistently attacked identity thinking as an expression of idealism or of positivism, he did not necessarily favor the particular over the concept, but favored a balance between the two and a modest positing of the concept. "Despite the inadequacy of philosophical concepts, Adorno advocated philosophical self-reflection, or reflection on the nature of thought itself. Since they are universals, concepts say both more and less than the particulars they subsume" (80). Any assertion of concepts should tacitly acknowledge this gap or excess entailed in using concepts.

13. Theodor Adorno, *Minima Moralia: Reflections from a Damaged Life*, trans. E. F. N. Jephcott (New York: Verso, 1974), 74.

14. Theodor W. Adorno, *The Jargon of Authenticity*, trans. Knut Tarnowski and Frederic Will (Evanston: Northwestern University Press, 1973), 24.

15. See Martha C. Nussbaum, "The Professor of Parody: The Hip Defeatism of Judith Butler," *New Republic*, February, 22, 1999, 37–45; and Susan Bordo, *Unbearable Weight: Feminism, Western Culture, and the Body* (Berkeley and Los Angeles: University of California Press, 1993), 289–94.

16. Judith Butler, "Variations on Sex and Gender," in *Feminism as Critique*, ed. Seyla Benhabib and Drucilla Cornell (Minneapolis: University of Minnesota Press, 1987), 128.

17. Judith Butler, *Gender Trouble: Feminism and the Subversion of Identity* (New York: Routledge, 1990), 145; hereafter abbreviated as *GT*.

18. For another example of what I consider to be a misreading of Butler that compares her work to that of Adorno, see Carrie L. Hull, "The Need in Thinking: Materiality in Theodor W. Adorno and Judith Butler," *Radical Philosophy* 84 (July/August 1997): 22–35. Hull argues that though there are many substantial similarities between the positions of Adorno and Butler, such as their critiques of idealism, Adorno would argue that Butler succumbs to identity thinking by subsuming the autonomy of the object into the subject by way of discourse. Although Hull partially falls into the mistake of reading Butler as a radical constructionist, she still acknowledges that Butler maintains that language and materiality are distinct even though they cannot be thought apart from each other (26). What is missing from her analysis is how gender functions as an ideology, and a virtually totalizing one at that. If this is the case, whatever bodies are in any natural or raw form, we cannot perceive them because they are prefigured for us in a discourse that makes them intelligible to us only as sexed and gendered. Hull also claims that Butler wants language to be able to correspond to reality, even "other" realities, and that this shows her sympathy with Hegelianism (27). According

to Hull, this position leads Butler into a key contradiction, "Butler has basically asserted that there is no distinct reality outside of discursive, social practice, yet we may one day know that reality" (27). However, Hull ignores Butler's shared goal with Adorno that what we need to do is to create new realities that are not there yet, new possibilities, ways of thinking and of creating the material world. In this sense, Butler is acknowledging the operation of materiality, and how gender specifically functions as a Kantian schema, but simultaneously hoping that that schema does not wholly determine our capacity for sight or insight. Last, Hull uses Adorno's acknowledgment of suffering as evidence that the material body has some ontological priority, while ignoring that possibility that gender itself could constitute a kind of suffering. The material body, which Butler does not deny, is always already socially conditioned in several ways. But, if my argument in this chapter works, suffering itself is socially conditioned and does not happen to just a body, but a woman's body, a Jewish body, a terrorist's body, and so on.

19. See Judith Butler, *Bodies That Matter: On the Discursive Limits of Sex* (New York: Routledge, 1993), 111–19. With Butler, I acknowledge that these contexts cannot be genuinely understood apart from each other.

20. Randy Shilts, *And the Band Played On: Politics, People, and the* AIDS *Epidemic* (New York: St. Martin's, 1987).

21. Alexander Garciá Düttmann, *At Odds with* AIDS: *Thinking and Talking About a Virus*, trans. Peter Gilgen and Conrad Scott-Curtis (Stanford: Stanford University Press, 1996), 1–2.

22. Düttmann, *At Odds with* AIDS, 28.

23. See Donna J. Haraway, "The Biopolitics of Postmodern Bodies: Constitutions of Self in Immune System Discourse," in *Simians, Cyborgs, and Women: The Reinvention of Nature* (New York: Routledge, 1991), 203–30.

24. Haraway, "Biopolitics of Postmodern Bodies," 221.

25. John Nguyet Erni, "Ambiguous Elements: Rethinking the Gender/Sexuality Matrix in an Epidemic," in *Gendered Epidemic: Representations of Women in the Age of* AIDS, ed. Nancy L. Roth and Katie Hogan (New York: Routledge, 1998), 3–4.

26. Barbara Ehrenreich, "Welcome to Cancerland: A Mammogram Leads to a Cult of Pink Kitsch," *Harper's Magazine,* November 2001, 44.

27. Ehrenreich, "Welcome to Cancerland," 43.

28. Ehrenreich, "Welcome to Cancerland," 44.

29. Ehrenreich, "Welcome to Cancerland," 50.

30. Margaret Atwood, *Bodily Harm* (New York: Anchor Books/ Doubleday, 1981), 93.

31. Atwood, *Bodily Harm,* 197.

32. Atwood, *Bodily Harm,* 278–80.

33. Atwood, *Bodily Harm,* 279.

34. Cornell, *The Philosophy of the Limit,* 26.

35. Adorno, *Minima Moralia,* 44.

36. Adorno, "Culture and Administration," 116.

37. Theodor W. Adorno, "The Schema of Mass Culture," in *The Culture Industry: Selected Essays on Mass Culture,* trans. J. M. Bernstein (New York: Routledge, 1991), 64; hereafter cited as "Schema."

38. Judith Butler, "Imitation and Gender Insubordination," in *The Second Wave: A Reader in Feminist Theory,* ed. Linda Nicholson (New York: Routledge, 1997), 300–315.

39. Butler, *Bodies That Matter,* 7.

40. I acknowledge that there is a problem with the notion of a standpoint when we say that suffering, social forces, and the subject are all in flux. "Dialectics cannot be a 'standpoint' (*ND,* 4–6), an a priori method or an independent project of reason, for were it so it would be in contradiction with the claimed dependence of concept on object." J. M. Bernstein, *Adorno,* 230. By a critical

standpoint, I simply mean a changeable and fluid stance that finds some distance from proscribed cultural narratives to some extent. This critical standpoint would be a precondition of immanent critique, since immanent critique requires some distance from ideology, though still operates within it in order to happen at all.

41. Adorno, *Minima Moralia*, 95.

14
Unmarked and Unrehearsed

Theodor Adorno and the Performance Art
of Cindy Sherman

Mary Caputi

In his defense of modernist art, Theodor Adorno criticizes the way in which the mainstream aesthetic norms that characterize Western culture pass themselves off as universally appealing. Eager to dismantle the complacency of bourgeois society, he extols the jarring, undomesticated quality of modernist art precisely because it contravenes the predominant sensibility. Indeed, modernist art's frequently abrasive impact challenges the premise that art should be pleasing, relaxing, or an antidote to life's troubles. It utterly rejects the traditional assumption that art resides in an apolitical sanctuary, privileged by its disconnection from the social sphere. On the contrary, for Adorno all art must make social engagement its primary task, for art is an inquiry into political life. This explains his famous statement that to write poetry after Auschwitz is "barbaric," if by poetry we understand a delicately crafted verse meant to delight, appease, and divert.

Modernist art's ability to disrupt our ingrained assumptions and unsettle our complacency disallows its claiming apolitical intentions, for its oppositional status safeguards it from collaboration in what is "barbaric." Its power to shock is in fact a venue for healing change, for shock challenges the "feeble-mindedness [that] has by now established itself as common sense," and thus keeps alive the critical faculty that, Adorno feels, has otherwise been appropriated by bourgeois charm.[1] Art's ability to challenge the damage wrought by common sense thus clearly relies upon its retaining an undomesticated stance vis-à-vis the mainstream, for it freshens our responses only so long as it maintains autonomy from culture's more hegemonic forces. By extension, the aesthetic realm's domestication spells cultural death as the venues for political opposition are denied expression.

But what happens when even the avant-garde bears traces of appropriation, as inevitably it will, and can no longer claim autonomy from the society it critiques? What happens when, popularized and familiar, its contrapuntal qualities themselves become mainstream and thus lose their maverick, progressive edge? Here, I would like to examine this problem, of which Adorno was surely aware, by placing his aesthetic theory alongside the early feminist performance art of Cindy Sherman. Sherman's subtle, deliberately understated disruption of the status quo offers a way out of modernism's ingrained conundrum. This is because her art critiques bourgeois categories from within their own lexicon and offers a feminist reading of gender that unveils the profound instabilities that inhere in the mainstream itself. She seeks to implode, rather than explode, the "common sense" of gendered meanings by highlighting those meanings' unstable foundations and by demonstrating how the appearance of gender's domestication is itself merely facade. In sum, I would like to argue that Sherman's performance art, which foregrounds the undomesticated qualities of convention itself, offers an alternative to modernist art's untenable position. Hence, while Adorno claims that the avant-garde must always atone for its guilty measure of inevitable cultural appropriation, Sherman's work provides a critique of gender unhampered by such feelings of guilt. Thanks to the subtlety of her early work, she offers hope by illustrating how those unmarked, unrehearsed dimensions

of gender's conventions can in fact expose the deep anxieties that produced them.

Adorno and the Artwork's Atonement

In order to function as a repository for new cultural values, Adorno argues, modernist art must be disquieting, displaying an unmistakable resistance to the status quo. It must thwart the standard ideas about the
aesthetic realm's purpose and through its jarring impact awaken its audience's dormant social conscience. There can be nothing soothing or se-
rene in its delivery lest its powers be appropriated to anesthetize rather
than to subvert. Hence in *Aesthetic Theory*, he notes that "modern works
shoot toward the viewer as on occasion a locomotive does in a film. Ask
a musician if the music is a pleasure, the reply is likely to be—as in
the American joke of the grimacing cellist under Toscanini—'I just hate
music.'"[2] Indeed, Adorno's high praise for atonal, twelve-tone composers
such as Arnold Schoenberg and Alban Berg can be understood in terms
of these composers' ability to contravene our commonsense notions about
what makes music theoretically engaging or aesthetically beautiful. If the
grating dissonance of atonal music can liberate us from the grip of bourgeois assumptions through its own painful irresolution, Adorno argues,
then its social function is validated. Because tonal resolution always spells
surrender, music must intentionally avoid the dominant aesthetic norm
in order to serve its healing, transformative purpose.

Such validation demands that the artist remain "lonely" as he or she
doggedly resists absorption into the hegemonic mainstream. There must
be a concerted effort on behalf of the artist to avoid becoming a celebrity,
a cultural icon, or a folk hero lest his or her art lose its social "truth."
The cost is too great and the slippage too automatic when dissonance
becomes widely appealing, and art's truth morphs damningly into yet
another form of social control. "In an age of repressive collectivism, the
power of resistance to compact majorities resides in the lonely, exposed
producer of art. This power of resistance has become the sine qua non of
art; without it, art would be socially untrue."[3]

Only if art succeeds at disruption can it escape from the subject's immediate cognitive grasp, thereby refusing to participate in the standardized, anesthetizing practices of the culture industry. By challenging our

cognitive assumptions, truly progressive art can force a radical reconsideration of social norms, and thus exert the hopeful, revolutionary impact now missing from more conventional political practices. Consequently, there must always be something unrecognized in its expression, something unexpected and unclear about its performance that stretches the limits of our complacent imaginations and unsettles our intellectual categories. For if we can imagine a new form of cultural engagement, Adorno argues, we can similarly dream of a different social and political order unencumbered by capitalism's irrationality. We can imagine a world unpracticed in the brutalities of the Western tradition, brutalities with which Adorno, as a twentieth-century German Jew, was only too familiar.

The ability to confront and destabilize hegemonic forces allows the artwork to function metonymically, striving to unsettle the docile society at large as it surprises and disturbs the audience in front of it. For instance, the disquieting impact of atonal music not only confronts an audience expecting to be soothed and appeased, but also disrupts an unwitting, unrecognized cultural acquiescence which Adorno deems sorely in need of change. Such music is a "force field" capable of summing up the surrounding culture's irrationality while simultaneously opposing it. Modernist art both exposes a society's irrationality and embodies it as it purposefully runs counter to the audience's collective expectations. "The artwork is both the result of the process and the process itself at a standstill."[4] Importantly, then, by bringing the social order to a standstill and revealing its contradictions, art produces the insight that the reigning cultural paradigm, despite appearances, is eminently malleable.

Indeed, by thwarting the senses and unsettling our cognitive complacency, modernist art retains some promise of a different society, signaling a ray of hope, a chink in the armor of despair even amidst its own jarring disturbance. While art cannot offer a clear political agenda that will bring about social change, it can affect human consciousness in ways that encourage critical thinking and restore the transformative potential of the imagination. The intellectual distance and ironic edge that it allows can function as catalysts for profound internal change even when hegemonic forces appear so deeply ingrained, and their impact so thoroughly unrivaled. "[S]omeone sitting in a café who is suddenly struck by the music and listens intensely may feel odd to himself and seem foolish to others. In this antagonism the fundamental relation of art and society appears."[5]

Indeed, this ability to produce a significant change in human consciousness constitutes the artwork's political importance as it both brings together and radically opposes the existing social order. For art can awaken the public to the fact that current social relations are not immutable, that bourgeois culture is not synonymous with common sense but in fact engenders an irrationality that simply goes unchallenged. Oppositional art can adumbrate political change by critiquing the culture of which it is nevertheless a by-product. Hence the autonomous, revolutionary dimension of art has nothing to do with the audience's "appreciation" of it, for true art is not "culinary" in purpose, nor does it appease. Rather, the aesthetic function that Adorno extols insists on a painful dissonance so that the possibility of cultural healing might be kept alive within its own unlikely, undisciplined expression.

Adorno's enthusiasm for modernism's disruptive, progressive potential recognizes the limits of the autonomy of modern art and understands that its unassimilated voices always bear some relation to the status quo. He admits that aesthetic expression can only critique the existing social order from within that order's own categories and that in order to be meaningful, it must retain some dialectical interrelation with its opposite. Its contrapuntal impact notwithstanding, all art necessarily restates and reaffirms the very confines that are in question. The act of contesting social categories first affirms, if unwittingly, the far-reaching influence that such categories have had and upholds the success of the very ideology that is in question. Ironically, then, there is always a residual conservatism to even the most revolutionary art, as some measure of cooperation in the status quo remains embedded in its expression. For even as such art highlights its autonomy from cultural forces, it nevertheless displays the degree to which it remains enmeshed within the very system that it critiques. Its ability to be autonomous thus remains blunted, and it is "culpable" in that it always, to some degree, reaffirms given social relations.

Aware of this irony, Adorno concedes that even the jarring twelvetone music of Schoenberg, whose structure disallows the pleasing resolution of the seven-tone scale, confirms the appeal of the musical tradition that it strives to subvert. Atonality necessarily takes tonality as its point of reference, as its dissonance is interpreted only in relation to the pleasing resolutions of tonal music. Schoenberg, then, appears revolutionary only in the context of Brahms, Beethoven, and Chopin, such that performing Schoenberg's music necessarily invokes the classical tradition he strives to oppose. To posit atonal music as undomesticated, then, is to invoke the domesticated tradition that it necessarily addresses, just as to rebel against a musical tradition is to affirm that tradition's hegemony.

As an unwilling agent of conservatism, then, all modernist art ironically participates in "disaster," since it remains implicated in the reigning paradigm whose conventions it despises. The hope that modernism holds out for changed social relations always remains tainted by a pessimistic undercurrent, and its revolutionary potential can never claim complete autonomy from the powers that be. "At present, all works of art including radical ones have a conservative tinge, for they help reinforce the existence of a separate domain of spirit and culture whose practical impotence and complicity with the principle of unmitigated disaster are painfully evident. . . . By definition, art works are socially culpable."[6]

Ultimately, then, there can be no escape from the forces of production that give rise to revolutionary art's expression. The ambivalent nature of the avant-garde's potential will always resides in the fact that it emanates directly from the cultural order that it critiques. Hence the racism, anti-Semitism, and materialism that were so abhorrent to Adorno during his lifetime were necessarily restated in the artwork's efforts to discredit the same, and the new society he envisaged could only bear traces of the Nazi regime from which he fled. His famous work on the authoritarian personality, for instance, forever refers back to the authoritarianism it so assiduously criticized, ensuring that his experience of Nazi Germany would remain the framework within which he wrote.[7] Thus implicated in the forces of control, art—like other forms of social criticism—remains "culpable," guilty of participating in that which it denounces.

Such is the paradox of progressive forces, whose beguiled, beguiling double entendres hinder and diminish their oppositional status. "[A]s prisoner of its own form," Adorno writes, contemporary art "never entirely divested itself of its authoritarian inheritance, its unrebellious malice."[8] Caught up in such a paradoxical web, it will always display what Linda Hutcheon terms "irony's edge": the fact that irony always restates and thus reaffirms precisely what it is trying to subvert.[9] Modernist art thus retains a marked ambivalence, and its commitment to truthfulness ensures that it can never hide its guilty internal conflict, but must atone for its sin. Necessarily implicated within a conservative cultural network that alone generates its oppositional status, such intimacy, Hutcheon warns, "can always be seen as complicity."[10]

Nevertheless, the artwork's degree of autonomous berth gives it room for creative repentance: "the worthy ones among them try to atone for their guilt."[11] This atonement undoubtedly takes the form of its exaggerated abstraction and formalist retreat from conventional categories. By staying aloof, it can highlight the degree to which it remains unappropriated by the surrounding cultural forces, and hence meaningfully contrapuntal. Thus the atonality of twelve-tone music, the deliberate eschewal of everyday categories in abstract expressionist painting, the emphasis on material substance in modernist sculpture and architecture, are all efforts to heighten art's autonomy from bourgeois sensibilities, and thereby allow "the worthy ones . . . to atone." Yet this atonement is never absolute, as even the most unsettling art-work remains implicated in the very culture that it disparages.

Ed Harris's film *Pollock* (2000) dramatizes this conflict inherent in the avant-garde's mission. While the film's portrayal of Jackson Pollock's career illustrates his unique methods of expression and daring creativity, it also dramatizes the artist's conflicted relationships with two established pillars of the art world: art critic Clement Greenberg and wealthy patron Peggy Guggenheim. Pollock's love-hate relationship with these two persons is in many ways emblematic of how difficult it is to declare oneself entirely free of the reigning cultural order. To be sure, in its day abstract expressionism represented an innovative new genre, and those committed to its development—Pollock, Lee Krasner, Willem de Kooning, Jasper Johns, Marc Rothko—saw themselves as working independently from the established system. They believed themselves to be an enclave unappropriated by the mainstream, and thus unapologetically defiant of convention. And in many ways, they were. Nevertheless, artists such as Pollock needed the patronage and support of the art world's luminaries in order to be counted within the very society they wished to critique. Pollock needed access to the corridors of power, to journals, newspapers, and galleries, in order to challenge and undermine that same power. And if Greenberg and Guggenheim stood for the establishment, then Pollock was confronted with the troubling paradox of desiring what he opposed, of striving to embrace and find approval from precisely what he shunned. The film's director takes pains to dramatize Pollock's self-hating struggle as Pollock alternately seeks out and rejects the company of these people. Thus, he has a brief romantic interlude with Guggenheim, whose patronage surely helped advance his career. Yet, in an act of defiance, Pollock also urinates into a fireplace during an elegant party thrown by Guggen-heim, rendering her and her well-heeled guests speechless.

Still, Adorno does not overstate the artwork's social culpability and thus never gives up on the important if not unique revolutionary function that it serves. For if the voice of opposition can speak only from within the established parameters of power, how much more clearly it expresses the need for subversion. If its opposition depends on its acquiescence, how much more necessary its expression of dissent. As a repository for new cultural values, the aesthetic realm can never be read as merely com-plicitous in existing relations. Thus, even as he admits the guilt of the art work's conservatism, Adorno still concedes that art's atonement redeems its progressive edge. This atonement keeps the project worthwhile: while the aesthetic avant-garde cannot offer a clear revolutionary agenda to a public "kneaded into shape by the culture industry," it can provide the crucial insight of transformed perception that ultimately functions as a catalyst for social change.[12] The willingness to atone is thus the measure of artistic success, for modernism can rehabilitate its audience's sensibilit-ies only if it admits its own complicity in the forces of cultural conserva-tism. If its atonement truly challenges the limits of the reigning cultural order, then art can meaningfully function as a double agent.

Unrepentant: Cindy Sherman's Staid Rebellion

The early work of feminist performance artist Cindy Sherman offers a different interpretation of revolutionary art's role as double agent. For her, working within the rank and file of a system that the artist simulta-neously inhabits and critiques is far less problematic than for Adorno. Undisturbed and unapologetic about the artwork's indeterminacies, Sherman's photography and videotaped performances suggest that the atonement demanded by Adorno is unnecessary given that art's entangle-ment in the powers that be is not an impediment, but the very venue for a meaningfully subversive assault. Thus, as the product of one concerned with the cultural meanings of gender, Sherman's work is unapologetic about its deliberate replaying, restating, and reenacting of prevalent femi-nine archetypes to the point that her obvious cooperation in the system risks appearing as a simple endorsement. Indeed, the creative power of Sherman's work allows it to operate from within well-rehearsed, even hackneyed cultural stereotypes without falling "prisoner of its own form." Rather, it offers an effective mode of internal, immanent criticism that subverts as it mimes. Her work displays a confidence that the intimacy described above need not be read as complicitous in what it critiques, since it is precisely such intimacy that allows the double agent to go to work, to confound and confuse the familiar conventions that she is at pains to represent.

Indeed, the sheer volume of Sherman's videotaped performances and early photography reveals an ease with traditional feminine stereotypes, an ease that is capable of making these stereotypes work against themselves. Hence, as parodic ruse, she dresses herself up to replay the familiar female archetypes: the glamorous actress in dark glasses, the downtrodden housewife overwhelmed with responsibilities, the wide-eyed ingenue primping for a first date, the brazen femme fatale lying across a sports car. She is so adept at changing modes, at remaking and re-creating herself, that she never falls prisoner of any form. On the contrary, her ease with stereotypes facilitates her critique of them and thus she need never repent. There is nothing guilty in her replaying of femininity's most traditional guises, precisely because their very abundance does not ensure, but thwarts, that category's certainties. Their preponderance reveals instability, since the more the body is performed, the less clear its meaning becomes.

The deeper subject of Sherman's feminist performance art is not the female body variously presented, then, but the instability of "woman" as a cultural category. The more Sherman is in control of her art and adept in the demands of performativity—the more she changes her clothes, hair, and makeup and captures herself on film—the more fluid and open-ended that category appears. For this reason, there is a confidence in her ability to bring about a changed social consciousness without capitulating, unwillingly, to the status quo. Although her photography deliberately affects a certain unease, to be discussed presently, this does not diminish Sherman's overall confidence that her art will produce a changed social consciousness where the meaning of woman is concerned. Her art underscores the body's unstable meanings and gender's extreme tenuousness even as it replays society's efforts to mark femininity as stable.

Such a changed consciousness first of all demands that the body's biological reality not be conflated with a naturalistic reading of gender, or that the outward physical markings of femaleness be read as coextensive with a larger narrative about femininity's "truth." On the contrary, the narrative of gender is something humanly crafted, something that exists as the by-product of human agency and the ideological backdrop that informs that agency. In an effort to dramatize the weight of that ideology, Sherman thus highlights the performative aspects of gender such that every claim to femininity's "natural" meaning will be undermined, put into question, exposed as uncertain and provisional. Thus, while her work presents us time and again with a different rendition of the female form—glamorous, tired, dressed up, dressed down—the resultant saturation works to critique not only the body, but also gender (or the body as it participates in the construction of gender).

Indeed, performativity insists that bodies are read and not seen, that the reality of their biological immediacy need not obfuscate what is in fact the learned, acquired, culturally inscribed way in which we read them. Deaggregating biology and gender brings into focus the weight of culture's text, highlighting how pervasively its influence shapes our desiring imaginations. What seemed simply biological now becomes a politicized text, even when it takes the form of the conventional and everyday. Artists such as Sherman recognize that, while gender's narrative may be far-reaching and effective, its textual component always allows an interpretive space to challenge the manner in which it is received. If gendered meanings adhere to an overarching, yet ultimately insecure cultural narrative, this means that their display is always open to interpretation, always ready to invalidate rather than to affirm the pronouncements they make.

The term *performance* makes this analytic slippage particularly clear, for it invokes the tremendous room for maneuver afforded an actor when interpreting a role. If skillfully read, the lines he or she rehearses can be made to work against themselves and to invoke with a carefully regulated irony precisely the opposite of what they appear to convey. In the same manner, the discourse of gender is an assumed role, a narrative, the standard enactment of which can itself be the means of its own deconstruction. Such an ingrained irony gives rise to the performativity upon which a feminist interpretation depends. "There is no gender identity behind the expressions of gender," writes Judith Butler; "that identity is performatively constituted by the very 'expressions' that are said to be its results."[13] Thus, just as the expressions of gender cannot prove the authenticity of gender, neither can the outward "signs" of femininity verify its ontology, for these restless, mutating marks are nothing more than performative utterances whose claims to truth can be deconstructed on their own grounds. The healing, disquieting beauty of Sherman's early art rests on this fact as it dramatizes gender's deeply held insecurities.

It is the disquiet—be it sinister or humorous, provocative or shy—that allows Sherman's art to heal, reaching out even as it delivers an immanent criticism. To approach gender as one would a theatrical performance opens up interpretive vistas even as it unsettles the staid renditions of femininity and masculinity upon which we have long relied. As Amelia Jones explains in *Body Art: Performing the Subject,* there is "an anxious uncertainty put into play by the performative, theatrical dimension of meaning production," a tendency to draw attention to the unsteady foundation upon which cultural meanings rest.[14] This anxious uncertainty to which Jones alludes is surely played out in Sherman's tendency to collapse the boundaries between self and other (Sherman is both the model and the artist), viewer and viewed (she is the subject of her art, but also its creator), cultural critic and body-on-display (she is a performance artist going to work on herself). It blurs the distinction, in other words, between those roles that are traditionally assigned and thus highlights the anxieties of gender's profound uncertainty. "[W]orks of art . . . overtly stage their relationship to the viewer as corporeal, invested, mutual, intersubjective."[15]

Importantly, Jones affirms that the collapsing and blurring of distinctions can rehabilitate female agency and thus serve feminist ends. By highlighting the interpretive angle open to all gendered meanings, this collapsing empowers women to assume the role of critic even as they promote and replay the many guises of their cultural inscription. This admission of art's inscription within the very culture that it seeks to critique of course parallels Adorno's argument that the art both reconfirms and subverts bourgeois norms: art is implicated in the system that it contravenes. Yet for Sherman there is no need to atone for this implication, for it is only in mimicking gendered stereotypes that she can reveal the anxieties of their unstable existence, thereby rendering suspect the cultural order that promotes them. "Feminists have had much to gain from the narcissistic collapse of the boundaries between self and other, the distinctions between the public and the private, the difference between the signifier and the signified itself . . . (because) it has the potential of overthrowing the paternal function."[16]

*   *   *

In her early work, Sherman works from deep within traditional readings of gender to produce film stills and photography intent on unsettling the stereotypes she so playfully reenacts. The archetypes she works with constitute standard fare and often reproduce a seemingly hackneyed voyeurism in their perusal of women caught unawares. These women either do not realize that they are being watched by the camera or are ill at ease with its intrusive gaze. Thus in *Untitled Film Still #2* (1977) (Fig. 1), a young woman contemplates her image in the bathroom mirror, a towel wrapped around her, unaware that her image is being captured on film. Similarly in *#14* (1978) (Fig. 2), a glamorous woman in a black dress looks ready for an evening out yet does not know that she is the subject of some voyeuristic fancy. And in *#17* (1978) (Fig. 3), a prim woman appears to be visiting the downtown of a big city, but does not welcome the gaze that frames her face. While the pleasures of spying on women is a traditional motif in film, and surely constitutes a staple of pornography, Sherman's purpose in replaying this motif extends beyond a mere desire to jump on the bandwagon and be voyeuristic herself. To be sure, her voyeurism is not meant to simply catch women unawares and thus reinscribe them within the purview of the male gaze. Instead, her creative approach to gender's time-honored expressions is meant to register a profound uncertainty about the stereotypes being rehearsed, as seen in the uneasy, apprehensive, hesitant demeanor of so many of her subjects.

It is deliberate, then, that Sherman's film stills have anything but a reaffirming impact upon the viewer, despite their reference to familiar settings and situations. In *Untitled Film Still #2*, for instance, the woman wrapped in a towel appears worried, apprehensive, uncertain of what she sees in the mirror. She stands in an awkward position, with an awkward expression on her face. Her torso twists as if to imply a sudden gesture and a disruption in her train of thought. The towel begins to unravel from around her body. This is a photograph that has certainly caught her unawares, but that also registers her deep uncertainty about her own image. The viewer subsequently shares in this uncertainty, all of which jettisons the standard scopophilic pleasure of the pornographic setting.

Thus, while the voyeuristic motif reconfirms traditional readings of gender, the image's profound uncertainties and internal ruptures allow it to work against those readings, and to allude to gender's frailty. The nervous disruption that predominates here precludes its simply replaying the pleasures of looking, for the looking that is foregrounded here is not entirely fun. Subsequently, this woman is not merely a body on display, a

Fig. 1   Cindy Sherman, *Untitled Film Still #2, 1977*. Courtesy of the Artist and Metro Pictures Gallery.

Fig. 2   Cindy Sherman, *Untitled Film Still #14*, 1978. Courtesy of the Artist and Metro Pictures Gallery.

Fig. 3   Cindy Sherman, *Untitled Film Still #17*, 1978. Courtesy of the Artist and Metro Pictures Gallery.

nude whose exposed flesh reinscribes femininity within patriarchal parameters. Rather, the apprehension captured in this woman's worried, curious, quizzical stance, along with the general awkwardness of the image, works to unsettle the hackneyed gender scenario that it mimes. Indeed, this bather is thus a double agent who both cooperates in and informs on the gendered meanings that envelop her by exposing that system's tenuous hold. For that system, like her towel, easily comes undone in a gesture that reveals apprehension.

This same nervous apprehension predominates in stills #14 and #17, serving an equally rebellious purpose within the context of seemingly everyday scenes. There is an eerie quality resembling Hitchcock's daring insight into everyday life's uncanny side that draws us toward the unstable aspects of mainstream culture, reminding us of the frailty and indeed potential collapse of those meanings that we construct for ourselves. In both instances, the women Sherman portrays are glamorously primed for their respective outings and have been dressed, coiffed, and made up in traditional fashion, complete with eyeliner and teased hair. The woman ready for an engaging soiree in #14 wears a classic black dress and pearls, yet her overtly sexual clothing cannot hide the hesitation and indeed anxiety made visible in her facial expression. Thus the openness to advances suggested by her clothing is thrown into question if not negated by her body language. As in still #2, we do not get what we expected. The downtown visitor in #17 offers an equally unsettling expression, as her strangely fixated glance suggests nothing short of terror. As Sherman the artist captures Sherman the subject on film, the rewriting of boundaries implies an instability echoed in the frightened anxiety we witness in her eyes. The visitor's flowered sweater and protective headscarf all imply the comfort and reassurance of controlled traditional categories, for the subject of this still is protected against the wind just as cultural categories presumably protect her from needing to reinvent or reinterpret herself. Yet this woman's facial expression tells us that she is on anything but stable ground as she visits the downtown, for there is something deeply unsettled and unsettling about this image.

While stylistically images #14 and #17 both confirm a traditional interpretation of femininity, then, the deep sense of uncertainty that pervades each still nevertheless manages to unseat any complacency into which this tradition may have fallen. Indeed, the women in both stills seem anything but complicitous in the events taking place around them but, rather, convey a frightened rebelliousness if not a desire to flee. Their eyes reveal great discomfort, especially in #17 where the chilling look of disquiet has an arresting impact. There is an uncanny quality to Sherman's expression here that lends the still a truly disturbing aura, for a prim and seemingly conventional woman appears privy to some sinister revelation that strikes horror in her heart. The extended eyeliner and eerie stillness endow this face with mysterious, gothic overtones that work against the contemporary setting. Reminiscent of much performance art, then, the body on display stands out and emphasizes her uniqueness by not supplying us with what we expected. She disrupts, rather than confirms, the cultural order that her appearance so readily invokes, and thus subverts the scenario that she herself has helped create.

Peggy Phelan has commented on how performance art allows a unique body to stand out in relief and declare its autonomy from the appropriating patriarchal system, wrongly impressed with its own authority. In *Unmarked: the Politics of Performance*, Phelan uses language that parallels that of Adorno's critical theory, explaining how the uniqueness of both a given body and a given performance resist absorption into larger cultural tropes in ways that successfully undermine the assigned meanings that strive to engulf individuals. For what is unique, idiosyncratic, and committed to a singular performance or an unusual interpretation does not lend itself to the shared meanings of cultural metaphor. Instead, like Sherman's early stills, it highlights all that resists the mainstream's grasp, all that remains "unmarked" by standard readings and hackneyed conventions. "Performance's independence from mass production, technologically, economically, and linguistically, is its greatest strength," writes Phelan.[17] Performance art thus forever insists that, despite appearances, the body is not inscribed within a hermetically sealed text. Rather, it stands ready to signify oppositional meaning, devoid of conferred narratives or preassigned values. The body in performance art is resistant, empty, a "loss" within a society that is more a fractured totality than a seamless whole. In its uniqueness, it reveals subversion rather than compliance. Always assigned a cultural role, it can present the world with aspects of itself that do not comply with the expected performance, displaying unexpected, unrehearsed elements that defy the usual routine.

> Performance approaches the Real through resisting the metaphorical reduction of the two into the one. But in moving from the aims of metaphor, reproduction, and pleasure to those of metonymy, displacement, and pain, performance marks the body itself as loss. Performance is the attempt to value that which is nonreproductive, nonmetaphorical.[18]

Hence, in Sherman's art, the exhaustive, creative use of well-rehearsed cultural norms functions not to prolong their imaginative control, but to undermine their credibility as sources of cultural authority.

Indeed, Sherman's art overwhelmingly proclaims that the female body, deeply inscribed in the text of femininity, stands capable of disrupting that text thanks precisely to its own inscription. Only by speaking within the confines of tradition's norm can the female body's performance demonstrate the tenuousness of that norm; only its status as a double agent can reveal the unmarked, unrehearsed dimensions of our identities. Performativity unleashes the double-sided meanings that accompany cultural inscription, thereby drawing attention to the slippage that occurs between the general and the particular, the overarching social order and the individual on whom cultural meaning rests. Capable of rebellion, the individual performer need not repent as he or she demonstrates that order's propensity toward implosion. For without question, Sherman's conventional readings of the female body are only deceptively staid: she mimetically undercuts femininity's meanings, and, thanks to this mimesis, is spared the worries of appropriation that plague Adorno's modernism.

If Sherman's photography seems unwilling to repent, the same can easily be said of her witty videotaped *Interview with Cindy Sherman* (1980), which is part serious, part spoof—that is, part bone fide interview, part performance art. Sherman goes through the motions of being a job interviewee, showing up in an office suitably dressed for the occasion. Yet as she begins to talk about herself and her work, her appearance constantly changes right before our eyes in ways that amaze, confuse, and humor us. Everything about her appearance morphs into something radically different: blond hair becomes brown, reading glasses become sunglasses, a formal chapeau becomes a silly hat, and business attire becomes a bathing suit. Thanks to this ongoing transformation, the interview ultimately seems unrelated to a job, as a profound instability comes to occupy center stage. Indeed, Sherman talks about her art in ways that confuse what is happening, and the setting loses its original formality to take on a slippery, open-ended, uncertain feeling that nevertheless keeps the viewer not only entertained, but intellectually challenged by the sight of gender's frailty.

Importantly, though, the interview's playful deconstruction never causes Sherman to lose control of the process. As she discusses her training, her rise to success, and her hopes for the future, the free fall induced by her constant metamorphosis in fact becomes the subject of the performance. The topic is simultaneously "Cindy Sherman" and "Cindy Sherman?" And despite the overriding ambiguity that this produces regarding the artist's identity—is not the point of an interview to make oneself known to another?—she never lets go of a confident tone in speaking about her art's creative purpose. True, she avoids making definitive statements about the specific intent of her art. Yet the indeterminacies of her ever-mutating identity themselves reveal the emancipatory power of the unmarked, unappropriated dimension of identity, and Sherman successfully affirms the subversive, healing power of the imagination. Thus, as the interview comes to a close, the interviewer states, "It's been nice meeting all of you." And as the panoply of Sherman's assumed personae flash on the screen in all their various guises, a voice strives to identify their collective ensemble, failing and succeeding at the same time: "That's her."

*   *   *

The feminist performance art of Cindy Sherman thus presents the aesthetics of the female body in ways that parallel Adorno's understanding of modernist art's redemptive potential. Her art shares in the hopeful dimension of Adorno's aesthetic theory inasmuch as it, too, displays a refractory quality vis-à-vis the reigning cultural paradigm. By drawing attention to the unharnessed, undomesticated residual of current gender roles, the thematics of performativity hold out hope for rearranged social meanings much as Adorno holds out hope thanks to modernism's unappropriated cultural stance. As Adorno saw true potential in the atonal music of Schoenberg and Berg, so does Sherman's art move forward as it affirms, from within, the possibility of something different.

Importantly, though, Sherman does not share Adorno's anxieties about the dark irony of emancipatory art. While Adorno feels that modernism's investment in the powers that be make it necessary to atone—that is, to be all the more radical, all the more dissonant, all the more painfully irresolute—Sherman reveals a confidence and ease as she works comfortably within the established lexicon of femininity's meanings. She operates from within gendered meanings in order to reveal their uncertainties, for only those on intimate terms can act as double agent and expose the Achilles' heel. Unrepentant, she sets in motion a staid rebellion, eager to demonstrate that within the thematics of gender, things are not what they seem.

Notes

1. Theodor Adorno, *Aesthetic Theory*, trans. Robert Hullot-Kentor (Minneapolis: University of Minnesota Press, 1979), 13.

2. Adorno, *Aesthetic Theory*, 13.

3. Theodor Adorno, "The Autonomy of Art," in *The Adorno Reader*, ed. Brian O'Connor, trans. C. Lenhardt (Malden, Mass.: Blackwell, 2000), 248.

4. Adorno, *Aesthetic Theory*, 179.

5. Adorno, 253.

6. Adorno, 252.

7. See Theodor Adorno, *The Authoritarian Personality*, in collaboration with Else Frenkel-Brunswick and Daniel Levinson (New York: W. W. Norton, 1993).

8. Quoted in Linda Hutcheon, *Irony's Edge: The Theory and Politics of Irony* (New York: Routledge, 1994), 29.

9. Hutcheon, *Irony's Edge*.

10. Hutcheon, *Irony's Edge*, 30.

11. Adorno, "The Autonomy of Art," 252.

12. Adorno, "Arnold Schoenberg, 1874–1951," in *The Adorno Reader*, ed. Brian O'Connor, trans. C. Lenhardt (Malden, Mass.: Blackwell, 2000), 282.

13. Judith Butler, *Gender Trouble: Feminism and the Subversion of Identity* (New York: Routledge, 1990), 25.

14. Amelia Jones, *Body Art: Performing the Subject* (Minneapolis: University of Minnesota Press, 1998), 39.

15. Amelia Jones, "Art History/Art Criticism: Performing Meaning," in *Performing the Body, Performing the Text*, ed. Amelia Jones and Andrew Stephenson (New York: Routledge, 1999), 41.

16. Jones, *Body Art*, 51.

17. Peggy Phelan, *Unmarked: The Politics of Performance* (New York: Routledge, 1993), 149.

18. Phelan, *Unmarked*, 152.

15

The Economy of the Same

Identity, Equivalence, and Exploitation

Gillian Howie

Recent feminist theorists, named by some as third wave, raise objections to the exclusive tendencies within feminist theory of the 1970s and 1980s. Through critiques of essentialism, third-wave feminists resist the "seductive" promise of inclusive identity, arguing that, far from providing the grounds for political agency, the assertion of commonalities among women leads to the neglect, and even eradication, of differences.[1] Elizabeth Spelman believes that much of Western feminist theory, when struggling to articulate common grounds between women, actually internalizes a general philosophical tendency to reduce differences to sameness—a tendency apparent in the classification of individuals into two kinds: "male" and "female."[2]

The dimorphic assignment of properties to bodies and then their representation in terms of masculine and feminine is considered to be part of an economy "that claims to include the feminine as the subordinate term in a binary opposition masculine/feminine" but actually excludes the feminine and produces it as that "which must be excluded for the economy to operate."[3] Indeed, Luce Irigaray believes that the existence of an object matters less than the simple effect of a representation upon the subject: its reflection in the imagination of a man.[4] But in response to these postmodernist theories, Toril Moi proposes that we should move away from the problem of "sex and gender" because it cannot provide a concrete historical understanding of what it means "to be a woman."[5]

Theodor Adorno's negative dialectics, I believe, does offer a way to develop such an understanding, while at the same time addressing some of the concerns identified by third-wave feminists. By maintaining that there is something true designated by the concept of girlhood, Adorno's materialist dialectics opens a way to think about the concrete nature of group identity and to explore the interests underlying the attribution (or construction) of common identity. His analysis of interests can help us to move away from the (merely) psychodynamic model of the economy, while showing how interests determine the conditions of experience. In an attempt to make these interests explicit, I shall revisit the question of how economic and gender interests might coincide and create contradictory position for feminine subjectivity. Negative dialectics, however, also allows us to think that a "girl" is something other than what we declare her to be, and I conclude by examining how Adorno might help us to reorient cognition in a way that would begin to tackle third-wave concerns. This reorientation would clarify the prior and consequent facts of sex-based identification as being constitutive of identity and, importantly, also suggest a way to think of identity noninstrumentally.

The Predication of Kinds

Our understanding that a physical object persists through time seems to be primordial and commonsensical. Yet questions such as, What is it for an object at one time to be the same as an object at another? seem to require an account of the identity of the object. Skeptical about traditional metaphysical notions of stable and consistent identity, Judith Butler suggests that the insistence on a stable subject actually generates multiple refusals to accept the category.[6] Yet, intuitively, one would like to respond that individuals are named and grouped together because of features they share and that this identity is neither arbitrary nor merely an effect of discursive practices. According to Moi, this intuition is shared by de Beauvoir, who questions whether the concept "woman" is really empty of content, as Enlightenment thinkers, rationalists, and nominalists would have us believe.[7] My argument is that there is a way to make sense of these "natural" groupings, a way that is sensitive to the fact that properties of objects are mind-independent, or real, and to the dynamic conditions that affect classification. I will attempt to demonstrate how we can use Adorno's materialism, which is not naively realist, to make sense of identity claims related to "being-a-woman." My point is that we can do this without having to resort to prurient forms of scientific or metaphysical essentialism.

The concept of identity is involved in the ontological claims that an object persists over time and that different objects can be grouped together. Identity is also an epistemological principle—it enables us to point out and then say something about an individual. Adorno makes an important contribution to the vexed question of identity at this point by insisting on the fact that the principle of identity has a necessary cognitive role. Thinking, according to Adorno, is tied to entities, and for thought to have any content an individual x must have already been identified as an X, which means deciding that it not a Y.[8] Indeed, we cannot think without identifying, because, apart from anything, any definition is an identification.[9] This means that when we think about an object and attempt to communicate something about it, we have to identify it: to release thought from this principle of identity would immobilize it. But Adorno then draws our attention to the fact that while definitions strive to communicate something about a particular object, other forms of cognition merely express what an object falls under. This is a critical distinction between thought that intends, and so identifies an x as X, and cognitive strategies that simply subsume individuals under universal categories: a distinction between intentionality and instrumentalism. My core argument is that contemporary, third-wave, antiessentialist arguments are similar to this analysis of instrumental reasoning and that

Adorno goes one step further by offering a way to think about real group identity noninstrumentally.

First of all, I would like to suggest a way to think about the nonarbitrary nature of the classification of individuals into groups, such as male and female. Following Jay Bernstein, I accept that "conceptualisation is the determination of an intrinsically indeterminate, but essentially determinable, albeit never fully determinate, fine-grained and dense experiential base."[10] In the process of determining, some classifications, for example, separating objects into two kinds, "hats" and "frogs," seem intuitively obvious, whereas other acts of discrimination, for example, separating individuals into groups, "men" and "women," are more controversial. There are two principal ways to justify classification: each individual exemplifies a common property or the group is defined through similarity relationships. Classification according to common property is, I believe, the proper target for feminist antiessentialists, while classification by means of similarity relationships offers a way to move beyond the constructivist/essentialist debate.[11]

A metaphysical realist would claim that where objects agree in attributes, or are significantly similar, there is some one thing they share, or have in common These things are called *universal properties* and can be exemplified by more than one individual, which means that a number of individuals can share or partake in the same universal properties. If these properties are necessary for x to be an X, the property is also described as essential to the identity of the thing. Essential properties are usually considered to be ahistorical, as beyond the influence of the social and historical world. Feminist critiques of essentialism tend to object to the notion that any property can stand outside sociohistoric processes and to the attendant assumption that every individual has properties in common with other individuals.[12]

Metaphysical and scientific realism about essences run into a number of well-documented problems, and so there are some straightforward reasons for rejecting these essentialist accounts of natural-kind groupings, without embracing an alternative metaphysical system.[13] First, an account of the essential nature of individuals is unable to chronicle change over time and thus, being little use in explaining natural kind groupings, is at best redundant. The second problem is that of reductionism. The problem of reductionism is well rehearsed in the philosophy of mind, where contemporary concerns tend to circle around the problem of eliminativism that is, whether talk of "mental events" should be eliminated.

The more general problem, with wider application, concerns the difficulty with reducing one level of description, for example, a social event to a biological occurrence. The description of essential natures in substructural terms overly compresses and then translates available information about the object. Finally, even if realism about essences could withstand these criticisms, it cannot really survive problems that arise when explaining why one individual ought to be assigned to one group rather than another, and it is this problem of demarcation that will drive our argument forward.

Defending a weak doctrine of natural kinds, John Dupré argues that questions concerning natural kinds can only be answered in relation to some specification of the goal underlying the intent to classify an object. Offering the example of an apparently straightforward classification of a piston in the general economy of the car, he points out that the unambiguous nature of the classification depends on context. If, instead of working on the car in a garage, we are at a football match, those at the gate will dismiss our arguments that the hard metal object in our hand is a piston and not a weapon or a hammer.[14] Dupré's argument has ramifications for the realist position, because it means that both the existence of groups offers no evidence for essential properties and that classificatory taxonomies are open to critical scrutiny. One can remain perfectly agnostic about essential properties, and common substructural features, and still entertain the idea of group identity.

Coming at the problem from a slightly different angle, Clare Hill denies that the abstraction required from individuals to form a group is innocent. "Abstraction process," she writes, "robs individuals of their individuality. The members formed by abstraction are identical, indiscernible, and interchangeable precisely because they have been logically stripped of whatever might distinguish them, the criteria by which any difference between the might be discerned having been disposed of."[15] Instead, she offers a defense of a similarity thesis, whereby group identity depends on similarities between individuals: individuals have a property in common only in the sense that each bears a similarity relation to every other member of the kind.[16] Hill argues that there is a fundamental difference between identity and weak forms of equivalence (similarity in some respects), illuminating this through an example of an organ transplant. Intensional factors, marking a difference between identity and weak forms of equivalence, come into play where it is vital to differentiate between organs that are alike in some but not all respects, here healthy rather than diseased parts. Intensional considerations mark a difference between unwanted strict identity and an equivalence that is powerful enough to stop the substitutivity of the organs from breaking down: "to say of organ x that it has properties in common with organ y essential for successful transplant is to make a weaker claim than to claim that they are identical."[17] Or, indeed, that they share identical properties.

The grouping of individual things into organs, whether healthy or diseased, is thankfully not arbitrary and is restrained by the natures of the objects in question. Various descriptions and properties, however, can be predicated of any object. Although there is a limit to the range of classifications—x cannot both be a hat and an elephant—x can be classified in a number of ways. Classification depends on the selection of properties (in which ways are x and y similar enough to make them S? How do x and y differ to make them S but not R?) and this selection of relevant properties takes place according to criteria related to our interests. Natural kinds are made up of individuals that are similar enough, in relevant ways, to make the group cohere. The criteria for deciding similarity imply relevance, which means that attention is focused on the properties that are associated with the context-bound function of the object. The implication of this is that we can simultaneously maintain that individuals are grouped together into the kind "woman" because of similar features and that the focus on these features, what makes these features relevant, is related to (social) function, explained in terms of human interests. Before I explore the character of these interests, there is a preliminary issue to address, one raised by third-wave feminists. If it is the case that natural-kind identity is best explained through similarity relations, then why do we think that individuals are identical (i.e., the same) in some respects? Once again we can find a way to answer this in Adorno's *Negative Dialectics*, where he unpacks the relationship between judgments of identity and the phenomena of reification—as elaborated by Karl Marx through his theory of value.

The Predication of Value

The proposition "This hat is £10.99" predicates a property, "£10.99," to the hat. In *Theories of Surplus Value and Capital*, Marx terms this type of property a *value* and distinguishes between use value and exchange value.[18] Goods have uses dependent on their particular qualities and prop-erties and, because of these uses, a good can enter into exchange relation-ships. The good, now a commodity, stands in a relationship to other commodities: a ratio of magnitudes. If, for example, two chairs can be exchanged for one table, then the table has twice the value of the chairs. Marx's entire theory of value is an account of how we quantify values so that goods can stand in a specific ratio.

A ratio between commodities is a ratio of quantities, in this case 2:1. According to Marx, measurement is only possible because the commodi-ties all share something. As they have differing, sometimes incommensu-rable, uses, the common feature must be found elsewhere. Signifying the break from market economics, Marx argues that the universal feature is that they are products of labor. The measurement in all cases is of the same thing—labor—but the measurement distinguishes between amounts of labor. Reformulated, this is the claim that although value indicates different quantities of labor, it measures the same quality.

Refining this somewhat, Marx investigates how labor can be quantified and suggests that the quantities are amounts of labor time it takes to produce a commodity. This is not a measurement of any particular pro-ductive endeavor but is an abstract or general measurement: the socially necessary labor time taken to produce a use value under conditions of production common in society. In order to make this judgment of general productivity, an average degree of intensity and of skill must be supposed, and, by abstracting from particular productive endeavors, we are left with the average amount of labor measured in units of time. The propositions "This hat is £10.99" and "This chair is £12.99" are related insofar as both predicate value and those values are differing magnitudes of the labor that is required to make the two goods in question.

The simple predication of value, according to Marx, disguises an im-portant social fact. Capitalism is a system of production in which, in the process of exchange, value, now converted into money, is generated and accumulated (M_1-C-M_2).[19] Given that the value of any commodity is only the sum of past and present labor, measured in units of time that are socially necessary to the production of the object, an explanation has to be offered for the difference in magnitudes, and for the apparent genera-tion of values. Marx contends that the value of past labor (machinery, materials) is simply transferred to the new commodity, which would leave present labor adding value, that is, current labor produces values addi-tional to the value of "dead" labor in the system of production. This would mean that current labor must generate all value, including surplus values. For there to be a surplus available in the system, the value of labor must differ in magnitude from the exchange values of the commodities produced by labor. The value of labor must be worth less than the values that labor produces: exploitation. The value of labor is an exchange value, and like any other such value, it is the time taken to produce it: the commodification of labor. This time tends to be "cashed out" in terms of the values the laborer consumes to sustain him- or herself and his or her family. Incidentally, this means that when a worker receives a fair wage, s/he receives a wage equivalent to his or her value: the bundle of sustaining commodities. The rate of exploitation is the difference between the value of labor and the values that labor produces.

The propositions "This hat is £10.99" and "This chair is £12.99" predicate exchange values, which are measurements of units of production time. The predication of value is permitted through the abstraction of general indicators from particular endeavors and depends upon the commodification and exploitation of labor. The simple predicative judgment not only neglects the use values of the object but also, and more significantly, treats a social relationship (labor and its exploitation) as though it were a natural property belonging to the thing itself: reification. The judgment of identity, in this instance, depends on it being the case that unlike things, for example, distinct goods or particular productive endeavors, appear as if they are alike or equal and quantifiable. Bourgeois society, explain Adorno and Horkheimer, makes the dissimilar comparable by reducing it to abstract quantities.[20] Frederic Jameson notes that judgments based on sameness are above all judgments premised on the equivalence of value: "the possibility we have historically constructed of comparing them when in terms of their use value they remain incomparable."[21]

According to this characterization of the production process, each individual experiences the commodification of his or her labor, the loss of initiative, creativity, sociality and control. Because this process alienates the individual not only from other individuals but also from the object, the individual cannot see that the value of an object originates from his or her labor. Mistaken about the origin of value, the individual infers that the value of an object must rest with the object as a natural property and thus goods appear to be exchanged with one another according to their own natural qualities. The world comes into sight as inverted, which means that essential relations of production are mystified. This appearance of identity, where dissimilar objects are exchangeable and exchange value predicated as a natural quality, is, for Adorno, reification—both a social phenomena and a way of thinking.[22]

From the predication of price we can infer social facts, social relations supporting standard equivalence, and an explanation for the superficial simplification of these facts. Indeed, this is why *Capital* begins with an analysis of the commodity form. A simple judgment F (x), where x is a commodity and F is its value, predicated as a natural property, is only possible because the object is abstracted from its (productive) relations. Adorno suggests that a particular cognitive orientation is a consequence of the experience of this way of living and producing; from the preceding commentary, we can recognize that abstraction, simplification, and a tendency to see the dissimilar as similar, and the similar as identical, are the principal features of this cognitive orientation. For the sake of my argument, the salient point is that a particular kind of cognitive orientation is a consequence of a form of production, as is the move from the cognition of similarity to that of sameness. Specifically, this cognitive orientation also enables the interests governing production to be disguised. If we accept this account, then it is possible to make some move toward offering an alternative to the psychic explanation for judgments of sameness and identity.

Similarity and Exchange Relationships

In thinking how it might be possible for a number of individuals to talk about "being-a-woman," I have focused on the concrete nature of group identity and argued that group identity is best explained through similarity relations and then offered an explanation for why similarity relations became perceived in terms of sameness. My suggestion so far is that if we take two propositions, "This is a hat" and "This hat is red," the various groupings *hat*, *red*, and *red hat* are determined by a selection of similarities, guided both by interest and context. Why, for example, might I select its color as being essential to its group membership? A red hat may be the only hat to wear to a particular football match, because it marks identity of a slightly different kind. Identifying something as a particular kind of thing, grasping similarities according to our interests, suggests, for Adorno, an uncontroversial aspect of thought.[23] If, however, I attempt to offer a fuller description of a hat that I will be wearing tonight, I might comment on its properties and say that it is woolly, warm, and red and cost £10.99. In this latter case, the natural appearance of economic value disguises the social fact that the value of the hat embodies the exploited and alienated labor, which produced the hat in the first place. Because I can predicate exchange value to the object, it is likely that when I consider the hat I will also overly simplify the relationship between the object and its other predicates. So, I will tend to abstract the object and my consideration of the object, from its context as well as conceive similarities where there are principally distinctions. The shift, outlined in the previous section, from the apprehension of similarities to the identification and subsumption of different particulars under a common universal (concept or law), has been explained as an effect of a particular form of production. Now, I would like to explore how cognition guided by the conception of similarity could be so easily overwritten and distorted.

The idea that we group together objects into kinds, which give shape to, and determine, the world, according to our interests is a version of pragmatism. Describing Robert Brandom's *Making It Explicit* as a milestone in theoretical philosophy, Jürgen Habermas insists that Brandom is leading a pragmatist revival by taking, as a starting point, the notion that behavior is guided by way of implicit knowledge according to norms of speaking and acting. The content of a concept, its meaning, is also determined by normative linguistic and social practices.[24] The vocabulary of logic makes explicit what is already known practically, but implicitly. According to Bernstein, "know-how," shown through practical inferences, depends upon classifying and identifying objects, and the criteria by which objects are grouped together depends on human interest.[25] Meaning and comprehension are only possible if the context and consequence of the utterance are grasped. For example, if I see someone bleeding badly, then I (know that I should) apply a tourniquet.[26]

Material inference, rather than material implication, is when a move from one proposition to another is guided by the content of the concepts, rather than by any first-order logical rules concerning validity and bivalence. The steps in implication can be spelled out formally, which means that if I wished to secure the "ought," to justify the inference, I would formulate an explicit rule. When reason considers that it alone supplies the rules that guide thinking, it removes all external (ethical and social) authorities, and then subjects its own principles to scrutiny. This results in a way of thinking commonly associated with instrumentality: a form of reasoning, which prioritizes the gaining of an end and concentrates on discovering the most efficient means for achieving that end. So it is the presentation of the social or ethical claim as a formal principle that opens the way for an ultimately skeptical rejection of the moral inference: "for the reduction of ethics itself to an instrumental and, sometimes inhuman, remnant."

Detecting a historical modification of practical to logical inference, Bernstein's account returns him to the Enlightenment and he argues that the key with which to understand the claim, appeal, and authority of logical inference is to grasp how the authority established itself, culturally and institutionally. In the *Dialectic of Enlightenment*, Adorno and Hork-heimer bring into play Marx's theory of value and reification to explain this tension between the pragmatic and instrumental nature of thought. Their historical account notes an original pragmatic orientation of thought and observes how this practical and material orientation of thought became masked, until the conception—perhaps even perception—of the unlike as like, as well as a general tendency to think instrumentally (abstraction, simplification, quantification, and efficiency) became the norms of modernity and instrumental reason became the organizing principle of capitalist societies.[27] Picking up the distinction between reason as activity and reason that masks this activity, Bernstein develops the historical movement from practical to logical inference. He argues that the key with which to understand the claim, appeal and authority of logical inference is to grasp how the authority established itself, culturally and institutionally.[28]

To summarize the argument so far, because conceptualization, predication, and identification depend upon selecting relevant properties, and relevance is related to human interest, thinking tends to be pragmatic. If those interests, which determine the world and carve it at its joints, reflect the contested nature of social interest, then the determination of the world will mirror interests of the dominant social forces. The theory of reification explains how we became estranged from our own productive activity, so that the shape and organization of things in the world is observed to be the consequence of apparently objective, natural, and necessary laws. Additionally, it demonstrates the hidden nature of the interests giving shape to the world and explains the conflictual makeup of the social interests. The argument is not just that classification is interested but that because of the type of interests in question certain sociohistorical changes were effected, and these managed to disguise the interests and to alter the manner of cognition. The theory of value discloses how the perception of similarities became the perception of sameness through the subjection of individuals to the exchange mechanism, where even the unlike can be exchanged for one another, according to the abstraction of general properties from particular endeavors or products. We now have a fairly thick explanation for ways in which all thought is implicated in an antagonistic social base. This establishes more clearly how the move from judgments of similarity to judgments of sameness is linked to the development of capitalism, and reasserts the economic nature of the "economy of the same."

Exchange Relationships and Gender

Due to the pragmatic nature of thought, feminist antiessentialists are right to be skeptical about the existence of natural kinds and to be concerned about the political impact of arguments that explain the (moral) organization of the world in these terms. Essentialist justifications, metaphysical and scientific, for natural kinds tend to presume that classification can be premised on uncontested logical principles, that the original neutral act of discrimination, between the unlike and alike, is informed by these principles and that there are fairly stable individual things, which may have properties shared by other individuals things. The classification of x or y as male or female depends, in the main, on positing specific qualities essential to x's identity and claiming that these qualities are common to all individuals grouped together as X. The later scientific interpretation of essentialism took these properties to be biological features (having wombs, breasts, child-bearing capacity), which are causally related to primary sexual characteristics, principally chromosomes and hormonal excretion: a form of substructural organization. The dimorphic distribution of social roles and benefits has been historically justified by secondary sexual characteristics, which are taken to be a necessary causal consequence of primary characteristics.

Any justification for classifying individuals into two groups, male or female, by virtue of essential properties, reproduces the form of arguments for natural kinds discussed and rejected above. I have argued that problems with this type of essentialism need not push us into rejecting the concrete nature of group identity because a qualified similarity thesis is more convincing anyway. If a qualified similarity thesis is the most convincing explanation of kind identity, then arguments that posit essential natural qualities of femininity and masculinity—and explain the distribution of social goods accordingly—are either false or redundant.[29] I believe that two antiessentialist accounts of kinds, gender as seriality, whereby women are united passively as a series, and gender as genealogy, whereby individuals are located within complex genealogical filiations, are versions of the similarity thesis.[30] But—and this is an important caveat—any similarity thesis concedes that properties, according to which individuals are considered to be relevantly similar, have to be selected. This requires an assessment of how selection is interested, organized, and embedded.

If the principle of identity does find its social model in exchange, where nonidentical individuals and performances become commensurable, we would expect to find that features of the object come to stand, metonymically, for the whole object and that various individuals are classified as the same according to common and "natural" properties. A social selection of properties constitutes the kind "woman" and, almost certainly, qualities are selected because they endorse a sex-based hierarchy. The presentation of qualities as polar opposites is "heavily imbricated in the patriarchal value system: each opposition can be analysed as a hierarchy where the feminine side is always seen as the negative powerless instance."[31] Actually, a few properties do invoke the whole individual; indeed, metonymical representation defines pornography. As goods, in the sexual economy, women find that their (exchange) value is indeed a social property: all that supports a particular image of masculinity.

The cognitive orientation, associated with capitalist exchange, at the very least facilitates gendered classification and determination. It also manages to disguise the contingent and social determination of the world, presenting it as natural and necessary. First, the choice of criteria for organizing individuals into groups is related to social interests and this interested nature of judgment has been obscured and hidden from view (reification). Second, the organization of individuals into these groups, and the consequent effects of such an organization, is contingent. To think that it is either natural or necessary would be another example of reified thinking, the result of alienation. Extending Adorno's analysis of the Enlightenment, one could argue that putatively neutral, scientific frames of reference managed to mask gender bias during the Enlightenment in similar ways and, perhaps through the same institutions, as the authority of logical inference was established.[32] This would mean that we could bring together the work of certain feminist epistemologists, such as Linda Alcoff and Vrinda Dalmiya, with the work of certain critical theorists, such as Jay Bernstein, to discern the gendered implication of the move from practical to logical inference; from "know how" to "know that."

I have named a style of thinking, which abstracts, simplifies, and takes similar individuals to be identical, as instrumental, but these same features are also present in thought described as "phallogocentric." This is a term used for a style of thinking that presumes three principles of logic and then classifies things into two kinds, establishing a (gendered) hierarchy between them.[33] Those who argue either that thought is instrumental or that it is phallogocentric would agree that interests govern discrimination and classification.[34] However, an analysis of the (social) interests, driving classification, might result in an economic description of those interests, or focus on their gendered nature, or examine the intersections between economic and gender interests. These differences produce the same puzzles that absorbed radical and dual- and single-system Marxist and socialist feminist theorists of the "second wave." So far I have argued that capitalism facilitated a way of thinking about the world that protected and reproduced a gendered hierarchy. In what follows, building on the questions elaborated here about identity thinking, I will show how the questions raised by second-wave Marxist and socialist feminists are, far from being displaced by the problem of globalization, critically relevant to an understanding of "being-a-woman" in "post" modern global economies.

Globalization, Feminization, and Rationalization

Working with a Marxist frame of reference, Adorno offers us a way to consider the connection between group identity and interests, and it might be tempting to argue that because the frame of reference is modernist it is anachronistic, revealing nothing about the contemporary quality of "being-a-woman" within a newly transformed global economy. Although I am remaining agnostic as to the various permutations of the causal relationships between gender interests and economic interests—because here all I wish to indicate is that these problems need to be revisited—I do believe that there is nothing "post" about our modern economy.

Globalization has many and varied meanings. It may be taken to refer to a newly integrated market; to the integrated operations of distribution and political order; to the sense that the world, through information technology, has contracted; to the domination of a particular type of productive commercialism; and to a restructuring not only of the market, but also of the state and civil society—processes that are mediated through local economic and political structures.[35] Yet aside from all this, concentrating on the features of global economies, David Harvey notes that the principal characteristics of "post-Fordism" are flexible accumulation and flexible labor and argues that they are perfectly consistent with, and entailed by, the growth-oriented, and technologically and organizationally dynamic, features of modern capitalism. If this is the case, then growth in real values still depends upon the commodification and exploitation of living labor: the gap between the value of labor and values labor produces. Thought, which has never been immune from these processes, is as implicated in its social context as ever.

Self-defined third-wave feminist Jodi Dean describes how global technoculture affects women. She defines *technoculture* as "the rise of networked communication [such as] the Internet, satellite, broadcasting, and the global production and dissemination of motion pictures; . . . the consolidation of wealth in the hands of transnational corporations and the migration and immigration of people, technologies and capital; and . . . the rise of consumerist culture and the corresponding sites of impoverishment, violence, starvation and death."[36] However, arguing that technoculture heralds the end of patriarchy, Dean notes that these economic changes are in the interests of (some) women, affording them the benefits of a choice of living pattern, control in relationships, and the power that accrues to the occupation of the traditional role of family provider. To the extent that global capitalism delivers on liberal aspirations, offering, for example, access to education and fairness in the labor market, the feminist fight for equal opportunities seems to have been won. Alternatively, one could argue that flexible labor, as one of the main features of global capitalism, marks the feminization of the laboring process. The term *feminization* relates to features within the restructuring process that depend upon existing inequities, so, for example, the activities of the global financial market involves the emergence of a feminized "internationalized," largely casual and insecure service economy, in which male, but principally female, migrant labor, plays a significant role.

Lisa Vogel, a second-wave feminist theorist, comments on the structural role of women in the labor market; her insights can shed some light on these apparently diverse strands of global capitalism. There are, she contends, some straightforward effects of the tendency within capitalism to minimize necessary labor over the long term—to ensure the maximum availability of labor force participation—while simultaneously requiring the reproduction of labor power. Individual reproduction of labor is necessary to the smooth running of capital and yet is antagonistic to the tendency to appropriate surplus labor. The reproduction of labor includes all that is within the "private" sphere—domestic labor, parenting, and caring for elderly relatives—and the tendency to reduce this necessary labor is witnessed in various ways, for example, in the expansion of child-care provision and labor-saving devices. But these are the "private" responsibility of the individual producer, and so consumption is increased and the stratification of the labor market further embedded. The fact that the reproduction of labor (childbirth, child care, and domestic labor) is antagonistic to the creation of surplus value, which requires an expanding field of producers, goes some way in explaining the contradictory pressures experienced by women, who, in the main, still occupy these roles.

Global restructuring will, among other things, aggravate the tension between the structural tendency toward the free availability of labor power, and thus the equalization of male and female labor power, and the domestic labor required for the reproduction of the labor force. Gayatri Spivak comments that "the worst victims of the recent exacerbation of the international division of labor are women. They are the true surplus army of labor in the current conjuncture. In their case, patriarchal social relations contribute to their production as the new forces of super-exploitation."[37]

The Cultural Logic of Late Capitalism

In the attempt to break the spell that captures female identity within a masculinist sexual economy, feminist criticisms of essentialism center on how individuals are subsumed under universal concepts. Throughout the preceding discussion of identity, abstraction—including its philosophical equivalent in logic and in the form of universals—has been revealed, at another level, to be at one with the logic of equivalence and exchange: the logic of capital.[38] The underlying argument, then, is that beyond all forms of social differentiation, the abstraction implicit in the market system represents the domination of the general over the particular and accounts for the organization of similarities and differences into sameness and equivalence. This is where feminist antiessentialist arguments and Adorno's analysis of instrumentalism coincide, with a materialist underpinning. Although the form of cognition is at one with mechanisms of exchange, classifications, guided by social interest, preexist this particular form of production. Sexual difference is also a fact.[39]

The discussion in this chapter began with the suggestion that there is still useful content in the idea of "natural kind," but it also established that natural groupings can be best explained in terms of similarity rather than identity and that there was an historical shift from pragmatic to an instrumental orientation of thought, whereby the interests governing selection became hidden, groupings became naturalized, and similarity was viewed as identity. The conventional character of natural kinds does not make the groupings any less significant. Indeed, the way that we currently think about an object, the classifications and inferences drawn concerning behavior, say something true and false about the object. If, for example, one were to insist that there are two sex-based kinds, that is true, if one were to further insist that we can infer behavior from dimorphic sex distinctions, that too is generally true; that is, it is the case that individuals identified as women undertake most of the world's domestic labor. It would, however, be false to take this to confirm the original assumption of natural dimorphism, because it is also the case that the structures and mechanisms imposing specific similarity relations, and creating the situation in which it is possible to predict likely behavior, are contingent and thoroughly interested.

The individual really does experience the processes simultaneously as natural and disinterested and as interested and conventional. This is why the categories *essence* and *appearance* still have theoretical work to do. Essence is that which makes the facts what they are,[40] and appearances, although they conceal their conditions, are nonetheless real.[41] Thinking about properties in this way enables us to distinguish between propositions. For example, just as the claim "a fair day's wage for a fair day's work" is false, so too is the claim that women's reproductive organs suffer when they are educated.[42] Similarly, just as the predication of value to a commodity is real, so too is the predication of particular properties to women. If we can develop the parallel further, the description of properties occurs after a more original determination of relevant properties and the consequent "interpellation" of the individual into various social mechanisms and practices. The effects of the constituted world are real and can be accurately represented. Epistemologically, the "non-involved, distanced" knower can then assert transparent correspondence between proposition and world, and the world will confirm the truth-claim.[43] Hence, propositions can be confirmed by evidence, but this confirmation is only at the level of appearance.[44]

In the same way as exchange value abstracts from particular productive endeavors, yet is still in thrall to them, one can detect the similarities and differences underlying abstract dimorphic sex-gender categories. And in the same way as exchange is a dynamic and ruthlessly totalizing mechanism, reason reaches out to organize the individual data of cognition, stamping homogeneity on the heteronomous.[45] According to Adorno and Horkheimer, the schematic relationship between the general and particular, of concept and universal case, is "ultimately revealed in contemporary science as the interest of industrial society."[46] I have tried to insert into this analysis of the schematic relationship a gender dimension.

Cognitive reorientation is a term coined by Bernstein to indicate how we might make the implicit explicit and figure something like the (original) pragmatic way of thinking, which would help us to "hear the object speak." To do this, however, thought faces a complicated task. It must be aware of the mechanisms of abstraction, the effect of these on the production of similarities, and their presentation as identical, while also taking account of the tensions created at each and every moment of abstraction. It needs to express the object as distinct from the criteria of selection, while also recognizing how the object is mediated by the processes that operate with those criteria. Bernstein believes this type of cognitive approach must jettison bivalence and move toward what he describes as particularistic pluralism.[47] This term refers to a reoriented cognition, which is sensitive to the aspect of the object that preexisted any attempt to communicate something about it, and which endeavors to express the object through a constellation of appropriate concepts. It means accepting that an object is not just one thing or another. Assuming this orientation would lead an individual to keep in mind that an object can belong to a number, although not an infinite number, of kinds, while at the same time making explicit the rules, conventions, institutions, and interests governing the determination of groups of objects according to shared properties.

The nonidentical element in any identifying judgment, according to Adorno, is clearly intelligible insofar as every single object subsumed under a class has characteristics not contained in the definition of the class. It can also be discerned in the relationship between individuals endeavoring to achieve a quality predicated of them, for example, the quality "free."[48] The constellation of concepts, exceeding the individual's definition, within which an object stands, indicates the sedimented history that it carries within it. This history can only be unlocked by an awareness of the relationship that the object has to others and to the constellation of concepts orbiting it (163). No longer turning individuals into immutable objects (154), thought could attempt to mimic the identification present in the meaning of "to identify with" and this means being sensitive to the objective nature of contradiction (150).

This, I conclude, offers a way to think about constitutive identity. The subject is also an object (of thought, of selection, of exchange) and her dissonant experiences calls for an investigation into the reflexivity of nonidentity. This subject, whose dissonant experiences are testimony to the contradiction between her own definitions and the roles she is expected to occupy, can only harmonize her beliefs and experiences with the general system through concerted manipulation and, on her own, cannot eliminate the objective contradictions and their emanations (153). Adorno, however, does offer a way to make sense of dissonant experience and to grasp the contradictory nature of the conditions, thus taking us beyond a merely academic analysis of instrumental reason. Immanent critique, which is concerned with a totalizing system without itself being total, can be put in the service of an individual struggling to make sense of her own contradictory location.

Thought of the nonidentical is a thought against binary simplification, abstraction, equivalence, and instrumentality and by bringing into question not only objective contradictions but also the conditions for the contradictions, is a thought against the gendered processes of global capitalism. It is with Adorno that an individual subject can begin to reconfigure a concrete and historical understanding of what it really means for her "to be a woman" within an economy that imposes equivalence and identity, and it is the thought of the nonidentical that can accommodate the concrete nature of contradiction and indicate a way to the spell of the economy of the same.

Notes

1. See Margrit Shildrick, "Sex and Gender," in *Third Wave Feminism: A Critical Exploration*, ed. Stacy Gillis, Gillian Howie, and Rebecca B. Munford (London: Palgrave, 2003), 67–71.

2. Elizabeth Spelman, *Inessential Woman: Problems of Exclusion in Feminist Thought* (London: Woman's Press, 1990), 2–6.

3. Judith Butler, *Gender Trouble: Feminism and the Subversion of Identity* (London: Routledge, 1990), 36.

4. Luce Irigaray, *Speculum of the Other Woman*, trans. G. Gill (Ithaca, N.Y.: Cornell University Press, 1984), 207.

5. Toril Moi, *What Is a Woman?* (Oxford: Oxford University Press, 1999), 4.

6. Butler, *Gender Trouble*, 4.

7. Moi, *What Is a Woman?* 179.

8. Theodor Adorno, *Negative Dialectics*, trans. E. B. Ashton (London: Routledge, 1973), 103.

9. Adorno, *Negative Dialectics*, 103.

10. Jay Bernstein, *Adorno: Disenchantment and Ethics* (Cambridge: Cambridge University Press, 2001), 296.

11. Diana Fuss argues much the same thing but uses the Lockean distinction of real and nominal essences, where real essences could either be something like microstructural features or simply unknown (if not unknowable) and nominal essences are the linguistic expressions of common identity. Diana Fuss, *Essentially Speaking: Feminism, Nature, and Difference* (New York: Routledge, 1989).

12. See Hilary Putnam, "Refutation of Conventionalism" in *Nous* MR 8 (1974): 25–40. For a clear discussion of how issues pertaining to natural kinds and essences can affect talk of categories, see John Dupré, *The Disorder of Things: Metaphysical Foundations of the Disunity of Science* (Cambridge, Mass.: Harvard University Press, 1995), 23–28; and Christopher Norris, *Hilary Putnam: Realism, Reason, and the Uses of Uncertainty* (Manchester: Manchester University Press, 2002), 40ff.

13. There are numerous alternatives in metaphysics to the theory that there are objects and structures that retain coherent identity over time, including Heraclitean flux, event ontology, Nietzchean will to power, Deleuze's "new materialism," and even basic Humean empiricism.

14. Dupré, *Disorder of Things*, 5.

15. Claire Hill, *Rethinking Identity and Metaphysics: On the Foundations of Analytic Philosophy* (London: Yale University Press, 1997), 48.

16. For a further discussion of natural kinds and the qualified similarity thesis, see Eli Hirsch, *The Concept of Identity* (New York: Oxford University Press, 1982), 264–86.

17. Hill, *Rethinking Identity and Metaphysics*, 52.

18. See Karl Marx, *Selected Writings*, ed. David McLellan (Oxford: Oxford University Press, 2000).

19. Karl Marx, *Capital: A Critique of Political Economy*, vol. 1 (Middlesex, U.K.: Penguin, 1986), 247–57.

20. Theodor Adorno and Max Horkheimer, *Dialectic of Enlightenment*, trans. J. Cumming (London: Verso, 1986), 7.

21. Frederic Jameson, *Late Marxism: Adorno; or, The Persistence of the Dialectic* (London: Verso, 1990), 23.

22. Gillian Rose, "How Is Critical Theory Possible? Theodor W. Adorno and Concept Formation," *Sociology in Political Studies* 24 (1976): 75.

23. "A thinking whose course made us incapable of definition, unable even for moments to have a succinct language, represent the thing, would be as sterile probably, as a thinking gorged with verbal definitions." Adorno, *Negative Dialectics*, 165.

24. Robert Brandom, *Making It Explicit: Reasoning, Representing, and Discursive Commitment* (Cambridge, Mass.: Harvard University Press, 1998); Jürgen Habermas, "From Kant to Hegel: On

Robert Brandom's Pragmatic Philosophy of Language," *European Journal of Philosophy* 8, no. 3 (2000): 323.

25. Although there are clear distinctions between Habermas and Brandom, the former also pursues the interested nature of reason. It would be worth investigating the link between this and the "need" in thought, the connection between self-preservation and the control of nature. Jameson, *Late Marxism*, 96.

26. Bernstein, *Adorno*, 265.

27. Gillian Rose, *The Melancholy Science: An Introduction to the Thought of Theodor Adorno* (London: Macmillan, 1978), 20.

28. Jameson, *Late Marxism*, 103.

29. Dupré, in *Disorder of Things*, argues that as the idea of essential properties does little or no work in the explanation of kind identity, one can remain agnostic.

30. For a discussion of Young's view of women as a series and a defense of genealogical identity, see Alison Stone, "On the Genealogy of Women: A Defence of Anti-essentialism," in *Third Wave Feminism: A Critical Exploration*, ed. S. Gillis, G. Howie, and B. Munford (London: Palgrave, 2003), 85–96.

31. Toril Moi, *Sexual/Textual Politics: Feminist Literary Theory* (London: Routledge 1985), 104.

32. For a discussion about the congruent nature of events that embedded a distinction between "know how" and "know that," a move that managed simultaneously to deauthorize traditionally female practical knowledge and to exclude women from new knowledge by excluding them from medical institutions, see Vrinda Dalmiya and Linda Alcoff, "Are Old Wives Tales Justified?" in *Feminist Epistemologies*, ed. L. Alcoff and E. Potter (London: Routledge, 1993).

33. Moi, *Sexual/Textual Politics*, 134.

34. I would argue that this would be true even if one were to decide that the driver behind the classification is "desire."

35. M. Marchland, "Gendered Representations of the Global," in *Economy and the Changing Global Order*, ed. R. Stubbs and G. Underhill (Oxford: Oxford University Press, 2002).

36. Jodi Dean, "Feminism in Technoculture," *Review of Education, Pedagogy, and Cultural Studies* 23, no. 1 (2001): 1–25.

37. Gayatri Spivak, *In Other Worlds: Essays in Cultural Politics* (London: Routledge, 1988), 167.

38. Jameson, *Late Marxism*, 28.

39. Adorno and Horkheimer, *Dialectic of Enlightenment*, 111.

40. Adorno, *Negative Dialectics*, 167.

41. "The theoretical levelling of essence and appearance will be paralleled by subjective losses." Adorno, *Negative Dialectics*, 170.

42. For a discussion about different truth-values with reference to appearance and essence, see Norman Geras, "Fetishism in Marx's 'Capital'" *New Left Review* 65 (January/February 1971): 69–85.

43. Catharine MacKinnon, "Feminism, Marxism, Method, and State," in *Feminist Theory: A Critique of Ideology*, ed. N. Keohane, M. Rosaldo, and B. Gelpi (Brighton, U.K.: Harvester, 1982), 22–23.

44. Adorno, *Negative Dialectics*, 187.

45. Adorno and Horkheimer, *Dialectic of Enlightenment*, 81.

46. Adorno and Horkheimer, *Dialectic of Enlightenment*, 84.

47. Dupré's version of this is promiscuous reality.

48. Adorno, *Negative Dialectics*, 150. Further page references are cited parenthetically in the text.

Selected Bibliography

Benhabib, Seyla. *Critique, Norm, and Utopia: A Study of the Foundations of Critical Theory.* New York: Columbia University Press, 1986.

Benjamin, Jessica. "Authority and the Family Revisited; or, A World Without Fathers?" *New German Critique* 13 (Winter 1978): 35–58.

———. *The Bonds of Love: Psychoanalysis, Feminism, and the Problem of Domination.* New York: Pantheon Books, 1988.

———. "End of Internalization: Adorno's Social Psychology." *Telos* 32 (Summer 1977): 42–64.

Coles, Romand. *Rethinking Generosity: Critical Theory and the Politics of Caritas.* Ithaca, N.Y.: Cornell University Press, 1997.

Cook, Deborah. *Adorno, Horkheimer, and the Search for a Rational Society.* New York: Routledge, 2002.

Cornell, Drucilla. *The Philosophy of the Limit.* New York: Routledge, 1993.

Dews, Peter. "Adorno, Post-structuralism, and the Critique of Identity." In *Mapping Ideology,* ed. Slavoj Žižek . London: Verso Press, 1994.

Engh, Barbara. "Adorno and the Sirens: Tele-phono-graphic Bodies." In *Embodied Voices: Representing Female Vocality in Western Culture,* ed. Leslie C. Dunn and Nancy A. Jones. Cambridge: Cambridge University Press, 1994.

Grant, Judith. *Fundamental Feminism.* New York: Routledge, 1993.

Halsema, Annemie. "Sexual Difference and Negativity: Irigaray, Derrida, and Adorno." In *Against Patriarchal Thinking: Proceedings from the Sixth Symposium of the International Association of Women in Philosophy.* Amsterdam: V. University Press.

Hull, Carrie L. "The Need in Thinking: Materiality in Theodor Adorno and Judith Butler" *Radical Philosophy* 84 (July/August 1997): 22–35.

Mills, Patricia Jagentowicz. "Feminism and Ecology: On the Domination of Nature." *Hypatia: A Journal of Feminist Philosophy* 6, no. 1 (1991): 162.

———. *Woman, Nature, and Psyche.* New Haven: Yale University Press, 1987.

Nicholsen, Sherry Weber. "The Persistence of Passionate Subjectivity: Eros and Other in Marcuse, by Way of Adorno." In *Marcuse: From the New Left to the Next Left,* ed. John Bokina and Timothy J. Lukes. Lawrence: University Press of Kansas, 1994.

O'Neill, Maggie, ed. *Adorno, Culture, and Feminism.* London: Sage, 1999.

Phelan, Shane. "The Jargon of Authenticity: Adorno and Feminist Essentialism." *Philosophy and Social Critique* 16 (1990): 39–59.

Salecl, Renata. "The Sirens and Feminine Jouissance." *Differences* 9, no. 1 (Spring 1997): 14–36.

Wilke, Sabine, and Heidi Schilpphacke. "Construction of a Gendered Subject: A Feminist Reading of Adorno's Aesthetic Theory." In *The Semblance of Subjectivity: Essays in Adorno's Aesthetic Theory*, ed. Tom Huhn and Lambert Zuidervaart. Cambridge, Mass.: MIT Press, 1997.

Contributors

PAUL APOSTOLIDIS is an Associate Professor at Whitman College, where he teaches critical theory and U.S. politics. He is the author of *Stations of the Cross: Adorno and Christian Right Radio* (Duke University Press, 2000) and co-editor of *Public Affairs: Politics in the Age of Sex Scandals* (Duke University Press, 2004). He has published articles and essays on Adorno's critiques of radio, Cultural Studies in the United States, and conservative anti-gay and anti-welfare discourses. He is currently writing a book titled *Hegemony and Hamburger: Immigration, Rights, and Radical Democracy in the U.S. Labor Movement*, a study of Latino meatpackers' narratives of immigration, work, and union activism.

MARY CAPUTI is professor of political theory at California State University, Long Beach. She publishes in the areas of feminist theory, psychoanalysis, critical theory, and postmodernism. Her book on American political culture and melancholia is forthcoming from the University of Minnesota Press.

REBECCA COMAY teaches in the Departments of Philosophy and Literary Studies at the University of Toronto. She is the coeditor of *Endings: Questions of Memory in Hegel and Heidegger* (Northwestern University Press, 1999) and editor of *Lost in the Archives* (Alphabet City Media, 2002). She has authored numerous essays on modern continental philosophy.

DRUCILLA CORNELL is professor of political science, comparative literature, and women and gender studies at Rutgers University. Cornell has authored many books, including *Defending Ideals* (Routledge, 2004), *Between Women and Generations* (Palgrave, 2002), *At the Heart of Freedom* (Princeton University Press, 1998), *The Imaginary Domain* (Routledge, 1995), *Transformations* (Routledge, 1993), and *The Philosophy of the Limit* (Routledge, 1992). Currently, Cornell is collaboratively directing a research project in South Africa in an effort to deepen the role of African jurisprudence through ideals such as *ubuntu*, to inform constitutional clauses and legal interpretations in the ongoing building of the new South Africa.

JENNIFER EAGAN received her PhD in philosophy from Duquesne University in 1999. Her dissertation was titled "Justice and Judgment: A Re-reading of Kant's Second and Third Critiques." She joined the faculty at California State University, Hayward, in 1999 in a joint appointment with the Departments of Philosophy and Public Affairs and Administration. She is the author of "Philosophers and the Holocaust: Mediating Public Disputes" (*International Studies in Philosophy* 29 [Winter 1997]), which features the work of Theodor Adorno. Currently, Eagan is doing research in the areas of feminism, postmodernism, and democratic politics, focusing on the figures of Adorno, Michel Foucault, and Luce Irigaray.

MARY ANNE FRANKS currently teaches philosophy and world religions at Quincy College, Massachusetts. She received her PhD from the Modern Languages and Literature Faculty at Oxford University in January 2004. Her research interests are psychoanalytic theory, ethics, aesthetics, feminism, human rights, and cultural theory. Her publications include "Obscene Undersides: Women and Evil Between the Taliban and the U.S.," which appeared in *Hypatia: A Journal of Feminist Philosophy* 18, no. 1 (2003); "Von Sex und andere Akte" (Of Sex and Other Acts), in *Über Žižek: Perspektiven und Kritike*, edited by Erik Vogt and Hugh Silverman (Verlag Turia and Kant, 2004); and "Controlled Exposure: Courbet's *L'origine du monde* and the Woman-Thing," in *Exposure: Revealing Bodies, Unveiling Representations*, edited by Kathryn Banks and Joseph Harris (Peter Lang, 2004). Dr. Franks is currently working towards a JD at Harvard Law School.

EVA GEULEN teaches German literature at the University of Bonn, Germany. Her publications include work on philosophical aesthetics, literary theory, and literature from the eighteenth to the twentieth century. Recent publications include a book on the end of art (forthcoming from Stanford Press 2005) and essays on Wedekind, Adorno, Stifter, Thomas Mann, Walter Benjamin, and others.

SORA Y. HAN is currently a fellow at the Center for the Study of Law and Culture at Columbia Law School. She recently received her JD from the School of Law, University of California, Los Angeles, with an emphasis in critical race studies. She is also a PhD candidate in the Department of History of Consciousness at the University of California, Santa Cruz.

RENÉE J. HEBERLE is an associate professor of political science at the University of Toledo, where she is active in the Department of Women's and Gender Studies and the Program in Law and Social Thought. Her publications include "Deconstructive Strategies and the Movement Against Sexual Violence" (*Hypatia* 11, no. 4 [1996]: 63–76); "Law's Violence and the Challenge of the Feminine" (*Studies in Law, Politics, and Society* 22 [2001]: 49–73); and "Postmodernism and the Repudiation of Grand Theory," in *Encyclopedia of Government and Politics*, ed. Mary Hawkesworth and Maurice Kogan (Routledge, 2004). She is currently researching constructions of "the will" in modern and poststructuralist thought to explore what feminists might make of this apparently quite nonfeminist concept.

ANDREW HEWITT is a professor of Germanic languages and comparative literature at the University of California, Los Angeles, where he currently heads the Department of Germanic Languages. He is the author of *Fascist Modernism* (Stanford, 1993) and *Political Inversions* (Stanford, 1996). His latest work, *Social Choreography: Ideology as Performance in Dance and Everyday Life* (Duke University, 2005).

GILLIAN HOWIE is a senior lecturer in philosophy at the University of Liverpool, U.K., and director of the Institute for Feminist Theory and Research. She is author of *Deleuze and Spinoza: Aura of Expressionism* (Palgrave, 2002), editor of *Women: A Cultural Review*'s special issue on gender and philosophy (Ashgate, 2003) and coeditor of *Gender, Teaching and Research in Higher Education* (Palgrave, 2001) and *Third Wave Feminism* (Pelgrave, 2004), publications from the institute's conference series.

LISA YUN LEE is cofounder and director of the Public Square in Chicago. She is the author of *Dialectics of the Body: Corporeality in the Philosophy of Theodor W. Adorno* (Routledge, 2005). She is the organizer of the Vista 360 Festival in Jackson, Wyoming. She serves on the board of Ms magazine, the Chicago Humanities Festival, and the Woodrow Wilson Foundation.

D. BRUCE MARTIN is an administrator at New Mexico State University at Alamogordo, responsible for institutional research, assessment, and strategic planning. He also teaches political science courses, including those on American government, international relations, and politics and film.

LAMBERT ZUIDERVAART is professor of philosophy at the Institute for Christian Studies in Toronto and an associate member of the Graduate Faculty in Philosophy at the University of Toronto. His primary interests lie in philosophy of discourse, social philosophy, and continental philosophy, and he does specialized work on German philosophy from Kant through Habermas. Zuidervaart is currently completing a book on cultural politics and conducting research into theories of truth and theories of globalization. He is the author of *Adorno's Aesthetic Theory: The Redemption of Illusion* (MIT Press, 1991) and *Artistic Truth: Aesthetics, Discourse, and Imaginative Disclosure* (Cambridge University Press, 2004); coauthor of *Dancing in the Dark: Youth, Popular Culture, and the Electronic Media* (Eerdmans, 1991); and coeditor of *The Semblance of Subjectivity: Essays in Adorno's Aesthetic Theory* (MIT Press, 1997) and *The Arts, Community, and Cultural Democracy* (Macmillan/St. Martin's Press, 2000).

Index

Philosophy of the Limit, 34
Pickford, Henry, 20 n. 14
plastic surgery, cultural differences concerning, 215 n. 49
Plato, 51–54, 63 n. 9; mimesis and, 143–44, 157–58
play, art as form of, 163–66
Playboy, 203–4, 207, 209, 211, 213 n. 22
pleasure: in culture industry, 194–213; pornography and degradation of, 206–13; sexual violence in context of, 198–213; of thought, Adorno's concept of, 127–36; *Urgeschichte* of, 102–5
political theory: Adorno's discussion of, 36–38; aesthetic autonomy and, 268–72; body as agent for change in, 116; culture industry and, 262–66, 275 n. 24; ecofeminism and, 145–50; of inclusive democracy, 234–40; instrumentalization of art towards, 16; intersectionality and, 178–83; mimesis and, 142–50; suffering and, 217–30
Pollock, 307
Pollock, Jackson, 307
pornography: Adorno's discussion of, 28–33; as caricature, 205–6; Cornell's discussion of, 28–33; culture industry's effects on, 13–14; economic statistics of, 207–8; materiality of women's bodies and, 9; sexual violence as, 198–213, 213 n. 22; Zee's discussion of, 30–33
Pornschlegel, Clemens, 98
positivism, identity thinking and, 283–86, 297 n. 12
post-Fordism, 335
postintersectionality, concept of, 174–75
postmodernism: Cartesian dualism and, 131, 139 n. 43; concept of suffering in, 218–30; feminist artists and, 94 n. 3
power: artwork's atonement for, 303–8; of culture, 292–96; fascism and, 56–57, 70–94, 94 n. 2; mediation and, 69–70; women's alienation from, 79–94
praxis: Adorno's philosophy and, 8–9, 11, 114–36; dialectics in communication and, 245–52
predator-prey interaction, 152–54
price, Marx's theory of value and, 329
Principles of Scientific Management, The, 121
production, Marx's theory of value and, 328–29
property, linear time and, 112 n. 21

prostitution: Adorno's discussion of, 29; consensual sex issues in, 206–13
pseudoindividuality, aesthetic autonomy and, 264–66
psychoanalysis: Adorno's rejection of, 100, 103, 260–61, 297 n. 9; freedom and, 281–82, 297 n. 9; jouissance in, 207; mimesis and, 150–54
public patriarchy, 252

racism: intersectionality and, 179–83; in labor issues, 247–52; Nazi cult of body and, 119–20; pornography and, 199–213; radical ecology and, 149–50; in Western canon, vii–ix
radical ecology: critical theory versus, 168–70; mimesis and, 145–50
radical feminism, aesthetic autonomy and, 260–61
radio, Adorno's writing for, 111 n. 2
rape: culture industry as anesthetic to, 198; distribution as pornography, 199–213; intersectionality of racism and, 181–83
Raw Deal: A Question of Consent, 200–201
Rawls, John, veil of ignorance concept of, 23
reading, ethic of, 185–89
Reagan, Ronald, 287
reality, Adorno on, 5–6
reason: critical theory view of, 229–30; mimesis and, 144–50; nature and, 42–43
reconciliation: of love and death, 105–8; mimesis and, 84–85, 95 n. 7
reductionism, object identity and, 324–26
Reich, Wilhelm, 94 n. 2
reification, 331–32; Adorno's philosophy and, 161–66
representational theory: in *Dialectic of Enlightenment*, 72–94; Irigaray's critique of, 157–58; pornography and, 31–33; suffering and, 34–36
repression, mimesis and, 142–50
reproductive aberration, Adorno's discussion of, 53–58
Republic: afterlife discussed in, 63 n. 9; mimesis in, 144
"Resignation," 137 n. 7
resistance, Adorno's pessimism concerning, 24, 233–34
ressentiment, Nietzsche's theory of, 34–35
rhetoric: communication through, 243–45; in inclusive democracy, 237, 239–40